# UNCLAIMED HARVEST

# UNCLAIMED HARVEST

## An Oral History of the Tebhaga Women's Movement

Kavita Panjabi

zubaan

ZUBAAN
128 B Shahpur Jat, 1st Floor
NEW DELHI 110 049
Email: contact@zubaanbooks.com
Website: www.zubaanbooks.com

First published by Zubaan Publishers Pvt. Ltd 2017 in collaboration with the Indian Institute of Advanced Studies, Shimla



10 9 8 7 6 5 4 3 2 1

ISBN 978 93 83074 54 9

Zubaan is an independent feminist publishing house based in New Delhi with a strong academic and general list. It was set up as an imprint of India's first feminist publishing house, Kali for Women, and carries forward Kali's tradition of publishing world quality books to high editorial and production standards. *Zubaan* means tongue, voice, language, speech in Hindustani. Zubaan publishes in the areas of the humanities, social sciences, as well as in fiction, general non-fiction, and books for children and young adults under its Young Zubaan imprint.

Typeset in Adobe Garamond 11/13 by Jojy Philip, New Delhi 110 015
Printed and bound at Raj Press, R-3 Inderpuri, New Delhi 110 012

*To my mother Sushil*
*whose life now shows me*
*why to cherish the worth of memory.*

# Contents

*Foreword: Histories of Our Own* — V. Geetha ix

*Thanksgiving* xxxv

*Introduction* xli

APPROACHING

1. '*Sholte Pakano*'—The Rolling of the Wick: The Mahila Atmaraksha Samiti and the Women's Movement in Tebhaga 3
2. The 'Retroactive Force of Interiority': The Conscience of Oral History 53

ENGAGING

3. '*Ektu Phyan De Ma*'—Mother Give Me Some Rice Water: The 'Man-Made' Famine and Women's Responses to Hunger 85
4. '*Meyera Andolane Antarikata Aanlo*'—Women Brought an Inwardness to the Movement: Redefining Political Agency, Forging Affective Comradeships 128
5. '*Atiter Jed*'—The Persistence of the Past: The Santals and the Times of Revolution 185

6. '*Premer Jomir Khoje*'—In Search of the Terrain of Love: Alienation in a Politics of Violence 220

RETROSPECTION

7. '*Bhije Matir Gandhe Naach Kori Anande*'—In the Fragrance of the Wet Earth We Dance in Joy: From the Aesthetics of Liberation to the Wreckage of History 269

*Interviews Conducted* 284

*Appendix: Literary Representations of Tebhaga* 291

*Bibliography* 293

*Index* 310

# Foreword

## Histories of Our Own

V. Geetha

IT IS HARD as well as gratifying, embarrassing as well as pleasurable to write a foreword to a book that I've waited for avidly and read along the way. If, in the process, I am able to point to some directions that it opens up for us, I would have repaid the faith that Kavita Panjabi, the author, and Urvashi Butalia, the publisher, have both reposed in me.

I would like to begin with a short note on history and history writing.

Since the 1970s, a decade that witnessed the emergence of women's groups across the country, feminists have asked questions about their own practice. Such questioning involved two distinct groups of women, the first being those who had founded women's groups or forums in cities and towns, and the second comprising those who worked with mass organizations, including trade unions, peasant groups and Dalit forums, and were active in struggles concerning land and environment. These groups were not hermetically sealed off from each other and there existed constant traffic between the two. But their concerns were different. On the one hand, both groups were acutely aware of the 'women's question', as an earlier usage would have it. Both asserted the importance of attending to what women had to say about their concerns, anxieties, needs and rights. Both acknowledged the fact that women's political expectations centred as much around their role in the family and included issues like alcoholism, violence at home and childcare.

Where the two groups differed was on the question of who and what constituted the feminist subject of politics: the articulate, emancipated woman who could speak her mind about a range of issues that had seldom been spoken about or considered pertinent, belonging to the realm of the 'personal', 'sexual' and the 'familial', or all those 'other' women, peasants, agricultural labourers, Adivasi mine workers, fishers and Dalits, who struggled at home and outside, in their workplaces and within communities for survival, fair livelihood practices and dignity. This was an issue that did not admit any easy resolution. Some, particularly feminists in urban contexts, sought to mark their 'difference' by proclaiming that women were oppressed as much by patriarchy as by feudalism and capitalism. Feminists working with mass movements and sometimes women from these movements wondered if feminist practice, centring on family, sexuality, culture and religion was relevant to all women, and if women ought to indeed insist on the salience of gender amidst the clamour of those who foregrounded class, caste and tribe.

Not all of these thoughts and misgivings, such as they might have been, were voiced aloud. And when they were, in public debates and conversations, they did not appear polarized, as they do in written descriptions of them. Eventually, these latter found their way into books and essays that feminists produced with alacrity from the late 1980s onwards and well into the early 1990s. It was as if, even as they plunged into practical action in the streets and courts, their poky offices and in spaces that were home to various democratic movements, they took a mirror to what they were doing and wrote about themselves, incessantly.

Gail Omvedt's early essay 'Rural Origins of Women's Liberation in India' in the *Social Scientist* (1975) and the chapters on women's movements in her latter-day *Reinventing Revolution* (1993:76–99), Chaya Datar's study of women *bidi*-rollers and their movement,

*Waging Change* (1989), Ilina Sen's *A Space within the Struggle* (1990), Nandita Gandhi and Nandita Shah's *The Issues at Stake* (1992), which examined the theory and practice of women's activism, and Nandita Gandhi's *When the Rolling Pin Hit the Streets* (1996) were published in the wake of feminist engagements with law, health, labour, the state and environment on the one hand, and women's substantial presence in mass politics on the other. At around the same time, feminists also re-examined the past as they looked for histories of their own, of women like themselves, whose lives and politics spoke to their concerns. The most important text in this respect was Stree Shakti Sanghatana's (SSS) *We Were Making History* (1989). It stood poised between a progressive socialist past that it wished to understand from the point of view of women's experiences—the importance of which was self-evident for the feminism that it espoused—and a feminist present that it understood to be linked to a broad progressive politics of the left, but which yet desired its own space and autonomy.

This looking to the past while being mindful of the present was also mirrored in the relationship that women's movements—in the late 1980s and after—had with the parliamentary as well as the militant left, at least in parts of India, and especially in Andhra Pradesh, home to the SSS. On the one hand, women's groups in Andhra, Maharashtra, Delhi, Bihar and West Bengal were alive to the fraternal attractions of left politics and theory; on the other hand, they clearly did not want to be absorbed into it. This made for interesting, contentious conversations, whose density and richness have been so richly captured for us in a range of texts, from Gail Omvedt's early work that I have cited earlier to Anuradha Ghandy's reflections in the 2000s (*Scripting the Change*, 2011) on feminism and the Indian women's movement.

*We Were Making History* and those texts that examined women's place and roles in mass movements in the present (Omvedt, Sen, Shah and Gandhi) raised important questions about the relationship of feminism to wider struggles: Does the presence of women in these struggles change their character, objectives and everyday practices? If it does, is it possible to claim such struggles for feminist politics? What are the stakes involved in claiming or not claiming, as the case may be? These questions were raised in other forums as well, as is evident in the literature published in *Manushi* in the early years of its existence. However, these arguments did not lead to new directions in history scholarship to do with these matters (though it made for much contention and liveliness in everyday politics of the left, feminism and mass movements). Within feminism, history and historiography had emerged as crucial contexts for battling patriarchal and established approaches to the past, but the history and practice of communism in India—or for that matter other progressive movements—did not attract as much critical attention as they deserved. Theoretical arguments to do with Marxism and feminism, however, did. Interestingly, those who wrote on social movements—very few feminists did—did not really go beyond the terms of argument set in this instance by Gail Omvedt and Ilina Sen in the 1980s and thereafter, though Omvedt broke new ground in *Reinventing Revolution*, in which she considered the immediate history and contexts of social movements in post-1960s India, including the women's movement, in their relationship to socialism.

Interestingly, other histories were being written during the same time—in the 1980s, that is. In the wake of the Shah Bano controversy, the reform debates that took place in various Muslim forums in the 1930s, prior to the passing of the Dissolution of Muslim Marriage Act in 1939, were invoked by those who were actively invested in this issue. However, feminist interest revolved around Muslim personal law, its suspension, supercession or reform did not spill over into examining this other history for what it tells us about the emergence of the women's question in late colonial and independent India, and how it may hold lessons for the present. Sadly, this history remained trapped by the context that had prompted its recall.

The 1990s saw a return to the past through a kind of haunting: the violence that rocked Punjab through the 1970s and 1980s, particularly the ruthlessness exhibited by the Indian state in its approach to the so-called Khalistan problem, the anti-Sikh riots of 1984, the unspeakable acts of terror that the Indian army and its ancillaries committed in Kashmir and the Northeast, and the horror and abuse visited on Muslims in the 1990s—all these made a turn to the history of the partition years inevitable. And the result was a set of astounding books published in the late 1990s—by Urvashi

Butalia, Kamla Bhasin and Ritu Menon—that helped us understand how the birth of the nation-state heralded a new and violent politics of gender and identity.

Another kind of feminist investment in the past—and present—of progressive movements was visible in the late 1990s and early 2000s in the wake of nationwide Dalit militancy and assertion. Feminists politicized by these events came to write on anti-caste and Ambedkarite politics, more specially on what the late Sharmila Rege has described as 'Dalit counterpublics'. Some of them went on to produce new and startling historiographies of the late colonial period, specially the years leading to independence. Gail Omvedt's work provides a continuum between these new efforts and early feminist attempts to write histories of our practices. For, more than anyone else, it was Omvedt who insisted on locating the women's question in our times within a broader history of social transformation, be it the peasants' movement in Maharashtra, or the anti-caste and Dalit struggles in the state. Subsequently, and in some ways coevally, Urmila Pawar, Pratima Pardesi, Sharmila Rege, Wandana Sonalkar, S. Anandi, Uma Chakravarti and I have all produced work that forces us to look for our feminist 'origins' in places where we had not looked before: the philosophy and practice of anti-caste radicalism.

Kavita Panjabi's work must be seen in the context of this unfolding history of ideas and practices, to do with the past (and present). For one, she positions herself within this tradition, quite unselfconsciously, as she sets about to identify and draw the contours of a useable and relevant past. Second, her work picks up from where *We Were Making History* left off, both literally and in a substantive sense, as she seeks to rework, in the context of the early twenty-first century, our sorrow over the unfulfilled promises of socialism in this country and our faith in the redemptive power of feminism. Meanwhile, her book does other things: it is responsive to the caste–gender conundrum, forefronted by feminists working on—and in—the tradition of anti-caste radicalism, and is equally sensitive to the so-called communal question and its implications for women's lives and choices. It also carries forward a persistent feminist concern with the state and nation, and women's anxious and embattled relationship to either.

## Tebhaga: Intersecting Histories

The fundamental question that this book raises has to do with the elided history of women's participation in the great Tebhaga struggle, led by the undivided Communist Party of India, and the value and importance of this history for feminists today. Kavita Panjabi's approach to this past is suffused with wistful nostalgia, which is, however, held in by her very robust sense of what separates the feminist in our times from those who fought alongside peasants and sharecroppers, agricultural labourers, and Adivasi and Muslim rural workers. She has no use for that enormous condescension that the present often reserves for the past; yet, she is not unaware of the wisdom that is history.

What she does, then, is summon that history through the voices of women, who recall it and whose memories conjure up a time that appears out of joint, almost as if it did not and would not sit easily within the narrative framework that standard left historiography has accorded it. Remembering in this sense does not merely 'restore' women to a past out of which they have been written out, except for descriptive accounts of their 'contribution' to it, but actually enables the author, who is invested in this memory, to align it to other histories and to ask other questions about Tebhaga itself.

Why did Tebhaga happen? The sharecroppers' struggle to retain two-thirds of the harvest might seem a modest demand, but from the women's accounts, it becomes clear that its value lay elsewhere, in the fact that it was urged forth at a time when great hunger had barely ceased to walk the land. For it was these very same peasants who had watched each other die, who had to sell themselves—husbands sold wives, adults traded children—to eat, even as their grain filled the warehouses of Allied troops and enriched black marketeers. The demand to retain their rightful share of the harvest was in effect an assertion of the peasant's right over food, over his and her means of survival. At once elementary and cosmic, the exercise of this right created a culture of resistance that sought nothing less than a remaking of self and the social order, and whose dream of the future was utopic and exuberant. Importantly, this resistance happened as much in domestic and intimate spaces as it did in the fields, streets and courts of law.

Panjabi's manner of relating the larger 'public' history of Tebhaga to this lesser-known, but equally germane 'interior' history of the movement is the fulcrum on which her narrative turns. She notes that Tebhaga is best understood through the many histories that brought it about and the new political subjects shaped and moulded by these histories. There is the history of peasant resistance, directed from the 1930s onwards by the communists, but there is equally an older memory of fighting back from the fields, which influenced Santals to throw in their lot with the communists. Then there was the ecumenical history of Islam and Hinduism in the region: while caste barriers were stubborn, religious differences were negotiable and, as Sabitri Ray's classic novel, *Harvest Song*, reveals, a nomadic Vaishnavism sat well with local Sufi and folk religiosity in the region. This made it possible for Muslims and Hindus to form alliances at a time that argued the impossibility of Hindu–Muslim coexistence. The author does not dwell overmuch on this history, but she certainly points to it, while noting that communist practice and the precedent set by its cadre made possible the persistence of Hindu–Muslim comradeship.

Longer histories, which have their origins in nineteenth-century debates about women's place, education and reform of their intimate lives, also fed into Tebhaga. Women whose lives had been transformed by these developments had already begun to make their mark in public life: abiding by the Bengal revolutionaries of the early twentieth century on the one hand, setting up and running educational and other supportive institutions for girls on the other. Some of these women had subsequently turned to the more expansive and less militant Indian national movement, while others retained their revolutionary ardour and became communists in the wake of Tebhaga. This older generation of women mentored younger women, who in turn were already politicized by Gandhian nationalism. The Bengal famine proved a turning point, for it enabled all those women who were active in a major or minor manner in public life to transit to an active social culture of care and nurture, which, over time, translated into both a rich ethics and politics.

This work is particularly important in this respect. There exist accounts of women's care work during the famine and after. In

English, we have Manikuntala Sen recalling that time in her account of the Mahila Atmaraksha Samiti (MARS), which was set up in the famine years, and in the wake of Allied troops being stationed in Bengal. There are clearly other accounts in Bangla (2001). What Panjabi offers us is an absorbing account of how care work proved political in the most fundamental sense of the term and helped build a basis for communist organizing, both in the cities and districts. In her reading, care work ceases to be a 'feminine' task that the party entrusted to its women and instead becomes a rallying context for new political subjects to come together. For now, relief workers, familiar with the struggle for independence and the Communist Party's freedom from fascism slogan expanded the idea of liberty by claiming freedom from hunger as one of their chief objectives. Later on, as famine relief led to communist organizing in the districts, freedom from feudal oppression emerged as an additional and important political value. Working to protect themselves from sexual violence on the streets, let loose by Allied soldiers, they ranged themselves against sexual servitude routinely imposed on underclass women. Care work, thus, proved decisive in women's understanding of liberty and, as we shall see, justice and fraternity as well.

She also points out that Tebhaga is best understood as a constellation of times and happenings, and that it was this unique intersection of several impulses and times that enabled peasant and underclass women to articulate their politics. And they did so not as wives of peasants merely or nurturing mothers who 'naturally' were drawn into a politics of food and sustenance, but as workers who desired to make their rightful claim on what they had laboured at and helped produce. Further, this sense of productive worth was resonant with righteous anger at sexual oppression—now directed against the routine and extractive sexual servicing that was expected of them by *jotedar*s and others who held them in thrall. In effect, for the protesting underclass woman, it was her bodily integrity that was at stake, and her insistence on defending it, the author makes clear, was honed in the devastating experience of the famine, as well as the expansive world created by MARS and communist politics.

Feminists need to reckon with this history, which is rightfully theirs—and not only by virtue of the fact that MARS at one time had around 40,000 members. Tebhaga is feminist history because the women of Tebhaga, from across classes, castes and faiths, imagined and attempted to realize a new world that straddled domestic and public contexts, economic and social realities, and political and cultural realms. Whether the Communist Party intended this is not as germane to Panjabi's enquiry—in fact, she makes it clear that the party did not really have a worked-out policy to engage with the unprecedented female presence in its ranks. Instead, she demonstrates, through her skilful sifting of women's memories, how work, resistance, comradeship and compassion were tightly woven together in their consciousness. This appears important also because we have been prone in the past to proclaim, with unreflective ease, that struggles such as Tebhaga did not really consider the women's question so to speak, and instead accommodated it to the class question (see Gangoli 2007:17). The work of MARS has also been discounted in this context and assigned a 'relatively minor role' (Basu 1992).

Importantly, in this analysis, the Communist Party is not merely an object of critique. Rather, it is accorded the centrality it deserves, but it emerges less as a monolithic entity and is actually visible as a party in 'movement', inventive, alive to the contingent and unashamedly idealistic. She argues that the party's strength lay in its power and ability to persuade women, in fact rural plebians as a whole, that they were historical agents, capable of making their future—both middle-class activists and peasants were thus actors in historical time, not agents of a primitive fury or anger. Consequently, for the author, the party's subsequent 'failure' becomes an instance of thwarted female idealism, of a failed tryst with a history it had helped set in motion, in however unreflective a manner. Through her analysis, we see how this happened, how the partition of India, violently anxious nation-states and a disastrous Comintern directive, as much as the party's own recourse to violence, collapsed its hard-won gains for women. Her sorrow, however, is reserved for the party's disastrous turn to militant violence. Communist leadership might look back on that turn and resignedly note that it was an instance of 'mistaken' strategy, but, as she points out, for many, especially women who lived through that period, these mistakes signified nothing less than the end of hope and political good faith.

It has been more than twenty-five years since *We Were Making History* was published. For the feminists who came of age in the 1970s and later, the book was a veritable charter and we were grateful that it alerted us to the unfulfilled promises of a revolutionary past that thousands of women from diverse social contexts and communities 'made' and owned up to. In doing so, the book had asked a range of questions to do with the writing of history, its public character and private silences, the ways in which some things may be said but not others, the value of experiences that are not granted the dignity of a name or political meaning and identity. Further, it had 'read' women's recall of lives led in the shadow of the Telengana armed struggle in and through the discontinuities, silences, elisions and subterfuges that constituted it.

While affirming the importance of grasping women's experiences during Tebhaga and the relevance of oral history, however fragmented, and its power to redeem mainstream history, this book goes on to do something else: it identifies a set of key events to do with women's participation in the struggle and builds a different story around each of them. Together, these stories raise a set of important questions about why women did what they did, the balance of forces and choices that shaped their lives, and their expressive sense of what their struggle was all about. It is not merely women's experiences that are at stake here, but the nature of their recall, what they remember, what they would rather not, what is 'forgotten', what evades recall and, finally, what memories speak to us, who wish to hear them now, in the present and why. As history, in the sense of the past, and memory that relives and, therefore, remakes that past, come together, mix, match and collide, we discover a time that 'lives' and which we may yet make our own.

## Moments of a Comradeship: The Making of the Female Subject of Resistance

What sort of political subject did Tebhaga create? In raising and addressing this question, Panjabi breaks new ground. Care work that middle-class women carried out during the famine, the role that peasant women played in housing and protecting communist men and women, the 'terrain of love' that women in the party sought to hold on to, as they forged startling intimacies across class, caste, faith and other differences that did not go away, but which, at times, appeared irrelevant—all these produced an 'ontological' bonding that is simply not reducible to class unity or an idealistic comradeship fostered by communism. In what follows, I would like to unpack her notion of an ontological bond in terms of related historical debates on resistance, socialism and revolution.

She identifies four important moments in the bonding and comradeship that emerged during the Tebhaga years: the moment of the famine; the 'interiority' that enabled activists and supporters to own up to the struggle from the depths of their being; an emergent terrain of love for all human beings; and, finally, the moment of memory, which, in retrospect, illumined the stubbornness of comradeship forged in struggle. These moments do not exist in isolation, and in her argument relate to and highlight each other in emphatic ways.

I would like to examine each of these in some detail and place them in the context of debates and research that help us annotate them further.

## ♦ *The Moment of the Famine: Who Eats, Who Starves?* ♦

The author observes that the famine, as noted earlier, seemed a cosmic wrong and a symbol of the ultimate alienation of the producer from the products of her labour. For those who undertook famine relief work, the experience proved deeply unsettling and for some epiphanic. I quote these lines from the chapter on the famine (Chapter 3 in this volume) to indicate how she conceptualizes the 'moral' force of relief work:

> It was the starkness of right and wrong stripped down to a nakedness that could not be avoided, neither could it be borne. Systematic and continued deprivation had emptied human beings of their dignity, destroyed their volition, rendered them non-human, beyond representation. If dignity is also the name for the quality of humanity that is capable of morality, for the ability of human

> beings to choose their own actions, then this was a naked reality that also demanded choice on the part of those who witnessed it; and it demanded a choice that went beyond any relative value, a choice between what was clearly, radically, right or wrong. The dignity of the perceiver lay in making that choice. To not make the right choice would be to render oneself non-human. Thus witnessing the non-humanity of the other, her inability to be human, impinged on one's own implication in being human. The opposition between who eats and who starves translates into who can be human and who cannot. To deny the other the possibility of dignity, that is, of being human, would be to empty oneself of dignity, of being human. The moral force of this politics was such that it posed a radical challenge of choice: between a response made in the preservation of one's own human dignity and the annihilation of it.

Historians writing on food scarcity, including famine-like conditions have cautioned us about representing women's role in struggles for food as an expression of their 'nurturing' function. There are two points of view that are germane to our understanding of what happened in Bengal in the wake of the famine.

The first is stated with great lucidity by the historian John Bohstedt (1998), who has studied food riots in England over a period of thirty years (1790–1810) and in different cities. He observes that women are present in these riots, but are not always in the forefront. When they are, it is possible to establish that they have consistently staked their claims to food on the basis of their productive worth, on a perceived sense of their own centrality to the process of production, income creation and survival. In short, they have clamoured for food and against those who seek to hoard it or trade it away, as workers who deserve their grain. He terms these protests that had women in the vanguard, often along with men, as belonging to a 'protoindustrial' economy, in which women were present actively in manufacture and moved between home and workplace easily. He goes on to note that in such an economy, women and men's work was neither necessarily equal nor interchangeable, but women's contribution to the family income made all the difference between subsistence and destitution. The household economy in this scheme of things, thus, stood halfway between an older 'moral' economy and the market, production and reproduction, and exchange value and use value (ibid.:38). Housework, he suggests, was not alienating as it would become under capitalism, and instead overflowed into creating social networks with other women, best exemplified in the sort of 'mutual aid' cultures that developed in these contexts.

The second point of view is one best articulated by the historian Temma Kaplan (1982), who suggests that women agitating for food forefront their roles as mothers as those who fulfil the ordained task of feeding—it is not so much about women being 'essentially' nurturing, but about them being located within a division of labour where it is their role and duty to procure food, and when that function is thwarted, they protest and rebel. Kaplan notes that in such instances, women exhibit 'female consciousness'. In her lexicon, this is as much a feeling that emerges in the doing of protest, forging solidarities with other women, all of whom are united in everyday associational action as well, sharing food, washing clothes together, taking care of each other's children and supporting each other through ill health.

Both Kaplan and Bohstedt are agreed that women protesting over food in public spaces are intensely conscious of their role in provisioning their families and act out of that sense of importance along with other women (and men). Kaplan's studies have been of women protesters, whereas Bohstedt's are of what he terms 'plebian' protests that included a large number of women. While Kaplan suggests that women across space and time might be said to respond in a spirit of female consciousness, Bohstedt limits his analysis to suggesting that food riots reveal women's capacity for setting the scales of justice right—he notes that, as food rioters, women agitated for a just price against the rapacious one fixed by traders, and does not attribute to them a transcendent class or 'gender' sensibility. He insists too that this mode of demanding justice worked as long as the protesters and the hoarders were locked in a face-to-face combat; when market forces turned more impersonal, as they did under early capitalism, rioters turned violent and inchoate.

Female consciousness is a tricky concept, but nevertheless of great heuristic value, since it helps us name and assess acts of resistance that evade easy political meaning and significance. If we are to align expressions of this consciousness to an ethics and practice of care, we are back within more recognizable political spaces, in this instance, the terrain of 'reproduction'. While socialized childcare, and social and financial support for motherhood have been debated from the point of view of policies and practices in the Soviet Union, and Central and Eastern European nations that laid down principles for state departments to create and enforce this support, hunger has not been part of the argument. But it was hunger, along with the socialist dream of socializing reproduction, that mandated the state take care of matters to do with the household in post-revolutionary Soviet Union. Alexandra Kollontai, who would go on to become Commissar of Public Policy, decided in early October 1917 and in the teeth of opposition, that she would send out bread to starving and impoverished women from 'counter-'revolutionary factions—she could not let children of counter-revolutionaries starve, she argued in *Pravda*, and thereby help fan further resistance to the Bolsheviks. She, thus, deftly combined 'revolutionary' reasoning and her own anguish at hunger, which, in this instance, led to the setting up of public kitchens to provide for the hungry and the desperate beaten down by war and revolution (Farnsworth 1980:130–31).

In Tebhaga, it would seem that women's experience of the famine forced them to respond in both ways that I have outlined: relief workers exhibited a consistent measure of 'female consciousness', moving from domestic to social motherhood, as Panjabi felicitously phrases this transition. They created networks that included women from across the political spectrum and generations, through actual acts of setting up public kitchens, milk dispensation centres and places where women could learn a trade to rebuild their lives. The associational life that they grew familiar with stood them in good stead when later on women belonging to the communist-inspired MARS moved to the districts when the party issued the call for Tebhaga.

At another level, peasant women and agricultural women workers came together, along with men in their contexts, forging powerful 'class' bonds. While the great hunger reaped several thousand deaths, the terrifying experience of the famine also transformed the consciousness of at least some of those who survived its onslaught. Like the food rioters of Europe, these survivors gradually learnt to define their own worth and stake their claims to equality and justice on that basis. As this work points out, a peasant woman who was 'sold' off was indignant that there was a market for bodies such as hers. She was upset not so much at her husband selling her, but by the commodification of hunger, which appeared a far greater evil than sexual servitude, which, in her situation was a 'given', for there was always the looming figure of the *jotedar*. Later on, this anger, an expression of utter alienation, would rouse peasant women and female agricultural workers organized around the issue of sharecropper rights into demanding their due as workers who laboured equally and alongside men. Thus, at the height of the Tebhaga struggle, women would put forth their demands, not as mothers or as peasants, but as producers who were both—and this, suggests Panjabi, was because the famine years had made them witness to their own annihilation and paradoxically fostered in them a sense of their worth in the interlinked spaces of home and the field.

It was from this position of confidence that they bonded with middle-class women and welcomed them into their homes. While these women brought with them the consciousness and necessity of communism as idea and ethic, their everyday lives and struggles embodied a spirit of resistance that overwhelmed and inspired middle-class activists. This was no easy comradeship, as we shall see, but it was one that they were prepared to risk and pursue.

Is this comradeship understandable as revolutionary class consciousness? From being a class that endured exploitation and humiliation, the Tebhaga sharecroppers and workers became a class that was determined to stand its ground and fight for its due. How much of this consciousness was due to its consistent sense of itself as a class that was antagonistic to feudal landlordism? And how much of it was due to this class's experience of hunger on the one hand and sexual servitude on the other? Is it possible to speak of class in and through a politics of the body and the alienation that it endures on account of hunger and humiliation? Panjabi's narrative suggests that as far as the women who were active in Tebhaga were concerned, the sense of being a 'class' was everywhere resonant with the claim for sexual dignity. By saying 'no' to sexual servitude without, and domestic abuse within, these women stood tall, as peasants, workers and as women, conscious and mindful of their bodily integrity.

In Telengana too, class action of this kind appears to have been present—*We Were Making History* refers to the tribunals of the Communist Party that listened to and acted on instances of wife beating, sexual abuse and rape, and in at least one instance condemned a rapist to death (SSS 1989:16). Women's memories of Telengana also draw attention to the party's role in arbitrating relationships, including romance, issues to do with sexual irresponsibility and promiscuity. However, these instances are underlined to make a different argument: that the politics of the left did not consider these tensions political; rather, they were analysed either from a pragmatic point of view or a moral position. Panjabi makes a different point—she reads the demands for sexual justice and for the dignity of persons as exemplifying an emergent *female* political subjectivity, which the party may or may not have heeded. Notwithstanding that, she notes, this self-consciousness marked women as political beings in their own eyes.

## ♦ *Moments of Joy and Love: Eros, Politics and Women's Lives* ♦

This brings me to the second and third moments that formed the core of the comradeship that Panjabi considers characteristic of the Tebhaga years: the moment of interiority and the emergence of a terrain of love. The Tebhaga struggle meant that women were more mobile than before, though in some ways the conditions of the struggle required them to be circumspect and even secretive. But their mental space expanded in exponential ways (Manikuntala Sen [2001] notes that women experienced the 'taste' of freedom), as is evident in the story of that iconic heroine of Tebhaga, Bimala Mahji, a young widow, who remarried and became one of the most articulate peasant leaders. This was why women described that time as one of '*shanti*' (peace), '*ananda*' (joy)—much like the women of Telengana wistfully recalled that 'magic' time. Guarding crops, passing on messages, confronting jotedars or the police: none of this was easy and, besides, the struggle was shot through with violence, even before armed struggle became an official dictum with the Communist Party. Yet, for women, it appeared as if they were on the brink of something extraordinary.

Unsurprisingly, Telengana activists recalled their fighting days as 'that magic time': 'There was a lot of difference between these days and those. What was there then? Like the proverb which says, "One is peace, and two is comfort. Either we lived or else we died"' (SSS 1989:171). This sense of the present as all, as that which ends as well as begins things, is perhaps what created the 'magic' of existence. There is a certain breathlessness even in the recall of events, whose unstated and whispered message is, 'We did it, but we don't know how we did it.'

This utopic sense made for, even as it was shaped by, complex and expansive social relationships. It was not easy to earn the peasants' trust or win the hearts and minds of the Santals, but as both Manikuntala Sen and Ila Mitra have pointed out, communist women worked hard to create trust and goodwill, and in turn those who sheltered them or decided to accept the Communist Party as their own, also accepted the necessity of disciplined action and daring. Literacy classes, cohabitation, commensuality, fighting the jotedars together, keeping the police at bay, forming new friendships, secret meetings and planning: comradeship emerged in and through a range of related practices and experiences. Panjabi has this to say about how collective life and the 'inwardness' that women activists spoke of coalesced in Tebhaga:

> Collective activity … begins to transform intimate experiences of activists' lives at the core, such as freedom from sexual exploitation; the happiness of equal partnership in conjugality; the unprecedented joys of finding acknowledgement of their labour as workers; the fulfilment of personal needs and political desires in the public sphere of the movement.

What did this interiority in tandem with being part of an intensely experienced collective life achieve? It made possible Anima Biswas's, 'terrain of love', which men and women experienced in their intimate relationships, and made the basis for a greater affection that encompassed all those who stood with them and the cause for which they were willing to love and risk so much. It created, literally, even if for a brief window of time, 'new' men, who related to women in ways that appeared inspiring to Panjabi, as she listened to the renowned

Amal Sen of the Bangladesh Workers' Party, heir to Tebhaga in some ways, and to Heleketu Singha. Further, the movement helped women who were marginal in their social contexts, such as the so-called promiscuous young widow Phuli, to lead meaningful and rich lives. While the national movement, the Gandhi ashram in particular, too drew widows and so-called 'fallen' women, the communist movement was singular in the '*mazaa*' (enjoyment) it made possible.

The other side of this 'mazaa' was fierce loyalty, and Panjabi's account of Ila Mitra and the Santal Harek is a veritable fable of comradeship. It is this relationship that she terms an instance of 'ontological bonding', which was rooted in but went beyond party loyalty and fidelity to a greater cause, and was affirmed at the level of bodily being. As she notes, this loyalty persisted in Santal collective memory and brought over 100,000 of them to the borders of Bangladesh during the fifty-year celebrations of Tebhaga in 1996 because they wanted a glimpse of Ila Mitra, their legendary leader. For Mitra this witnessing of a bond through time was highly emotional and she attributed it to the 'stubbornness of the past', to the fact that memory insists on its own claims, whatever the actual course of history. After all, many of the Santals who had gathered on that occasion had not even been born when Tebhaga happened.

Ila Mitra's resilience in the face of severe and terrible sexual torture, the Santals' equally obdurate dignity and refusal to name her as their leader, as the one who instigated them to commit violent acts and the fact that not one Muslim peasant or worker in rural Bengal (then part of the newly formed nation of Pakistan) could be found to testify against her: all these instances, this work points out, are poignant markers of resilient comradeship in the context of freshly drawn and fiercely policed identities and borders. Tebhaga, she notes, existed as an event that memory owned up to in ways that history did not and could not, a time of unspeakable trust and love.

Interestingly, the discovery of an 'interiority' that was intensely political and joyful, present and yet transcendent, was experienced in other movements where women were active in large numbers: in the Tamil self-respect movement, for example, women owned up to the ideas and practices of the latter in heartfelt ways, as evident in the excitement that marks their writings and speeches. Interiority is central to those dreamers of a new day, of whom Sheila Rowbotham (2011) writes about so eloquently. These women, from both the middle and working classes in England and the USA, drawn to socialism and various versions of feminism, worked, struggled and sustained visions of the future that included transformed domestic and intimate lives. More important, they carried their domestic and affective concerns into the public realm. Many of them, for instance, were active in local government, and used that space to plan for childcare support for poor mothers, free health clinics and better schools for the poor (ibid.:19–24).

This interiority notwithstanding, women were sometimes uneasy with what they had to contend. When interviewing those who had been steadily active through the Tebhaga years, the author had to engage with what she describes as 'the retroactive force of the past'—its ability to exercise its hold on memory such that women could not bring themselves to speak outside of the collective identity the past had made possible. While eventually some of them did, and pointed to the tensions that underwrote their relationship to the events of their time and the Communist Party, this was, of course, in retrospect, when it seemed all right to do so. Even then, Ila Mitra, notes Panjabi, could not bring herself to analyse the violent turn taken by Tebhaga and which compromised its gains and diminished the ardour of some of its cadres. In the case of Anima Biswas, the weight of the past was such that she could not speak about it, at least not consistently and steadily.

So, while as feminists we are invested in coming to terms with female subjectivity caught in the moment of change, we are forced to note the uneven terms on which, perhaps, some of these transitions happened. As I have pointed out earlier, the challenge for the feminist historian is, how does one do this without belittling and reprimanding the past, without being condescending towards it? Panjabi does neither; instead, she measures the past against its own utopic moments—her account of Anima Biswas' tragic fate, which was exemplified in the disappearance of that terrain of love she claimed for herself and communism is important.

In this instance, what this work does is essay a somewhat different trajectory than say the SSS researchers did with respect to Telengana.

In the late 1980s, building feminist solidarity in a political context that was shaped by left politics, it seemed important to return women's experiences to history. While the voices of women spoke in a myriad tongues, the analysis from a feminist point of view marked certain tensions in their narratives as pertinent: their disillusionment with the manner in which the armed struggle was called off, their dismay at being returned to their homes and kitchens, and their bewilderment with the party's refusal to own up to the women's question.

What did not appear important in terms of argument and analysis in that volume, but which looms large in this book is the fact that women activists were shaped as much by class politics as by their gendered inwardness. That they were peasants and agricultural workers dispossessed by the jotedars was central to their understanding of justice. As for middle-class women, anti-fascism on the one hand and the example of the Soviet Union and China on the other rendered socialism a very desirable ideal, and if they were to attenuate their class identity, in the long march towards the latter, like Manikuntala Sen, they did not mind it at all. For all women, class politics transformed into party loyalty, yet it was its own truth, and it was this sense of the 'truth' of class, along with the aligned dream of socialism that made it difficult for women to speak of their misgivings or unease as they probably experienced them all those years ago. It is almost as if it were unthinkable, unbearable even, to call that experience to account, for any such recall would be tantamount to betrayal.

Historians and writers who seek to come to grips with the silence of those who they expected to have spoken out against perversions of communist practice have pointed out this out. Victor Serge in his novel *The Case of Comrade Tulayev* has drawn unforgettable portraits of those who were victims of Stalin's 1930s purges. Each of them is deeply distressed by what Comrade Stalin does, but none of them can muster the will to protest his acts—and not only because that would have meant death. They feel burdened with the memory of revolution, by what they had wrought in 1917 and their dreams that were tied to it. To call attention to how it had perhaps turned horribly wrong appears to them a betrayal of the revolution itself.

## ◆ *The Moment of Recall: Silence and Dispossession* ◆

This is a good place for me to transit into examining the fourth and last moment that marked the experience of solidarity and love that Tebhaga made possible: the moment of memory. For Ila Mitra, remembering her trauma, however terrible it was, meant reliving that ontological bond with the Santals. For Anima Biswas, the Namasudra activist who fell out with the party over the question of armed struggle, memory appeared tinged with loss, sorrow and even a sense of anomie. When the armed struggle began, she had to flee for her life, both from the police who were hunting communists down as well as party members who were worried about dissidents and informers. Then there was the horror of partition, which forced thousands to cross borders amidst conditions of terror and fear.

In Anima Biswas's case, her forced relocation to West Bengal, as well as the forced abdication—even if self-abdication—of communist politics appeared nothing less than cataclysmic: she retreated into silence, left only with the bitter memory of a party that would not seek responsibility for its strategic new line and work with dissidence, and instead sought to silence it. Her silence resonates with that of many hundreds of women and men who were stunned by their party not heeding them or taking them seriously. This, in a sense, is also what we find with Serge's Bolsheviks who eventually died in Stalin's purges, but who, when alive, were left with no words to describe the perversion that unfolded before their eyes.

Panjabi points out that with Anima Biswas something else happened: her terrain of love actually collapsed without the sustaining presence of the party in her life. She and her husband, whom she had learnt to love and refine—he seemed to have been a rough-and-ready peasant—parted ways. Such a conjunction of eros and politics is the stuff of communist fantasy, one is tempted to argue. After all, there are other examples of those who felt hurt and lost in their erotic lives, but continued to be good comrades to their lovers—witness Rosa Luxemberg's relationship to Leo Jogisches, and Eleanor Marx's embittered love for the philanderer socialist Edward Aveling. But feminism has a stake in upholding the conjoined nature of eros and politics, especially radical left politics. And equally resolute communist women have insisted on the importance of linking the two. So there is great value in pondering over Biswas's fate, her extreme loneliness and quiet retreat into a life of service.

Panjabi adroitly links the disappearance of the terrain of love to the onset of violence: the silencing of opposition within the party and the murder of former comrades, she insists, disrupted that field of social affection, which was the very stuff of communist solidarity. While revolutionary violence has been endlessly interrogated, it has seldom been examined in relation to the ideal of broad and expansive comradeship that revolutions seek to create. There have been discussions on the impact of violence on inner-party democracy, how the onset of armed struggle can and does make it hard to forge broader solidarities, united or mass fronts, except when such fronts are already in place and armed struggle exists as one aspect of the struggle. There have also been debates about the usefulness of violence—whether it broadens resistance to capital and state power or invites reprisals that in fact make it difficult for resistance cultures to take root. The impact on violence as strategy on comradeship, on building a culture of solidarity that is open and dialogic, is yet to be fully understood.

There exist descriptive and narrative accounts, to be sure: Issac Deutscher's *The Prophet Armed* has poignant descriptions of the affection and comradeship that animated the Bolshevik leadership in the early days, in the months immediately following the storming of the Winter palace (1954:282–86) and even towards the end of the Civil War (ibid.:17–20). This contrasts with the culture of dissembling, fear, petty ambition and intrigue that marked the years of terror. The book does not posit a simple opposition between those who were for and against Stalin, but paints a detailed and nuanced picture of the utter perversion of relationships, of revolutionary comradeship, in the party in the wake of Stalin's campaign against his former colleagues.

The point about comradeship is not that it is cosy or romantic, but that it emerges in and through what Panjabi refers to as 'intersubjective' practice. To attend to a fellow comrade's life and experiences, to acknowledge her subjectivity, is seldom easy or final. It is a process, a practice that survives its unease as the author makes clear in her account of Ila Mitra's astonishing life and times. The loyal bonds that Ila Mitra and the Santals forged with each other, she notes, existed alongside and in spite of persistent prejudices. Mitra's characteristic references to how 'dirty' the Santals were cannot be wished away; on the other hand, they cannot be made the sole measure of her commitment to their cause, and while in prison, their persons. This work establishes that the bonds that Tebhaga helped make were *risked*—in Mitra's case, both she and the Santals together risked a comradeship that literally bound them together in a horrific common fate and enabled them retain their faith in each other in the face of severest torture and death. This is why the Santals felt summoned to the border in 1996 by their memory of that period and, in turn, it is Mitra's sense of that time, of what the Santals stood for and did when they were all in prison together that sustained her through the healing years. The terrain of love, then, was one that needed the party or at least shared memory to survive, and in her case, she had both, whereas the Santals had coded the past on their own terms and had managed to retain their love across generations for her.

In Anima Biswas's case, memory did nothing. When she fled the new state of Pakistan to India, she cut herself off from what had sustained her until then. Her memory of 'that' time, while fresh and goading, was forced to wait on an uncertain present. The party's disaffection with workers like her who had dared question its strategy of armed revolution, the impossibility of reviving comradeship—in spite of Amal Sen visiting her from across the border—and the collapse of her intimate world: all these rendered her 'silent' and dispossessed.

## The Uses of Tebhaga

Thus far I have attempted to elicit and annotate certain key themes in this account of the Tebhaga struggle. The question is: why Tebhaga now? As I have argued earlier, to seek out a past for our feminist struggles in the here and now has been central to our politics. We reach back to moments in that past that best speak to the present, and through means that address our concerns, needs and questions. Panjabi's turning to Tebhaga is on account of her interest in the women's movement and its pasts, as she makes clear. But she is also interested in the practice of history: what do we get out of exploring the past in the ways that we do? And by this she means the specific method that feminists, among others, have deployed in their conversations with the past—the method of oral history.

Oral history has many uses, and feminists who have long argued that women have been 'hidden from history' to use Sheila Rowbotham's felicitous phrase, have looked to oral history to capture an elusive past. Panjabi has recourse to this method for two reasons: one, her interest in Tebhaga and the presence of Tebhaga activists in her milieu; and two, her conviction that oral narratives are capable of yielding memories of the past that could well contrast with and offer a different reading of history or histories. While oral historians have been long aware of the tension between memory and history, and also memory and narration, she turns this tension to productive advantage. Drawing on Holocaust studies, especially the processes of memory that have produced testimonies about camp life and survivors' autobiographies, she argues that the slippery nature of memory ought to be seen as integral to efforts to understand the past, and that what is 'remembered' is as 'real' as what may have 'actually happened'. For memory is not precise recall, but a relationship to the past that is mediated through longing, loss, desire, fear and repression, as the case may be. In this sense, memory creates meaning, sometimes in tandem with what is officially recorded as having happened and sometimes against the grain of the official story.

As far as Tebhaga is concerned, oral history achieves many things: For one, the presence of an interlocutor, in this case Panjabi, makes memory 'speak' in certain ways. The 'present' of the women's movement defines the past as useful and urgent, even while it marks its difference from that past. This immediately sets the stage for a rich and contentious exchange, leavened by the trust and comradeship the oral history process sets in motion. Second, the interlocutor is not a neutral presence, but one who wants to know and is invested in the lives and times of older women. In seeking out the women of Tebhaga, she has created a situation where the past becomes a shared enterprise, something that implicates both the teller and the told (and, as with Rani Dasgupta, becomes a reason for her to break her silence around certain issues). Third, the memories that are sought, being of a time that had been rendered discontinuous by momentous and painful events, emerge as both precious and fraught, and the oral historian then becomes a 'reader' of not only what is told to her, but also of what is unsaid, left behind, not addressed. And in doing so, she brings the process of memory making in a full circle. For as she seeks to read the elisions and quietness behind her subjects' narratives, she does so from the point of view of what we, as feminists today, consider pertinent about women's lives, the Communist Party and feminist engagement with peoples' movements. Her volubility is thus as much on her account as it is an approach the past.

In this sense, Tebhaga returns to haunt us as we strive to make sense of struggles over land, hunger and dispossession in our own time, wonder about women taking to arms to defend their right to their environment and resources in the forests of central India, and rage over the fact that women engaged in guarding what is meagrely theirs are often subject to sexual violence, sometimes by those who are meant to secure their welfare—khaki-clad state personnel. For feminists, these are themes that have fallen behind since the decade of the 1990s and this book offers a valuable context and opportunity for us to return to these themes, enriched by all else that we have learnt meanwhile.

## References

Basu, Amrita. 1992. *Two Faces of Protest.* Los Angeles, CA: University of California Press.

Bohstedt, John. 1998. 'The Myth of the Food Riot: Women as Proto-Citizens in English Community Politics, 1790–1810', in Harriet B. Applewhite and Darlene G. Levi (eds), *The Age of Democratic Revolution*, pp. 21–49. Ann Arbor, MI: University of Michigan Press.

Datar, Chaya. 1989. *Waging Change.* New Delhi: Kali for Women.

Deutscher, Issac. 1954. *The Prophet Armed.* London: Oxford University Press.

Farnsworth, Beatrice. 1980. *Aleksandra Kollontai, Socialism, Feminism and the Bolshevik Revolution.* Palo Alto, CA: Stanford University Press.

Gandhi, Nandita. 1996. *When the Rolling Pin Hit the Streets*. New Delhi: Kali for Women.

Gandhi, Nandita and Nandita Shah. 1992. *The Issues at Stake*. New Delhi: Kali for Women.

Gangoli, Geetanjali. 2007. *Indian Feminisms: Law, Patriarchies and Violence in India*. Hampshire: Ashgate.

Ghandy, Anuradha. 2011. *Scripting the Change*. Delhi: Daanish Books,

Kaplan, Temma. 1982. 'Female Consciousness and Collective Action: The Case of Barcelona, 1910–1918', *Signs*, 7(3):545–66.

Omvedt, Gail. 1975. 'Social Scientist', *Rural Origins of Women's Liberation in India*, 4(40–41):40–54.

———. 1993. *Reinventing Revolution*. London: M.E. Sharpe.

Ray, Sabitri. 2005. *Harvest Song* (translated by Chandrima Bhattacharya and Adrita Mukherjee). Kolkata: Stree (originally published in Bangla as *Paka Dhaner Gaan*. Kolkata: Suprakashini, 1986).

Rowbotham, Sheila. 2011. *Dreamers of a New Day*. London: Verso.

Sen, Ilina. (ed.) 1990. *A Space within the Struggle*. New Delhi: Kali for Women.

Sen, Manikuntala. 2001. *In Search of Freedom*. Calcutta: Stree.

Serge, Victor. 1967. *The Case of Comrade Tulayev* (translated by Willard R. Trask). New York : New York Review of Books Classics.

Stree Shakti Sanghatana (SSS). 1989. *We Were Making History*. New Delhi: Kali for Women.

# Thanksgiving

The idea of launching a full-scale exploration of Tebhaga women's lives and visions first came to me in the course of intense conversations about women's involvement in political movements at the 1995 Jaipur conference of the Indian Association of Women's Studies. It's been a long journey from the first stirrings of that idea to the completion of this book, and it is finally a time for thanksgiving.

Jasodhara Bagchi, founder-director of the School of Women's Studies, Jadavpur University, Kolkata, held out enthusiastic encouragement and support, without which a once wistfully articulated wish would never have taken off. I still cannot believe that she will not be there to see this book. Most of the conversations with the Tebhaga women and men took place across four years, between 1996 and 1999. Nripen Bandyopadhyay extended valued guidance with much patience and largesse when I first began this work. He and Malini Bhattacharya also gave kindly of their time as members of an advisory committee. Shivani Banerjee Chakravorty joined me on this project for a year and was always there for me, both as a dear friend and as a wise colleague, at a time when I most needed her. Abhijit Sen, a virtual font of knowledge regarding women's writing in nineteenth- and twentieth-century Bengal, provided valuable leads to lesser known publications on Tebhaga. Several students and research fellows from various disciplines, now impressive professionals in their own fields, worked on the translation and transcription of the narratives; a considerable bulk of this was handled by Syed Tanveer Nasreen, Seemantini Gupta, Sougata Mukhopadhyay and Ruchira Goswami. Asmita Chaudhuri was exemplary, with her expertise and sincerity, in compiling the index.

The political commitment of Bangladeshi activists and scholars to our shared history of the Tebhaga movement, and their hospitality and support to someone from India who had come to research it, elicits profound respect. Each time, everywhere I went, in the fortnight-long trips that I made across four years to Bangladesh, I found myself being treated as an honoured guest. The constant refrain was, 'You have come here to work on the Tebhaga movement, you are our guest.' It was an overwhelming experience, but it also placed the burden of history on one's shoulders in no uncertain terms. There is no way my research would have made headway without the sustained support of more people there than I can possibly remember today. In Kolkata, Ila Mitra had given me just two introductory notes to take to Bangladeh—for Fazle Hussein Badshah and Mohammed Aakash. Badshah bhai introduced me to Tariq Rahman, who in turn roped in Nur Ahmad Bokul, and between them, these four not only gave generously of their time, knowledge and hospitality, but also paved the way for me seamlessly into homes and offices right across Dhaka, and the villages and towns of Dinajpur, Nachole, Narail, Rangpur and Mymensingh. The largesse, courtesy and shared commitment with which everyone there engaged with me, as did Maleka Begum and Mesbah Kamal in Dhaka, and Nazrul Islam in Narail, made our contemporary national borders seem facile.

The Sephis Grants Programme, the Netherlands, supported the fieldwork with a sensitivity to the cultural specificities of Bangladesh that is rare for a funding agency. Willem van Schendel kindly shared with me the official transcript of Ila Mitra's testimony that he procured from the Home Department, Bangladesh. The Centre for Studies in Social Sciences Calcutta (CSSSC), extended a visiting fellowship that proved valuable in terms of library research and discussions with colleagues there, especially with Anjan Ghosh, whose mischievous smile still reigns supreme across the lasting worth of his challenging arguments; and with Gautam Bhadra, who does not know how his excitement regarding issues of memory gave this work a new turn. The South Asia Fellowship of the Social Science Research Council (SSRC), New York, gave me the focused time needed to begin writing seriously; and Hamida Hossain and Itty Abraham's faith in the potential of this research reinforced my resolve at a critical juncture. In the best traditions of promoting scholarship, Jadavpur University extended generous institutional support that enabled me to take up the CSSSC and SSRC fellowships, of six months each, and the Indian Institute of Advanced Study (IIAS) fellowship of one year.

This work finally saw completion at the IIAS, Shimla, in 2012. My tenure there enabled me to dedicate to these narratives the focused and sustained attention needed for the writing of the book. Peter deSouza was an exemplary director in his shaping of the academic ethos of this institution—there was a healthy culture of intellectual sharing, and precious time for quiet reflection and writing. As a scholar, he saw the threads I had spun more clearly than I could myself at that time, picked them up and handed them over to me, thus speeding me on my way. As for the entire staff of the IIAS, their extreme courtesy, warmth and cooperation went beyond the dictates of officialdom and created the pleasant conditions that were so conducive to work there.

Tridip Suhrud was the first person to read the completed manuscript at the IIAS, hot off the printer. He has been an inspiration and a rock, intellectually, ethically and as an absolutely delightful friend. With Vrinda Dalmiya, it's been a time of learning, and her sincere generosity in discussing issues that underlie this work has meant a lot. Anupama Vohra was the most sensitive and genuinely warm study mate that one could have had in the turmoil of completing a manuscript. Gopal Guru's generous yet demanding engagement on issues of dignity and politics marked an important moment of growth for me.

Many cherished friends enhanced my thinking as this work took shape and evolved slowly across the years. Satya Mohanty, Debra Castillo and Chandra Talpade Mohanty had begun to nurture my engagement with narratives of women in political movements at Cornell University, as had Ann Rosalind Jones earlier at Smith College, even before I had begun to think of the Tebhaga women—their imprints remain. In Kolkata, Shefali Moitra and Supriya Chaudhuri posed intellectual challenges that I hope I will yet be able to rise to in the future. Sajni Mukherji exemplified the wisdom of celebrating pure affection and knitting communities of choice, as so many of the Tebhaga women had done. Anjum Katyal, with genuine curiosity and honed experience, held my hand through the various stages of searching for a way of writing this history that would not kill its spirit. Moinak Biswas bracketed the years of putting this book together with his thoughtful engagement in its early stages and valuable feedback once it was done. Animated conversations with Nilanjana Gupta across several decades underlie this book, and others, with Ruchir Joshi, Amlan Dasgupta, Swapan Chakravorty, Nilanjana Chatterjee, Indrani Chatterjee, Krishna Bandopadhyay and Sibaji Bandyopadhyay brought much joy and dimension to the effort of writing it. Dilip Simeon drew me into work on the Violence Mitigation and Amelioration Project, and then with Aman Trust, which enhanced my understanding of violence, and of the intricate connections between activism and academics. Vrinda Grover kept me going on the strength of a pact we had made with each other that I would complete my Tebhaga book and she her's on the Sikh riots—she's worked instead with such dedication and brilliance towards making feminist legal activism a force to reckon with in this past decade that I am compelled to offer her a spirited salute. As for Jojo Bose, Kunal and Rupa Sengupta, Shankho Chowdhury, Vahista Dastoor and Dolly Dadlani—they egged me on in feigned disbelief that I would ever finish this blessed book. How could I lose the bet? Shaio Bose, I have to admit, has always stood loyally by me—even in such battles.

The indomitable feisty solidarity of feminist scholar-activists that has been forged across this subcontinent in the last fifty years has rooted me in more ways than one. Their sense of collective investment makes short shrift of closely guarded individualistic professional boundaries that are so commonplace today; and this has been an inspiration, generating a sense of responsibility towards something much larger than oneself. Vina Mazumdar, who began to support this venture even before I had met a single Tebhaga woman, knew how to be exacting and admonishing in a way that paradoxically placed one on cloud nine. The impact of her scholarship, relentless drive and affectionate twinkling eyes will always be with me. Sharmila Rege's interest in this history has been a motivating factor; that she left us too soon for me to share this with her remains a cause of sorrow. In Pakistan, Tahira Mazhar Ali narrated her own history of the Mahila Atmaraksha Samiti in Lahore, with a powerful sense of belonging that conveyed to me the expansive spread and impact of this women's movement in the 1940s. She too is with us now only in spirit. In Bangladesh, Hamida Hossain graciously extended herself to put me in touch with Tebhaga scholars, and to share little known local histories; and, in several lively conversations across the subcontinent, Meghna Guhathakurta and Amena Mohsin alerted me to differently nuanced contemporary perspectives on this shared history of the two Bengals. Tanika Sarkar's work on women revolutionaries of Bengal opened up new ways of reading women's history for me in the initial stages of this work, and the excitement of its catalytic force remained with me even as I went in different directions. Kumkum Sangari's incisive theoretical analyses and her fine nuanced sensitivity as a person came to work together as a stimulus in my own attempts to forge ways of understanding women's shaping of history and culture. Uma Chakravarti, whom I have admired so much across decades for her wisdom and for carrying it so light, extended a thoughtful invitation to the Gender Workshop at the IIAS, and then firmly insisted that I apply for a fellowship to complete my book. I could not let her down. Urvashi Butalia's wonderful, pioneering work in oral history prepared the ground for mine. I have felt deeply honoured by her unflagging faith in this book across all these years, and the quietly enriching depth of her own reflections has meant even more to me, I suspect, than I understand as yet. V. Geetha's unbelievable generosity with my half-baked drafts, her camaraderie and her infectious intellectual excitement redoubled my investment in the tough, beautiful and poignant history of the Tebhaga women. It is the sheer joy of this sharing that finally propelled this book into being.

My father Jaikishan, my brother and sister-in-law Sumeet and Malini, and my nieces Kahini and Ishika kept me securely grounded with their affectionate teasing and indulgent acceptance of my eccentricities ... and that is important. The one person I would have wanted most to read this book is my mother—it is wonderful how she continues to grow, in my understanding of her, as I become more capable of such understanding.

Finally, I have been deeply moved by the generosity of all the Tebhaga women and men in Bangladesh and West Bengal, and their concerted efforts, both joyous and painful, to recall a time long past and reflect on its continued relevance. The power of their commitment, evident even in extreme disillusionment, and their sheer capacity for humane engagement will always stay with me. I sincerely hope that what I have to offer now would have lived up to their expectations had they lived to read it.

# Introduction

THERE IS A powerful prehistory of women's political activism in South Asia that has never found acknowledgement as a women's movement in the pages of history. Overwhelmed by nationalism and the coming of independence, which occupied centre stage in the Indian subcontinent, mainstream historiography elided the other theatres of liberation being waged on the sidelines. The largest ever participation of women in peasant struggle in Bengal was couched in one such crusade for liberation from below, the Tebhaga movement. An estimated 50,000 women—urban and rural—entered the fields of political activism in the course of this insurrection and played a prominent role in shaping it. Some left histories did proudly document not only Tebhaga but also the extensive contribution of women to the struggle; yet, they too fell short of recognizing that there was actually a unique women's movement, sculpting it firmly from within and infusing it quietly with an indomitable spirit.

The legacy of this women's movement did not shape ours because of the ruptures of history—the partition, the armed revolution of the Communist Party (CP) and the violent crackdown of the state; even the very knowledge of it did not come down to us. The exigencies as well as the politics of writing history are such that some histories never get written, while others get marginalized; and the irremediable absence of a history of the Tebhaga women's movement would have signalled a critical loss for the history of this subcontinent, as well as for our women's movements. Thus it was in 1996 when I began to grapple with the resources we still had available to us in the present for approaching a lived past fast slipping out of our reach.

The Tebhaga movement was launched during the harvest of 1946, three years after the Bengal famine, by severely exploited sharecroppers. It was led by the Communist Party of India (CPI) and spread across the vast span of undivided Bengal. In 1947, after independence, it was temporarily withdrawn. Despite the divisions resulting from partition, it picked up again in some districts of West Bengal and East Pakistan, and then entered a deeply contentious phase of armed struggle in 1948 that gradually ushered in its end by 1951. The movement was founded on a collective demand of landless tillers of the soil against feudal landowners for a greater share of the crop, and it grew to involve large numbers of urban men and women too in a powerful left solidarity with the peasants.

A spiralling in women's political activism had already taken place in India in the nationalist movement, especially in response to Gandhi's leadership, and in Bengal in retaliation against threats of sexual violence posed by the entry of the US and British soldiers during World War II, as well as the attacks by the Japanese. Even more compelling a reason in Bengal was the devastating impact of the 'man-made' famine of 1943, which led to a massive coming together of women across divides of class and caste, village and city. For peasant women, the experience of the period had included witnessing the starvation of their families, sexual exploitation by rich farmers and sometimes even being sold by their own husbands for food. Urban women, moved by the sight of emaciated peasants flooding the cities and dying before their very eyes, and by their own experience of the marauding soldiers targeting women in the cities, had come together with rural women to mobilize solidarity, resistance and survival. They did this through the organization of self-defence committees, initiating hunger marches demanding food and clothing, and working in the *langarkhanas* or soup kitchens for the famine stricken in the war and famine years. In the course of events, they continued with their activism into the Tebhaga movement, forging solidarities across the rural–urban divide. Only a small percentage of the women who participated in Tebhaga were from urban contexts, largely activists, of the Mahila Atmaraksha Samiti (originally the Women's Self-Defence League) of the Communist Party (CP), who, politicized during the famine work, had ventured out further to set up and work with women's groups or *mahila samiti*s in the villages. The majority were peasant women, largely from the middle and lower castes, leading movements for crops, protesting against sexual exploitation by the *zamindar*s and *jotedar*s, and taking on the leadership of entire villages when the men were arrested.

It was clearly a major social and political revolution in the 1940s in Bengal, marking the emergence of new subjects and unique subjectivities. Even the little bits of the known history of women's participation indicate that they must have played a considerable role in shaping the Tebhaga movement. Research on the gendered nature of their participation and the unique social transformations they forged on a ground receptive to their actions further reveals that there had flourished within Tebhaga a robust women's movement that had marked, for all the women who participated in it, a radical rupture with the past. This movement was as much grounded in the emergence of new subjectivities for women through the upheavals of the 1940s as it was itself rich ground for the flourishing of these subjectivities; and knowledge of these is the legacy the Tebhaga women have bequeathed in their narratives to our movements in the present.

Personal desire had found rich fulfilment in politics, enabling what the women recalled as experiences of *shanti* (peace), *nasha* (intoxication) and *ananda* (joy); and political desire had taken on 'magic' dimensions, fuelled by personal desire, transforming, it would seem, every dimension of lived experience. A fusion of eros and politics had brought with it a sense of fullness experienced but rarely in human history. It had truly been a time of harvest, especially for the women in the movement. Yet the harvest remained unclaimed. For then the violent turn taken by the armed struggle unleashed a ruthless destruction of the radical vision of social change that Tebhaga had shown was possible in both the personal and the political fields of life.

The existing accounts of women's mobilization in the left historiography of Tebhaga largely comprise descriptive elaborations of the ways in which they had formed women's brigades, organized marches against the zamindars and jotedars, thrown chilli powder in the enemies' eyes, or warded them off with household or agricultural equipment. Inspiring stories of courageous peasant women, like Ahalya and Batasi of Chandanpidhi, who died fearlessly in the face of gunfire, have found pride of place in these histories. But these accounts too remain straitjacketed within the conventional framework of martyrdom. There is little in them about how women had experienced the Tebhaga movement, the struggles they had waged from the standpoint of women, the nature of their solidarities, what their hopes, visions and transformations may have been, or their disillusionments and critiques. And the question of how they may have shaped the movement is never addressed seriously. How, then, could one begin to understand the transformations of this period and their significance from the point of view of women's lives as well as for political culture in general?

Some of the reasons this history was never written also have to do with the nature of materials considered to be valid resources of historiography, as well as with the gendered blind spots of scholarship. Conventional historiography, sourced from archives and newspapers, could certainly not rise to the challenge of an unrecognized and quietly radical women's movement, specifically because the Tebhaga women's movement calls for a recasting of existing frameworks, not only of history but also of gender, in order to be grasped in at least some of its complexity. It required, as I began to realize, certainly the resources of oral history, but also of memory studies and close literary reading, as well as of nuanced understandings of the different ways in which gender works across cultures of collectivity and cultures of individualism.

The decade beginning with 1989 had marked a watershed in both South Asian historiography and in feminist scholarship. As a result of this, several trajectories had begun to intersect in my thinking about women's collective political attempts to transform their worlds. Three remarkable works were published in India—the Stree Shakti Sanghatana's *We Were Making History: Women in the Telengana People's Struggle* (1989) alerted us to the radical relevance of women's political activism in our own histories; and Ritu Menon and Kamla Bhasin's *Borders and Boundaries: Women in India's Partition* (1998), and Urvashi Butalia's *The Other Side of Silence: Voices from the Partition of India* (1998) foregrounded the historical and political significance of women's lived experience of partition.

In Latin America, on the other hand, by the 1980s, the *testimonio* had gained ground as a new form representing women's participation in revolutionary political movements. It had crystallized as a genre, especially in the context of women's perspectives, narrated in the form of first person eyewitness accounts of collective political struggle from below that had been launched against dictatorships in power right across Latin America in the seventies. I had been working on such Latin American testimonios of women's political activism in the late 1980s, namely Barrio's 1978 narrative *Let Me Speak! Testimony of Domitila, a Woman of the Bolivian Mines* (which had also worked as a distinct influence in the making of *We Were Making History*, as acknowledged by the editors); *Sandino's Daughters: Testimonios of Nicaraguan Women in Struggle* (Randall 1981); *I Rigoberta Menchu: An Indian Woman in Guatemala* (Menchu 1984); and *The Little School: Tales of Disappearance and Survival in Argentina* (Partnoy 1986), a concentration camp testimonio of the 'Dirty War' in Argentina. What interested me about the testimonio was that it gives voice to women's hitherto silenced perspectives and their first-hand experience of politics; it is not to be confused with the factual evidence of testimonies delivered by witnesses in courtroom trials as the name might imply. It can be written directly by an activist or narrated by her to another person (as is more often the case). And in its narration, it nurtures collective identity and consciousness; it articulates the pulse of a culture, its modes of resistance, its dynamics of transformation, all this from the lived standpoint of women.

What most of these accounts—Indian and Latin American—shared was an engagement with orality, memory and unwritten histories; and they also gave us a clear indication that, given the gendered lacunae of both existing archives and historiography, the turn to oral resources had become inevitable for retrieving lost histories. Women's testimonios had already begun to make their mark in India too, even if not actually acknowledged as a distinct genre as yet (Panjabi 2004, 2009) and this was clearly evident not only in the case of *We Were Making History*, but also in the context of Dalit women's narratives in Marathi, such as Baby Kamble's *Jina Amucha*, 1986 (The Prisons We Broke, 2008) and Urmila Pawar's *Aaydan*, 2003 (The Weave of My Life: A Dalit Woman's Memoirs, 2009), and of Naxalite women's prison narratives in Bangla too, such as Jaya Mitra's *Hannaman* (1989) (One Who is in the Process of Being Killed: Prison Memoirs of Indian Women, 2010) and Meenakshi Sen's *Jailer Bhetor Jail* (Prison within a Prison, 1993). Another thought-provoking book that came out, even as I was well into working on these narratives was Sharmila Rege's *Writing Caste/ Writing Gender: Reading Dalit Women's Testimonios* (2006). All of these demonstrated that women's lives and activism demanded new methods of historiography; they had to be grasped not just as a series of events viewed from the outside, but as the events were lived out, and from women's standpoints, in order to be understood. At the end of the twentieth century, then, when I had started thinking of the history of women in the Tebhaga peasant movement of the 1940s, it became a natural choice to plumb the memory of it—in the memories of those who had forged the movement—before it faded out forever.

So I set out between the years 1996 and 1999 in search of the only sources of lived memory that were available then: oral narratives of the women and men who were still alive in West Bengal and Bangladesh. Most of these narratives, of more than sixty Tebhaga activists, leaders and theoreticians, urban and rural, Muslim and Hindu, and across caste and tribe, were collected across the districts of Nachole, Narail, Rangpur and Dinajpur in Bangladesh; Jalpaiguri, Mednipur, Malda and Kakdwip in West Bengal; and, of course, in and around Calcutta and Dhaka.

Three concerns became central to this exploration—gender, history and memory. The initial impetus was to understand the movement from the perspective of the women who participated in it and transformed it. The second was to explore a history that is no longer alive in public memory. And, as I gradually began to delve into the cumulative memory of this movement, it threw forth another challenge—to claim this history for a feminist vision of radical social change.

A full-fledged women's movement had been at work in Tebhaga, but it was certainly not feminist in the contemporary sense of the word, especially in the absence of any explicit critique of patriarchy. Yet, there is much wisdom in Ilina Sen's observation that: 'Perhaps women in the movements of toiling people have a longer view of history and are able to conceptualize levels and stages of struggle much better than their analysts are willing to give them credit so for…' (1990:14). This became excitingly relevant for me as, thanks to the Tebhaga women, I began to learn to see their movement and ours together, from other conceptual standpoints, in a longer view of history. The oral narratives of these women—and men—bore out that there were other sophisticated modes women had forged of engaging in culture and politics that had transformed the ethos of their times, and that can well extend and enrich what we mean by feminism in South Asia today.

The lived past of the Tebhaga women had become, in its remoteness, a 'foreign country' to the present; yet, why did it seem so critical, especially for the feminist concerns of our own times, to salvage it?[1] And how was I to salvage this lived past? These two question persisted; they haunted me through the years of this work and shaped it.

As I began to immerse myself in the times, trying to understand what life must have been like for them, other, more direct, questions emerged. What were processes of subjective transformation by which women located themselves in the Tebhaga movement? What were the transformations that they in turn effected and in what ways did this inflect the nature of Tebhaga? And what significance, or even challenges, do these subjective transformations, at both the individual and collective levels, carry for our understanding of women in history and women and history today?

[1] This is an echo of the name of David Lowenthal's book *The Past is a Foreign Country* (1985).

I deliberately desisted from mapping a comparative perspective on women in political movements in South Asia because I had begun to sense that it was not just a large-scale participation of women but a full-fledged women's movement that had been active within Tebhaga, and would thus require a different set of approaches. When I started engaging with the Tebhaga women, there were already some extremely rooted and impressive studies relating to women in political movements. There was, of course, Stree Shakti Sangathana's *We Were Making History* that I have already mentioned; Ilina Sen's edited collection *A Space Within the Struggle: Women's Participation in People's Movements* (1990), ranging from the Sarvodaya-led movements to the Naxalite Revolution, and including trade union struggles of fisherfolk and *bidi* workers, as well as Adivasi movements; and also Gail Omvedt's *Reinventing Revolution: New Social Movements and the Socialist Tradition in India* (1992) that discusses the anti-caste, women's, farmers' and environment movements from the 1970s to the early 1990s. More recently, there have been others such as Urmila Pawar and Meenakshi Moon's work on on Ambedkarite women, *We Also Made History* (2004); Srila Roy's *Remembering Revolution: Gender, Violence and Subjectivity in India's Naxalbari Movement* (2012); and Mallarika Sinha Roy's *Gender and Radical Politics in India: Magic Moments of Naxalbari (1967-1975)* (2012). Unlike these, however, Tebhaga was a pre-independence movement that had continued into the early years of the new nation-states of India and Pakistan. There seemed to be a radically different and unique quality of feminism here, unrecognized as such, yet actively supported by men too, that was quite unlike much of what we know about contemporary women's movements in South Asia. Hence, I was very wary of straitjacketing the Tebhaga women's movement with the questions of my time, feminist, historical, political, so distant and so different from the times narrated by these activists. I did not want my exploration of this movement to be framed by our contemporary debates and frameworks of analysis either, at least not to the extent that I could help it. I had yet to figure out what my approaches were going to be; all I knew was that I wished to start with a focus on the standpoints asserted in the lived realities of Tebhaga.

Neither did I want my understanding of the Tebhaga women's

movement to be inflected by fictionalized perspectives. Thus, I also held back from addressing the modest but rich body of literature in Bangla on Tebhaga, including Sabitri Ray's wonderful *Paka Dhaner Gaan* (1986), a novel extremely nuanced and sensitive to the women's perspectives; from Bangladesh, Akhtaruzzaman Elias' magnum opus *Khwabnama* (1996) on the sharecroppers' struggle and partition, and Selina Hossein's novel *Kaanta Taare Projapati* (1989) about Ila Mitra, the legendary Tebhaga leader of Nachole; and a host of stories, and some poems and plays from both sides of the border.[2] So I refrained from any engagement with either the comparative, historical, movements approach or comparative cross-readings of oral and literary representations because I felt that it would have been premature for this yet unknown history, and could overdetermine my exploration of it. I decided, then, to lend myself centrally to the perspectives of the women and men who had forged Tebhaga, and read them in relation to the first-person narratives, local lore and local histories that were available. I hope future studies will take Tebhaga into account in analyses of women's movements in South Asia and that others will engage with the fine literary representations of the movement too.

I found myself focusing instead on forging a set of comparative approaches to plumb the activists' narratives—beyond what the eye could see or the ear could readily hear. They recounted their pasts as they had lived them, yet the significance, for them, of these events that they were remembering with such intensity, seemed to be hovering beneath the words and, of course, the silences, not fully accessible to me. I began to cross-read each activist's narratives in relation to another's, in the context of local documentation of the struggles, and also in relation to diaries and first-person narratives written by some of them, and popular songs, slogans and sayings of the time, all of which narrativize memory in different ways as crucial repositories of history. Each set of concerns in consequent phases of the movement, right from its prehistory in the famine to its tragic,

[2] *Paka Dhaner Gaan* has been translated as *Harvest Song*. *Khwaabnama* is literally untranslatable into English, but it means a chronicle/epic of visions/dreams. *Kaanta Taare Prajapati* translates as a butterfly trapped in barbed wire. See also the list of literary representations of Tebhaga in the Appendix.

uneasy culmination in the armed struggle, compelled me to look for more adequate ways of comprehending their recall and in fact also their *modes* of recall in the present, which ranged from impressive analytical narrations, proud celebratory nostalgia, barely suppressed chuckles and sad wistfulness, to furtive looks, self-contradictory confusions and sudden terse, grim outbursts amidst troubled, edgy silences.

The nature of memory shared too covered a wide range, from confident recall, both joyous and critical, to troubled, conflicted efforts to call to mind repressed aspects of the past, to other kinds of struggles against forgetting. There were also radically different modes of memory, as of the Santals, inflected with a powerful temporality completely distinct from that of historical time. All this gradually took up a critical place in my attempts to understand the cross-cultural dynamics of the past through the lens of memory.

Approaching a lived past such as this was a humbling task. It became a labour of love, of respect for many who forged it; and it required lending oneself, above all, to their standpoints, their visions and their disillusionments, in the context of their times. Perhaps what humbled me most was the trust with which they placed the stories of their lives as they saw them in my hands. The force of the commitments I shared with them, and also of the friendships with some, demanded that the ethical codes of scholarship be further extended to include the ethical codes of solidarity and friendship. The meaning of ethics in scholarship took on a deeper significance as I tackled this double burden. It extended from respecting their privacy where they expressed the need for it, to committing myself to stepping into their shoes, not only as a rational scholar, but also as a sensitive feminist comrade, and sometimes friend too, to understand the complexity and nuances of their standpoints as well as I could. It also meant that I had to continue to keep one foot firmly in their shoes, with the other in my own, as I began to represent them. I have tried my best to live up to their trust, not only in terms of keeping confidentiality and withholding the identities of speakers where requested to do so, but also in trying to do justice to their lives, their histories and their visions.

As I began to enter into long conversations with the Tebhaga activists in both the cities and the villages of West Bengal and

Bangladesh, it began to dawn upon me that what I was engaging with was not just an instance of women's participation in a political movement, but an actual women's movement—and that it had been forged through rich processes of bridging across various social divides, of caste and class, of ethnicity and religion, and of urban and rural locations. This finally led me to the realization that the insights of each woman's and man's testimonio, positioned differently across such divides, would have to be understood as a part of a shared history in relation to that of the others if I was to garner a sense of their collective vision and actions as facets of a women's movement. So what I have eventually tried to do is plumb the activists' standpoints on self and politics that the testimonios yield, and then woven their perspectives together, across often trenchant divides and varied locations, to recreate a lived sense of the women's movement that had once flourished in the fields of Tebhaga.

This is an attempt to understand a lived reality, and life is not, like academia, split into disciplines; it thus called for a comprehensive approach, in which the various dimensions of life could find representation through a transcending of disciplinary boundaries. This, then, is what this exploration is about. It is an attempt, not to address every factual aspect of this history, but to comprehend the women's lived negotiations with history both in realms of interiority and in the external world. What it represents is a grappling with the resources we have in the present for approaching, comprehensively, a lived past slipping out of our reach. It comprises a process of identifying and grasping their conceptual approaches; and of weaving together, or even reading against the grain of each other, a range of insights and perspectives of feminist scholarship, memory studies, history, oral history, Holocaust scholarship and comparative literary studies. The theoretical chapter titled 'The Retroactive Force of Interiority' maps a conceptual trajectory of this process. This chapter may be of interest to those concerned with the issues that find place here, and those working with oral narratives themselves; those who wish to follow only the story of the Tebhaga women may skip it without experiencing any break in the story line.

One way of anchoring my understanding in the perspectives of the activists was by keeping track of articulations that found resonance across those of others, as they seemed to be relevant to a wide range of women's lives; another was to explore the lived signification for them of the critical motifs of the movement—of motifs such as hunger, *mazaa* (enjoyment) or ananda (joy), *antarikata* (inwardness), *atiter jed* (the persistence of the past), *anchal* (the end of the sari with versatile uses, including sheltering another), motherhood and *premer jomi* (the terrain of love). The chapters are named and organized around such resonant articulations and recurrent motifs that represent the mobilizing forces of their times, as they experienced them, as they shaped them and as they spoke them. And if there is no articulation I could find that bespeaks the final disillusionment of those who quietly withdrew themselves from a collective shaping of history, then that silence too has to be telling.

Thus, I reached out from my own field of comparative literary studies and of course women's studies, to history, then oral history, on to memory and then Holocaust scholarship, holding on, all the while to anchors such as indicated earlier in their narratives. The first-person histories that already exist of the Mahila Atmaraksha Samiti, like those of Manikuntala Sen and Renu Chakravartty, were, when read in conjunction with the histories narrated to me by the Tebhaga women I'd met, exciting and easy enough to address. The first challenge though came with these very same women's narratives of the famine, written ones by the former and oral of the latter: there was a deeply moving and haunting quality to all of them, combined with a powerfully determined sense of women taking up public responsibility in a collective way that was unprecedented, at least in the history of Bengal, both in quality and in number. Collectively, they comprised a memory of the famine, the likes of which I had never come across before and which doesn't find place in accounts of production and distribution.

This memory of the famine had to do with profound affective aspects, the terrible moral abyss that it had opened up, and the collective ethical responses this elicited from the activists. The approaches of history were again inadequate for grasping the devastating lived reality of the time; and all the approaches of literary studies could not enable me to comprehend the collective rallying power of the metaphor of the anchal, the figure of motherhood, the sayings, songs and memories the women shared with me. Neither could they help me tackle the agonized questions the written narratives raised. I needed to understand ways of approaching these narratives from the vantage point of affect, as well as lived memory and oral history, also in order to grasp the motivations that had mobilized urban women into claiming political power in the interests of rural women, men and children they had never set eyes on before, having hitherto been separated from them by boundaries of class, caste and location.

I needed to comprehend too what it was about the nature of the interactions between the urban and rural women that enabled them to forge relationships of mutual respect and bonding that continued well into the Tebhaga movement in the face of daunting social hierarchies. In fact, the understanding of an ethics of care that had mobilized an entire movement during the famine—and of how this ethics, from being an affective interiorized acknowledgement of another's suffering, became a shared structure of feeling, and then transformed into a shared politics across urban and rural divides—began to crystallize only in the course of prolonged reflection upon the interrelations between the many narratives that I heard.

I had begun to understand that the Tebhaga women had been part of an extremely dynamic women's movement that predated Tebhaga and continued into it; I could also sense, from the exuberance and pride with which many recalled it, as well as from the deep unease and stubborn silences of others, what the power of their visions must have been and that it must have shaped Tebhaga in significant ways. The ananda, or joy, in their spirit of recall became a driving force for me—what was it that was so powerful that it had survived as joy in so many women, a full fifty years after the movement had died out? The other of memory as exuberant ananda, however, is memory as troubled reticence—and plumbing reticence is what proved to be the toughest challenge. The uneasy ambiguity of Ila Mitra's response regarding her explicit court testimony of the sexual torture she was subject to after being arrested in the armed struggle or the studied silence of Anima Biswas, who had been forced to flee to West Bengal from Narail for her opposition of the violent line, all became important in the process of making memory 'speak to' and interrogate the past in different ways. Practices of oral history led me to cross-readings of narratives of activists in the attempt to establish some objective sense of the repressed histories, as in the case of Anima. And in the difficult case of Ila Mitra, years of honing in the field of literary studies and close readings finally came to the rescue, proving that where direct articulation failed, the construction and interweaving of multiple perspectives in one person's narrative, and the recurrence of critical motifs too, could reveal deep ontological structures of bonding that made for powerful camaraderie and unshakeable resistance.

Ways of making sense of complex, elusive representations of violence and trauma began to open up after some reflection on the paths that the analyses of Holocaust narratives had forged, albeit in a very different context. The insights of such scholarship, and my own experience of the women's silences, ultimately led to the acceptance that there could never be any closure, any sense of finality, in explorations of memory, representation and oblivion, because of the erasure underlying every act of recall:

> Whenever one represents, one inscribes in memory, and this might seem a good defence against forgetting. It is, I believe, just the opposite. Only that which has been inscribed, can, in the current sense of the term be forgotten, because it could be effaced. (Lyotard 1988:26)

If, as Lyotard observes, memory is an apparatus by means of which human suffering can be tempered, contained or even expunged, then what was the horror of that which could not even be inscribed in memory?

For well over a decade of reflecting on Tebhaga, one word, antarikata, had remained the biggest puzzle for me in relation to the everyday contribution of the women. In their direct articulations of what their collective visions may have been, the women largely reiterated the anti-imperialist and anti-feudal ideologies of the CP, and at most discussed their fight against sexual exploitation by the jotedars and zamindars—they rarely had any sharp perspectives to offer on any other collective vision they may have forged as women. It seemed that they had not thought about political activism from the point of view of women transforming a movement—except for one woman, Bina Guha of Dinajpur, who said to me with quiet conviction that women had brought antarikata (a genuine, inward, heartfelt quality) to Tebhaga. On the surface of it, it seemed but natural; of course, women—who were the worst affected by the famine, both as nurturers of children and menfolk in the family, and were also exploited both economically and sexually by the zamindars and jotedars—would naturally participate in the movement in a heartfelt manner. Yet, there was a depth to Bina Guha's quiet conviction that told me otherwise, that told me she meant much more than just that.

The need to understand the significance of antarikata persisted stubbornly, and I was plagued by the steady refusal of every narrative to shed light on its meaning. It was only in the last stages, when I began pulling together the insights garnered from all the women's lives, that the apparently ordinary everyday relations of women began to reveal extraordinary significations, their intimate negotiations with each other, and with others across barriers of gender, caste, class and ethnicity, began to reveal critical transformations at widespread social levels, if only for a short-lived moment in history. In confronting the political challenges of their times, they had transformed their own selves and that of large numbers of their men. The women may not have thought about how they would shape the movement as women, in self-reflexive ways as we might in our times, but they had clearly responded to the needs of the times in radical, inwardly transformative ways. The narratives began to speak to each other, and it was gradually and only with a cumulative understanding of these recollections that the profoundly extraordinary quality they had brought to the movement came into focus. The Tebhaga women's movement forged unique ways of transcending social divides and led to a sense of transcendence in the secular sense—of being able to influence the march of history. And it went beyond the lives of women and touched men's lives as well in profound ways. It had truly been a revolution within, in the realms of interiority.

There was a pressing sense I experienced, that going beyond the factual knowledge of the Tebhaga women's movement, and understanding the *values* and *processes* by which it transformed politics, may shed critical light on a crucial period of our political history and have bearings for contemporary women's movements in India. This pertains especially to the role women played in the forging of intimate comradeships in a left unity across caste, class and community, and to their response to the hunger and violence of their times. There are evidently no links between this politics and ours; yet, across this break in the political legacy of women's movements in South Asia there are nevertheless powerful continuities—of modes of gendered exploitation, of forms of social marginalization, and of both determined and joyous modes of resilience, bonding and striving. Across this matrix of continuities, then, it may be meaningful to reconnect with a prehistory that could well have shaped us, that may yet awaken us to renewed understandings of ourselves in our movements today. It may be meaningful for others beyond our women's movements too, for other men and women with whom we also walk this world and share concerns of equality, dignity and justice, to reconnect with that which forged such an enabling moment in history—and also understand why it is no more.

# APPROACHING

# 1

# '*Sholte Pakano*'—The Rolling of the Wick

## The Mahila Atmaraksha Samiti and the Women's Movement in Tebhaga

*In the evening before lighting the lamp you have to prepare the wick. This wick was prepared by the Mahila Atmaraksha Samiti.*

– Bina Guha of Dinajpur

'Tebhaga andolan jodi prodeep hoye taahole MARS holo sholte pakano.' If the Tebhaga movement were a lamp, then the Mahila Atmaraksha Samiti (MARS) represented the rolling of the wick. Bina Guha, general secretary of the Paschimbanga Mahila Samiti in 1997, thus summed up the relationship between the women of the Tebhaga peasants' movement, launched across undivided Bengal in 1946, and MARS of the time.[1]

By the time Tebhaga started, a critical factor had been at work that had prepared both urban and rural women in Bengal for participation in peasant struggle. This was the experience of joint political work in an organized women's movement coordinated by MARS since 1942, and the sustained interaction of urban MARS

[1] The Paschimbanga Mahila Samiti is the women's wing of the CPI.

and Communist Party (CP) activists with a devastated rural populace in the relief work and political marches during and after the Bengal famine of 1943. This historical experience of MARS had marked women's participation in Tebhaga as qualitatively different from those in the pre-Tebhaga agrarian movements such as the Tanka, Hattola and Adhiar in which peasant women had already become politically active by 1937, though not in such large numbers as in Tebhaga.[2] The relevance of MARS' work and its rapid expansion across undivided Bengal also explains the significant increase in numbers that Bina Guha spoke about:

> We had prepared the wick; [MARS] paved the way for women to participate in the Tebhaga movement, in the peasant struggle. We did not have to try hard. Women were more than ready to take the plunge. Earlier there had been movements like the Adhiar, or other movements to take over the market places, like Hattola—women had come then, but only a few. But these numbers swelled up like tidal waves during Tebhaga. Like a flood they came.[3]

A vast majority of the activists, including women, were peasants, especially from lower caste or tribal communities.[4] In Kakdwip and Mednipur, there were the Mondals and Majhis; in Narail the

[2] By 1937, the Hajong peasants of Mymensingh, organized by the *kisan sabha* (farmers' committee), had already begun demanding a lowering of *tanka* or produce rent, which the tenant farmers had to pay in a quantity fixed by the landowner; the Tanka movement itself was launched in 1946 winter (Sen 1985:119). In the Hattola movement (1939), poor peasants in Dinajpur, Jalpaiguri and Rangpur refused to pay the *hat tola* or levy exacted from them by landowners when they came to the weekly market to sell rice or vegetables. In the Adhiar movement, also in 1939, in Dinajpur and Jalpaiguri, the main demands of the sharecroppers were the right to an increased share of the crop, from one-third to half the harvest, the reduction of interest rates on paddy loans, and the right to bring paddy directly to their own *khamar*s (threshing floors) instead of taking it to the jotedars' (ibid.:85–89).

[3] Unless otherwise indicated, the quotes are from the interviews of activists conducted in the Tebhaga areas. See Interviews Conducted for a comprehensive listing.

[4] See Cooper (1988) for a detailed account of the participation of different Scheduled Caste groups in the Tebhaga movement.

Namasudras; and in Rangpur and Dinajpur the Rajbangshis.[5] In the case of tribal communities, the Oraons comprised majority of the activists in Jalpaiguri, as did the Santals in Nachole.[6] Some Muslim

[5] While the title Mondal was associated with a range of largely depressed castes, the Majhis were a subgroup of the Mahishyas, who formed part of the rural population in Mednipur and Kakdwip. These Mahishyas were agricultural peasants of middle castes, somewhat better off than the Dalit Namasudras and Rajbangshis (see Bandyopadhyay 2004:68). The Namasudras, originally known as the Chandals, an untouchable or lower caste (opinions differ on this), were a fishing/boating community in the marshy areas of East Bengal, who improved their lot as pioneer cultivators and emerged as an upwardly mobile settled peasant community with the rapid reclamation of these areas. In 1911, over 98 per cent of these peasants were rent payers (*ryot*), sharecroppers or farm servants (Bandyopadhyay 1989:170). See also Bandyopadhyay (1998:1):

> The two most important communities which dominated Scheduled Caste politics in colonial Bengal were the Namasudras and the Rajbansis. The Namasudras, earlier known as the Chandals of Bengal, lived mainly in the eastern districts of Dacca, Bakarganj, Faridpur, Mymensingh, Jessore and Khulna.
>
> When these districts were ceded to East Pakistan, the inhabitants were forced to migrate across the new international boundary to the state of West Bengal in India. At the same time, a section of the Kochs of northern Bengal, living in the districts of Rangpur, Dinajpur, Jalpaiguri and the Princely state of Cooch Behar, came to be known as the Rajbansis from the late nineteenth century. Of those districts, Rangpur and parts of Dinajpur went to East Pakistan, while the rest remained in West Bengal. In other words, so far as the Namasudras and the Rajbansis were concerned, the international political boundary that came into existence in 1947 did not correspond by any means to ethnic boundaries, and resulted in the uprooting of these two groups of people from their territorial anchorage. Incidentally, according to the 1901 Census, the Rajbansis and the Namasudras were the second and third largest Hindu castes respectively in the colonial province of Bengal.

The Rajbangshis occupied, since well before Tebhaga, an ambiguous position between tribe and caste. Bodo-speaking tribes in origin who underwent a 1,500-year transformation from Bodo speech to a Sanskritic language, they registered themselves as Kshatriyas in the 1921 census, yet are now classified as Scheduled Castes in Bengal. See Nandy and Raman (1997) for a detailed account of the Rajbangshis.

[6] Categorized as Scheduled Tribes in India, the Santals are one of the largest marginalized communities and original inhabitants of the eastern region of the Indian subcontinent. They played a critical role as forest-clearing labourers of Bengal and Chota Nagpur in colonial times. The history of the Santals from the colonial period

women also played an active role in the movement, especially in Mednipur and Narail.

Accounts of the widespread participation of women as activists and leaders in the Tebhaga movement are to be found only in left histories. Yet, even these are inadequate because of their use of criteria modelled on formal leftist male activism. They subsume women's political issues and activities under the conventional rubric of their contribution to Tebhaga as an anti-feudal and anti-imperialist struggle. They depict women's roles as being 'additive' or merely supportive of agendas set by the CP and the *krishak samitis* (peasants' committees), and are devoid of any understanding of the significance of women's gendered demands, or of the ways in which they transformed the movement.[7] Peter Custers' book, *Women in the Tebhaga Uprising* (1987), on the other hand, is marked by a surprising lack of class

---

onwards has been one of a continuous struggle to resist the encroachment of their land by the colonial government and the *zamindari* system (Banerjee 2002:244).

This feature of women's participation cannot be read in isolation from the fact that lower-caste and tribal women played an important role in agricultural and income-generation activities (such as the selling of produce), and hence enjoyed greater autonomy and mobility than did their middle-class counterparts. They were less limited by constructions of gender regulating the sexuality and mobility of middle-class women right through the history of the reform movements and the era of nationalism in India.

[7] The writings of Sunil Sen (1985) and Arati Ganguly (1992) document that Tebhaga was marked by the participation of a large number of women, unprecedented in any agrarian struggle before in Bengal. They record the formation of women's brigades (*naribahinis*), and document that women also became leaders of the movement, carried rice-processing equipment as arms in some forces (*gaynbahinis*), used chilli powder against the enemy, built up an espionage system, and so on. These works, though, are not informed by a *gendered* perspective that is capable of dealing with the ways in which gender politics is inflected by class, communal and nationalist politics. And Kunal Chattopadhyay's (1987) work, which *is* sensitive to some of these aspects, does not recognize that there was a grassroots women's movement at work during Tebhaga; hence, the perspective is one of women in political movements. Renu Chakravartty's *Communists in the Indian Women's Movement* (1980) and Manikuntala Sen's memoirs *Shediner Katha* (1982) clearly project an understanding of a women's movement, but Tebhaga is only one of their concerns—Chakravartty takes into account an entire span of the country from the late 1930s to the 1950s, while Sen, though she does focus on Bengal, and is the most nuanced of the lot, covers a range of issues and movments from the late 1930s to the early 1960s.

perspective, rather simplistic views of patriarchy and notions of the 'spontaneous militancy' of women, all of which are limited and often verge on inaccuracy.[8] Adrienne Cooper's impressive work, *Sharecropping and Sharecroppers' Struggles in Bengal: 1930–1950* (1988), has the most analytical approach to issues of gender, but this constitutes, unfortunately, only a minuscule portion of the book.[9] So, while there is a substantial body of historical writing on Tebhaga—including Barman (1997); Dasgupta (1995); Dutta (1985); Ghatak (1984); Ghosh (1987); Haoldar (1996); Majumdar (1993); Niyogi (1996); Rasul (1982, 1989); Sen, S. (1993); Siddiqui (1987); Singha (1983); and Umar (2004)—it is marked by a stark lacuna vis-à-vis gendered perspectives on the movement. There has been virtually no sustained gender-sensitive analysis of women's political activism in terms of Tebhaga or how it shaped our histories.

The Tebhaga movement signals a critical juncture in history with both, the largest participation ever of women in peasant struggle in Bengal and a major coming together of urban and rural women. It was marked by distinctive democratizing conditions within which women's contribution to political culture could not only flourish, but

[8] The major problems with this odd study are the lack of a class perspective, an unproblematized hypothesis about the 'spontaneous militancy of women', and a simplistic view of patriarchy, communalism and nationalism. Custers' view is that the Communist Party, through its patriarchal bias, prevented the joint efforts of the women from developing into a far more effective force, which could have contributed to an assumed revolutionary situation at the national level. He completely ignores the role played by the British colonial government, and the liberal nationalism of the Congress leadership, in diffusing the potential of liberation struggles (including women's movements) from below. His argument also lacks evidence and historicizing, and sets up an easy polarization between a 'patriarchal CP leadership' and 'spontaneously militant women'. He does not even touch upon the question of whether their political experience helped the women overcome their own patriarchal conditioning, and if so, how?

[9] This book has but a few pages of a chapter that deals with women in the Tebhaga movement, yet it shows by far the most mature, though still inadequate, approach evident in these works. Cooper is sensitive to ways in which class and communal politics, and patriarchy, intersected in the Tebhaga movement. Also, acknowledging that the demands of Tebhaga were not won immediately, she still asserts its historical significance in that the movement changed people's lives and struggles in other ways. However, her discussion ends exactly at the point where the investigation should begin for a gendered historical understanding to develop.

actually give it unique shape. The women's movement, that developed in the Mahila Atmaraksha Samiti and in the mahila samitis set up by the CP in areas where MARS did not exist, and the Bengal Provincial Krishak Sabha led by the Communist Party both mutually reinforced each other during that period. The widespread establishment of mahila samitis was, however, the result of a gradual process of politicization across the decade, leading up to Tebhaga, and it was as much the temper of the times that made possible the unique left unity of Tebhaga, across gender, class, caste and tribe, and urban and rural locations. How women gradually equipped themselves across the famine and the 1940s to forge a movement and gain the political confidence that ultimately led to their dynamic participation in Tebhaga is sadly no more a part of a lived memory of politics, far less of official history.

## The Discovery of New Subjects in the 1940s: A Gendered Perspective

*The dream of socialism was in the air and the young shared it.*

– Manikuntala Sen

Manikuntala Sen's sentiments reverberated in powerfully poetic, nostalgic and pained echoes across all the interviews with the Tebhaga women. A member of the CP and a stalwart of MARS in Calcutta, she had been active in the students' movement and then in the women's movement. She travelled widely across Bengal during and after the famine working for the CP, and to extend the work of MARS to the towns and villages in the far reaches of the state, and later during Tebhaga too. Activists I met spoke of her with affection, one even recalling the shadow theatre she had brought to their village in the pre-Tebhaga years.

The 'magic' of the times lay not only in the women's experiences of joyous subjectivity, such as mazaa and antarikata, or ananda and shanti.[10] Travelling across the cities, towns and villages of West Bengal

[10] The first two articulated by Poko Oraoni, a peasant woman of the Oraon tribe of Jalpaiguri and Bina Guha, an urban leader of Dinajpur, and the last two by Phuli Goldar, a Namasudra peasant activist of Narail.

and Bangladesh, in conversation with scores of Tebhaga activists, I realized that in order to understand the women's movement in Tebhaga, one would first have to lend oneself to this dream, and then pull oneself out of it to analyse it from the hindsight of history in a way Tebhaga women could never have done in their own times. It also took me time to cut through the magic of this utopia and to recognize what the limitations of this dream could have been for women.

What were 1940s like on which this dream was nurtured? Major upheavals had led to crucial and widespread transformations in gendered social sensibility. It was an already richly layered sense of ethical transformations that created the grounds for the massive participation of women in these struggles for equality and justice in Bengal. The writings of Manikuntala Sen, Ashoka Gupta, Sabitri Ray and other women are testimony to these transformations. The intensity came from famine experiences, which brought urban activists and rural masses together in effective bonding and political collectives; the intersection of literary and political cultures in Bengal, the force of the CP, the Progressive Writers' Association, the Indian People's Theatre Association and the Anti-Fascist Writers' Union; the formation of MARS; the powerful force of women's education, with large numbers having gained access to colleges and universities; and the changing contexts of middle-class women's lives. Among other factors was the powerful force of elite nationalism, the massive mobilization of women in the Gandhian movement, albeit as *sahadharminis* (wives; literally, those who participate together with their husbands, in the upholding of *dharma* or religious duty) in political struggle; and national liberation movements from below, a polarization of identities, Hindu and Muslim, and a simultaneous rejection of such communal polarization in the moves towards class unity. All this culminated in partition: massive dislocations, the armed struggle of the CP and the violent crackdown of the state. The coexistence of several contrary and uneven impulses lent this period its powerful vibrancy as well as its dynamically transitory character that ushered in unprecedented experiences of history.[11]

[11] Some of this was worked out in conversation with V.Geetha.

It was a decade marked by a secular modernity of political perspectives, most evident in the critique of power. There was a renewed investment in freedom, such that the logic of national emancipation became the ground for the emancipation of women too. Significantly also, there was people's own analytical wisdom garnered from the lived experience of the grimness of the times, ranging from harsh colonial repression and feudal exploitation to the devastating Bengal famine and partition, as well as from the layered political experiences of tackling them. Severe injustice often becomes the basis for the emergence of powerful ethical forces in culture. Remarkable about this decade was also a powerful ethical imperative underlying a culture of radical openness to contending political philosophies, an ability to imbibe from apparently contrary ideologies—anti-fascist and left to Gandhian. This non-partisan openness eventually became a crucial factor in drawing women from varied walks of life and political persuasions into the women's movement.

What was extraordinary about the women, and especially the peasant women, was the unalloyed *modernity* of the political perspectives in their critique of power. Their discussions of oppression, exploitation and emancipation were never framed in terms of cosmogonic transformations, nor in terms of expectations of protectionism and consequent betrayals by the lord, king or ruler, as has been observed in many a peasant movement in Indian history. Underlying every single discussion was the questioning of political power, be it at the local level, that is, of the local feudal head, the zamindar or jotedar, or at a more national or even international level of imperialism.[12] The intensity and spread of this questioning

[12] With the introduction of the Permanent Settlement Act of 1793, the British liquidated most of the hereditary rights of the old zamindars, who, as powerful feudal lords of Bengal, had become political obstacles to the growth of British power. In their place were instituted a new class of zamindars who were under an obligation to pay a fixed rent to the government. As a result of this, a majority of the cultivators lost their ownership of land, reducing peasants to the state of semi-serfs. Across time, and especially with the absentee landlordism resulting from the mass migration of zamndars to the cities, there emerged a new class of intermediaries, the jotedars, who were a landed class that leased land from the zamindars and sublet it to landless sharecroppers (Majumdar 1993:17–21). Jotedars also engaged sharecroppers

of power, which was also extremely gendered, transcending by far the Gandhian woman's role of the sahadharmini in politics, was, as Passerini (1996:132) puts it, 'a way of recognizing *transcendence in the secular sense*', and a 'shared project of...*forcing the march of history* by means of a participation *capable of interpreting* it and restoring objectivity to it thanks to an affirmation of extreme subjectivity' (emphasis added).

I would argue that the nature and spread of the prolonged history of exploitation in Bengal, which led to an organic questioning of power among the peasants, also contributed to this transition to the secular. One explanation for such transformation could be that this was a result of the interventions of the CP, which had already been working in these areas for more than a decade when the Tebhaga peasants' movement was launched. The Bengal Provincial Krishak Sabha, which initiated the Tebhaga movement led by the CP, had originally been founded within the Congress Party, but was extended primarily by radicals who had been imprisoned for terrorist activities and were released in the 1930s. Thus, by the late 1930s, the peasants had already been organized by the krishak *sabha* (Cooper 1988:5).

The experiences of the 1930s ranged from the peasants' direct understanding of the workings of feudal power as revealed to them in their political activities right through the protests of the Tanka movement (Mymensingh, 1937–46), Hattola (Dinajpur, Jalpaiguri and Mednipur, 1939) and the Adhiar Andolan (Dinajpur and Jalpaiguri, 1939). On 21 March 1940, under the patronage of the ministry of Fazlul Haq, the *Report of the Bengal Land Revenue Commission* (popularly known as the Floud Commission) recommended that two-thirds of the crop should go to the tillers of the land (Majumdar 1993:29).[13] The krishak sabha had also taken up the task of mobilizing peasants all over Bengal to demand the

---

independently for their own lands. In Bengal most of the landlords were Hindus and the tenants Muslims or lower-caste Hindus. Also see Chaterjee (1997:57–66) for an account of the land relations that led to the severe exploitation of sharecroppers.

[13] It was a landmark report in that it also recommended the abolition of the zamindari system and the elimination of the *bargadari* or sharecropper system, stipulating that the *bargadars* be regarded as tenants with definite rights to the land that they tilled.

implementation of the Floud Commission, but before that could happen, the famine hit Bengal. The experience of the famine itself, witnessing the role played by the hoarders in this, the continuing food scarcity, the mounting oppression of the jotedars through the inflation of the war years, and the nexus between the imperialist forces and the jotedars that resulted in crackdowns on the peasants by the British police, intensified the peasants' critique of both feudal and imperialist power. What is especially noteworthy is that when I spoke to the Santals of Nachole they too launched into a fierce critique of the CP as, they asserted, it had been narrated to them by their predecessors in their political terms; it was a critique of the lack of vision of the leadership, articulated not in cosmogonic or anti-feudal terms, but in the language of contemporary political strategy.[14]

Various contrary political influences had fed into the making of MARS. Renu Chakravartty and Manikuntala Sen, two of the most reputed communist leaders of Bengal, and founder members of MARS, started their accounts of political influences in their lives, unexpectedly, with Gandhi. Chakravartty asserts, on the very first page of her book:

> Gandhi had the foresight to comprehend that only with the active participation of women could the unlettered home of the peasant be a bastion of the freedom struggle. Had this not been done, a major part—perhaps the majority of the population—would have been left out of the vortex of our liberation struggle. (1980:1)

Manikuntala Sen, on the other hand, recalls, 'Gandhiji's civil disobedience movement moved me deeply.... I said, "Why shouldn't we respect a man who himself lives like an ascetic, leading his countrymen on the road to freedom?"' (2001:25). Citing the 'defiance' with which 'women in their thousands' participated in the

[14] The Santals of Nachole (now in Bangladesh) were uncompromising in their critique of the CP, holding it squarely responsible for the lack of vision that had led to the devastation of an entire population of Santals. Under the leadership of the CP, the Santals had killed a Muslim *daroga* (guard) of the British police. The British police took full advantage of the tensions that ensued, and attacked all the Santal villages in the area and razed them to the ground. This also led to the mass migrations of the Santals to Malda (now in India).

non-cooperation movement of the 1920s and the civil disobedience campaign of the 1903s, as well as courted imprisonment on a mass scale, Chakravartty goes so far as to claim that that this is what 'laid the foundations for a dynamic and powerful women's movement in this country'. (1980:2)

In fact, she points out with acute perceptivity that 'women's equality with men was effectively asserted in India, not through legislation at first, but through the ordeal of the freedom struggle' (ibid.). That their massive participation in the nationalist movement created the very conditions of possibility for the MARS women of the 1940s to even conceive of the original and dynamically transformative roles women could play in politics is something she acknowledges in no uncertain terms. She attests to the fact that the value of freedom that was the impetus of the nationalist movement had created the social basis for a valuation of freedom for women too, emphasizing that: 'It was in this climate of freedom for womanhood that my generation was brought up in our country' (ibid.). This privileging of freedom becomes simultaneously the font as well as the primary goal of political activism for most Tebhaga women also, as is evident in the very naming of '*Swadhinatar Swad*' or 'The Taste of Freedom', the most famous essay by the legendary Ila Mitra of Nachole. It is the pivot of Manikuntala Sen's political philosophy too, as the name of the English translation of her memoirs, *In Search of Freedom*, indicates.

Two other 'contradictory pictures', as Chakravartty (1980:3) aptly puts it, made a powerful impression on that generation of women:

> If the Soviet revolution aroused an irrepressible interest beginning with curiosity, [then] the ugly face of Hitler, fascism with its war against culture and women's emancipation, in the land of Goethe and Beethoven, Thomas Mann and Einstein, evoked repulsion in many of us.[15]

It is no wonder, then, that in stark contrast to fascism's reactionary approach to issues of gender, the Russian Revolution became the

[15] She also says: 'I hated Hitler's dictum for women: "Kinder, Kirche, Kueche"—Women were meant for bearing children... praying in the Church... [and] working in the kitchen' (Chakravartty 1980:4).

big inspiring force for women, as did Lenin's 1921 International Women's Day speech, from which Chakravartty quotes: 'The masses cannot play their part in political life unless women are brought into it' (ibid.).

Sibarani Dikshit, a college-educated activist and one-time president of the union board in Mednipur, in fact the only woman in Bengal to have ever become union board president, also cited the influence of Russia on the women of Bengal as she testified to their increasing awareness of international movements for the emancipation of women and simultaneously located the women's movement in Bengal within a larger international trajectory of emergent women's movements of the time.[16] She said:

> Russia showed us the way to women's emancipation. We all came to know about it. Books were published. Speeches were heard. We got all these from a variety of sources, we studied all of them. Yes, I did too. I do not remember anything now ... but we had to study.... It would not do otherwise. Each and every subject. We had to study all the subjects. Women worldwide prepared themselves for movements for their emancipation. Worldwide. They prepared themselves and started to fight. Amongst them [the countries of the world] our country, India, fought the hardest. In India, movements were being waged, women were being educated. In Calcutta, in the zonal office—people came to take classes—both women and men came. Women were gradually becoming international. Do you think this [the women's movement] could have happened here in isolation? It was a reflection of what was happening in the international arena. They also started fighting against injustice, and things were beginning to change. If there were no movements elsewhere, would there have been any movement here in India alone? No. This was a reflection [of what was happening worldwide].

Ironically, however, since communist literature was sealed off from India during most of the 1930s, Indian students and intellectuals abroad, geographically closer to the gruesome impact of

[16] The union board was an administrative unit of the village self-governance scheme, controlled by the government under the village Self-Government Act (Chatterjee 2003:98). It ran on the strength of volunteer corps comprising the National Service Workers' Union under the guidance of the National Service Board (ibid.:52).

Hitler's fascism, and with easy access to the literature of the Soviet revolution as well as the progressive resistance movements of Europe, were better equipped to begin conceptualizing, in the context of international politics, a new left culture, politics and social order for India.[17] This crossfire between communism and fascism over the role of women in society and politics facilitated a sharpening of vision, both in relation to class politics as well as gender in their linkages with nationalism. So, on the one hand was a perceived need to transfigure the exploitative class structure upon which rested the edifice of the nation, and about this Chakravartty (1980:5) records:

> I came to realize that our fight for freedom must bring social justice for the down-trodden, poverty stricken and the oppressed in our country... this has to be safeguarded not only by laws, the constitution and the whole state apparatus, but by *an awakened populace.* The entire structure of present society, based on exploitation and amassing of wealth for individual enjoyment must be brought down. (emphasis added)

On the other hand, national independence was conceived of as a powerful ground for the emancipation of women:

> Many in my age group ... could realize the link between our urge for national independence and the objective of a social order where true emancipation would be achieved for the mothers and sisters of my great country. (ibid.:4)

What is significant is that, for some MARS leaders, like Renu Chakravartty, there was also clarity about not just the intersectionality of issues of nation and class, and nation and gender, but about gender in relation to both nation and class. Drawing together both these insights in relation to international politics of the time, Chakravartty, then, concludes on a stand that also represents the evolved political platform of MARS:

> It was a fight against both feudal and capitalist exploitation, as well as against foreign rule in India and against forces of reaction in the world at large. If the happiness and dignity of women were to be

[17] Refer to the Indian Progressive Writers' Association that was launched in a Chinese restaurant in London in 1934 (Mir and Mir 2006:1).

> won and the security of the life of their children and their families were to be ensured, they must win this struggle. Women's liberation could not take place or be separated from the struggle of the toiling people for a better life. (ibid.:7)

Having located the project of women's liberation not just within the nationalist movement but also squarely within class struggle, MARS may have started off as an urban organization in Calcutta, but it was also conceptually well equipped for the political work that followed among the 'toiling people' of villages across Bengal right through the famine and Tebhaga years.

This was not just the perspective of highly educated women leaders; others, like Rani Dasgupta of Dinajpur town, who had interrupted their studies to work full time in the movement, also articulated similar political views. They had clearly left behind the old clichéd left view that women's equality would follow the revolution, as they worked actively with the CP in setting up women's organizations. Rani Dasgupta said:

> So, that was one of the communisms ... just as communism aspires for the liberation of workers and peasants, it also wants women's liberation. My reading made me realize this. I joined the party not for this sole reason; whatever little I read made me realize that our freedom will come along with the freedom of workers and peasants. This was also the precept of our party and I understood this precept even more clearly ... later on in my party life. While I was still a student, I went to work among the students as well as among the peasants, and of course, among the middle-class women ... we were doing the relief work, and while we were doing it, our party instructed us to build up women's organizations. P.C. Joshi was the then all-India general secretary of our party. He issued a call when our country came under the threat of Japan's attack ... I mean, when the bombings had started, he urged us: 'Our motherland is in danger. So, every mother and sister come out and work for the sake of the country ... to save your life, to save your children's lives and to save this country'... or something like that.

Within the nationalist framework, on the one hand, there was the deep respect for Gandhi; on the other, the imprisoned revolutionaries too won sympathy and were held in high esteem as courageous nationalists by the MARS women. Manikuntala Sen remembers her fiery defence of the 'terrorists' and their 'work' to members of her family: 'I regard this work as holy. I respect those who can court execution like this for the sake of the country because they attain spiritual release by sacrificing themselves for others' (2001:25). She also writes about Gandhi's visit to her hometown Barisal, where, upon hearing that a town as small as this had 300 'prostitutes', he had them invited to his public meeting, whereupon he rejected the conception of them as 'fallen' women and offered to take responsibility for their livelihood if they would 'sacrifice [themselves] for the country' (ibid.:27). Despite the fact of Gandhi having drawn in fifteen to twenty of the 'prostitutes' into the nationalist movement, and having initiated the culture of weaving *khaddar* into their village and, consequently, the home too, the affective power of the sacrifices of the revolutionaries had a powerful immediacy about it. It made Gandhian politics seem inadequate in the eyes of these young women, compelling them to look beyond the nationalist politics of the Congress Party and experience the stirrings of a new form of political desire, still rooted in deference to Gandhian ideals, yet seeking more dynamic confrontational action.

Manikuntala Sen also recounts being torn by her devout brother-in-law's pressure to make a choice between religion and politics at this time, and recalls the affective pull of the latter:

> I began to grow restless.... Conversely, I could see a clear perception of patriotism in my mother. One day, Ma had sat down to eat when the newspaper arrived with the news of Dinesh Gupta's execution. I saw Ma's eyes brimming with tears. She sat with the plate before her for some time and then just got up without eating anything. Ma's cries of 'Oh the poor child!', whenever she got such news, hammered at my heart. I had seen Ma being similarly affected by the news of Khudiram and Bhagat Singh's executions. I had gathered some pictures of some of the revolutionaries of Chittagong who had fallen under the sepoys' gunfire. Amongst these was also the picture of Preetilata. I gazed at these pictures secretly and felt an immense desire to follow in these people's footsteps. (2001:26)[18]

[18] Dinesh Gupta, Khudiram and Bhagat Singh were all young revolutionaries hanged by the British. Preetilata Waddedar was the first woman martyr of the freedom

Simultaneously, the language of women's collective responses to the crises of the times as evident in the *prabhat pheris* (early-morning singing squads) that came out in areas such as Pabna, were as reminiscent of the Gandhian women's modes of enacting civil disobedience as was the practice of *mushtibhiksha* of Vinobha Bhave's Sarvodaya.[19]

The fact that both Renu Chakravartty and Manikuntala Sen write candidly about the coming together of such contrary political forces, as the Gandhian and the revolutionary, in a snowballing impact attests not only to a political culture of openness, of respect across differences of ideology, but a willingness to engage across those differences within the women's movement.

The move beyond the scope of the Gandhian political role for women, however, also signifies a deeper motivation than the affective pull of the dynamic, heroic revolutionaries, which may not have been articulated specifically by them at the time, but is certainly evident in their political activity in the years that followed. This relates to the transcending of the limitations of both the elite discourse of modernity as well as the confines of nationalist politics for women. Sekhar Bandyopadhyay has argued (2004:165) that despite Gandhi's sensitivity to women's issues, especially from the time of the Non-Cooperation Movement onwards, 'in the mainstream nationalist discourse, the question of women's welfare and upliftment was subordinated to and became contingent upon the liberation of the nation' (ibid.). The fact that a more radical quality of women's activism than was available within the nationalist movement was forged within the economically lowest rungs of peasant politics is also logical given that the disinherited peasant had received short shrift in the mainstream nationalist movement. So, women in peasant politics were clearly not obliged to subordinate

movement. She joined the revolutionaries led by Masterda, and after conducting the Chittagong armoury raid, she and other survivors escaped to the jungle. An reward was announced for her arrest. After this, she also attacked the European Club on 24 September 1932, killed one person and wounded many. She committed suicide to evade capture (see Sen 2001:33).

[19] Mushtibhiksha literally meaning a fistful of alms, in this case rice, donated by each house in a locality.

their activism to the project of national liberation; also, the levels of impoverishment of the poor peasant woman and her family were so acute, and the conditions of their exploitation so severe, that it necessitated a far more radical politics than nationalism's framing of women's issues in terms of 'welfare and upliftment'. Thus, women in the Tebhaga peasants' movement were not only free to move beyond Gandhi and the confines of the dominant nationalist movement, it was incumbent upon them to do so. Their collective activism may not have been feminist in the contemporary sense of the word, in terms of a direct confrontation of patriarchy, but it certainly did transcend the patriarchal framing of women's roles within the nationalist movement.

## Emergence of the Mahila Samitis

In December 1941, the World War spread to Asia, the Japanese launched their offensive through South-East Asia, and one by one the countries of this region began to be subjugated by them. As the Japanese advanced towards the borders of India, the hazards of war began to be felt here too. The British fled back in the face of these attacks and made Bengal their base. Rangoon fell to the Japanese army in March 1942. Burma rice became unavailable as the British destroyed all the country boats in the coastal belt and banned agriculture as part of their defence preparations. In addition to massive food scarcity, a rapid escalation of food prices and extensive hoarding resulted; unemployment also soared. In the midst of large-scale evacuations and fear of invasion, the Allied forces began to arrive, villages began to be mowed down and airfields began to be constructed in their place in the interior areas. Calcutta was bombed five times by the Japanese in the week of 20 December 1942, leading to panic and mass evacuations, intensifying the turmoil (Chakravartty 1980:16–17).

In the midst of such extreme calamity, the British 'tommies' and the US army GIs who had come to guard the Indo-Burma front, and had then spread their bases across the state, began to increasingly subject women to atrocities. This 'news' was, of course, never published in the papers, especially due to wartime censorship, but spread rapidly by word of mouth and also through songs. The following song, composed in Rangpur, was sung to me in 1997 by Nirmala Rai in Baidyerbazar village. She said that it was circulated later by MARS in Calcutta to villages right across Bengal, informing peasant women about the loss of women's honour during the Japanese invasion of Manipur in 1942:

> What do I hear o *shaila*[20]
> What do I hear *kisani*[21]
> Its being said that in Manipur
> The Japanese robbers
> Have abducted the virtuous *kulobodhu*[22]
> And dishonoured them
> . . . . . . . . . . . . . . .
> To ward off the Japanese,
> This is our only weapon
> Beware, never let its edge be blunted

Once sung widely among MARS women in Bengal, this song articulates a political critique of sexual exploitation by the Japanese enemy in Manipur. It is about the violation of 'honour' of the kulobodhu, the upper-class, upper-caste, 'virtuous' wives; and it was sung also to the kisani, the peasant woman in the villages of Bengal. What is interesting is that despite the wide difference in class, and often caste too, such songs were sung by Nirmala and other peasant women as *their* songs, in the hope of uniting women. The precise nature of the 'weapon' is unclear in the recording I have of Nirmala singing, but it is clear that it is a song of resistance against the atrocities of the Japanese. That the nation is being invoked is also implied in the 'our' that extends at least from the kulobodhu of Manipur to the kisani of Bengal. Songs such as this indicate that upper-class urban and poor rural perspectives, as well as those across divides of caste had found a common ground in the sexual exploitation of women; and given that these protests were directed against the Japanese as

[20] Close female friend.

[21] Peasant woman.

[22] The one who maintains the honour of her clan.

well as the British and the US soldiers, they in turn helped in forging a sense of community amongst women across the nation.

The response to such sexual violence and to the call for the war against fascism was considerable. On the one hand, there was a concrete experiential ground from which women began to articulate an anti-fascist critique of the Japanese invasion of India; on the other, they began learning to defend themselves against the British and American soldiers who were flooding into the towns and villages of Bengal.

Chakravartty records that local women had reported cases of atrocities in the villages of Noakhali, which led her and other women to initiate a signature campaign and send it to the viceroy. Seven self-defence committees were started in Barisal to impart first aid and lathi training. Closed-door meetings or *baithak*s were held in Mymensingh to discuss the role of women in the war against fascism. Prabhat pheris, poster exhibitions and meetings were organized in Pabna. In Hooghly and in 24 Parganas, women's self-defence committees were formed to alert women to the impending threats to their 'honour' and their country, and women's meetings began to be organized in Calcutta too (Chakravartty 1980:20). Albeit 'scattered and spontaneous', these responses nevertheless contributed to the sense of a movement spreading, and Chakravartty recalls that 'a new type of mass organization of women was being born… it drew in women from the peasantry, the bustee working class, as well as the middle classes' (ibid.:20–21).

Thus, during the anti-fascist movement and in the relief work of the first stages of the food shortage that built up to the 1943 famine, a women's movement had begun to emerge, in the form of scattered but numerous local women's groups, in affected villages, mofussil towns, as well as in parts of Calcutta (ibid.:21; Sen 2001:73–74). Manikuntala Sen testifies to this, and to the growing need for linkages between the groups, especially to address the growing food scarcity:

> During the anti-fascist movement, some groups had sprung up in a few localities in Calcutta and in some mofussil towns and villages, but none was connected to another. Now the need was felt for an all-Bengal association. There were many workers, and a massive section

> of the female population was looking to us for guidance. We would have to come together, and they too would rise in revolt against the famine. (2001:74)

It was with the aim of organizing and coordinating this scattered mass movement that the Mahila Atmaraksha Samiti was set up, initially as the Women's Self-Defence League, on a very modest scale in Calcutta in April 1942. A handful of communist and other activist women of Bengal, such as Renu Chakravartty, Manikuntala Sen, Kamala Chatterjee and Shanti Sarkar, were its founders, with its organizing committee office in the house of Ela Reid, who became its first secretary.[23] Manikuntala Sen recalls the discussion regarding its naming at the first meeting:

> What would the samiti be called? Renu said, the men are doing 'people's protection', our samiti will be for women's *atmaraksha* or self-respect. Thus was the Mahila Atma Raksha Samiti born. (ibid.:75)

Kamala Mukherjee, one of the founder-members, points out the convergence of two factors, the smuggling of women and the smuggling of rice, that was evident in the landmark hunger march of 5,000 women, and that necessitated the coordination work of MARS:[24]

> Many of those 5000 women had joined [the *Bhukh Michhil*] spontaneously. We set up the Mahila Atma Raksha Samiti… almost at the same time. At that time girls were being smuggled—girls from good middle-class families—they were being sent … to the soldiers.
>
> Being a woman, don't you understand soldiers demand women? Because of sex—that is dangerous…. Just as the traders were smuggling rice to create famine, there was smuggling of girls as well. We had to keep awake nights to guard against such troubles.
>
> All soldiers were foreign. At that time, Calcutta was the chief centre of the Eastern Command…. There were agents. I saw the complete loss of morality during the war. People [hoarders] wouldn't give food to their own countrymen during the famine, and the girls were being sent…. Schools and colleges were all closed.

[23] Ela Reid, daughter of the late Dr Mrigen Mitra, was married to John Reid, a journalist at the reputed English news daily the *Statesman* (Sen 2001:74).

[24] Her maiden name when she helped set up MARS was Kamala Chatterjee.

> [MARS was established] … so that women could defend themselves. I remember, once Shanti [Basu] and I—women did not come out after evening, there was no way either, there were no trains or buses—we couldn't return home. We dared to go out because we were daredevils—women wouldn't normally come out then. Women were being abducted; they were sent away to villages by their families for safety. Calcutta was deserted.… Why only girls? Family after family. Houses were lying vacant—of the women only a few like us didn't leave.…
>
> [The training for defence involved] lathi and knife sports—what else? Actually, that some of us were going out was an act of great courage. There were problems to be faced in darkness. The training was imparted in order to ensure some safety for women, so that they could protect themselves if they were caught.

The Women's Self-Defence League was soon renamed the Bengal Provincial Mahila Atmaraksha Samiti, and gradually spread to small towns and villages right across undivided Bengal, addressing the needs of millions of rural folk affected by the Bengal famine of 1943. As hundreds of branches came up and MARS spread to every single district of Bengal, the notion of atmaraksha took on wider dimensions relevant to the villages too (Sen 2001:74). It began to cover a range of meanings and activities, from physical self-defence to self-defence against hunger, exploitation, ignorance and violence.

The felt need for a shift in class focus, to working-class and peasant women, was another reason for the formation of MARS, despite the fact that the All India Women's Conference (AIWC), a large nationwide organization of women, was already well established. Manikuntala Sen (ibid.) asserts: 'We felt the AIWC would not suffice any more. We would form our organization primarily with middle class and lower middle class, working and peasant women.' Rani Dasgupta, a prominent activist of Dinajpur, also confirmed this, saying: 'This had become the barrier.… They agreed to take in middle-class and lower-middle-class women, but rejected all possibilities of any intake of peasant and working-class women … the leadership of AIWC.' The needs MARS was addressing had necessitated this shift of focus, and its work then began to centre around tackling the impact of the famine and also training the women to acquire income-generation skills (Sen 2001:74).

A group of Muslim women including Nazimunnesa Ahmed, Rabeya Begum, Muksuda Begum, Laila Ahmed and Tasmina Khatun also joined MARS. Sakina Begum, the only woman advocate in the Calcutta High Court in 1935, who was well known as the *mataji* (mother) of the Dhangar scavengers and had been one of the leaders of their strike on 26 March 1940, also contributed to the work of MARS (Chaudhuri 2006). In Dinajpur too, Bina Guha recalled, Muslim women like Shahzadi Begum and Nurunnissa had joined MARS, and the latter, also a member of the Muslim League, had become a member of the district committee too.

Work started in collaboration with Women's Emergency Volunteers, and later the People's Relief Committee and the Janaraksha Food Committee. Registering volunteers, and teaching first aid and fire fighting were the initial tasks; with the food crisis, the work also extended to distributing relief (Chakravartty 1980:21). Eventually, the movement focused on three main 'planks': anti-fascism, independence and the famine: 'First, defence of the country; second release of the imprisoned leaders and the formation of a national government; and third, defence of the people from starvation and death' (ibid.:22).

Although MARS had been founded by communist women, it was marked by an ideological catholicity and continued to engage and work across various political divides in the interest of women. The release of national leaders became imperative because it was clear that without it there would be no independence. It was understood by now that women's emancipation could be achieved only with the freedom of the country and a government that would ensure people's welfare. Chakravartty (1980:24–25) records that 'from its very inception the MARS in West Bengal carried the "Release Gandhi" campaign right into the rural areas', demanding that national leaders headed by Gandhi had to be released and a national government must replace the present one 'propped as it was by the British'. Right through February and March 1943, huge meetings were organized by MARS women, from Dacca district to Rajshahi, from Bankura to Howrah to Barisal, for the release of Gandhi and other imprisoned leaders.

These meetings would draw women in numbers ranging from 200 to 1,500, and the meeting held in Bankura on 3 March 1943 saw 6,000 men and women, students and women workers join the demand for Gandhi's release. A year later, at the district conference meeting held in Dinajpur on 26 March, Rani Dasgupta, Bina Guha and other young members of the movement moved a condolence resolution on the death of Kasturba Gandhi, a protest resolution against the ban imposed on Congress Party member Sarojini Naidu to prevent her from public speaking, and yet another demanding the release of political prisoners (ibid.:51). Muslim women leaders like Shahzadi Begum and Sabeda Khatun, and the well-known Congress activist Snehalata Ganguly also attended this meeting. Chakravartty notes, 'This was the first conference which women of all classes, parties, and communities attended' (ibid.).

Meanwhile, the question of people's survival in the face of the hazards of war, as well as the acute food scarcity, demanded immediate attention. With the impact of the famine and rampant disease, the single most important task for the period became saving lives and caring for the famine victims. Chakravartty (ibid.:23) says of this period: 'Humanitarian work and political work became one and indivisible.'

The first significant meeting point of the urban and rural women's groups was in 1943 in the context of the Bengal famine. Starving peasants streamed into small towns like Dinajpur, and MARS set up langarkhanas for them. Kalyani Dasgupta, an urban activist of Tebhaga and schoolteacher in Jalpaiguri town, explained to me how the movement spread, with painstaking work, from home to home, *basti* (slum) to middle-class locality, from training in sword fighting to lessons in weaving:

> We first started working in a mahila samiti as members of the Mahila Atmaraksha Samiti. Now, how did we do it? We went to each house. During [19]42, we were the first to conduct home visits to talk about the mahila samiti. The Congress had a mahila samiti which worked among the urban middle class. And we started from the slums and the colonies. In the suburbs we worked in the peasant areas in the towns also among the middle class. What did we do? The name Mahila Atmaraksha Samiti in itself expresses

> our activity. We taught sword fighting, stick fighting to women. We made arrangements for women to learn weaving, we rented a room near colony para so that women could make *gamchhas*, mats etc. Though the quality was not very good, nevertheless we at least started making them.[25]

And upon being asked how all this related to atmaraksha or self-defence, especially when there were no British or US soldiers stationed in Jalpaiguri, Dasgupta retorted:

> Does atmaraksha mean only defending oneself against soldiers? It is self-defence against poverty, self-defence against disrespect; economic self-dependence is also a form of self-defence. The word atmaraksha has to be used in a wider sense. Then, simultaneously, we started the langarkhana because the famine had begun. In Jalpaiguri, around the station, and in the Dinajpur area, I saw women lying on the streets. Apart from working in the langarkhana, we distributed medicines, powder milk and some clothes with the help of the Red Cross. We also conducted the mushtibhiksha.... In each locality we started a mushtibhiksha unit.

As urban women, many of them communists, began working at the grassroots level, peasant women started to express a deep desire to organize themselves as well, even in the most backward of villages. 'That was the greatest contribution that communist women made,' says Renu Chakravartty (1980:34). Gandhi's vision of *swaraj* (self-rule) may never have taken root in India, but the wisdom of it was not lost to the peasant women, and despite the substantial communist leadership of MARS, the organization acknowledged the deep relevance of the Gandhian political programme, of at least the *charkha* (spinning wheel) for the reconstruction of rural society. Chakravartty recalls on this note that during the severe cloth crisis that accompanied the famine,

> at Kurigram village in Rangpur district, five MARS branches were set up. They demanded charkhas and cotton as the women wanted to weave their own cloth to hide their shame. The leaders of the movement of Rangpur were all peasant women, and not from the

[25] A gamchha is a long piece of cloth used for drying the body; also worn by men, tied around the waist.

> town. In this district alone, in 1943, there were already 3000 women in the samity. (ibid.:35)

In fact, the very language of women's collective responses to the crises of the times speaks of the non-sectarian catholicity of the women's movement, and its openness to a range of social and political practices and ideologies. The prabhat pheris that came out in areas such as Pabna against the exploitation of women were reminiscent of the Gandhian women's modes of mobilization in the Civil Disobedience Movement (Taneja 2005:146) and, in turn, of the Sikh custom of collective affirmation; so was the practice of mushtibhiksha, in response to the famine in places like Jalpaiguri, evocative of Vinobha Bhave's Sarvodaya practices of collective support (in Bahuguna), which came from Buddhist customs of offering alms. The responsiveness of the clearly left-oriented MARS to such varied cultural and political elements, as well as such rooting in indigenous cultural practices, would certainly have gone a long way in drawing in women from a wide range of social and political contexts. They would, thus, also have contributed to the phenomenal growth it experienced in the famine years.

Gradually, MARS started up more mahila samitis in small towns to continue with the relief and income-generation work in the aftermath of the famine. While urban communist women set up MARS in various towns, peasant women's participation in Tebhaga was a result of the latter's demands. This is reinforced across various narratives, as in Bina Guha's about the peasant women of Dinajpur:

> We were at a meeting in the party office. At least ten to fifteen women came… they had seen the play and our work. Their language was different. They said, you're going to hold women's meetings only in the cities and not in the villages? Come, come to our place too. You won't come?! We'll break your legs if you don't! They would then say in this [good humoured but insistent] manner.
>
> We finally said fine, we would go. We were wondering whether we would be allowed to go to the villages. Manida said, yes you can go. Go to the villages. So I went to the village for the first time in 1943. In 1943, with my cousin [Manida].
>
> At that time there was no conveyance other than bullock carts—or you had to walk. I was going to the village with Manida in 1943;

> on the way our bullock cart broke down. The bullocks would not stir. They just didn't stir. The peasants were there with us. They said, 'Comrade now you'll have to walk.' Fine, so we'd walk. We started walking—mile after mile in the scorching heat [laughs]. We asked them—how far is it? Just here, after this *kandar* [field] there's another one, and then … anyway we crossed about ten fields and then they said, see there's our village. We looked afar and saw the trees and the sky mingle with each other—but not a single house was to be seen anywhere. I told Manida, 'Manida I can't take it any longer' [laughs]. Manida said, 'Come along. Let us sing.'
>
> We reached there at about eleven in the night. We had started at about eight in the morning and reached there at eleven in the night. A women's meeting had been organized and all the women were waiting for us since afternoon. They hadn't strayed an inch. This was my first experience.

Her account demonstrates not just the absolute sincerity of the peasant women's interest in working in the mahila samitis, but also the ordeals urban women had to adjust to upon venturing into the rural areas.

Rani Dasgupta also narrated how peasant women drew upon the anti-imperialist dimension of MARS and harnessed the nationalist vocabulary of *swadeshi* to justify their own entry into politics. They would come to the women leaders in Dinajpur town clamouring for the setting up of mahila samitis in their areas. Their demand was, '*Amrao swadeshi, amrao swadeshi korbo!*' (We are swadeshi too, we want to participate in the Swadeshi Movement too). At the same time, Dasgupta's account demonstrates that the peasant women, in identifying themselves as swadeshis demanding a mahila samiti, far from mistaking the left movement for elite nationalist politics, clearly saw these women's groups as a forum for nationalist activities at the local level. Thus, even though they may have been involved only locally, such articulations reveal a maturity of political vision that comprehended the continuity between local and national politics, and the complex identity formulations that extended beyond that of the immediate community to encompass nationalist and anti-imperialist visions.

By the time of the Barisal conference in May 1944, Renu

Chakravartty (1980:53) claims, the fight against famine and pestilence had played a considerable role in expansion, and 'MARS had become one of the bigger mass organizations of women with a membership of 43,500, and branches in every district'. The fact that its openness in working across ideological divides, and specially those of political parties, had played a significant role in such an expansion was clear. Attending this conference were Congress veterans such as Nrityamoyee Debi, Amiya Debi and Nirmalabala Sanyal, all freedom fighters. Also present was the wife of the secretary of the Bengal Muslim League, Abdul Hashem, and greetings came in from Hamida Momin of the Muslim League too. And despite the fact that MARS had felt the need for a separate women's organization in the face of the urban, and middle- and upper-class bias of the AIWC, they continued to work in close contact with it; Kulsum Sayani, the secretary of the AIWC sent greetings for this massive conference (ibid.).

Emphasizing its non-sectarian character and striving to become a mass organization of women across all political divides, Chakravartty cites another powerful example from 1944 that elaborates the power of MARS' commitment to unity:

> At the beginning of the conference news had come in that Mahatma Gandhi had been released, and when the president Hajrah Begum announced the news there was thunderous clapping. Had not the MARS carried out a big campaign for his release together with others? It was an outstanding example for the women of how unity in action can and will in the final analysis be victorious. (ibid.:54)

In fact, Jyotirmoyee Ganguly, the reputed Congress leader who presided over the third conference of the All-Bengal MARS in November 1945, had also acknowledged the importance of forging links in the interests of women across political parties that MARS clearly upheld. At this conference, she had said: 'Many think this organization to be a part of the Congress Party. But I believe nobody wants to keep the samiti in their pocket. There are many well-known communists here, but they want that women of all parties should join it and make it strong' (ibid.:81–82).

That concern for the well-being of women was the overriding

factor, beyond ideological considerations, is evident also in the context of what Kamala Mukherjee called the 'constructive work' of setting up Nari Seva Sangh, a shelter and training centre for women abducted during the war or rendered destitute by the famine:

> Then, we started the constructive work.... So we set up the Nari Seva Sangh—do you know of it? It was famous. It was set up to give shelter to many women in [19]44... we did it. First, we had the centre. The government gave us a home. We brought back girls who had gone away from their homes to the centre at Lake Road... girls had been made to entertain soldiers at tea parties—there had been incidents like that. Most of the girls of the well-to-do parents were taken back.

The far-sightedness of communist women like Kamala Mukherjee and Renu Chakravartty is impressive. They safeguarded the autonomy of the Nari Seva Sangh, especially from political parties; and the choice of a committed, efficient and respected person like Sita Chaudhuri, who could rope in the efforts of a large number of women and lead it through the various political upheavals of the times, was strategic. Kamala Mukherjee recalled:

> Renu and I, we decided we could not run it. It is in Renu's report—we ensured it had an apolitical character. The first person we approached was Sita Chaudhuri.... We were almost of the same age. Sita was a homemaker with three or four children. We asked her to run it. Sushobhan babu, one of her husband's friends, he also went with us. Somehow we managed to convince her.... Eladi was there all along. She had a great deal of influence. She could also write in the papers, in English. At that time, all the mahila samitis worked together. We started the Nari Seva Sangha.
>
> Women suffer most during war—as we have seen in Korea, Japan.... However, we contacted Shyamaprasad babu, Bidhan Roy, Justice Charu Biswas, Sisir Biswas, and asked them for advice. They became our patrons. Sita was made the secretary and her mother, the president—she gave us Rs 10,000. Renu's mother was also there from the beginning.

The wisdom of focusing on the critical needs of women beyond ideological preferences became crystal clear when the CP launched its armed struggle in 1948, was driven underground, with all its institutions and activities banned, and its leaders and activists, including Kamala Mukherjee, imprisoned:

> It was a good choice because I was arrested again in [19]48. Though I was the founder-member.... Sita carried on the work well, and all social workers of that time participated in it. I was released in [19]51 and went back there again. Fortunately, this was not a party organization—so it survived.

MARS samitis had proliferated in all the districts of Bengal by the time Tebhaga started. Yet more branches were set up at the demand of peasant women who wished to participate in the movement through mahila samitis in their own villages. And in places where MARS had not yet reached, such as in remote villages of Narail and Kakdwip, yet other mahila samitis were set up by peasant women themselves with the encouragement of the CP. All these samitis also became political bases from which women then operated and contributed to, and shaped the Tebhaga movement.

## The Tebhaga Movement

In 1946–47, in the aftermath of the 1943 famine, exploited sharecroppers across undivided Bengal agitated to reduce land rents to *tebhag* (one-third) and to keep two-thirds instead of half the crop they cultivated on land sublet by zamindars and jotedars. The movement was launched in September 1946 during the harvest season by the Bengal Provincial Krishak Sabha, calling for a mass struggle among sharecroppers to keep tebhag of the harvest. As the fields came alive to the cries of '*Nij kholane dhan tolo*' (Take the paddy to your own storehouse) and '*Adhi nai tebhag chai*' (Not half, we want two-thirds), the movement spread from its starting point in Dinajpur to nineteen districts of Bengal. (Majumdar 1993:48, 101). Soon after the arrests of the first poor peasants, leaders of the CP went into hiding to guide the movement (Sen, S. 1982:106–7). Abani Lahiri, one of the most prominent and respected of Tebhaga leaders also explained that gradually, with the awareness-raising and systematic mobilizing efforts of the CP leaders, first men, and then women too, Tebhaga also became part of a strategy of the left to widen its base in the rural areas, as part of its fight against imperial powers. It also crossed communal barriers, with sharecroppers organized in a collective class struggle against exploitation and for greater control over land and crops. The movement was launched by impoverished peasants, led by the CP, and drew about 5 to 6 million activists into its fold (Ghatak 1984:35; Kamal 1996:2; Rasul 1989:142).

What is less discussed, however, is that Tebhaga also marked the largest participation and leadership of women in rural political struggle in Bengal. It has been estimated that approximately 50,000 women took part.[26] Urban women from the CP and MARS united with thousands of peasant women to shape the movement and lend it force (Cooper 1988; Chakravartty 1980; Chattopadhyay 1987; Ghatak 1984; Sen, M. 1982; Sen 1985). In relation to the solidarities forged between urban and rural women too, Tebhaga witnessed the largest coming together of women in the history of Bengal.

For all the women who participated in the movement, Tebhaga marked a rupture with the past. For peasant women, the experience leading up to the period included sexual exploitation by rich farmers, witnessing the starvation of their families and sometimes even being sold by their own husbands for food. The response was powerful—for they came together, across the rural–urban divide, to mobilize survival, solidarity and resistance through the formation of local mahila samitis and self-defence committees. It was at their insistence that the rampant sexual exploitation by upper-caste landlords and jotedars, especially of lower-caste and tribal women, was brought to feature centrally on the agenda of the movement, and even put to an end, particularly in districts where Tebhaga was more powerful, as in Dinajpur. The women also transformed the very texture of village society, at least in areas such as Dinajpur and Narail, by enacting

[26] Approximately 10 per cent of the primary membership of the Bengal Provincial Krishak Sabha, which spearheaded the movement, were women (Ghatak 1984:125). Since the membership was 255,000 in 1945 and 217,304 in 1946 (ibid.:119; Rasul 1982:174), there seem to have been approximately 21,000 to 25,000 enrolled women activists. As the actual number of activists was much larger—estimated to have been 5 to 6 million—it seems more likely that approximately 50,000 women participated in the movement.

shifts in notions of chastity, and by facilitating the emergence of a new, more egalitarian family.

Tebhaga occupies an important place in the history of both land reform and local national liberation struggles from below in India. It is marked by four phases. The first was from its beginning in October 1946 to January 1947. The second was from early January to the end of February 1947, when the movement intensified in unorganized fashion upon Chief Minister Fazlul Haq's announcement of the Bargadar Bill on 4 January 1947, and its consequent publication in the *Calcutta Gazette* on 22nd January 1947, to prevent the eviction of the *bargadars* and ensure two-thirds of the share of the crop for them (Majumdar 1993:50; Sen, S. 1993 :115).[27]

The third phase was from the end of February 1947 to independence, the phase of intense state repression (Majumdar 1993:118). After the creation of India and Pakistan in 1947, the CP initially suspended the Tebhaga movement in the interests of negotiation and national unity. However, after the betrayal of the promise of independence for peasants and workers, the CP shifted away from the nationalist position. Meanwhile, the 'Indian situation' had also become matter of debate in international communist forums.

Finally, after fierce internal dissent, the CP chose a tactical line based on the Telengana experiment and, with the slogan 'the Telengana path is our path', it launched its fourth and final phase, as a programme of armed revolution, at its Second Congress in February 1948 under the leadership of BT Ranadive (Majumdar 1993:118; Sen 2001:186). This decision was also in keeping with the influence of the Yugoslav Communist Party, represented by Edward Kardelj at the Cominform, that advocated armed revolutionary struggle against the national bourgeoisie (Umar 2004:40). This fourth and final phase of Tebhaga lasted from 1948 to 1950, with the party line being changed yet again in 1950 after the publication of the Cominform thesis of 1950 that now disapproved of B.T. Ranadive's violent revolution and the programme of overthrowing the state (ibid.:124).

[27] Bargadar refers to sharecroppers, so literally, the Sharecroppers' Bill.

The Tebhaga movement did not have any immediate consequences in terms of legislation. As stated earlier, the Floud Commission of 1940 had recommended a Bill to ameliorate the sufferings of the bargadars, which, sabotaged by the zamindars, was relegated to the archives of history.[28] The shelving of the Bill, however, served to increase the unrest. The Bengal Bargadars' Temporary Regulation Bill was published in January 1947, but was not immediately passed as an Act, leading to a spurt in the movement from February 1947 (Majumdar 1993:153–54). After independence, the zamindari system was abolished in India, and the main demands of the related Tanka movement conceded in East Pakistan, but it was only in 1950 that the Bargadars' Bill became an Act in West Bengal (ibid.:161). Yet, it was only after the redistribution of surplus land above the stipulated ceiling levels under the Land Reform Act of the 1970s that the realization dawned that hundreds of thousands of small sharecroppers still remained vulnerable to high rents and recurrent evictions. Operation Barga, implemented between 1978 and the mid-1980s, finally secured for the landless sharecroppers legal protection against eviction by the landlords, inheritance rights and a due share of the produce.[29] Thus, the Tebhaga sharecroppers' struggle did finally lead to the acknowledgement of the importance of tenancy and tenancy rights in the Indian agrarian situation, and ultimately resulted in both tenancy and land reforms in West Bengal. These are the most progressive measures in South Asia to date (ibid.:257–58; Cooper 1988:9).

This struggle for the right to a greater share of the food grown on

[28] Jyoti Basu, the Communist Party of India (Marxist) stalwart and chief minister of Bengal for almost three decades from the late 1970s onwards, had also been active in the Tebhaga movement. In his memoirs, he states:

> A draft bill had been readied and circulated. But this had been swept under the carpet later on. I asked Suhrawarddi as to why this has been done. Suhrawarddi told me that he did not know that we had so many landlords in his party! In other words, he admitted that it was these Zamindars who had forced the Bill to be sabotaged. The farmers waited for years. When it was realised that the Bill was only a pipe dream, it was then decided that the Tebhaga demand would have to take an agitational route. (2009: chapter 8)

[29] See Bandyopadhyay's (1981) study for an evaluation of Operation Barga.

land translated—over decades—into the most important land reform programme in India to date, but the peasant women's participation in active political struggle died out. It gathered strength once again only during the Naxalite movement, which, as the urban world often forgets, was also centred initially around food. In fact, one of the key songs of the Tebhaga movement, Salil Choudhury's '*Hey samhalo*', became a banner of the Naxalite movement of the 1960s:

*Hey samhalo dhan ho*
*kaaste ta dao shaan ho*
*jaan kobul aar maan kobul*
*aar debona aar debona*
*rokte bona dhaan moder praan ho*

(Protect the crop
sharpen the scythes in glory
our lives and honour on the line
never again will we give up
our crops planted in blood, our life.)

## Women's Entry into Tebhaga

In their narratives, documented in *We Were Making History: Life Stories of Women in the Telengana People's Struggle*, the women of the Telengana people's struggle explicitly take male comrades to task for patriarchal practices within the CP. Their critiques include accounts of inequality or injustices, such as the exclusion of women's perspectives from theory lessons; women being blamed for leading men astray from the cause by forging relationships with them or by becoming pregnant; and also women being forced into abortions in the absence of husbands or lovers. The Tebhaga women's testimonies are not marked by such a sharply articulated feminist consciousness. The reason for this seems to lie in the fact that their perception of their relationship to the male leadership of the CP was largely one of being nurtured in politics by them. The ways in which the Tebhaga women shaped the movement, however, have much to tell us about deeply impacting feminist transformations of political struggle, as I was gradually to learn.

Abani Lahiri, the Tebhaga leader in charge of north Bengal, confirmed that there was no conscious decision on the part of the CP to involve peasant women in the movement. Their participation was initially spontaneous; it was only later that the party took notice of the fact and strengthened its efforts to involve many more of them. In the context of urban activists, middle-class communist men were members and leaders in almost all the major krishak sabhas in the Tebhaga areas. And while many middle-class urban women worked in the villages, those who joined the peasant organizations as full-timers, such as Rani Dasgupta and Bina Guha of Dinajpur, Ila Mitra of Nachole, Kalyani Dasgupta of Jalpaiguri and Rani Mukherjee of Rangpur, were rare. All the urban women cite the experience of the famine as one of the central reasons for joining the movement. Many of them had come out to extend their services to the langarkhanas set up in north Bengal by the CP to provide meals for the famine stricken. The sight of emaciated and starving women, men and children lining up for food, and witnessing starvation deaths had exposed these urban women to the dire inequities of class society and propelled many of them to join MARS and the CP. From within these ranks, some of them moved on to working in the villages, organizing peasant women in the local mahila samiti branches of MARS and later in the Tebhaga movement too.

Manikuntala Sen (1982:161–64) recounts that peasant women fought by the men for their rights during the Tebhaga movement right from the beginning. As police repression became increasingly brutal and the men were forced to go into hiding, the women formed their own militia. The *naribahini* or women's brigades grew out of experiences of combat, as women successfully deterred the police, hired thugs and fought relentlessly to protect not only their crops and homes, but also their leaders in hiding. The weapons they used were their own—the sickle, the cutting board, the broom, chilli powder, etc. They blew on conch shells to warn the men of the approach of the enemy, communicated with the leaders who were underground and engaged directly with the police. They jumped in to save their harvest set on fire by the police, were beaten and tortured, and yet hit back with whatever they could get hold of. They faced any amount of personal persecution, yet continued to protect their men and their leaders (ibid.).

Arati Ganguly (1992:105–15) records that women not only acted as volunteers, but also assumed militant and strategic leadership roles and formed groups of women activists. They guarded their territory and harvest with weapons, and the police were unable to penetrate their ranks. They were vital to the movement and saved it by sheltering workers, confronting the police and providing food to escaped workers.

The first hurdle they had to negotiate was related to the taboo against women's participation in political life in the villages of Bengal. In the interviews, Abani Lahiri indicated that the party was initially unprepared for women's participation, and spoke about the accusations of 'spoiling women' that progressive male leaders had to deal with when women began entering the movement. Starting with the exclamation, '*Amra to bhabini je hajar hajar meye nambe,* age-old restrictions *bhenge debe!*' (We didn't think that thousands of women would step out, breaking age-old restrictions), he explained how other political parties would focus on the participation of women in the movement to run down the CP:

> First, to be very honest, as one of the organizers I can say it was our mental backwardness. We who went to join the peasant organisations didn't understand the significance and effects of women's participation. What would be the condition of the families if women participated? What would be the reaction of the villagers? Also, the striking power of women was not very apparent to men.
>
> Actually, the problem in the beginning was that those with vested interests would spread propaganda about us '*Je meyeder tthang tthang kore nachachchhe*' [that we were making women dance vigorously to our tune], and that we did not want to deal with initially.

However, as Kamala Mukherjee pointed out categorically, these thousands of women did not begin participating overnight; nor did they suddenly start breaking time honoured restrictions. What Abani Lahiri narrated was the experience of his generation of the male leaders of the CP, who may not have had direct experience of the kind of political history that Mukherjee had spoken of:

> I am a political person. I was in the Jugantar Party.... In the movement of 1931, 200 to 400 women were jailed from every district of Bengal. Some were released soon after, some took six months.... If you don't know the background, it is difficult to understand the Tebhaga movement suddenly.... There is a continuity in it—do you understand? And that women were coming out, going to jail. In the beginning, they didn't keep women in jail.... Only later, they began to arrest women. When I was in jail ... I had been arrested in December [19]31 ... for being in the terrorist movement. All members of the Jugantar Party were arrested. We were released after six years. How can you ignore this movement ... the Mahila Atmaraksha Samiti could not have evolved suddenly. These women, in later times, carried on women's movements, set up women's samitis, as did Ashalata Sen, Lila Nag, etcetera in Dhaka.[30]

In fact, Mukherjee too, who had been imprisoned in British jails for six years for her involvement in terrorist politics and was initiated into communist ideology in 1938 to become the party's second woman member, did not hesitate to point out the importance of the Gandhian movement in Tamluk in terms of its role in drawing women into active political struggle:

> [Think of] these women, and then in 1942, when Matangini Hazra died, the women's movement in Tamluk. Think of it—how great it was. This movement was the background of Tebhaga.... There were also women who were not educated.... Imagine, 200 to 400 women had come out from every district. This was surprising. The contribution of the movement lies there. Not that everyone was educated. If you look at the movement of [19]42 in Tamluk, the British army couldn't enter that place for two and a half years—they tortured people outside, they raped the women, but couldn't enter.... For two and a half years, Sushil Dhara, Satish Samanta, didn't let the British enter their villages.... Then after the cyclone in Midnapore we went with relief—we saw the fire on one side and we entered from the other ... seventy-five women were raped by the soldiers in the [19]42 movement—all of them were taken back home by the *mahishyas*. The mahishyas were an advanced

[30] The Jugantar Party, comprising revolutionary freedom fighters, was founded by Surendramohan Ghosh and ultimately driven underground.

> militant group—all these factors strengthened the later movements. You have to understand this movement, you can't see Tebhaga as a sudden event.
>
> There is a history behind the women stepping out … someone or the other from their families had gone for swadeshi. In the communist movement too, you will find people of the Swadeshi Movement … the Civil Disobedience Movement, or salt *satyagraha*, how women had joined them. Most of them were illiterate. There is a history of all these struggles. In the case of women's movements too, if there had been no Gandhian movement, the later movements would not have taken place.[31]

In the face of the unpreparedness of the CP leaders, however, it was on their own initiative that women first began to join the Tebhaga movement. Their entry subsequently led men to realize the value of their contribution. Once this had been established, the CP gradually created a supportive space for women's activism, facilitating rapid social transformation in the process. However, the question of how the party dealt with masses of women joining the

[31] One of the unique features of the freedom movement in Tamluk, Mednipur, was the large-scale participation of women and the establishment of the women's volunteer corps, Bhagini Bahinis (Bandyopadhyay 2004:180). Matangini Hazra is a legendary emblem of women's resistance. She was a staunch Gandhian who had participated in the Civil Disobedience Movement and was arrested twice for breaking the salt law and protesting against the tax. As part of the Quit India Movement, she had led a huge procession, largely of women, to the Tamluk police station. Defying orders to stop and disband, she was shot at several times by the British police, and died clutching the Congress tricolour.

The arrest of Gandhi in 1942 during the Quit India Movement, the devastating shortage of food created by the diversion of rice for the war effort and hoarders too, the rampant shooting and killing by the British police to control the power of the Congress nationalist movement, and finally the cyclone of 6 October 1942 that took an estimated 30,000 lives, led to the decision of the Tamluk freedom fighters to set up their own government, the Tamralipta *jatiya sarkar*, or the Tamluk national government, and cordon it off completely from the British. The relentless onslaughts of the latter, the killing of several people, and gang-rapes of women finally compelled this non-violent movement to turn violent (see Mukerjee 2010:81–103 for a detailed account of this movement).

According to testimonies compiled by Ramakrishna Bari and others, forty-six women were raped in Masuria and the neighbouring villages of Dihi Masuria and Chondipur after the cyclone (ibid.:100).

movement, and the problems that accompanied this development, was left unanswered by her.

The beginning was rough. One of the CP leaders who had played a nurturing role in supporting women's activism was P.C. Joshi. Renu Chakravartty's book *Communists in the Indian Women's Movement* (1980) is dedicated thus:

> To the memory of P.C. Joshi who, more than anybody else, taught us with his unfailing enthusiasm, to work for the building of the women's movement as a militant contingent in the struggle for a free India emancipated from the shackles of poverty, ignorance and degeneration.

Manikuntala Sen (2001:95) too says of him in relation to the famine relief work the women had started doing:

> The person who first showed us how to do this kind of work was P.C. Joshi, the then party leader. In order to fight for the special rights of women we would have to organize all the women save those belonging to the uppermost rungs of society. Women would fight in the freedom movement with all the others. They would be the pioneers in the fields of class struggle. Women would have to be organized for constructive work. The priority would be the welfare of women and children. Other struggles would continue side by side: anti-fascist campaigns and the movement for [the] release of political prisoners. These were some of the things P.C. Joshi taught us.

However, within the year, there was to be a major setback. At the All India Peasants' Conference held in Netrakona, Mymensingh, in April 1944, the same P.C. Joshi launched a public attack against the women. Sen (2001:145) records her stunned response to it:

> The accusation, roughly, was against us, the middle class women who were present there. Our fault, apparently, was that we had not mixed with the peasant women the way we should have. We might have been in the wrong. But he made many other complaints which I would not like to mention. We listened to this harsh criticism with our heads bent.

The women did not protest. That they did not, reveals a clear hierarchy, on grounds of an imposed 'party discipline' and by virtue of the fact that they had been newly initiated by the same person who had chosen to criticize them so harshly in public. Sen goes on to explain:

> Manorama Mashima and many other elderly women workers, who worked specially in peasant areas, were sitting behind me. They were upset by the criticism and repeatedly asked me to protest. But I did not do so because I had been taught to accept whatever the party leader told me and not to protest. Moreover, at that time we had a great regard for Comrade P.C. Joshi. We, the workers of the Women's Front had been trained by him to do the work of the Front, and were proud that we owed its success to him. Therefore, despite the fact that such criticism was extremely painful to me, I did not feel like protesting. We were truly upset because he had chosen to vent his criticism in a public assembly. Had he called us aside or said the very same things at a party meeting, we would not have felt so bad. It was the rule that leaders should come forth with their criticism at party meetings. But this was a public meeting. I don't know why he criticized us like that. (ibid.:146)

There is, however, an implicit criticism built into Manikuntala Sen's response. The sense of pain and puzzlement voiced here is not only personal, it is also about a violation of principles of comradeship. Sen clearly says that had he voiced the same criticism in private, or at a party meeting, as was the rule, it would not have been so bad. Between the lines here is a charge, or at least a reproach, for she had adhered to the party discipline and not protested; but he had violated both the party discipline and the codes of comradeship by humiliating party colleagues—significantly women—in public.

At best, it was bad political strategy, for not only was it shaming members of one's own party in front of a public whose support the party was out to win—hence risking a clear loss of confidence of the public in the CP's women members—it was inexplicable behaviour, a mode of public betrayal that could not serve any constructive purpose. And Sen confirms this: 'We felt extremely disheartened. We could not figure out anything; we did not know whether we should continue with the work we were doing or do something else.' Kanak Mukherjee, one of the prominent full-time party workers, retired from her position as a full-time worker of the party, completely 'demoralized'. Sen herself took a long time to 'regain confidence', was 'troubled by feelings of guilt and had doubts about working for the Party'. It was clearly an experience of a culture that silenced dissent, for she says, 'While I was a Party worker I had not even discussed these incidents of Netrakona with anybody in the Party, let alone talk about these incidents in public' (ibid.).

Ultimately, Sen says, she was 'able to overcome these negative feelings with the help of Comrade Bhawani Sen' (ibid.). The question, however, was why should such a recovery have to be wrought at the personal level? Why could P.C. Joshi not have been asked to explain his actions and make amends at a consequent party meeting? However nurturing a leader he may have been for women, there was a clear and damaging ambiguity in the articulation of stands that shows a complete lack of gender sensitivity, of even the kind that Bhawani Sen may have shown to Manikuntala Sen in person, or that is evident in Abani Lahiri's response to me regarding P.C. Joshi's criticism of urban women activists that I include in the next section. The CP had begun to welcome large numbers of women into its membership, but it seems clear that neither had the male leaders given any thought to the ways in which they needed to involve women, nor did the party acknowledge the need to give gender issues enough importance to challenge a male leader's actions and lay out some principles for engaging with the growing number of new women members.

It is only in retrospect, in her memoirs first published in 1982, that Manikuntala Sen becomes confident about articulating her critique of this untoward humiliation of women workers—and it is significant that she sees in it a much deeper malaise of power that made its presence felt, sometimes even in the early, truly progressive years of the CP. She articulates her critique not in personal terms against Joshi, but in a perceptive critique about the CP's relationship with power as evident in its party structuring and codes of discipline:

> Today, as I write about it, I hesitate just for one reason: P.C. Joshi is dead. Under such circumstances it is perhaps not correct to raise this topic, but I feel the need to say something. It now seems to me that the unlimited power which the topmost leader of the Party enjoys is not desirable; and the consequences could be serious. We know the

> extent of damage that the misuse of power could cause: the Soviet Union and China provide painful lessons. (2001:146)

Women, thus, had to overcome a culture of silence around the ambiguous, often contradictory, gendered behaviour of their male comrades. That this was so evident in one of the most supportive and progressive of male leaders is indication that it would have been the case with other male colleagues too.

Within this culture of silencing, which continued unobtrusively until well after this incident of 1944 and was visible again during the armed struggle of 1948–50, there is evidence of sophisticated conceptual approaches and strategies that women developed to gain acceptance as equal comrades in the movement, at least at the ground level, as I will show later. Meanwhile, women also had to also inure themselves to the opportunistic gendered hostility of other parties. Lahiri narrated an incident that demonstrated how opposition parties tried not only to alienate women from the CP, but also to malign the CP on grounds of what would amount to indecency by urban middle-class standards of morality:

> Later, when women came en masse, then they [other parties] spread such propaganda. One example was at the Congress MLA [Member of Legislative Assembly] Nishit Kundu's meeting that we had attended so that we could have our say there. One of their leaders said [in slang] that the *lal jhandawala*s [bearers of red flags] have thought hard and come up with this, that if peasant women raise their arms to say '*inquilab zindabad*' [long live the revolution], as is done in the krishak samiti, then the cloth of their *bukhni*s [piece of cloth wrapped around the body and tied under the arms] will ride up too! Savouring the thought with great amusement, he said, 'So the lal jhandawalas have started this programme to destroy the *izzat* [honour] of the peasant women.'

Such were the initial barriers to drawing women into the political fold. And Abani Lahiri, exclaimed repeatedly, 'I was nonplussed!' After all, it was no easy task for young 30-year-old leaders like him to deal with such an accusation.

On the other hand, in conversations with women members of the CP, a central contradiction persisted regarding comradeship between men and women. Every woman, including Rani Dasgupta, Bina Guha, Anima Biswas, Ila Mitra and Kalyani Dasgupta, said that despite the egalitarian ideology of communism, the male membership of the party was decidedly patriarchal; *yet*, that she herself had experienced no discrimination personally. Each time I came up against this contradiction in account after account, I found myself driven into the perplexing wedge between representation and experience.

It was after months of questioning different women that, with Bina Guha's narrative, I began to come to some understanding of this apparent contradiction. She claimed that though women were doubly exploited—as women and as poor peasants—they faced no discrimination within the home or in the party. Their opinions were asked, they could criticize anything, they were encouraged to analyse themselves and others, allowed to take decisions and so on. At that time, in the pre-independence period, the party nurtured women, helped them evolve as communists in order to facilitate a mass movement and increase awareness. Thus, it was a period of support and exposure, a new experience for women, a transitional phase, a learning phase.

That men within the movement had begun to appreciate women's contribution to the movement, and readily admitted so in the present, testifies to the effective transformation of the gender ideology of male activists during Tebhaga. This was evident in the progressive views of both urban and peasant CP leaders of Dinajpur such as Abani Lahiri and Heleketu Singha respectively; it was also reflected in the views of Muslim leaders from Narail. Nurul Akbar, a peasant leader of Tebhaga, commented on the indispensability of women to the movement, proclaiming that, 'Men needed to be guided and alerted by women at every step.' And Mohammed Mominuddin Mullah, another peasant leader from Narail, said:

> Women acted as the messengers. They received all the information and guided all the activists in hiding. *Meyera jinish gopon rakhte jaane* [women know how to keep secrets]. They never let out anything to anyone. Women were very important for organizing this movement.

This is an emphatic inversion of the accusation that women are not to be trusted, '*Meyeder pete kichhu thake na*' (women can't keep secrets). Even if this is a reversal of stereotype, it does indicate that once women joined them as comrades, there was a shift from men's typical undermining of women for their 'feminine' failings to an appreciation of their political abilities. And Mominuddin ended decisively, '*Meyera jodi andolane na name, tahole kono* party *shrinkhalabaddha thakte pare na*' (If women don't enter movements, no party can maintain a well coordinated structure).

Regarding the high morale of the women Abani Lahiri recounted that even when the women were arrested and made to sit in the jotedar's courtyard, the effect was 'electrifying' because

> the women ... did not surrender. The first thing that was asked was whether any of them was crying and the answer was that none of them was; in fact, their morale was high. The police had arrested women separately, and none of them was crying, that itself became very important news for the peasants. Then it so happened that after such an arrest other women from another village would land up to wage a demonstration at the site.

He further observed that the increasing participation of women had a 'terrific effect' in increasing the male membership of the movement too:

> As more women joined the movement, word went around that a women's brigade [*mahilabahini* or naribahini] had been formed. This created such a sensation that at a particular time, within fifteen days, a large number of women joined. The news spread like fire.... If women are active, it has a terrific effect ... [men would think.] Men of the villages participate in krishak sabhas, but even women are joining the demonstration now? Then why should we be left behind?

As large numbers of men began to be arrested, women began taking over the political arena. In fact, the renowned Bangla litterateur Manik Bandyopadhyay is known to have observed that, with the large-scale arrests of men, entire village societies comprising children and the aged began to be run by women. The women gradually gained in confidence and boosted the morale of the village.

Thus, there was a gradual coming into consciousness to a point of no return.[32]

One of the reasons the gender hierarchy that continued to exist within the party was never questioned was partly because of its approach—liberal, open and encouraging towards women and their active participation. Another reason was that women were still new actors on the political stage. The time had not yet arrived for a sharp sustained analysis of patriarchal politics. In fact, Bina Guha's attitude towards the CP of that period was marked by a sense of deference, communicated through a telling metaphor of the party as a mother who gave birth to communist women:

> We were trained by the party about what we have to say, what we should do, what the party stood for, what socialism meant, we attended class after class learning all that. The party literally gave birth to us as communist women.

## Partition, the Crackdown on the CP and the Decline of the Mahila Samitis

While women had found the experience of Tebhaga an extremely rewarding one, the realization, though only semi-critical at this stage, did exist that they were drawn into the struggle because the movement needed them rather than for the sake of women's empowerment. This was clear in the account of Bokul*er ma* (Bokul's mother), a peasant woman of Ranisainkel, Dinajpur. She recollected that men encouraged the establishment of a mahila samiti in her area. Then, with a chuckle that conveyed an amused but nevertheless critical perspective, she emphasized that this was so that women could bring up the vanguard and prevent the men from being beaten up by the *daroga*s (guards) in encounters!

The trauma and the massive dislocations of the partition of India, and of Bengal into West Bengal and East Pakistan, dealt a severe blow to the CP in both countries. The women's movement was truncated with the dissipation of Tebhaga and the severe ruptures of partition.

[32] Narrated by Manik Bandyopadhyay's brother, Ramen Bandyopadhyay, to Nripen Bandyopadhyay.

Most of the women who had been leaders in East Bengal were Hindus who migrated to India, leaving a vacuum in the leadership there. The CP too was irreparably debilitated by the split. It was not only divided across the borders, it was also declared illegal in 1948 in India and experienced severe repression in East Pakistan, forcing most of its leaders to go underground in both countries. The mahila samitis disintegrated in most of the rural areas and the same left that had created the unprecedented conditions of possibility for their radical gendered politics during Tebhaga failed to reconstruct them after partition. The strengths this movement could have grown to in a more amenable gendered context are now a matter of conjecture.

The process of reconstruction after such truncation was arduous on both sides. Yet, when it did take place, the left parties, which had been instrumental in the emergence of the movement in the first place, paid scant attention to women's issues in both East Pakistan and India. In the 1950s, the focus of the left in Bangladesh shifted from the agrarian question to the language movement launched against the imposition of Urdu by Pakistan, and in the late 1960s, the Bangladesh War of Liberation consumed all the energy of the progressive parties. The reconstruction of the mahila samitis remained a dead issue. In fact, most of the younger women interviewed in these areas voiced surprise when they learned of the existence of these samitis and of spirited women leaders in their own communities in the past.[33] Bina Guha testified to the active endeavours of a revolutionary CP in undivided Bengal to draw women into the party in the late 1940s, and simultaneously pointed out the sharp contrast in the ruling left party's neglect of the issue of women's membership in contemporary West Bengal in the 1990s:

[33] In fact, one very interesting distinction that some young women of Hatiara, Narail, made between the mahila samitis set up by the villagers in the past and those set up by foreign-funded non-governmental organizations in the present was that they denied the latter the very status of mahila samitis. Despite their ignorance of their own histories of women's activism, what this distinction implies is the association of the notion of a mahila samiti with a politics from below, based on peasant women's own initiatives. Thus, despite the absence of concrete historical knowledge, traces of the grassroots political consciousness that informed Tebhaga can still be found in the present.

> Now this [active effort to enrol women] does not happen, as the left party has formed the government. In West Bengal now its membership is 21 lakh [2.1 million].... At that time, there were two clear enemies, the zamindar/jotedars and the British government, and the country had to be freed from imperialism, [but] now the situation is different.

In the case of Dinajpur, Abani Lahiri cited the painful phenomenon of partition as the reason why the mahila samitis did not survive Tebhaga: ranks were divided, leaders dislocated and the party weakened. But at the local level, Heleketu Singha, a peasant leader of Dinajpur, said, 'The fact that we failed to preserve the mahila samiti, that's our failure, my failure. We are party workers, but we couldn't get conscious enough about the need to preserve [the mahila samiti].' Amal Sen, one of the most dearly loved Tebhaga leaders of East Bengal, too echoed the same sentiment, reiterating the failure of the party to retain and develop such transformative power as Narail had witnessed in women such as Sarala Singha, Anima Biswas and Phuli Goldar.

Thus, this history also begins to fracture a claim of continuity of the communist women's movement. Kanak Mukherjee, a committed activist since the famine period, a prominent member of the Communist Party of India (Marxist) and leader of its women's wing, the Ganatantrik Mahila Samiti, in the 1990s, argued in an interview with me for a continuity in the history of women's activism in the left and between the mahila samitis of the Tebhaga period and now.[34] This was clearly not the case in areas like Kakdwip, and among the tribals of Jalpaiguri, where the samitis disappeared completely. In urban areas, like Calcutta or Jalpaiguri town in West Bengal, where the samitis had managed to survive, they continued functioning in diminished form till they were revived later or were set up afresh after the CP split into the Communist Party of India (CPI) and the Communist Party of India (Marxist) (CPM). In Bangladesh the picture was even more drastic, with virtually no mahila samitis of the left in existence in the four areas I covered. On the other hand,

[34] The women's group associated with the Communist Party of India is the Paschimbanga Mahila Samiti.

prominent male leaders of Tebhaga, such as Amal Sen of Narail, Heleketu Singha of Dinajpur and Abani Lahiri of north Bengal, conceded, with responses ranging from deep regret to cautious acknowledgement, that the CP had indeed neglected women's issues and mahila samitis in the process of reconstruction in both countries.

So no direct trajectory could be traced from the Tebhaga women's movement to women's political activism in later years. Despite the claims of both the Ganatantrik Mahila Samiti (CPM) and the Paschimbanga Mahila Samiti (CPI) of a direct continuity with the mahila samitis of the Tebhaga movement, the ruptures of partition and the period when the CP was banned from 1948 to 1950, as well as the disruptive impact of the state violence that followed, demonstrate otherwise for most of the rural areas I visited. In fact, in many cases, even the families of the Tebhaga women, their children and grandchildren joined us to hear for the first time the details of these women's political activism in what seemed to be an earlier life. It is, thus, extremely difficult to see any significant connection between the activist histories of the Tebhaga women and the political activism of later years, or even any direct impact, except in the case of urban women who became members of the Paschimbanga Mahila Samiti of the CPI and continued to lend force to the refugee movement, the teachers' movement, etc. Yet the transformation had been major, especially in terms of thousands of rural and urban women entering the field of political activism and shaping it together. It was clearly a major social and political revolution, marking the emergence of new subjects in the 1940s in Bengal. How do we begin to understand the transformations of this period and their significance from the point of view of women's lives?

Upon arriving in Calcutta after partition, many of the erstwhile leaders of the Tehbhaga women's movement in East Bengal threw themselves into political activity. This was largely representative of the people who came here. They participated in the refugee movement and the school teachers' movement, and later worked as members of the National Federation of Indian Women. One of the slogans of Tehbhaga was translated directly to the slogan of the refugee movement: '*Jaan debo toh dhaan debo na*' (I can surrender my life, but not my crops), translated into '*Jaan debo toh ghar debo na*'

(I can surrender my life, but not my home) because of the repeated onslaught on their shanties and slums (Sen 2001:180). It became a question of having a roof over your head. Many new samitis came up in the colonies, but Manikuntala Sen, who worked actively amongst the refugees of East Bengal, records that, 'None of these new samitis affiliated themselves to the Mahila Atma Raksha Samiti, they wanted to maintain their independence' (ibid.:82). Later, however, these samitis coalesced with the remaining MARS towards the formation of the National Federation of Indian Women.

As refugees too, the Tebhaga women continued to show their mettle. Many, like Rani Dasgupta, brought their families across to West Bengal, but steadily refused the identity of the refugee with fierce pride. Yet this rejection was obviously not of thwarted class aristocracy; it was a typical political self-respect. Dasgupta protested: 'Why should we be called refugees? I feel very strongly about this since I was very young. Our country, you have partitioned it—we had to leave and come away from it. That was our *desh* [land]. We were born in Dinajpur, everything was there.' She never went back to the place she came from, but she never really left it behind either. Her friend and comrade, Heleketu Singha, helped her take the last train across the newly formed border and she started life anew in West Bengal. She died with her wish to see the land of her birth once more unfulfilled.

The work of these left activists among the East Bengal refugees also carries import in relation to the stemming of communal politics. Sumit Sarkar, stressing on this in comparison to parallel work in north India, says in his introduction to Abani Lahiri's book, *Postwar Revolt of the Rural Poor in Bengal*:

> Abani Lahiri also rightly emphasizes the long term historical significance of relief and rehabilitation efforts organized by Bengal Communists in subsequent years among East Bengal refugees. Their counterparts in North India among whom similar work from an utterly different ideological perspective had been carried out by the RSS, had become a major support base for the Hindu Right. Things have been significantly different in West Bengal so far. (2001:xlviii)

The demise of Tebhaga was a tragic story for all who waged it—and even more so for the women. It was painful witnessing how an increasingly conservative gendered post-Tebhaga scenario, and the devastating violence and dislocations of the times had diminished the confidence and transformed the once radical subjectivity of these women. Urban women like Rani Dasgupta and Bina Guha were still determinedly committed to their work with women's organizations, but with a confidence in the younger generation that was almost desperate. Anima Biswas, the dynamic peasant activist of Narail who had fought to bring her friend Phuli Goldar, a 'licentious' young widow, into the movement, had withdrawn into a cocoon of silent disillusionment in a suburb of Kolkata. In Narail, an aged Phuli, ravaged by Parkinson's disease, was still ready to mobilize women again, even though, as she said ironically, 'I can jump into the fray ... but I can't walk!' Her fiery optimism rang hollow in a village where the young stood gaping in disbelief at her stories of the past, and where no mahila samiti had existed since Tebhaga. And the regret that she voiced continues to echo into the present its poignancy: '*Keu to ekhon daakena*' (Nobody calls us today).

Almost seventy years have passed since the inception of the Tebhaga women's movement, but the stark lacunae in our understanding of it as a movement still persist. Archival records of the gendered perspectives of peasant women are non-existent. There are fine memoirs by male leaders, but even those of the most enlightened, such as Abani Lahiri's, do not yield gendered insights about the movement. One of the reasons for this is the separation of the personal from the political, sometimes even the suppression of the personal, in most communist memoirs. In fact, Sumit Sarkar even comments on this in his introduction to the English translation of Abani Lahiri's memoirs, saying:

> One wishes Abani babu had spoken more about his boyhood, and about his personal and family life in general—but as in most Indian Communist memoirs, there remains a considerable reticence at that level. The modesty and dignity underlying the reticence of an evidently outstanding political leader compels respect, but there is also a separation of the political from the personal that remains

> problematic—and not unconnected with the general silence about the gender question in most such male reminiscences. (2001:xlii)

All we had by way of written material then, when I first began this work, were a few first-person accounts penned by some of the urban women leaders. The only other resource was memory. Alternate modalities such as oral history, based on oral narratives that do not shun the personal in a privileging of the political thus became invaluable; they became a resource for reconstructing both, women's history *in* Tebhaga, as well as a gendered history *of* Tebhaga.

# 2

## The 'Retroactive Force of Interiority'

### The Conscience of Oral History[1*]

I picked up the phone to find Ajoyda's voice on the other side: 'Kavita, your Ranidi is no more.' I slumped into a chair in silence. She had passed away five days ago, when I had been on my way to Shillong for a workshop. In fact it was the very day when my car had swirled three 360-degree turns and almost flown off the mountainside. I had thought it was my last day on earth—instead, it turned out to be the day on which she had breathed her last. This was in September 2002, and of all the women who had been in the Tebhaga movement, Rani Dasgupta was the one whom I had begun to care for the most. I went to her memorial service in Abanindranth Sabhagriha in Kolkata. It was a full house. People from all walks of life were there—from a

[1] I take the term 'retroactive force of interiority' from Benjamin's 'Theses on the Philosophy of History' (1969b:245). Interiority, as used here, relates to one's inner self or mental and emotional being. Its nature is shaped by the rational as well as affective impact of events in intimate, private and public life, and in response to them. It involves an ineffable internal processing of layers of experience and desire, and exists virtually as an internal chamberhouse of echoes, with a selection of them coming into play—and interplay—in specific circumstances. It is neither absolute nor static, but a continually transforming process. As I see it, the quality of interiority underlies self-formation and agency—and thereby history making too.

political party, of which she and her husband Ajoy Dasgupta had been members for half a century; from the Paschimbanga Mahila Samiti in which she had been active to her last day; from the refugee and teachers' movements of the past, and the women's movement in the present; neighbours, ex-students and friends whose lives she had touched; and also her husband's niece, a leader of another political party, reaching out across all political differences to pay her last respects—for that was the kind of love and regard Ranidi elicited. On the way back, I held on to the frame of her black-and-white photograph, staring unblinkingly at her smiling face, still in denial. Five years ago, when my mother had passed away, it was Ranidi who had called me every three days, straining to catch my words with ears that could barely hear. Today, I was straining to hear her. Ajoyda and his niece's voices floated into my ears from the back seat in a steady drone, till it suddenly registered that they were talking about her in the past. Fortunately, I was in the front seat and they did not see the tears that muddied her smile, still resplendent through the glass of the frame.

What was this relationship that had developed between her and me across the past seven years? I had first gone to her, as I had to many other women and men, as an academic on a research project and more so as an activist in search of a collective past of the Indian women's movement that I was convinced was to be found in the Tebhaga movement. Rani Dasgupta of Dinajpur had been a leader of women in the Tebhaga movement. As Rani Mitra then, she had been one of the few single young urban women who had played a prominent role in it. Our friendship in the present had grown across two years of intense conversations, most in her sparse two-room home in a modest old government colony and a few at my apartment in a multistoreyed building of a modern residential area.

She had also come with me to Baroda to speak at a seminar organized by the Indian Association of Women's Studies on the occasion of the fiftieth anniversary of independence. Travelling together in a cab in Bombay, she had asked me why I had never married and narrated, with a twinkle in her eye, the response she had received from Ajoyda when she had asked him to think of a suitable partner for me. He had retorted: 'Not on your life! The only young men I know are the ones in politics, and the less said about them these days the better.' A sad reflection, true, considering Ajoyda's perception of the young men, who, of course, could not live up to his sterling principles in these changed times, but the twinkle in Ranidi's eyes had subverted the very content of her question to me and forged one of those many unspeakable bonds we shared.

At the seminar too, she had reached out across language and geography, to befriend another tiny woman from Gujarat—Kesariben, who had taught Kasturba Gandhi how to read and write in prison, and who spoke no Bangla or English, even as Ranidi spoke no Gujarati. Ranidi had also reached out to speak to us across time, conjoining her history of activism in Tebhaga with ours in the women's movement.

How was I to relate to women like her, whom I felt so close to, in writing about them? There was a shared political commitment linking their past to our present and the rich intersubjective bonds of friendship. Would these help me develop richer insights into their lives or would they become obstacles in the way of critical analysis?

## Engaging with Otherness, Grasping Difference

When I had first started meeting the activists of the Tebhaga movement, scholar Nripen Bandyopadhyay, who had shared valued insights with me, had asked me: 'Have you thought about how you are going to reach out to them across all the differences of culture and class?' I had told him then about the role that I had effortlessly found myself in—part of a younger generation of women to whom history was being passed down by word of mouth. I had got some of the best 'stories' lounging around on the floors of homes rather than sitting formally on chairs—if there were any—looking up at the woman or man talking, often slipping into the easy interactions of a younger person teasing and bullying older people—like aunts, grandmothers, grandfathers—into telling their stories. Without consciously realizing it, I had slipped into a familiar traditional mode of oral cultures. The implicit hierarchy of the narrator's age, the stature of the interviewee as storyteller imparting counsel (Benjamin 1969a), and the mutual enjoyment of this exchange helped us circumvent, to a significant degree, the problematic hierarchies of interviewers over interviewees. Hierarchies yes, and—so I'd thought—differences too.

When other scholars too had asked me to think about how I'd negotiate the divides of location and differences of perception between, say, the extremes of my position as urban feminist academic 'subject' and the peasant, or even urban activist, and her history as 'object of enquiry', I had been uncomfortable with the binarism underlying such a positioning of my relationship with the women I interviewed. For I had begun to develop a sense of bonding with many regarding our investment in the women's movement, albeit from very different locations in time and space, and with a few it had also become an emotional, personal friendship. This subject–object binary clearly did not stand, but neither did my assumption that such bonding or friendship naturally overcomes the distances of history and location. Our relationships had to be understood in a place of overlap between these two extremes, of a distanced 'othering' inherent in the former and strong identification implied in the latter. The cultural premium of their age and experience that inflected our oral interactions did help me negotiate the hierarchies of the researcher and researched somewhat, as did friendship the differences. Yet, one had to work hard at grasping the standpoint of the other, beginning with an acknowledgement of a certain otherness in the first place. This, however, was not easy, especially in relation to the urban activists I found myself identifying with in personal bonding and shared political perspectives—of my investment in their histories, as well as from their continuing activism in the Paschimbanga Mahila Samiti and mine in the women's movement.

Yet, shared political perspectives, despite creating a sense of shared subjectivity at a point in history, can actually signify radically different trajectories and diverse meanings for people differently located. The implications of the difference, across my location and history, and those of Rani Dasgupta and all the Tebhaga activists, were driven home as the significance of her initial refusal to talk to me about her personal experiences in Tebhaga gradually dawned upon me. She, and most other women leaders, when asked if the

CP had been patriarchal in its functioning, had replied 'Of course'. But each of them had also hastened to add that she personally had never felt discriminated against on grounds of gender. This paradox remained a big question mark for a long time till the dawning of a certain understanding regarding her earlier refusal to focus on herself. Recognizing this refusal as a retroactive force from the Tebhaga days and exploring its reason and import yielded critical insights.

Rani Dasgupta had been absolutely unwilling to narrate her personal experiences of the movement as one of the rare single young women who had taken on leadership of the struggle. She had willingly elaborated an extremely illuminating account of women's political activism in general; but regarding 'indulging' in personal accounts of experience in a collective struggle, her stand was that it amounted to self-aggrandizement—it was only the history of the movement that deserved attention. In fact, she had even wagged her finger threateningly at her husband, Ajoy Dasgupta, and said, 'I have told him that if he ever joins electoral politics I will divorce him!' This privileging of her collective sense of self at the cost of the individual, I realized later, actually defined the epistemic limitations of her approach in terms of developing a feminist understanding of the movement. Shaped by the demands of a collective, non-gendered, euphoric subjectivity, she and other Tebhaga women were resistant to the modes of being and knowing of an individual gendered subject, and to acknowledging the personal on equal standing with the political. This pre-empted the very possibility of making the linkages between the personal and the political that are the basis of feminist analysis. Consequently, the women were epistemically incapable of developing feminist perspectives on the patriarchal practices within the movement.

One of the central features of all narratives, and especially oral ones, I began to understand, is that the narrator's sense of self and relation to society become bases for the epistemic process. These determine what is considered to be valid as knowledge and what the possibilities of representing or challenging a specific reality may be. Thus, while narrative imposes a structure on experience, how experience is first structured as knowledge is determined by the narrator's specific sense of self in a particular context.[2] What one can know or not know depends to a great extent on how one perceives oneself and perceives one's relation to society. The epistemic process itself is limited or enabled by the relationship between self and society.

Fortunately, Rani Dasgupta changed her mind and did eventually narrate her story. The fact that she did so at her husband's insistence that it was her 'duty', otherwise the history of women in the Tebhaga movement would be lost to posterity and the contemporary women's movement, also attests to the egalitarianism that had characterized the 1940s and continued to lend stature to some of the CP men. An ethos of equality and gender-sensitive men, a party that was patriarchal, and a collective disposition that pre-empted any critique of the collective that was the party—all these contradictory impulses settled in together to reveal a palimpsest of the decade layered with contradictions of gender. I eventually recorded her narrative across a period of over two years—she yielded enough to lend her personal history to textualization, but the retroactive force of history that had preempted a feminist critique prevailed.

So I came to understand why Rani Dasgupta—and other women like her—were unable to to develop a feminist critique of patriarchy. But the more important point I wish to make here is about the flip side of the situation, about my own ability, or rather inability, to grasp the significance of these women's narratives, about the limitations of one marked by a culture not of a collective, but of contemporary urban individualism. If the privileging of a collective self and consciousness can impose such limitations on the epistemic process, and on one's understanding and critique of history, as I realized was happening with her, then, in the reverse case, what were the epistemic limitations at work in my own privileging of an individual sense of self over the collective? This is a grey area that we, as academics and scholars, rarely admit and have not yet begun to explore. At this point I can only raise certain questions: Did I, who generally privileges notions of the individual self, have adequate access to the realities of those whose identities are inextricably linked

[2] This is not to straitjacket human beings into rigid oppositional categories of collective or individual subjects, but to recognize that the privileging of the collective or individual self in a particular context shapes the relevant epistemic processes.

to that of a collective in struggle? What were my limits of knowing and how could I even recognize them? It was this humbling reality that made me realize that an epistemic chasm divided me from the women I had begun to relate to as friends, with whom I shared certain political perspectives; and it was a chasm across which I had to build bridges of understanding.

On the other hand, when one came up against silences, contradictions and incomprehensible actions, the sense of 'otherness' became only too evident and demanded other ways of exploring the activists' making of meaning. Such was the case with urban women like Ila Mitra, the legendary leader of Tebhaga in Nachole (now in Bangladesh), with whom too I had spent hours in intimate conversation in Kolkata, and with peasant women such as Anima Biswas, a dynamic leader of Narail (also in Bangladesh now), who had retired into virtual oblivion and complete silence by the time I looked her up in Barasat, a suburban town of Kolkata. Their otherness became crystal clear to me as the contradictions and silences came in the way of our communication with each other. Then the question really loomed large: How does one write the scripts of a 'lost' history? Of a collective and critical history of women that was never written, only carried in the memories of thousands of activists? While oral narratives prove to be a critical source of history, they involve not just representations but also the silences of memory, as well as its multiple contradictions across the layering of time. How may these be plumbed?

## The Prism of Subjectivity

Oral narratives, I began to see, communicate also through the dynamics of their recollection—of joy or nostalgia, of hesitation or self-contradictions, of pain or disillusionment, of gesture and tone, and also of silence. For these spoke to me as much as the content of the narratives did. I began to see how the significance of the narratives gradually filtered across to me through the *subjectivity* of the speakers, which, if read closely and across different accounts, spells out the varied hues of power, politics, patriarchy and militancy, as well as sexuality, agency and intoxication. The dynamics of human subjectivity, thus, became a focal point of this oral history. The term 'subjectivity', as I use it here, refers to the historically and socially constituted subject, and not as an abstraction but as the *embodied* female subject of history, hence also constituted materially.[3] Further, this subject of history is not just subject to, and thus constituted by, the forces of history, but also one capable of agency, a thinking, knowing, affective subject, that in turn shapes history. Thus, subjectivity also 'connotes the area of symbolic activity that includes cognitive, cultural and psychological aspects... [and] forms of awareness such as the sense of identity and consciousness of oneself' (Passerini 1998:54). In this, it also relates centrally to the dynamics of interiority that responds to affect.

Predicated, then, on the workings of agency, cognition and interiority, as well as the socially, historically constituted subject, subjectivity also proves to be a useful lens of analysis for establishing the relations between the cognitive dimensions of the personal and the political significations of the collective. As such, it 'embraces not only the *epistemological* dimension but also that concerned with the nature and significance of the *political*' (ibid., emphasis added). The subjectivity of the speakers provides access to both epistemological and political standpoints, specially in the accounts of women activists, because their narrative subjectivities are layered with their perspectives of how they understand history as it unfolds for them in their politicized realities, and how politics is in turn textured by their standpoints and agency. Subjective articulations also express the collective significance of the political realm in these narratives by representing ways in which subjectivities are transformed by, and also transform, political movements.

The aim, then, is to read the narratives for an understanding of how the subject and the collective are constituted, rather than to approach both as mere reflections of party positions, or of ideologies, or of misplaced surrender to or trust in the party. This is an important

[3] In this sense, focus on the subject is as an 'effect' of power and disciplines, after Foucault, and as being ideologically interpellated in the Althusserian sense. I do not include in my analyses the notion of the psychoanalytically constructed subject—the focus here is on the socially constructed subject.

aspect of reading recall, and this is also why subjectivity serves as a critical prism for the analysis of oral narratives, for it transcends the narrower, more bounded, limits of identity. Identity functions in the nature of a limited and temporary fixing for an individual of a specific mode of subjectivity; it is constituted by a certain degree of identification or self-recognition by the subject, an assumption of what one is; and it restricts the multiple possibilities of subjectivity intrinsic to a social field, limiting a subject to a restricted sense of who she/he is in relation to notions of belonging determined by a specific set of values or ideology. Subjectivity, on the other hand, constitutes a field much wider than identity and is also the ground of repressed desires, un-self-conscious identifications premised on unacknowledged needs and wishes, as well as modes of interpellation by social and political forces that may well be outside the spheres of cognition, yet shape the subject in significant ways. All of these find their way into narratives in ways unintended, spoken or unspoken, in gesture, look, tone or even pregnant silences.

Since subjectivity includes the interplay of unintended responses to history too, its workings involve a dynamic dialogism capable of revealing the emergence of new visions and practices, as well as tensions and negotiations, both of the time and in the time of recall. The study of oral narratives also becomes crucial for feminist scholarship because it is in narration that the desire for the imaginary, the possible, contests with the demands of the actual, the 'real'. Further, women's lives are also shaped by the tension between different notions of identity—between the idea of a feminine identity (what women 'ought' to be normatively) and that of a feminist imperative (what women need and desire), paralleling the contest between the possible and the actual. This rich gendered dialogism in their oral narratives provides vital access to the standpoint of women, constituted by them as female subjects located in hierarchies of gender, class, caste, ethnicity and community; yet, it also enables access to the nature and significance of their subjective liberation, as well as of the limits of such liberation—both clearly areas not adequately taken account of in history writing.

This duality of the lens of the subject/subjective that constitutes subjectivity thus facilitates discussion of both subjectification and liberation. It is significant that Foucault too, in his later years, extended his notion of the subject to one also constituted by liberation—in a 1984 interview, he emphasized:

> I do indeed believe that there is no sovereign, founding subject, a universal form of subject to be found everywhere. I am very sceptical of this view of the subject and very hostile to it. I believe, on the contrary, that the subject is constituted through practices of subjection, or, in a more autonomous way, *through practices of liberation*. (1988:50, emphasis added)

That the subject can be constituted by liberation too opens up the possibility of conceptualizing a free subject. It is this dynamics of liberation, not just of the collective but also of the individual within—and maybe also sometimes against—the collective that I wish to tap in order to grasp the nature of both—the liberatory as well limiting nature of the movement and the woman activist's gendered negotiation with this tension.

Thus, rather than following the locus of an already determined set of values, which I had assumed underlined our shared politics in the contemporary context, I learnt to pay attention to each person's standpoint from her location, the point from which her values were constructed or interpreted. These locations were, of course, multiple, for the subject of Tebhaga women's standpoint was multiple and heterogeneous, with individual subjects at times even at a tangent to others in the collective. The category 'Tebhaga woman' was far from uniform, ranging from the Adivasi Santal and Oraon, and the lower-caste Namasudra peasant women to the urban Muslim or upper-caste Hindu women. Thus, the standpoint of each of them was not always in consonance with that of the others in the struggle together and depended on her social location within the collective.

Such solidarities as the Tebhaga women forged across trenchant divides transcended the ultimately debilitating privileging of difference, of 'authenticity' and narrow 'identity politics' that are still the focus of much current debate. In the context of contemporary Dalit feminism, Sharmila Rege has forcefully argued that that the issues underlined by the new Dalit women's movement go beyond a privileging of the 'difference' of Dalit women to call for a revolutionary epistemological shift to a Dalit feminist standpoint, one that must be shared by non-Dalits too:

> The dalit feminist standpoint which emerges from the practices and struggles of dalit women, we recognise, may originate in the works of dalit feminist intellectuals but it cannot flourish if isolated from the experiences and ideas of other groups who must educate themselves about the histories, the preferred social relations and utopias and the struggles of the marginalized. A transformation from 'their cause' to 'our cause' is possible for subjectivities can be transformed. (1998:45)

The actual transformation of subjectivities across social hierarchies is, however, an exercise requiring much self-reflexivity. As V. Geetha (2008:5) asserts, in engagements regarding caste that involve both Dalits and non-Dalits, 'Caste invariably ends up as a "dalit" concern—it is never really seen as having to do with caste Hindu privilege, with what non-dalits are.' As non-Dalits today educate themselves into taking on Dalit feminist standpoints, so upper-caste/-class urban women had questioned their complicity in hierarchies of social privilege and extended themselves to taking on the standpoints of Tebhaga women.

The concerns of these current debates about averting a narrow identity politics and unlearning upper-caste/-class privilege to forge comradeship across difference had already been put to the test—and successfully so—by the Tebahaga women in the late 1940s. Even as they were carefully attentive to the standpoint of situated identities, they forged a richly democratic activism, averting isolationist and conflictual identity politics. In fact, contemporary feminist movments have much to learn from the Tebhaga women's exemplification of the ways in which solidarities may be forged across social divides. The latter's modes of sharing, and the trials and tribulations through which urban and rural, Hindu and Muslim, and upper-caste, lower-caste and Adivasi women came together, reveal the workings of complex analytical, affective and intersubjective processes that may be lost to lived history, but are fortunately still available to us in their narratives; I discuss in Chapter 4 on antarikata how these are recalled by women like Manikuntala Sen, Rani Dasgupta, Bina Guha, Bimala Majhi, Ila Mitra and others.

The Tebhaga women's liberatory project was also the subject of other such projects of caste, class, gender and sexuality, all of which construct each other. This further opened up the Tebhaga women's standpoint to various emancipatory challenges and transformations. I show, in the discussions of Dinajpur women and also in the chapter on antarikata, how they also began to harness egalitarian leftist and anti-imperialist ideologies in the project of empowering themselves and gaining acceptance of their gendered demands, as well as their activism and leadership.

Even as urban women learnt to educate themselves and unlearn their privileges of class and caste in lived history, to stand with the Tebhaga peasant women, I too, across significant divides not just of location but also time, began attempting to build epistemic bridges of comprehension, the nature of which I hope will emerge in the following pages and chapters of this history.

The meanings of each event for the activists, as may be expected, were not always easily available to me. For, in the work of oral history, 'knowledge is not simply a factual given, it is a genuine *advent*, an event' (Laub 1992:62, emphasis added). It involved a process of arriving at, or facilitating, the emergence of particular kinds of knowledge, of finding oneself trapped in epistemological pitfalls and then learning to work one's way out of them. This process of grasping their meanings thus involved conscious intersubjective reflection, of working one's way into other modes of being and knowing. In a way, engaging with another subject's orality is like being in a relationship across a period of time and gradually uncovering layers of meaning—replete with contradictions, sometimes forever baffling and sometimes fostering intellectual and human understanding of an other.

At the level of engaging with a range of women and a multiplicity of identities that constitutes a collective, such work also amounts to what Passerini (1996:xi–xiii) has termed 'the study of the history of subjectivity ... the impact of social and cultural change'. The subjectivity of the women accessible in these oral narratives in turn also bears critical import for a theoretical reassessment of what constitutes history itself. The epistemic privilege of hitherto marginalized women derives from their specific gendered locations and roles in historical struggle.[4] Further, such narratives are 'necessarily embedded in wider explanatory theories of history' (Mohanty 1998:235). Thus, their alternative visions relate not only to an understanding of the specific movement in question, but may also pose challenges to established practices of historiography. The central point about oral history, then, is not about the epistemological challenge of otherness, though that certainly needs to be tackled, but about coming to terms with and engaging with difference, with the perspectives that may interrupt the flow of given narratives. In doing so, the omitted stories may allow us to rethink the historical itself and through it the political. One's interest in the subject is not to straitjacket it within one's own sense of the political, but to restore to the larger picture, as part of one's legitimate history, the significance of the multiple perspectives, as well as of the hitherto unspeakable, that history has elided so far.[5]

## History, Memory, Intersubjectivity

History seemed not to have a place for such narratives and for the dynamics of narration. Its rupture with the lived pasts of the activists had made it too remote from the past that still continued to shape their memories and lives. Its objective approaches failed to grasp the significance of their experiences and standpoints. Its privileging of factual veracity crushed the very impact of events that transformed the subjectivity of a people and fuelled historical transformation. And its preoccupation with temporal continuities, and relations between periods, left one defeated in the attempt to grasp the import of a movement that in itself had marked a break between the lived realities of the past and the obsession of a present rapidly moving into the future (Nora 1989:8–9). History also had no time for the languages of gesture, tone and silences, for the contradictions and

[4] Mohanty also cautions that the claims of epistemic privilege need to be evaluated, as any social and historical explanation should be, and for this task he relies on 'such a conception of reason as both evaluative and empirically grounded… universal in scope, but necessarily context sensitive' (1998: 251).

[5] This was evolved in conversation with V. Geetha.

the stories underlying 'false recollections' and distortions. There was evidence of complex negotiations with lived history that history writing could not accommodate.

In 1997, in Kolkata, Ila Mitra had read to me from Maleka Begum's biography of her, her own testimony of grim sexual torture in East Pakistani state prisons that she had delivered in court in the early 1950s. Maleka Begum, when I met her shortly after that in Dhaka, had looked at me with surprise and asked me twice over: 'Did Iladi say it was *her* testimony when she read it out?' For when Maleka Begum had shown it to her a few years ago, four decades after its delivery, Ila Mitra had looked mystified and asked, 'Is this really my testimony?' History writing, with its privileging of objectivity, would spare no time for such distortions of memory and the stories of repression they may have to tell. And it would be quite unthinkable that history would have any room for the guilty giggles or furtive looks with which peasant women in Narail talked about their 'enjoyment' of the cross-gender solidarity in the fields of politics, or for the secretive tone in which an urban woman in north Bengal recounted the romances in the CP. The fact that these guilty, furtive and secretive modes of communication were actually a telling comment on the conservative gender politics of the 1990s when I was interviewing the women in these villages would be lost to history. What the activists were sharing were their memories of the past as they had lived it and as it had continued to inform the present. Yet, contemporary modes of history writing did not allow any significant way of grappling with the meaning the past carried for the activists. In fact, history, with its focus on dispassionate analysis, had no room for the very memories through which I was accessing their rich grasp of a lived past. Pierre Nora's eloquent assertion of the distance between memory and history kept echoing back to me right through my attempts to grasp the import of these narratives. Whether this distance between memory and history has indeed, as Nora (1989:2) maintains, reached a 'breaking point' now or been mitigated by the turn to memory in scholarship in recent decades may be debatable, but not his claim that, 'At the heart of history is a criticism destructive of spontaneous memory.... Memory is always suspect in the eyes of history, whose true mission is to demolish it, to repress it. History divests the lived past of its legitimacy' (ibid.:3). The lived past had become a 'foreign country' (Lowenthal 1985) to history; yet, why did it seem so critical, especially for the kind of feminist work I was doing, to salvage it? This question persisted; it haunted me through the years of this work and shaped it.

What was it about the past, then, that was being divested of its legitimacy and why was it so important? What these narratives deliver to us in the present are the actual processes of meaning making, the impact of historical events that mobilized masses of women into action, the gendered processes of empowerment and equally gendered trajectories of disillusionment. And all these had been played out in the rich dialectics of *interiority and politics* that their memories carried, subjectively, into the present.

Ila Mitra refused to renounce her politics to buy freedom from devastating sexual torture and came back to the fields of politics even after a prolonged nervous breakdown because of atiter jed, the persistence, or even stubbornness, of the past, which was the memory of the Santals' dream of freedom and the lives they had sacrificed for her, their leader. Urvashi Butalia's account 'The Persistence of Memory' (2001) too reinforces the mobilizing force of memory. In this, Bir Bahadur Singh, a survivor of partition violence of Muslims against Sikhs and Hindus, continues to be plagued by the memory of his family's unforgiving rejection of the offer of protection from close friends from his home village of Saintha during the violence of Thoa Khalsa just because they were Muslims. It is the persistence of his memory that compels him to go back across the Indo-Pakistan border on a journey of reconciliation more than fifty years later. The connection between memory and the present is that the sense of lived history continues to inflect and inform the present in a sense of continuity, and thus motivates or animates the present.

These are dimensions of the past, even counsel (see Benjamin 1969a), that face complete elision if approached exclusively through the lens of a history that distances itself from both memory and subjectivity. Yet, they stare one in the face, resound in the ear, when one lends oneself to these narratives of the Tebhaga women and men. Of what worth could this engagement be if devoid of the complex processes of struggle and change waged in the intimate realms of self? Could one really understand these pervasive historical transformations that involved the participation of women in politics right across Bengal on such an unprecedented scale if one were to disregard the internal revolutions of subjectivity, which were not just catalysed by but in turn also catalysed these very transformations into being? Memory was pivotal to the narration of these pasts and to their very significance; it could not but be pivotal to the writing of them too.

Yet, I was also invested in retrieving a history of the Tebhaga women—did engagement with subjectivity and memory necessarily jeopardize historical credibility? Nora (1989:3) distinguishes between memory and history as follows:

1. memory as a continuous yet dialectical process, and history as the mode by which 'modern societies organize a past they are condemned to forget because they are driven by change';
2. the former as extending from the past into the present and directing the future, and the latter as constituted by a definite break with the past; and
3. memory being that of a specific collective yet of the individual too, but history, characterized by a problematic universalism and a professionalism, as that which affirms its own logic rather than that of the past.

Yet, while memory does throw up critical challenges for history, can a sincere historical engagement with the past not open itself up to the logic of other times too and circumvent the problems inherent in a generalized universalism, especially if it is sensitive to the sense of the lived pasts that rooted memories hold in store for us? The supposed 'chasm' between history and memory can be bridged, and should, for neither can do without the other in understanding how the past speaks to the present. The more complex problem here is of grasping the specific ways of relating to the past. For if one does understand the impossibility of grasping any sense of an 'authentic' past, and also one's inability to grasp it in terms of its exact organicity for the narrators of memory, then one cannot but agree with Benjamin (1969b:255) that: 'To articulate the past historically does not mean to recognize it "the way it really was."' How, then, can we understand our investment in our past given such an approach? The answer can be found only in the specific possibilities, maybe even the lost possibilities, to which the memory of the past can lead us.

The biggest challenge was to find ways of understanding the narratives of violence and trauma of the armed struggle launched in 1948 and of the consequent reprisals of the state. I had come upon a rich body of Holocaust scholarship (Friedlander 1984; Laub 1992; Koch 1997; Young 1997) on memory and history that continued to echo in my thinking about these issues, in seemingly unrelated, uncomprehensible yet persistent ways, across a couple of years. The context was so different—the horror of the genocide and the modes of torture, the unspeakability of it all, as well as the compulsion to speak of it, the fear of forgetting and the impossibility of doing so, the struggle to establish the historical veracity of the events in the face of denials and of accusations about the fallibility of memory—none of these seemed to be directly relevant. Tebhaga had thrown up other questions regarding memory. I was trying to understand an event not even known to younger members or neighbours of some of the activist families, struggling to coax memory into the open from people who had opted out of the public gaze, asking questions about matters that had long been silenced by the CP, given their changed stance on a number of issues. Finally, I was simply interested in how people lived the struggle: what did it mean to be a woman or a man in those times, to forge powerful comradeships across social divides in the shared endurance of hardships? And how were the dreams of utopic comradeship cruelly shattered? Neither public memory, nor official history, nor left historiography has asked these questions; and neither has the women's movement reckoned adequately with women whose presence in public life and public work were motivated by considerations that are not ours. I was, therefore, at a loss as to how to deal with them, till it dawned on me that the relevance of the Holocaust scholars' work lay for me in the modes in which they foregrounded their own relation to the survivor's memory, forged new standards for the writing of repressed histories, and resisted ideological closure; and equally so in the modes in which they plumbed the narratives of survivors, for the unspoken, or even the unspeakable pasts, from the point of view of representation. These finally enabled me to reach out to that which had been rendered unspeakable, yet had continued to simmer in precarious unease under the surface of a largely triumphalist left narrative of Tebhaga.[6]

Finally, I found my ground in more ways than one. The first was in relation to the role of the activist's memory and my own role—this was in Friedlander's insistence on integrating the survivor's memory and the historian's voice, leading, 'not to an abandonment of historical standards but to a deepening of them' (Young 1997:51). Survivors' memories are not just important but indispensable to a historical understanding of their time because 'it is their voices that reveal what was known and what could be known.... Theirs were the only voices that conveyed both the clarity of insight and the total blindness of human beings confronted with an entirely new and utterly horrifying reality' (Friedlander 1997:2, cited in Young 1997:50–51). While all of the reality of Tebhaga was not horrifying, some of it definitely was; and the sense of it being a 'new' experience was certainly pervasive.

Second, Friedlander's insistence on the 'restoration of the historian's reasons for writing such history to the historical record' (Young 1997:50), as well as his perception of the historian's task as one that could 'serve to disrupt the facile linear progression of the narration, introduce alternative interpretations, question any partial conclusion, withstand the need for closure' (Friedlander 1992:53, cited in Young 1997:50) were also centrally relevant to my own investment in this past as a feminist. The fact that my own subjectivity has been at work in these attempts to grasp meaning, in constant interrogation and in wariness of ideological closure, was foregrounded again, taking me back to Laub's understanding, discussed in the previous section, of knowledge in oral history being not a given, but an advent, to be arrived at. I realized that this engagement had to involve a process of conscious intersubjective reflection. This oral history, then, began to map the contours of an intersubjective process across women's concerns of the 1940s and my feminist concerns of the present.

[6] I would like to emphasize that I draw upon Holocaust scholarship here for understanding the role of representation and memory in oral history. It is certainly not to indicate any correspondence between two such disparate histories as that of the Holocaust and the Tebhaga movement.

## Narrative, Aesthetics and History: The 'Poetic Truth' of Oral Narratives

The other significance of Holocaust scholarship for this work, as I have indicated, was in relation to its engagement with the survivor's narrative as a mode of *representation* that provided access to the complexities of a conflicted past. From the framing and structuring of the narratives and narrative voice, from the intertwining of voices and the dialogic character of the narratives, from the ellipsis, pauses and contradictions, from the context of the narrator as 'storyteller' and her role in offering 'counsel' (Benjamin 1969a), from careful cross-readings of narratives as well as silences, and above all, from the workings of the *aesthetic* impact of events on the subjects of history and from a hermeneutic reading of the narratives for the significance they had to impart. While the insights of historiographers and, of course, oral historians were critical, the work of making meaning became, primarily, a mode of exploratory intersubjective work in literary readings of the narratives.

Given the interventions of history and the vicissitudes of memory, it is in any case difficult to make *direct* use of oral narratives for *explicitly* revealing facts and events. Two insights of oral history played a central role in this context. One is that a critical significance of orality is to be found in the recognition of the *symbolic* character of representations, and even distortions and 'false memory', rather than in the simply direct or even reflective significations (this recognition is what Laub [1992:62] would call the advent of knowledge of the event). The other is in relation to the impact of the events represented 'in the recognition of their potential influence on forms of actual behaviour' (Passerini 1989:191). It is here that the epistemological bridging becomes crucial—in learning to recognize how events impacted people, what their *aesthetic* response was that mobilized them into certain kinds of action, and what it was that made them consequently shape their own history in the ways they did. The tragedy is that more often than not we remain limited to our own epistemological standpoints and become mere chroniclers of our pasts as seen from our point of view—not the least for the demands of factual veracity made on oral history.

A central challenge for the analyses of oral narratives, then, lies in the recognition of the influence that the narrated events may have had on forms of actual behaviour. As Young (1997:55) asserts, historians often miss crucial data when they ignore or devalue testimony as 'historically inaccurate', for such historians 'also ignore the very reasons the witnesses and survivors, as well as victims, responded to the events as they did. Ultimately, to ignore this is to ignore the highly contingent reasons why events actually unfolded as they did.' Oral narratives need to be read in terms of a search for 'the truth of possibility' rather than the 'truth of material events' (Portelli 1998:38). This 'truth of possibility' is what constitutes the 'poetic truth' of the recall of memory in oral history, and secures its ground in the face of charges of factual inaccuracy. For the charges may certainly be valid in the logic of scientific precision, but are misplaced in relation to the lived understanding of the past that memories, both collective and individual, can yield. Take the case of Subhadra Kumari Chauhan's famous poem, 'Jhansi ki Rani' (The Queen of Jhansi), with its refrain '*Bundele harbolon ke munh, hamne suni kahani thi*'.[7] The historical relevance of the poem lies not in the verifiability of the factual details of the heroic anti-imperialist leadership of the queen that is narrated in the poem; it derives from the fact that the Bundelis *perceived* her to have led a war of independence against the British in 1857, which in turn contributed to the mobilization of the nationalist movement in the 1940s. *How* the Rani of Jhansi is commemorated in public memory is far more important than whether she really jumped onto a horse and injured General Walker. An understanding of this also facilitates an understanding of the link in public memory between the First War of Independence in 1857 and the nationalist movement in the 1940s, a period that was rife with retellings of this legend.

Thus, factual accuracy is not the central premise of oral history. As Portelli too established in *The Death of Luigi Trasulli* (1991), it is not the factual accuracy of memory but the nature and meaning of memory that becomes significant in oral recollections of the past. It is the 'poetic truth' of events to which oral history lays claim. So rather than focusing on the accuracy of dates and facts, I stress

[7] Literally translated this would be: 'From the mouths of Harbols of Bundel, we'd heard this story.'

the importance of broadening the notions of historical validity and credibility to grasp this poetic truth of historical and political events for those very actors who shape history—for it is the significance of these events in people's lives that inspires their consequent actions that in turn shape future histories. It does not matter whether the Rani of Jhansi had really been a brave anti-imperialist fighter; the reason why this legend played an inspirational role in the nationalist struggle in India was that she was perceived to be such in public memory. This signals the aesthetic potential of events, past or present, to influence behaviour in the present. Oral history tries to retrieve the 'why' and the 'how' of such mobilization in relation to the meaning the event carries for people, why they are moved or affected by it, and how they act as a result of this aesthetic affect. Aesthetic response, thus, becomes a crux of historical transformation. So the aesthetic potential of events comprises the affective impact of events that mobilizes history, as well as the aesthetic response to these transformations that in turn mobilizes future histories. Together, they constitute the poetic truth of events, which is also a historical truth of affective mobilization, bearing an explanation of a process of historical transformation. This, of course, may not be the only explanation of human transformation, but it is certainly one without which any understanding of personal or collective transformation would be radically deficient. Therefore, poetic truth is central to a comprehensive understanding of historical human transformation.

What such engagement with oral narratives involves, then, is the move from a factual 'knowing' of events to an interpretive 'understanding' of them, that is, from the generally epistemological to the more specifically hermeneutic (Koch 1997:395). One draws upon hermeneutics to engage with how the knowledge of events is understood, and the specific potential of this understanding to shape future acts and commitments. Koch clarifies the difference between these approaches in relation to the Holocaust, in terms of its import for our understanding of history. On an epistemological level, she observes that:

> This skepticism [about knowledge] applies not so much to the existence of facts as to our own ability to grasp them.... On this level there is no special need to prove the evidence of the Holocaust

> insofar as we regard it as a fact along with other facts.... On this level it is a fact we are convinced to be true, and not a metaphor. (ibid.)

On a hermeneutic level, she asserts that:

> Whatever knowledge we have in terms of facts that we believe to be true remains 'dead' as long as we fail to make use of it to interpret, communicate and mediate those facts. The real 'life' of knowledge, which goes beyond mere factual information, in this sense then is that which enables us to understand or explain meaning, intentions, personal acts, emotions and reasons. (ibid.)

A central reason for the entry of hundreds of urban women into the Tebhaga movement relates to the 'life' of one such fact. Almost every urban woman I spoke to pointed to the Bengal famine of 1943 as a turning point in her life. This was a time when thousands of starving peasants were flooding the towns and cities of Bengal in search of nourishment. The cry of '*Ektu phyan de ma*' (give me some rice water, mother) was heard on every street, and emaciated peasants would turn up outside kitchen windows in the hope of some phyan. Often women cited having seen men, women or children dying from starvation. The deep impact of this was what all the urban women referred to as the reason for first joining the langarkhanas as volunteers for distributing food, and then joining study groups and meetings to understand the politics behind such devastating hunger in a time of plenty, for it was a famine caused by 'man-made' scarcity, not by natural drought. And it was the memory of such distress and injustice that propelled them into political activism and dreams of a just future. Thus, the famine remains 'dead' as a fact in relation to urban women, until we interpret its meaning for those who were affected by its impact and whose future acts were shaped by it. Poetic truth steers clear of dead facts and gives us access to the mobilizing forces of history in the very realms of interiority. Such a poetic truth of history is premised on subjectivity in the sense of the affective, aesthetic response to events; yet, the mobilizing force of history to which it gives us access does not inhabit the shaky ground of individualized subjectivity. For when such poetic truth animates an individual and mobilizes her into historical action, it is an event of an order that has the capacity to animate entire populations. The factity of such poetic truth resides in the impact of history on the future, in the concrete mobilization of acts, be they of leadership, resistance or survival.

Poetic truth grounds the historicity of survival and resistance, but may also be harnessed as justification of hierarchical impositions, strife, vengeance or even devastation. The poetic truth of historical mobilization is not ethically value laden in itself; it only bears an explanation of mobilization on the basis of a perception of an event and its affective impact, and there is every likelihood of a clash of poetic truths occurring in volatile, contested contexts, especially where the social, political or economic stakes are high. And, as indicated earlier in the case of the legend of the Rani of Jhansi, it is often near impossible to prove the factual veracity of a legend, or folk memory, or even a contested event in contemporary public memory—and that is not, in any case, the central focus of oral history.

Yet, factual veracity, its distortion or even complete erasure, does play a role in the kind of oral history under discussion here in relation to understanding the human dynamics underlying historical change due to the impact of experienced events. The representation of 'factual' truth in testimony can be intrinsically contested, conflicting, repressed or even withheld completely; and the search for the reasons for the tensions underlying such dynamics often reveals significant complexities of response to historical events, especially traumatic ones, as will become clear in the later chapters of this book relating to Ila Mitra and her biographer Maleka Begum, and Anima Biswas and her mentor and leader Amal Sen. In such cases especially, cross-reading narratives becomes an indispensable mode of squaring off the discrepancies of memory, and hence of poetic truths too, across different versions of the past; and a foregrounding of the motivations underlying these discrepancies may in turn not only produce more accurate accounts, but also histories more richly layered with the complexities and intrinsic compulsions of the period in question.

In most cases though, the 'truth' that has to be weighed is barely touched by the minor deviations of factual evidence. The analyst Dori Laub discusses the contested terrain of 'truth' in testimony in relation to the inconsistencies of memory, in the context of a survivor relating her memories of an uprising in Auschwitz. In an intensified moment of passion during their conversation, she had claimed, 'All of a sudden we saw four chimneys going up, exploding. The flames shot into the sky, people were running, it was unbelievable' (Laub 1992:59). Historians claimed the testimony was not accurate because, historically, only one chimney had been blown up, not four, and that 'the limits of the woman's knowledge in effect called into question the validity of her whole testimony' (ibid.:61). Their concern with accuracy did have strong grounds, for as Laub himself acknowledges, 'it was utterly important to remain accurate, lest the revisionists in history discredit everything' (ibid.:60).

For the analyst however, the 'truth' of the account lay not in the empirical fact of the actual number of chimneys. His view was that the woman was testifying

> to something else, more radical, more crucial: the reality of an unimaginable occurrence. One chimney blown up in Auschwitz was as incredible as four. The number mattered less than the fact of occurrence.... The woman testified to an occurrence that broke the all compelling frame of Auschwitz, where Jewish armed revolts just did not happen, and had no place. She testified to the breakage of a framework. That was historical truth. (ibid.)

Laub's concern was, thus, not merely her subjective truth, but also the very historicity of the event, for the woman had testified to resistance, to the affirmation of survival, to the '*breakage of the frame of death*' (ibid.:62, emphasis added). This was her way of surviving, of resisting. Attention to her subjective articulations, thus, revealed the epistemological process—how she had grasped the knowledge of the chimney(s) blowing up as an act of resistance that enabled survival. This 'truth', it is important to recognize, was not only a 'subjective truth' for one woman, it highlighted a critical political process that did take place in Auschwitz, as well as the historicity of the event, of the breaking of the frame of the concentration camp.

Factual veracity, that is, the exact number of towers blown up, the exact date on which an event may have taken place, the precise number of people present, or even the specific words spoken or deeds done, is important, especially in the politically contested terrain of multiple contending versions that history is. However, the historian's emphasis on factual veracity runs the danger of erasing more complex 'truths'—history needs to open up to the oral historian's concern with the historical truth of *transformation*—for what enabled the victims of the concentration camp to regain their agency and find the motivation to stay alive, and finally survive the place is no less than a historical truth.

In the context of Tebhaga, most historians would write off the inconsistencies such as that between the Tebhaga leader Amal Sen's account that the peasant activist Anima Biswas was the one who drew the man she loved into both the movement and marriage, and her version that she joined Tebhaga at her husband's instance. Even Amal Sen would say that her account was 'not true'. The point is not to shelve such inconsistencies in the name of untruth, but to ask why Biswas had narrated a 'distorted' version of the truth, which actually even she seemed to have begun to believe. What did this version of events enable her to do in life? Could it have been a gendered negotiation with the anxieties that impact women under patriarchy?

The affective impact of events on the subjects of history and their aesthetic response to it is the central concern here. The ways in which history affects subjects determines their aesthetic response to it. Such aesthetic responses to events may catalyse revolutionary processes in the realms of interiority; these in turn mobilize populations and give history direction. Such analyses, of aesthetic response to historical events, thus provides access to the transformative forces of culture and history in ways that factual truths may not. Aesthetic responses of this kind then comprise a basic truth of history—one that is much neglected by historiography and deserves recognition as being central to political and cultural transformations. So the affective and aesthetic life of the actors of history must be restored to historiography.

The status of such truth, which may be attached to individual perception, has in fact been a concern of modern aesthetics from the very beginning, as Bowie explains, drawing upon Baumgarten, one of the pioneers of modern aesthetic theory:

> Baumgarten values aesthetic truth as the *Wahrscheinliche*, that which *appears* as true, even if it cannot finally be proved to be true, whereas the sciences can only ever claim truth for what is clear and distinct. The problem with the sciences is, then, that they exclude most of

> the content of what Edmund Husserl will later term the 'life-world', the untheorised horizon of our everyday experience, from any kind of truth. (1990:6)

Of course, in the context of modernity's circumscribing and limiting of truth to what Bowie (ibid.:9) terms a subject's 'capacity for objectifying the world in science', such transforming aesthetic experiences, that are clearly subjective, cannot aspire to being 'true', for scientific rationality allows only distinct objective factuality the status of truth. Yet, the truth of our modes of relating to the world is constituted as much if not more by our everyday experiences, by what is termed above as the 'life world' and 'the untheorized horizon of our everyday experience of the world'. According to Bowie, Baumgarten too saw individual perception in the 'life-world' as an inherent part of the truth of our relationship to the world and, thus, insisted upon including aesthetics as an integral constituent of philosophy (ibid.:6). Fortunately, our subjective everyday experiences are not so 'untheorized' anymore; the everyday world has been the focus of much attention as the contested site of materiality and gender upon which standpoints are developed, as has been evident in the work of standpoint sociologists such as Dorothy Smith, and of feminist philosophers from Sandra Harding to Nancy Hartsock for almost three decades now. Given that the everyday world is the locus of these women's accounts, the memories narrativized in orality need to be seen through the combined lens of both subjectivity and aesthetics.

The very structure of the narrative too has the potential to yield critical historical insights that may not be available even through reflective or symbolic readings of a woman's account, as I will show later in relation to Ila Mitra's experience with the Santals. Young's (1997:50–51) observation about our role as oral historians in relation to the survivors of the Holocaust is relevant here to the Tebhaga activists too: 'By recognizing the role their own narratives may have played in their lives, we acknowledge that their ongoing narrative grasp of events was very much a part of the historical reality itself.' As I will show later, the intertwining of the voice of Harek the Santal with her own voice in Ila Mitra's narratives reveals a level of her identification with the Santals that she herself may have been unaware of, and this has the potential to explain the extreme resilience and refusal of an upper-caste urban woman to betray her Santal comradres. Thus, the very structuring of the narrative may reveal 'the possibility of historical causes and effects otherwise lost in our projection of a hindsight logic onto events' (ibid.). Through close attention to aesthetics and structuring, to the activist's 'narrative grasp' of events, one has a chance of bridging the rupture of history with the lived past; one has a chance of accessing the past in terms of the significance it held for the activists, how they shaped it, and why they did so. Thus, one may be able to find the reasons for the ways in which the past was transformed—hovering in and around the narrators' acts of remembering the past—reasons yet to be accessed so that we may understand not just how 'the realities themselves, as they actually unfolded, owe an essential debt to those who lived and remembered them' (ibid.:51), but also how our realities came to be what they are.

## The Retroactive Force of Interiority: Calling History into Question

What is unique about oral history, then, is that it gives us access to expressions of how events are experienced and received *aesthetically*, and how this subjective reception of events in turn *mobilizes* future possibilities, future histories, in ways that the mere objective factual *incidence* of events may not. Oral narratives lead us to these subjective, aesthetic and affective dynamics of interiority that mobilize entire collectives into political action. Consequently, they also allow ways of understanding how the success or failure of such action refuels the dynamics of both interiority, and, in turn, of the narratives too.

This lived dynamics between the workings of interiority and the politics of a collective rarely find place in any other genre or discipline. Neither does any single disciplinary approach enable access to this absolutely basic force of human subjectivity, which combines both the standpoint of subjects and the effective loci of their subjective, aesthetic responses, upon which a movement and a people turn. Literature deals with the fictional imaginary, philosophy with theoretical abstractions, autobiography has the individual—not the collective—as its locus, anthropology focuses on the cognitive nature of socialization, without addressing the experiential dimension of a lived reality, and history has long eschewed both subjectivity and memory. It is left to an integrally interdisciplinary oral history to interweave the approaches of the social sciences and the humanities—to challenge and transform some and harness others—and break new pathways into the workings of human subjectivities that mobilize and sustain movements.

The dynamics of human subjectivity in shaping history, therefore, becomes a focal point of oral history. This attempt to approach the history of the Tebhaga women too is premised upon the fact that narratives are informed by the subjectivity of the speakers. In addition, subjective reality also has its own history and multifaceted relationships with structures of power (Passerini 1998:55). So the questions that can be addressed in readings of narratives that traverse half a lifetime or more, and across the articulations of multiple activists, include those that involve processes of historical change in the realms of interiority. Thus, it is from the relations between interiority and the world of political action that I come to the questions of gendered transformations: through what processes of subjective transformation did women locate themselves in the Tebhaga movement? What were the transformations that they in turn effected and in what ways did this inflect the nature of Tebhaga? And what significance, or even challenges, do these subjective transformations, at both the individual and collective levels, carry for our understanding of women *in* history, and women *and* history today?

Maybe there is, after all, a way of suturing the rupture between history and the lived past, of grasping the repressed, of accessing excluded dimensions of gendered political standpoints. Benjamin, in his 'Theses on the Philosophy of History' (1969b), observes that class struggle is for 'the crude and material things without which no refined and spiritual things could exist'. Yet these 'refined and spiritual things', the very stuff of ethical ideals and historical visions, also do make their presence felt in political struggle, not in the form of the spoils that fall to the victors, but in the very dynamics of the struggle: 'They manifest themselves in this struggle as courage, humour, cunning, and fortitude' (ibid.:254). These aspects of struggle may be intangible, yet they persist and may be experienced even decades later in the realms of interiority. They constitute the inner voice of humanity capable of calling history into question, for they 'have retroactive force, and will continually call in question every victory, past and present, of rulers' (ibid.:254–55).

The uniqueness of oral history work is that it enables access to what Benjamin (ibid.:254) calls the 'retroactive force of interiority'. It is that which is manifest in expression and tone, look and gesture, and even in the silence that continues to underline narratives of activists long after the movement/history in question is past. It is immaterial, impalpable, imperceptible, yet experienced powerfully enough to persist across a lifetime—it is what survives. This force of interiority that challenges the past also assesses the present in the realms of memory and recall. It defies the possible repressions of contemporary politics and acts as midwife for the emergence of historically suppressed perspectives. This retroactive force is the conscience of oral history.

Benjamin's poetic insight speaks thus of this retroactive force of interiority, this much neglected impetus of history: 'As flowers turn towards the sun, by dint of a secret heliotropism, the past strives to turn towards the sun which is striving in the sky of history' (ibid.:244). It is in the awareness of 'this most inconspicuous of all transformations' that some of the 'secret heliotropism' of the repressed history of the gendered transformations of the 1940s in Bengal may hopefully be brought to light in our times too. The retroactive force of the Tebhaga women's narratives may yet break through the controlled calm of the official story and turn towards the sun striving in the sky of history: their remembrances may yet release in the terrain of politics that which never saw the light of this sun and realign some dimensions of history.

# ENGAGING

Rani Dasgupta, Dinajpur

Bina Guha, Dinajpur

Abani Lahiri, Dinajpur

Bimala Majhi and Sibarani Dikshit, Mednipur

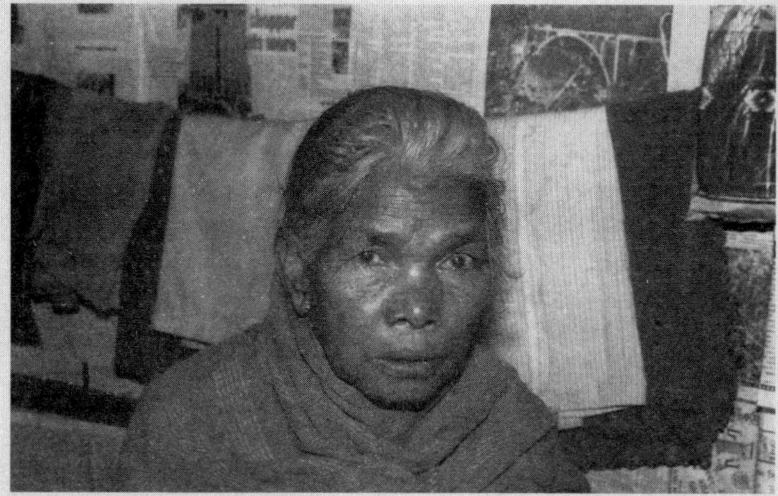

Poko Oraoni, Jalpaiguri

Kalyani Dasgupta, Jalpaiguri

Ila Mitra, Nachole

Ila and Ramen Mitra, Nachole

# 3

# '*Ektu Phyan De Ma*'—Mother Give Me Some Rice Water

## The 'Man-Made' Famine and Women's Responses to Hunger

The source of my inspiration was the famine. I learnt to understand that it was a man-made famine and I could see helpless people die in thousands. Actually, I did not have any plans to join politics. I used to be busy with my music, drama, sports etc. But then I saw the famine, and heard their cry for *phyan* [rice water]. Once I gave a woman phyan and she died the instant she had it. I saw it. Actually, after one has starved for many days, even a little food is dangerous. I experienced this when I was in jail myself. There we went on a number of hunger strikes, and when we had to break one, we never did so with solid food. We used to take liquid for seven days and then gradually move to solid food. But at that time I knew nothing. I saw her die with my own eyes.... Gradually, I had come to know that this was all created by the English people. They had large amounts of rice, but they were sending it to soldiers and creating the famine. Then I saw that the women of the Mahila Atmaraksha Samiti were serving these poverty-stricken people in Bidhan Sarani and other places. I joined them spontaneously. (Ila Mitra, urban activist, Kolkata)

> I joined the movement out of hunger. I cultivate paddy and the *mahajan* [moneylender] reaps the profit.... My husband, what could he say? I was fighting against hunger ... there were so many days my children starved. (Tulsi Samanta, peasant activist, Budhakhali, 24 Parganas)

In 1943, the streets and bylanes of Kolkata resounded with the haunting cry of 'Ektu phyan de ma', as thousands of starving peasants streamed in from the villages, all in search of food. Urban women did not even have to step out of their homes to witness this hunger, for emaciated peasant women would turn up at the kitchen window, desperate to save a dying child. This was the condition in the other towns and cities of Bengal too. What moved the urban, upper-caste and middle-class Ila Mitra so deeply in Kolkata was far from a rare occurrence during the Bengal famine. The Tebhaga movement came three years later, and almost every urban woman who had been an activist in it highlighted the profoundly affective experience of witnessing such starvation as the prime catalyst for her politicization. As for peasant women, the singular reason, as Tulsi Samanta too said, was the injustice of 'hunger'—and the terseness with which they articulated this word was clearly underwritten by grim memories of a terrifying reality.

Three million people died due to starvation and in the epidemics that followed the famine (Cooper 1988:51; Dreze and Sen 1993:5); 4.8 million rural poor had turned destitute. In all, 6 million were affected. Families had sold their children, husbands their wives, and women and girls had taken to prostitution to raise money for food (Cooper 1998:52–53). Renu Chakravartty adds: 'What destitution meant for women could be gauged from the statistics supplied by Dr Sourin Ghosh, the government doctor in the department of venereal diseases. The number of brothel inmates increased from 20,000 to about 45,000' (1980:28). The Bengal famine of 1943 clearly marked a rupture in which the rural poor became the most vulnerable, and, as Greenough observes, 'patterns of abandonment began to emerge, marked by the snapping of moral and economic bonds upon which rural society had hitherto been erected' (Greenough 1982:138, cited in Chaudhuri 2012).

Given that women were closest to the processing and serving

of food, and to caring for the sick, the dying and the violated, the hunger, disease and the escalating prostitution that were at the core of this famine proved to be a critical mobilizing force for them. Thousands of them came together, as activists of the CP or MARS, or as beneficiaries of the langarkhanas. As the langarkhanas and income-generation projects set up by MARS multiplied across Bengal, its membership increased rapidly: in the course of just the one year of the famine, it jumped from 500 at the first conference in Calcutta on 27 April 1943, to 43,500 by the time the second conference took place in Barisal in May 1944. Renu Chakravartty (1980:53) records that by the time of its Barisal conference, 'the MARS had become one of the bigger mass organizations of women with a membership of 43,500, and branches in every district.'

This famine, like many others, was not the result of drought; instead, and like many others, it was 'the historic counterpart of abundance'.[1] To use Dreze and Sen's terms, in 'slump' famines, starvation is accompanied by general economic decline; in contrast, and despite the Mednipur cyclone of 1942, this was a 'boom' famine, related to the growing economic affluence of middle-class traders in the context of the uneven nature of the war boom (Dreze and Sen 1993:5, 46). The experience of this 'man-made famine' (ibid.:46) marked a watershed in the transformation of subjectivity across undivided Bengal. It brought with it the experience of 'hunger in a time of plenty' (Chaudhuri 2012), a paradox that demanded explanation and ultimately led to an unprecedented growth of political consciousness too.

Various factors had contributed to the 1943 famine and most were related to the market economy of World War II. After the fall of Burma in 1942, the loss of rice imports had created an additional demand in Travancore and Cochin, which were the worst hit by it. This enabled sellers to demand a higher price. Combined with the rise in prices that had already occurred during the war, cultivators began 'to meet their cash obligations by selling a smaller quantity of their produce than formerly'—they began to wait for even better prices by withholding supplies from the market. An artificial situation of

[1] See Fernandez-Armesto (2001:230) for an account of other such famines.

scarcity was thus created. The *Famine Inquiry Commission Report* on Bengal states: 'Buyers are anxious to buy before a further rise occurs and therefore increase their purchases, while sellers are reluctant to sell because they wait for still better prices' (Woodhead 1984:79).

This situation of dearth was further compounded by the absence of any measures of control by the colonial government of Bengal for ensuring equitable distribution of what *was* available at affordable prices, so that even if each got less, none would starve. Severe inadequacies had resulted in the colonial administration due to policy clashes in the British War Cabinet (Mukerjee 2010:xxxiv). In fact, Mukerjee's study holds the British primarily responsible for this famine, claiming that even as they opposed the barbarism of the Nazis and the holocaust of 6 million Jews, they were simultaneously responsible for the death of 3 million Indians due to starvation and disease (ibid.). Hoarding by traders came as the final nail in the coffin. Highlighting the pervasiveness of a 'psychology of greed and fear', the famine report asserts that 'there was a moral and social breakdown as well as an administrative breakdown' (Woodhead 1984:78–79). Thus, the politics of the market economy underlined the 'man-made' famine at various levels—of the jotedars and zamindars as the powerful producers capable of inflecting the market prices, the traders as hoarders, and the empire as multinational consumer and regulator.

Janam Mukherjee's recent work also demonstrates how communal identities hardened during the famine in the crossfire between the ruling Muslim League and the Hindu Mahasabha, and in the communalization of relief work (Mukherjee 2011:264–73). Mukherjee also discusses the role of the state in facilitating this congealing of communal identities:

> But because famine victims were the most marginal citizens of empire, the record kept of corpses collected by the authorities in Calcutta was extremely limited. In fact, the sole criteria used to classify the dead, as in the case of the bombings, was religious affiliation. In some definite sense, that the state only recognized these nameless corpses as 'Hindu' or 'Muslim', was merely an extension of the simplistic binary with which they were wont to categorize the population more generally. That corpses were thus understood, however, lent a certain

> biological 'proof' to the long advanced discursive argument that this distinction, alone, was paramount in understanding the Indian population. Together with the cheapening of life that famine and war entailed, the contention that communal affiliation adhered to the very *bodies* of the citizens of Bengal represented a dark foreshadow of the violence to come. (ibid.:15–16)

The Irish famine too, as Eagleton (1995:26) says, was 'a matter of politics and property relations rather than of an all merciful providence'. And what he observes about the impact of the famine on the consciousness of Irish society, almost exactly a century ago in 1845, becomes relevant to the Bengal famine too:

> Because of the Famine, Irish society undergoes a surreal speed up of its entry upon modernity; but what spurs this process on is, contradictorily, a thorough traditional calamity. Part of the horror of the famine is its atavistic nature—the mind-shaking fact that an event with all the pre-modern character of a medieval pestilence happened in Ireland with frightening recentness. This deathly event then shatters space as well as time, unmaking the nation and scattering Irish history across the globe. (ibid.:14)

If for Ireland the famine 'unmade' the nation, for the peasantry of Bengal it 'unmade' both feudalism and the empire, as what had been perceived as feudal 'relations of dependency' between the sharecropper and the zamindar/jotedar revealed themselves in no uncertain terms to be relations of exploitation. Kalyani Dasgupta's (1997) account of the peasants of Sundardighi, Jalpaiguri, confirms the impact of this consciousness—she recalled that a common refrain amongst them was: '*Elay mora jagichhi, aar soshan chalbe na*' (Now we are awakened, no one can exploit us any more). And at the international level, the critique of empire paved the way for loyalties to the international communist vision of equality. For women too it signalled a time to move into the fields of politics, both economic and sexual.

As the Irish famine helped lay the economic ground for independence from the British (Eagleton 1995:17), the Bengal one similarly paved the way for the Tebhaga movement, which was as much anti-imperialist as it was anti-feudal. Still reeling under the impact of the famine, impoverished sharecroppers finally launched the movement in 1946, against the jotedars and zamindars, for an increased share of the crop. The function of food as necessary sustenance had become the basis for the peasants' unification in struggle across caste and community. Resistance against the sexual intimidation of peasant women by the jotedars and zamindars also figured prominently on the agenda (Cooper 1988:102–3). Sharecroppers were organized right across undivided Bengal under the Bengal Provincial Krishak Sabha, a communist-led organization, to reduce land rents from half to one-third of the share of the crops (ibid.:2; Majumdar 1993:1).

The crisis of the famine had rendered one perception crystal clear: what was food for the peasants was primarily capital for the zamindar and jotedar. Their greed was the perverse counterpart of the formers' hunger. On the one hand, there was a boom in the market economy of the war; on the other, there was a complete collapse of whatever vestiges of a 'moral economy' there may have been in terms of economic choices and practices being guided by considerations of morality.[2] This inverse relation between the market economy and the moral economy of the time, it can be argued, is intrinsic to the nature of capital and the maximization of opportunity in times of crisis.

It seems to me, however, and specially in the context of the Bengal famine and the consequent social transformations leading right up to and shaping the Tebhaga movement, that rather than look for possibilities of moral practices in the economics of the market, it would be more useful to focus on the nature of the moral imperative in the secular sphere within which this imperial market economy of the war functioned, and the ways in which it may have exerted pressure on the latter. As Supriya Chaudhuri (2102) asserts:

> One could, further, argue that while market economies are generally characterized as being non-moral in that their operations are ostensibly freed of moral compulsions, the secular sphere in which such economies operate may promote an increased social

[2] See Chaudhuri (2012) for an excellent discussion of the concept of 'moral economy'.

> compulsion to achieve 'universal' wellbeing, which then comes to inflect the apparently unregulated pursuit of profit at the cost of others.

What I hope to show here is that not only was there an 'increased social compulsion' to achieve well-being in the face of the exploitative greed that had brought on the famine, but also that it took on powerful new contours, especially through the relief work of women. In fact, it led to a unique mode of politicization for women—one that was rooted in concrete practices and an ethic of care rather than in a theoretical one of justice, with the former revealing the concrete workings of power, and putting on the table critical needs and demands to give embodied form and compelling urgency to the more abstract ethic of the latter.[3] Involvement in the concrete processes by which life is sustained demands that the notions of entitlements and human capabilities be translated into human practices. It was from the most basic level of saving the lives of famine victims, and taking on the responsibility to ensure that resources for their continued survival were available, that the women succeeded in challenging the mechanisms of power. Eventually, the attentiveness and responsibility that the relief work required, as well as the huge numbers of women involved

[3] I refer to care here as a practice that involves reaching out beyond oneself in specific actions 'to maintain, continue and repair our "world" so that we can live in it as well as possible' (Tronto 2009:102–3). Vrinda Dalmiya (2007:300) elaborates it further as:

> A receptive and affectively induced engrossment in the cared for's reality is the beginning of caring. This underlies a grasp of another's expressed and inferred needs without which no ethical response is possible. The next step is motivational displacement—a redirection of the carer's energy towards the projects of the cared-for … and a crucial third condition of reciprocity… the carer must be cognizant of the effect of her caring on the cared-for and give the latter a voice in shaping the relationship.

Carol Gilligan (1982:19) makes a distinction between an 'ethic of care' and an 'ethic of justice' as follows:

> The conception of morality as concerned with the activity of care centers moral development around the understanding of responsibility and relationships, just as the conception of morality as fairness ties moral development to the understanding of rights and rules.

in it, led to the development of a pervasive political consciousness rooted in an ethic of care that infused the left public sphere with a distinctive grounded morality.

## The Dynamics of Food*

It is common to thematize food—or the lack of it—in various ways: in terms of a 'crop' or commodity to be produced or traded, or as 'famine' to be explained, as in economic histories; as an index of differentiation and changing class relations as in social histories; as shared 'cuisine' or as 'hunger' that shapes identities in cultural studies; as '*rasa*' (flavour) or '*abhaava*' (lack) that shapes aesthetics and subjectivity; as the 'raw' and the 'cooked' that defines groups in anthropology; and as that which in its distribution signifies the relationships of power in political science and international relations.[4] A schizophrenic contemporary academia, with its categorization of knowledge into discrete specialized disciplines, has split the material and cultural processes of food into its many avatars, each more isolated from the other than not. This, I argue, has pre-empted our understanding of the degree to which the material and cultural processes of food organize the dynamics of our lives and how they do so. In other words, the specialist's approach to food—in terms of the narrow and often insular focus of each on commodity or cuisine or famine or hunger, or the 'raw' and the 'cooked'—prevents a comprehensive understanding of the mobilizing force of food in the lives of human beings.

What is unique about food is that it is the most basic material of *use value* (one cannot survive without it), as well as the most fundamental currency of *exchange value* (more basic than, say, clothing or gold, and in a chicken-and-egg relationship with labour—which came first?). It is *sustenance* as well as *capital*. Thus, that which is processed into food

[4] Fernandez-Armesto (2001:13) has listed some of this.

*An earlier version of this section and part of the next one also feature in my essay 'The "Man-made" Famine and Women's Responses to Hunger: The Pivotal Dynamics of Food in the Tebhaga Movement' in Uma Chakravarti (ed) *Thinking Gender, Doing Gender: Feminist Scholarship and Practice Today*, New Delhi: Orient Blackswan, pp 132–43.

is also exchanged as commodity. Food embodies one aspect of the duality of use and exchange—it serves the realm of use, but can easily be forced, as commodity, into the realm of exchange. And it is this duality of use value and exchange value that makes food the basis for various sets of sociopolitical dynamics, and especially gendered ones.

Specific to this famine was the fact that it was created by the *forced transactions* or *unnatural crossovers* between agents and processes of sustenance and of exchange/accumulation. What happens, for example, when women (who process crop into food) are exchanged as commodity (to feed the lust of jotedars)? Or when crop meant for basic sustenance (food) is hoarded as a commodity (for capital gains)? It is these 'aberrant' transactions that become the source of tension, that give rise to historical crises. Such an analysis cannot be based only on economic, or cultural or social perspectives—it needs to be posited at the intersection of these. I hope to develop here some understanding of the connection between the dynamics of food and women's participation in peasant movements.

An exploration of the multidimensional character of food and its dynamics also explains why historiography is dominated by relations of *production* (and distribution and political relations), while histories of the *reproduction* of cultural and social relations remain marginalized. While both men and women have been producers of crop, *processing* and *serving* food has traditionally been the premise of women, and *commodity exchange* and *distribution* largely that of men. Processing and serving of food, and caring for people, forms the basis of cultural and social practice, and women are critical to these realms. On the other hand, trade and distribution—and men—have largely pertained to the economic and political realms, which in turn dominate historiography. Thus, histories of *production* (from patriarchal perspectives), and of commerce and distribution, are privileged, while the *reproduction* of sociocultural relations (as involved in women's processing and sharing of food) receive short shrift. Consequently, women's history and gendered history have both been rendered marginal, as has the history of hunger. Yet, it is largely in the *reproduction* of cultural and social processes that women's agency and history are located—and it is from their location here that their political participation begins.

## Hunger and Political Critique

The dynamics of hunger during the Bengal famine initiated radical shifts in not just economic and political, but also social, cultural and gendered processes. The political consciousness of both class and gender deepened in the face of rapidly increasing inequalities, for famines are always divisive phenomena. Drèze and Sen (1993:48) emphasize this quality of a famine: 'Contrary to statements that are sometimes made, there does not seem to have been a famine in which victims came from all classes of society.' The pointed contrast between scarcity of food for the peasants and the abundance of rice hoarded by traders provided the grounds for a sharpening of class consciousness. What was *food* for the starving, was *capital* for the traders and the colonial government. In the villages, the zamindars' and jotedars' accumulation of crop continued to be experienced by the sharecroppers as want of food, as hunger, starvation and death. The former's control over the crop was perpetuated through a holding back by unfair means of what was due to the peasants (through the use of inaccurate measures for doling out rice, the levy of exorbitant interest rates payable in rice, etc.). And peasant women experienced a double exploitation, both economic and sexual (Cooper 1988:102–3). In classic left understanding, it is a consciousness of class—Luckas' description of the movement from class-in-itself to class-for-itself—that produces proletarian politics. The direct materiality of peasant politics, however, leads to food, land and the body being the very sites on which class struggles are waged. Thus, the consciousness of the class in itself and for itself is not one in transit, but is constitutively double-edged: its condition is its consciousness—this is what becomes clear from peasant women's reflections.[5]

One of the common refrains among the peasant women, indicating the pervasive sharpening of political consciousness, was, as recollected in the late 1990s by Anima Biswas and Phuli Goldar, both erstwhile peasant activists of Narail: '*Ora khaye dudh bhaat, aamra shaak bhaat o khayi na*' (They have milk with rice, we do not

[5] I am grateful to V. Geetha for this insight.

even get weeds and rice). In the world of the peasants, those who ate and those who starved inhabited the same moment.[6] The stark conditions of inequity marked, simultaneously, the consciousness of this inequity. These too inhabited the same moment.

The consciousness of the injustices of an exploitative system, combined with the paucity of food in the family, marked the entry of peasant women into the movement. The prehistory of the Tebhaga movement, of the famine's 'forced transactions' across categories of use and exchange of food, had resulted in a critical honing of the perception of class inequity.

Perceptions of gender inequality also came into sharp focus. What has been observed in other famines held for this one too, that 'one of the difficult fields of "food battle" is that of intra-family struggle' (Drèze and Sen 1993:50). Women faced systematic deprivation vis-à-vis men, and in Bengal the inequity extended to the point of women and girls taking to the sex trade, and even wives being sold by husbands for food, a cataclysmic fact of history that lives on in songs from areas such as Rangpur, and was remembered and sung by women right across Bengal up to Dinajpur. The 'man-made' famine transformed the subjective landscape of Bengal and this happened in unprecedented ways where women were concerned.

The jotedars' ownership of land and control of crop also extended to the sexual control, then ownership, of peasant women, thus marking another forced crossing of categories. Women, who were the processors of food and responsible for a large share of cultural reproduction, were increasingly forced into commodity status themselves. By the time the Tebhaga movement was launched, it had already become the 'tradition' in most areas that a newly-wed peasant woman would spend the first night at the jotedar's house. This was a marker of not just the class hierarchy, but also caste hierarchy, as the majority of the sharecroppers, other than the Muslims, were under-caste Namasudras or Rajbangshis, or Santal or Oraon tribals, and the jotedars and zamindars largely upper-caste Hindus. This right of the first night gradually spilled over into various attempts to sexually

[6] I adapt the phrasing of 'those who ate and those who starved' from Chaudhuri (2012), where it is used in reference to a 1965 poem by Birendra Chattopadhyay on the food riots two decades after the Bengal famine.

exploit peasant women, which is why demands to end this featured on the agenda of the Tebhaga movement right across Bengal, from Dinajpur in the north to Narail in the south.

Historical crisis, however, also became the springboard for a gendered critique of political conditions. Not unexpectedly, but rampant nevertheless with gruesome irony, extreme deprivation of food had led, in some circumstances, to a trading of wives. Thus, personal, cultural and social relationships underwent a radical metamorphosis in the realm of economic exchange. Nirmala Rai, of Baidyerbazar, Rangpur, would still sing this song in the late 1990s:

> I'm a woman of Rangpur
> Rangpur is my home
> My husband sold me
> For some rice....
> Rent with pangs of hunger
> My darling son, he cries.
>
> Great men we have
> The headmen we have
> And they all have mothers and sisters
> I, a woman, ask you all
> If my world remains in this state
> O if the world remains like this
> Mothers and sisters
> Will become slaves of others.

The word indicating the world in the second verse is *duniya*, but other versions of the same song used the word desh, indicating land or country. Given, however, that by 1943 the women were already familiar with the nationalist politics of swadeshi, and that desh in this case is located in a lexicon of critique of agents/sites of power ranging from the headman to the world, its usage here is akin to the signification of 'nation'. This song, composed in rural Rangpur, was widely sung during the months of Tebhaga, but it evidently dates back to the famine of 1943, told in the voice of a peasant woman. It enacts a socioeconomic critique of institutions ranging from family to nation to imperialism. What is significant is that though this is a song about sexual exploitation, its symbolic force operates at the level of village administration, nation and empire. It demonstrates the need to transcend the local, which is beyond one's control. In the process, it not only evokes a larger entity—that of the nation and empire—but also offers a rationale for women's solidarity in the struggle for national liberation from below.

The peasant woman, as the song demonstrates, was reduced to a metonym, almost a *phantasm*, of herself—the primordial female sexual body. The one skilled in the processing of food was sold for food, the reproducer of culture herself traded as a commodity. This grim exchange, of food for the female body, of the satiation of the peasant's hunger through satiation of the jotedar's lust, reveals a harsh equation in the history of trade, that is, between sexual appeasement and the appeasement of hunger.

The ontological consequence of the forced appropriation of food into the realm of commodity accrues further complexity when a woman's sexual body is traded for food, and this experience is yet another marker of the shifts in the subjectivity of that period. Manik Bandyopadhyay's story '*Chhiniye Khai Ni Keno*?' is an implicit response to what was supposedly Nehru's identical question 'Why did they not snatch and eat?' articulated by the latter in puzzlement about the passivity of the peasants. Writing about this story, Supriya Chaudhuri (2011) observes that the peasant narrator Jogi's response to this question indicates the ontologically paralysing effects of desire forced into the realm of hunger:

> [The] explanation... is rooted in the material difference of hunger and desire: hunger eats the self, desire eats the other... beyond that liminal point where the body crosses into the exhaustion and physical depletion of hunger, the body is its own food, hunger consumes it *like* an other, and in so doing it estranges and alienates the self, so that it appears to have no worldly recourse.

The peasants' experience of self-estrangement that occurs as a result of hunger consuming one's own body also transforms human relationships and challenges established morality at a profound level. Jogi's unquestioning acceptance of his pregnant wife after she had sold herself for food conveys an unspoken mutual understanding of the unfathomable alienation of self. It represents a deepening of the bond between husband and wife that upturns all notions of the normative in the realm of hunger.

This also explains why there was a greater intensification of class perceptions than a sharpening of the feminist perspective during the famine, and during the continued sexual exploitation of women by jotedars and zamindars in the Tebhaga movement. Even as Jogi understands his wife's dehumanized state of estrangement, so too evidently the woman of Rangpur her husband's, for the critique is turned not on the husband who sells her, but the 'headman' who consumes her. The impact of inequality can scarcely be felt deeper than in the entwined dynamics of food and sexuality: on the one hand, desire is consumed by the hunger that eats at the starved body; on the other, the hungry body of the peasant woman is consumed by the lustful desire of the 'headman'.

Manik Bandyopadhyay represents the poor as those who do not/cannot defy the law and assert their claim to food and, as Chaudhuri (2012) asserts, he is compelled to record the extremity of a situation where the moral economy fails. She argues that this collapse of the moral economy indicates, on the one hand, the triumph of a market economy and, on the other, the 'systems of power so deeply entrenched that the body of the subaltern is unable to resist their operation'.

## A Cross-Class Solidarity of Care and the Emergence of a Political Subjectivity

> Their heart rending cry 'Give us the rice water you throw away' still rings in the ears of those who witnessed the nightmare of those days. Women were just skin and bone and their children gasping for their last breath. (Chakravartty 1980:27)

> It was completely a man-made famine. You can't imagine it—people were eating raw, green pumpkins; rice floating down the drains—I've seen this with my own eyes. I used to feel as if I'd contract cholera just seeing them. From every house, starch and whatever else was possible used to be distributed. That's how we got involved in the work of society. (Dipti Bagchi, Thakurgaon, north Dinajpur)

Why did such experiences of witnessing starvation and death, as Ila Mitra, Renu Chakravartty, Dipti Bagchi and other women narrate, draw women into the political arena? One reason was that it was the women who prepared the phyan, interacted with the starving, handed them the nourishment, witnessed them dying. And the fact that the preparation of phyan ultimately involved not culinary but life-saving skills must have been a critical challenge that involved a transformation of a familiar art of cooking into a healing act. The ethic of care that they lived up to in attending to the starving from their very kitchen doors, thus, took on dimensions of public life-saving expertise. This link between the experience of witnessing starvation and harnessing one's domestic culinary skills to save lives clearly marked a shift in subjectivity that was to impact a significant number of urban women.

In the urban context, the sight of starved populations flooding the cities crying out for phyan stirred hundreds of women into joining the langarkhanas set up by the CP and MARS. With the public distribution systems rendered void by the merchants and colonizers, and the government relief kitchens being radically insufficient, (Mukherjee, 2011:263) these langarkhanas provided an alternative distribution system in the towns and cities—one based on social responsibility and community service in the face of the political economy of exchange and hoarding.

The affective impact of this devastating tragedy of mass starvation, and the critical knowledge that it was fuelled by economic greed, were two sides of the same coin. The central paradox of such hunger in a time of plenty led to a sharpening of the political consciousness of urban women. This transformation marked a transition from the domestic to the public realm. The urban women would cook the food and serve it themselves, interacting on a daily basis with the peasants. Rani Dasgupta of Dinajpur bemoaned her fragile constitution, but simultaneously revelled in the skills she did have in the work of feeding the people in the langarkhanas. She said, 'We cooked the food for them ourselves, and to tell you the truth that since I had extremely feeble health, I couldn't handle those big cooking pots; but nevertheless, I was quite an expert at jobs like serving food and so on.' The power politics behind the forcing of food into the category of commodity was writ large on the faces of the starving, and the urban women witnessed this at close quarters, experiencing the impact of this horrific reality in intimate ways. Bimala Majhi, a peasant leader of Midnapore, narrated one such incident that points to what Greenough (1982:138) refers to as the 'snapping of moral bonds' in the face of devastating hunger:

> Yes, when Monidi [Manikuntala Sen] came and organised a committee in Tamluk subdivision ... then it was decided that the women would run the langarkhanas. So a Karma Kendra was opened for destitute women and there were 140 milk centres. And the Red Cross—how much the Red Cross did those days. Say, each centre looked after 200 to 250 children—their medicines, clothes, food, blankets, everything was taken care of by the Red Cross. They would give us the supply and we would run so many centres. We would send 40 and 60 kg tins of milk atop buses to all centres. The mothers would come to these milk centres to take milk for their children, and in one such centre at Purva Chilka, where a mother had lost her child fifteen days back, so terrible was the famine that though the child had died, the mother continued to claim the milk for herself. One day I asked her, 'Hey, where is your child, you are supposed to have him drink the milk here.' Then the mother burst into tears and said, 'Ma, he is dead—died fifteen days ago.' 'So, what do you do with the milk?' [I asked. Her answer was:] 'I drink it.' So in the face of hunger the mother couldn't afford lofty thoughts such as this was the milk that my child, now dead, would have drunk. It was a terrible famine.

On the demand of the women, a subsidized rice shop was set up in Gariahat market in Calcutta, and the Janaraksha Samiti, comprising women from the CP and MARS, worked together to run it. Hundreds of men and women would come in by the 3 am train at Ballygunj station to wait for the rice. Hearing the clamour, MARS and CP women living in the neighbourhood would come out to organize them into queues and make sure they obtained the rice when the shop opened. Dividing their time into shifts, Manikuntala Sen (2001:71) says, the activists would stay near the queues as

> procurers from the sex trade would hover around young women who had to be safeguarded. Some women would give birth while

> they waited and would have to be looked after. Sometimes a woman would remain in the queue with a dead child in her lap, refusing to let go of her place: there were many such incredible sights.

Renu Chakravartty (1980:43) too recalls instances that were shocking in the moral ruptures they revealed. Some of them took place in Kalipara village of Khulna, such as:

> another mother, who, unable to bear seeing her hungry children's suffering, threw them into the river. Husbands leaving their wives, mothers snatching morsel of food from the mouths of their children, became a common sight.

And in other places:

> Half the women had no male guardians. So they fell victims to pimps or the jotedars.... In Dalitpur, a jotedar had bought six year old 'coolie' girl for Rs 10. In Baraganj a destitute mother sold her six year old daughter to a pimp.... In Lalmanirhat about 800 women were eating in the government-run gruel kitchen. But they were half fed. So they trekked to the nearby army camp, sold their bodies to fill their stomachs. (ibid.)

The urban women's experience of witnessing hunger and death; the close interactions with the women and children they cared for in the langarkhanas and the rare controlled-price shops; the experiences of being walled out by those who became numb to sorrow like the woman who continued to wait in queue with her dead child in her lap—all this led to a transformation of subjectivity. The cultural processes of cooking and sharing were extended beyond the domestic to the public sphere at a collective level, and the langarkhanas became the interface between the impoverished rural population and concerned urban collectives. The peasant women's suffering, both in terms of physical devastation and such intimate distortions of self that acute hunger wrought in the famine-stricken women, transformed both them and the women who became their caregivers. The work in the langarkhanas drew the rural and urban women into intersubjective processes, one to one, in which the destitute woman became a beneficiary of relief and care, but the woman caring for her was also transformed.

At another level, Manikuntala Sen also writes about profound challenges activists would have to grapple with in their work as they came to terms with the human implications of this economic and political crisis. One such situation was in relation to ways in which extreme deprivation can mark the limits of the work of political consciousness raising. Having compelled the sub-divisional officer (SDO) to start langarkhanas for the distribution of phyan in Midnapore—for the population here was too starved to be able to withstand the regular gruel or khichuri served in places like Barishal—she went from house to house to talk to the women. With all essential items disappearing during this period of crisis, cloth too had become scarce. Extreme corruption in the supply and distribution of cloth, and hoarding by blackmarketeers had made it inaccessible to impoverished peasants. The scarcity that was to lead to the peaking of the cloth crisis in March 1945 (Chakravartty 1980:77) had set in well before that. Sen recounts the human costs of this scarcity and its impact not just on political activity, but on basic human communication itself. On her visits to these homes, she had to come to terms with the ontologically immobilizing impact of this deprivation—both for the hungry and for the caregiving activist:

> You could not look at anyone, especially the women: the children were practically naked, and so were the women. That is why when we went into the rooms they neither looked up nor stood up. How could I speak to these people about politics or the release of prisoners? I was at a loss for words. (2001:90)

Similar stupefying experiences were endemic to the Irish famine too, of which Eagleton (1995:12) said, 'Starving families boarded themselves into their cabins, so that their deaths might go decently unviewed.' What Manikuntala Sen and other women like her witnessed, was a reality, which, 'in threatening to slip below the level of meaning itself, offers to deny you even the meagre consolations of tragedy.... What lingered on ... was ... the very different culture of shame' (ibid.). If for the urban women this was a reality that burst through the very bounds of representation, then for the rural families it was culture stripped to a level 'below meaning'; it defied signification itself. Such loss of dignity defied communication—how could one even reach out in caring?

The deep affective impact of such suffering, thus, led not only to a grim determination to combat it, but also to a questioning of the reasons for it. From the experience of the langarkhanas, women, young and old, went on to join the study groups—often clandestine—set up by the CP in schools, colleges and local clubs, and to developing a systematic understanding of class relations, imperialism and political economy. The experience Ila Mitra recalled had parallels in the lives of most of the other urban women, across Calcutta and other towns of Bengal, and specially of those who went on to become CP members and Tebhaga activists:

> And when I got admission in Bethune College, I joined the Girl Students Committee—there we began to discuss Marxism. There was a Qutbuddin ... who used to take our classes. We did this secretly. Gradually through my relief work I became a party member.

The langarkhanas, thus, became the sites for affective, subjective transformation, as well as launching pads for the awakening of political consciousness; and thousands of women began to join MARS and the CP.

The famine also led to widespread disease. More people died after the famine when food became available than during the famine itself—of cholera, malaria, smallpox and other epidemics. People's relief committees were set up across the state, and the women of MARS became primarily responsible for distributing relief there too. With the relief and income-generation work intensifying across Bengal, its membership too spiralled, as indicated earlier, leaping from just 500 to 43,500 women in just the one year of the famine.

While both the Congress Party and the CP had peasant organizations, the CP had already begun to establish much more intimate relations with the peasantry. Abani Lahiri (2001:41–42) recollects in an interview with Ranajit Dasgupta that:

> It was the experience and lessons of this one and a half years of living in hiding which were our capital, not only mine, but of all the comrades, for the peasant movement of later years. Previously, these middle class activists who went to work among the peasants

came back to the city after their work with the peasantry. This was possibly the first time that a kind of social relationship was established between us and the poor peasants. It was after the first year of the war, in 1941, that we went away to the villages. Our links with the city were virtually snapped. For a year and a half we lived among and with peasants, saw their way of life very closely, spent our nights sometimes in the cowshed or on the verandah of the kitchen. All this brought about a transformation in the ideas and thoughts of all our workers.

During the famine—and the food shortages had begun to be felt from 1942—the CP clearly focused on the impoverished peasantry. Its relief work aided the shift in loyalties from the Congress to the CP, and initiated widespread politicization amongst the peasants of Bengal.

Dipti Bagchi, an urban woman of Rangpur town, also spoke about the change of perception of the CP in the eyes of the peasants:

> The famine of 1350 [1943] that took some 500,000 lives brought politics to our area.... Before the famine, there was just the Congress, but after the famine the Communist Party became known. It had actually just been born. Initially, people used to be kind of terrified of the Communist Party, but the famine made the communists come closer to people and gain acceptance.

By March 1943, the price of rice had multiplied almost seven times, from Rs 4 or 5 a *maund* (approximately 37 kg) to Rs 28. The work of the MARS women and the CP youth in the langarkhanas and the subsidized-price shop had a spin-off effect in terms of the emergence of a cooperative public culture. Manikuntala Sen (2001:71) observes:

> Seeing the sincerity and tireless labour of party workers, many came to our aid, among whom were many well-known people. Funds began to pour in. People encouraged and helped us to open a canteen (langarkhana).... Canteens were opened in many localities. Or workers made the rounds of people's homes, asking for money or rice, and they would come back replete with supplies.

Rekha Pandey of Rangpur town recounts the widespread nature of the collection drives: 'We took rice from every house.... Lakhs and lakhs of people started coming to the cities from the villages'; and Asha *boudi* (sister-in-law) of Dinajpur testified not just to the efforts of the activists but also the generosity of ordinary citizens, like Asha's father, who contributed all that they had:

> We collected rice during the famine, we looked for everything that we could collect.... The mothers tried to save themselves—if they could only save their own lives, they could save their children.... During that time, my father gave away whatever paddy and rice we had.

Door-to-door collection became an integral part of the public culture. While women went on these collection drives in the conviction that it was their duty to save other women (Sen 2001:84), those rendered destitute by the famine became a part of the daily consciousness and practice of ordinary householders as they set aside a handful of rice for the former each day: 'The MARS went around collecting *mushti*[*bh*]*iksha*' (Chakravartty 1980:58). And while mushtibhiksha, the practice of keeping aside a handful of rice for the *bhikshuk* (mendicant) or the *sanyasi* (ascetic), was derived from both Buddhist and Vaisnava faiths, there had clearly been a shift from the religious to a humanitarian motivation of this practice in the famine years. MARS coordinated this activity for reasons far removed from the accumulation of religious merit—for such actions had by now taken on definite political significance.

That this work was political in nature, and neither charitable nor religious, was something that even the Congress Party leader Sarojini Naidu understood well and emphasized in no uncertain terms. Chakravartty puts on record that Naidu, when asked once if Congress members could join food committees that the government had later been compelled to set up in Bengal, had replied: 'Yes, but do not go there as slaves. Go as representatives of the people and fight for the people.' And Chakravartty adds: 'She had the political understanding to see the correct perspective of relief work when the worst ever food crisis had overtaken Bengal and the alien rulers had put all the national leaders in jail.... She summed up the political content of relief work, which even today some ultra Left opinion seems to underestimate' (1980:71). That such relief work acquired a quality of political action different from the vested self-interest that characterizes much of contemporary politics is clear. What needs to be understood is its ethical quality that made it distinct from both religious offering and charitable practice; and that, as inspired action arising out of a determined political will driven by the affective impact of human devastation, it also ran deeper than a sense of ordinary social responsibility or moral duty.

Other cultures of solidarity too had gathered force in the famine years, especially in the form of song and theatre performances, both at spontaneous village levels and in the more organized Indian People's Theatre Association (IPTA), which had an impact on the whole country, from Delhi to Bombay to Madras, and of which *Nabanna*, Bijon Bhattacharjee's play on the famine, and the IPTA musical production *Bhukha Hai Bangal* made a huge mark too. This intensified cultural activity succeeded in drawing more women into the field of activism, those who joined as singers or actors, as well as those who were impacted by these performances. Dipti Bagchi who lived in Thakurgaon, Dinajpur at the time of the famine recounted:

> I was in Thakurgaon. There was a Muslim gentleman called Haji Mahammad there—an excellent man. He was a Congress man, but since he was a good and honest person, he used to collect food, clothes—we used to like him very much. He used to tell us, 'Why don't you come and sing while I go out for collection?' So we used to do that … then I got involved in CP activities too … in the relief work.… The reason we developed connection is because we used to sing when we were young.

And Bina Guha talked about the impact of a play, which her husband Bibhuti Guha had written, on the acute food crisis and shortage of cloth, that she and others staged as a mime for local girls and women in Dinajpur:

> Our house was on the road—the main road connecting the town to the village. So many people passed by—all victims of situation—men, women, babies—it was so frightening. Then we went and told Rani Sen of All India Women's Conference, '*Kakima* [aunt], we would like to stage a mime here from the *mahila samiti*.' There were no clothes. If we called a meeting, maybe the mother would

> come and not the daughter, and after the mother returned home the daughter would come clad in that same sari. This was the condition. The women from the middle class never complained in spite of their dire distress. But we understood their plight.

While this shows an unspoken understanding between the activists and small-town middle-class women of the need to hold on to the last vestiges of dignity, the play itself also evidently reflected such sensitivity to deprivation—and Bina Guha explained how the aesthetic expression of such sensitivity across classes also became the grounds for affective bonding that drew more women in as active members of the mahila samiti:

> *Banglar Buke Kalo Chhaya* (dark shadows across the heart of Bengal) was the name of the play. You just won't believe it—the girls/women of the Dinajpur mahila samiti just thronged in to see the play. After the play was over, each and everyone had tears in their eyes. Everyone was crying. Rani Sen came and simply hugged me and said, 'Khuku, you all are doing a great job.' She gave us Rs 2,000.... She gave me Rs 2,000. I was mad with joy and went running to Rani [Dasgupta]—'Rani see. We have got Rs 2,000.' We also did relief work with our college girls. We had collected a lot of money. There were many girls who used to avoid us, we made a lot of effort to bring them in. Then Gita, Priti Banerjee—they all went there. Whatever it was, we netted in all the girls and did a lot of relief work together. All the girls, daughters of even government officers, SDO, magistrate—joined us for the relief work.

While huge numbers of ordinary citizens came forward to help with the famine relief work and the setting up of langarkhanas, it was still inadequate:

> As the food situation deteriorated, government callousness became clearer daily. Not more than 50 government controlled shops had been set up in the whole of Calcutta city. These could not cater to more than 20,000 persons at the outside, in a city whose population was 2 million at the time. In villages there was no food. Long queues in front of control shops, growing longer everyday, became an excruciating sight. Often people were crushed to death due to stampedes in long waiting lines. (Chakravartty 1980:29)

In the absence of adequate government action, the CP and women from the Calcutta MARS who were personally involved in running the langarkhanas found the need to take on the responsibility of finding food for the starving populations. In this they were joined by the Musim Women's Self-Defence League (ibid.). It is significant that the very women who had been deeply affected by the victims of the famine and worked intimately with them later took on the responsibility of ensuring the continued life and some degree of well-being of the latter. It was inherent in the logic of their care work that having once saved the lives of the starving peasants, they could hardly abandon them to die for continued dearth of food. In addition, as Ila Mitra and a majority of the urban women asserted, they had also developed a critical political consciousness through the study groups in schools, colleges and within the CP, to which their innate need to counter such injustice had led them.

The logic of their newly achieved political subjectivity demanded action as well. Thus, while unprecedented, at least in the history of Bengal, it was perfectly logical that it should be these women, the caregivers, whose planning and strategic action it was that finally mobilized the government, and also awakened the public into demanding responsible action of the government. The year 1943–44 witnessed the phenomenon of massive all-women hunger marches or ones in which large numbers of women participated. One of the first was on 17 March 1943 (ibid.) in Calcutta, in which 5,000 women just walked in through the gates of the Town Hall while the state Assembly was in session, demanding that they be sold rice at a reasonable price.

Sen (2001:72) recalls the women's reasoning thus:

> We did achieve something important. It was impossible to save people on rice acquired by begging from the better-off and khichuri or a gruel of rice and dal cooked in the canteens. The only way out was to bring down the price of rice and open ration shops. It would require a revolution and we got down to work. At that time the chief minister was Fazlul Haq. We decided that one day, while the assembly was in session, a women's procession would surround it and place its demand for rice.

This realization signals a clear emergence of the need for political activism, and a shift from public practices of charity to political practice. Kamala Mukherjee testified to the spontaneous participation of women, and even of beggars:

> While we were walking in the bhukh michhil [hunger march], women kept joining us on the way. I don't know who or what they were. We had an organisation. We had asked, on the advice of Bankim Mukherjee, for the gates [of the West Bengal State Assembly] not to be closed. So, 5000 women entered—it was a great movement. There was no food—you couldn't get rice—some of us had joined spontaneously. I remember, women were coming out of houses to join us even as we were walking—there were some beggars as well.

The care work that had been extended one to one from urban woman to famine-stricken peasant in the langarkhanas, now evolved into moves calling the state into question and demanding food for the hungry. The ethic of care transcended the personal intersubjective realm to take on political dimensions of no insignificant order, for it was no less than 5,000 women who ultimately made their way to the state Assembly, and they did so with the active and full support of the entire city's tram workers as well as of the guards of the Legislative Assembly:

> On the appointed afternoon a large group of women gathered in the Town Hall. They had come from all over Calcutta, and our leaders and workers were with them. If the workers of the tramways had not helped us that day, we would have been in trouble because the women had travelled without tickets. The tram workers' support cannot be forgotten. When those of us who had cards wanted to enter the Legislative Assembly, the guards opened the gates. The whole procession of 5,000 women entered the assembly in our wake through two gates. The guards didn't stop us at any of the gates; instead, they opened them wide. (Sen 2001:72)

The manner in which the urban women leaders consequently engaged with the politicians (some of whom were also their family friends) bears testimony to an admirable strand of the political culture of the 1940s—in firm persuasive dialogue and with self-confidence and dignity, all reminiscent of Gandhi's interactions with the British, and with a courtesy that bespoke the kind of respect across political differences that had marked Nehru and Gandhi's relationship:

> Fazlul Haq … appeared with some members, but they seemed dumbstruck. What could they possibly say? Such a thing had never happened before…. The women stood one behind the other, pointed to the money tied to their *anchals* [the loose end of their saris], and said, 'We haven't come to beg. Please give us rice at the price at which we used to buy it. We shall buy it.' Gita Mullick, Renu and Kamala went to the political leaders and said, 'Please have some rice brought before them, or you won't be able to leave the place.' (ibid.)

When the lorries arrived with the rice, within half an hour, the women were not asked for the money. 'Perhaps the politicians felt ashamed,' muses Sen (ibid.). In the half hour that it took for the politicians to summon the lorries of rice, they could also have chosen to call in a police force to disperse the women, maybe even arrest some of them for having 'disrupted' the proceedings of the Assembly. That they chose instead to accede underlines the fact that it would have been difficult to respond to the basic ethicality of the women's demand and their calm dignified approach with brute force.

A new stage of the movement had been reached—and that this was the perception of the CP and MARS women themselves is confirmed by Renu Chakravartty (1980:30). Women in other parts of Bengal too dealt with officials in a similarly cool, dignified, firm manner, refusing to take a negative response. Bimala Majhi, the unusually well-off peasant leader of Midnapore also recollected a similar incident of shaming government officials into complying with the needs of the famine stricken when she went to the local district magistrate demanding supplies of cloth for the women:

> Then came the Viswa Nari Seva Sangha—they came to the magistrate on deputation. The district magistrate was a nasty man. I told him the women are going naked—they have no saris to wear, we can't get clothes, kerosene oil, nothing. You will please give me 500 pieces of cloth from the shop…. So then he said, 'How can I trust you with so many pieces of cloth?' I replied, 'I will sell them—five rupees was the cost of each—and give you the money so that you can then pay whichever person it is from whom you've bought the cloth.' Then

> he said, 'But that's not possible.'... I was wearing gold ornaments worth five *bhoris* [approximately 11 g]. So I took them off and told him, 'I trust you. You are the district magistrate. You keep these ornaments and give me a receipt. If I don't come back and give you the money then you can sell my ornaments and pay for the cloth.' To which he exclaimed, 'Amazing, this woman is surely of the feline species—just like a cat—full of evil ideas. So young a woman, but look at her audacity—she takes off her ornaments and gives them to me!' Then he had good laugh with Sarat Ray and wrote out a slip for 500 pieces of cloth from a shop—Bhudura—Marwari—here in Burra Bazar [in Mednipur]—it's still there.
>
> He didn't accept my gold. He was pretty embarrassed. In fact he was quite insulted. That's why he said, 'You are like a cat.... Looking at her one wouldn't understand but she is quite a rascal! She takes off her ornaments just to embarrass me! You keep your stuff.' And so saying, he quickly wrote the slip. Sarat Roy was with me.

In the case of the 5,000 women who had gone to the state Assembly, the long weeks of their care work in the langarkhanas that the whole city had been witness to, and that had won them the tram workers' and guards' support, also seems to have finally succeeded in making the politicians acknowledge their own culpability and cooperate. That this was most likely the case is reinforced by the fact that the government kept the promise it made to the women: it opened sixteen fair-price rice shops in Calcutta and established several large canteens from where khichuri began to be supplied to the smaller canteens in every locality (Sen 2001:72–73). And maybe, as Sen suggests, the politicians had indeed been shamed.

Asha Chakravarty also talked of a *bhukh michil*, a hunger march, in Kurigram town of Rangpur district, in which both men and women participated under the leadership of men like Panu Pal, and recollected the slogan '*Main bhukha hun, de de khana de*' (I'm hungry, give, give me food). Samsunnehar Chowdhury Shanu of Kurigram recalled the cross-class solidarity and collective drive of the women led by Rani Mukherjee of Kurigram in another all-women hunger march:

> She led a procession of about 500 women from Badri Bazar to Kurigram during the famine. [At which point another person chipped in to say that at that time, tigers roamed around in Badir

> Bazar].... There was a dense jungle. She came with the demand for food and clothes. And they gheraoed the SDO's office the whole day. In the afternoon, they were given the clothes. She carried them on her head and walked back all the distance. She was very beautiful, the daughter-in-law of a very rich family.

Heleketu Singha of Thakurgaon recalls the bhukh michhil in Dinajpur, which Chakravartty (1980:77) records took place on 25 February 1945, with Bina Guha attesting that it had more than 2,000 women participating in it. This was another landmark in the genealogy of women's entry into the political arena, and Guha noted especially that women not only come together en masse across urban and rural divides, but that the entry of peasant women had actually become an inspiring force for urban women:

> The bhukh michhil was marked by a massive congregation of women. Two thousand peasant women gathered for this. We went to every village and talked to the women, requesting them to come. They were all eager to join. When peasant women entered the movement, city women broke out of the social constraints and taboos and joined the movement... the party supported this. Seeing those 2,000 women, women from other families too started coming out. My *barama* that is [my cousin] Sushilda's mother, came out in the lead saying—'I have come out. You too come out of your homes.' She was a famous lady. All the ladies from middle class homes shed their inhibitions and came out to join the march.... We felt united as women.

She also attested to the fact that it was on the strength of the relationships that had developed through the work of the samiti, relationships intimate enough for them to address the peasant women in familial terms, that they succeeded in mobilizing such a huge number:

> We mobilized women from each and every house of the villages and of the families, with whom we were on familiar terms, calling them *mashima, kakima, jethima* [aunts]... we told them that we had planned this and we would go to the magistrate and demand clothes and rice. These were our two demands and we also demanded that provisions should be made for initiating some small-scale handicrafts work to make the women self-reliant.

> Their response was—Well we can go but we have to pass the *cutchery* [administrative office] where our babus sit.... We told them, don't think of such things, we just have to go. There is no other alternative. You all have to come out. On the day of the march, Rani [Dasgupta] and I came out early in the morning. We called everyone. At about 11, about 2,000 peasant women—2,000 of them—gathered, raising the slogan, 'We want milk for our children and clothes to cover our bodies; we want food.'

Abani Lahiri explained that urban women could develop the close relationship they did with the rural women, and their joint campaign found acceptance in peasant households, because the CP had already established bases in these villages by 1942, and its men had already begun to cross class boundaries in meaningful ways. Yet, despite the fact that the men had established intimate links with the peasants even before the women did so, and despite the fact that it was a march organized at the suggestion of the CP, its magnitude and power was clearly something that took the CP men by surprise. It also left the women triumphant in a newfound confidence. Bina Guha described the humorous yet almost peeved responses of the men at having been left out of it:

> We marched for about 6 miles. We lead those 2,000 peasant women for 6 miles and went to the cutchery. We did not have microphones but we made do with improvised cones, and just like the men we shouted. Later on Manida and others exclaimed: 'You were all shouting into those?! [Laughs].... You couldn't get any men to raise slogans for you? You had to do it yourselves?'

She also narrated the story of the women's encounter with the district magistrate that marked the beginning of government action for providing rice and milk and arrangements for income generation for the famine stricken women in Dinajpur:

> Whatever it was, we gheraoed the magistrate. He came out, the district magistrate. We poured out our grievances. He assured us that he would make arrangements for rice. He kept his word. We also demanded that he should make arrangements for some cottage industry for village women. We demanded that the materials should be provided by him. He agreed. To make *shoti*—do you know what

> *shoti* is, it's like barley? Then the milk from the Red Cross. He also promised to make arrangements for milk. He did so. Milk booths were opened in villages and in the cities.

The magnitude of the march made not only the government but also traders succumb to its power. The contrast between greed and need too came sharply into focus in the modest nature of the women's demands—Bina Guha recalled that all they asked for was one-sixth of a sari to cover their bodies:

> The peasant women said, 'What about our clothes?' Clothes? There was a big Marwari businessman called Madanlal Agarwala. They all went to his shop. He knew us and our families. We said, 'Madanlal bring out all the saris you have at the controlled rate for these village women.' Then the women said, 'We will make do with one sari for every six of us.' They do wear it like that, they cut it and wear it like a *lungi*. [It is worn around the body, and in Dinajpur its called a bukhni.] They cut a sari into six pieces and showed us how to do it.... Madanlal Agarwala gave them blankets [and] saris.

Just one-sixth of a sari—dire need seems to have acquired the power of a truth that confronts one with an uncanny force, and one that cannot be denied. For though Bina Guha mentioned Madanlal's fear of his shop being looted, the word she used repeatedly to describe his reaction was not 'afraid' or 'threatened', but 'unnerved', implying that something in addition to a fear of large numbers had unsettled him:

> He had become quite unnerved when he saw the huge brigade of women. What if his shop was looted? He was really unnerved. He brought out whatever he had.... We gave away all the saris. We handed them over to Joymani, Phuleswari for distributing. The saris at the 'controlled rate' were distributed amongst the women.

It is significant that unmarried young women like Bina Guha and Rani Dasgupta, who were only student leaders then, had mobilized village after village in Dinajpur, led by Alaka Majumdar, who was also a college student. Having developed this sense of public agency at so young an age was clearly something the activist recognized consciously as a unique extension of her sense of self. And it was a matter of considerable pride, for Bina Guha framed her narrative of the michhil in cognition of this extended sense of self. She began with: 'We had organized the bhukh michhil. We were students then. We were activists in Mahila Atmaraksha Samiti.' And she ended her account of the march with: 'This was the first michhil of its kind [in my experience]. It was on the initiative of the students of Dinajpur, that this bhukh michhil was organized.'

Across the two months from January to March 1943, innumerable hunger marches and food meetings were held by women right across Bengal, from Bankura to Pabna to Madaripur, Jalpaiguri, Rajshahi, Mymensingh, Barisal, Mednipur and Faridpur (Chakravartty 1980:31–33). Such concerted action on the part of the women had wider repercussions too. Manikuntala Sen (2001:73) records that after the march to the Assembly: 'Fair-price food shops began to open in every locality. The public demand for fair price was such that shops selling coal, an expensive and scarce commodity, had also to be opened. Public opinion was of course in our favour.'

Thus, there was a snowball effect that had ultimately not just transformed political culture but also led to an amelioration of the devastated economic culture of the entire state of Bengal in the famine years. In fact, it was a move from which generations of citizens were to benefit in the coming years, for the fair-price shops were the beginning of the ration shops through which the West Bengal government continued to sell food right into the twenty-first century. In a poignant reminder Sen says: 'Today we are used to standing in the ration shop queues. It would be good to remember that poor peasant women had these opened for us' (ibid.).

## From the Anchal to the World: Social Motherhood

On one occasion, when Manikuntala Sen had contracted cholera while travelling, she had been offered hospitality in a home in Panskura. Recounting that her whole feverish body was wet with sweat, she remembers an old woman who kept wiping it away with her anchal and muses: 'The gentle anchal of a mother probably stays spread everywhere like this' (ibid.:90–91) The anchal of the mother becomes a metaphor for the intimate caring extended to another in the gentleness and concern embodied in this image; but it is not limited to the mother. It also figures as the anchal in which the woman of the house carries the cash for procuring food or the keys to the cupboard, in which she carries, tied securely, the means for the family's survival. As the women moved out from their homes to ensure the survival of the hunger-stricken ones on the streets, they carried with them the pride and dignity of those who take on the responsibility of ensuring the well-being of others tied safely in their anchals. This is reminiscent of Sen's account (quoted above) in the state Assembly in Calcutta: 'The women stood one behind the other, pointed to the money tied to their anchals, and said, "We haven't come to beg. Please give us rice at the price at which we used to buy it"' (ibid.:72). The fact that women should carry in this way the means of providing for a starving population must have stunned government officials in a way that few other images could. They had to acknowledge their utter failure in shouldering this responsibility. The pride and sense of responsibility as citizens that the women carried that day in their anchals must have been what put the government to shame and kept the ministers from charging them for the rice.

Combined with the metaphor of the anchal was the figure of motherhood; and even as the anchal had flown out of the precincts of the home to comfort and provide for the world, so too had motherhood transcended the confines of biology and family, and taken on much more complex social and political significance. Bina Guha, describing the bhukh michhil, recalled women's growing awareness of solidarity as well as a certain expansion of their sense, as mothers, to a sociopolitical motherhood:

> The urban women had wanted to join but there were social restrictions, codes—it took some time to break these.... Their dignity, women's dignity, was at stake. It was the same. I am a mother, they are also mothers [they would say]. This is why they also came out. In Dinajpur, so many women did not join the Congress movement. I have heard this. My sister-in-law [my husband's sister] was an activist—a leader in the Congress movement. Snehalata Ganguly, she was also there in the procession. She herself admitted

> this. What you did was unique. We have been working so long for the Congress but never could we gather so many women in this organized way [she said].... When peasant women entered the movement, city women broke out of their social constraints and taboos and they too joined the movement. We felt united as women, as mothers.

To explain what she meant by this, she went on: 'There were so many constraints, double-standards, we demolished all those myths and made women aware of their rights against political, social, and familial oppression, so that they could stand up for their rights.' This could well be an agenda for contemporary feminism in the subcontinent today and what is significant is that Bina Guha describes in such distinctly political terms the role of motherhood. Even if the vocabulary she used was of the late twentieth century, when the interview took place, the fact that a mother's domestic role of securing the well-being of the family had translated into a political role of securing the welfare of a hunger-starved populace by the mid-forties was reiterated across several accounts and contexts. And neither was it a deification—or reification—of woman as mother, for both urban and rural women would usually take care to refer to themselves in the twin phrasing of both women and mothers, indicating that they were invested in both, questions of women's dignity in the face of sexual exploitation and their role as nurturers.

Guha also recounted the argument put forward by rural women when they had come to the urban centre of Dinajpur town demanding that mahila samitis be set up in the villages too:

> They had been told by the farmers or peasant activists or the party members that there was widespread famine in other rural areas and they also had a part to play. They had heard all this. They had heard it from the party or the samiti.... So they actually stirred us into action, saying, 'You will only be active in the towns? What is the fault of the rural women? You are a woman, I am also a woman. You are a mother, I am also a mother.' They pointed at Baroda Chakraborty's wife as the mother. 'What is our fault? Why are we being left out?'

The fact that they were emphasizing their identities as women and mothers signals that it was not an abstract sense of social responsibility driving them—it was an affective, empathetic expression of a concrete understanding of what women and mothers were experiencing in the famine struck areas, and of their determined will to take action against such injustice.

Such translation of practices of caring into inspired political will became manifest in international women's forums too, such as the International Forum of Mothers. Sen recollects the role of mothers who had taken the oath after the devastation of World War II that there would be no more wars and had founded the Women's International Democratic Federation:

> The worst victims of the ravages of war are women. Their husbands and children are the first to be sacrificed. That is why, towards the end of the war, the first protests sounded from the voices of the women themselves; women who were weeping their hearts out amidst the devastation of Europe and Russia, looking for their dear ones, searching amongst bloodied and tattered rags to find out whether these belonged to anyone they knew. Around this time a group of women representatives from Russia and East Europe went to see what the situation was like in the countries ruined by war. They saw the most frightful sights. At a concentration camp in Warsaw, they came across a mountain of little children's shoes, which perhaps indicated the number of children who had been sent to the gas chambers. The latter were right beside the camp. I wondered whether those mothers had wept in front of them. Wouldn't their tears have frozen to ice and their hearts turned to stone? It must have been so. That is why they had steeled themselves and gripping those shoes had taken the oath: 'No more, no more wars, we cannot lose our children and our husbands in this way, nor will we allow others to suffer as we have.' (2001:229–30)

Motherhood here becomes emblematic of a caring rooted in an intimate love of one's children, and, from an understanding of the value of that caring, it also extends itself in identification with other mothers across the world. It begins to embody the value of caring translated into an international anti-war politics, for 'it was these mothers, bound by such an oath, who had built the Women's International Democratic Federation' (ibid.:230).

As the pledge of these mothers reached different corners of the world, women of Britain, France, Italy and Japan joined them. When their letter reached India, Manikuntala Sen says:

> We too were weary of war. True, our country had not been directly involved in the war, but within Bengal itself 35 lakhs [three and a half million] had given up their lives in the famine caused by the war, and there are no records of how many women were raped. We printed a few thousand copies of this letter. Collecting the signatures of a few million women, we sent these documents as a token of our wholehearted approval to the East Berlin office of the International Women's Organization. (ibid.)

The anchal also figures as the women's gesture of reaching out to the locality, the city and the world, creating the space in which the people's expressions of caring, their offerings, are gathered, to enable their moral will to prevail. The first conference of the Indian branch of the International Women's Organization, held in 1952, turned out to be a grand success, with people spilling out of the University Hall in Calcutta. Manikuntala Sen says: 'Without any help from the government, which, suspecting our Communist links, had kept strictly aloof, we had gone ahead. Our *anchals* had been filled with the offerings of people at large, which had enabled us to organize the conference on such a grand scale' (ibid.:231).

## A Politics of Care

> The joy that we felt in serving people at this time, sometimes going hungry ourselves, has never come again. (ibid.:71)

Manikuntala Sen captures the overriding sentiment of the activists in the immediate post-famine period. The affective impact of the suffering of the famine victims and the subsequent personalized care work in the langarkhanas had clearly resulted in considerable personal growth, enriched experiences, the ability to strategize politically and the confidence to take on the government. It had led the women to march to the state assembly, lead the numerous michhils across the state and compel the government to boost its relief programme. The intersubjective experience of caring for the famine victims had transformed the activists too. If there was any doubt that the joy Manikuntala Sen expresses may be pure altruism (if there is such a thing), then their own sense of confidence and political maturity that the women achieved, along with the charge of feeling united that Bina Guha talked about, should put them at rest. For the women, it was the joy of a unique, unprecedented and collective confidence in their ability to transform the world that was the hallmark of the 1940s.

The nature of the interactions in which women's responses to hunger, disease and dearth of cloth were manifest comprised an ethic of care that was rooted in concrete relief work. It involved intimate, everyday, intersubjective situations of nurture, caring, healing and saving lives. It was not just caring *about* people from a distance, or contributing rice or money, it involved the physical and emotional work of caring *for* human beings, not as objects of relief work, but as living beings whose very survival was in their hands and who also transformed them in turn. Moreover, since such care involves human relationality and its logic necessitates taking on responsibility for providing for the receiver, caring for the famine victims also translated into massive hunger marches and processions demanding food and clothing for them.

It is also important to remember that those devastated by the famine were once self-sufficient peasant families with dignity, not beggars. When they begged for the rice water one throws away, they were not asking for waste, but pointing out, in full self respect, the immorality of the fact that others were wasting what was food for the starving. The urban women, in turn, respected the dignity of the peasants. They started by reviving the starving peasants with phyan, but the moment the latter regained the strength to digest, the urban women demanded proper food—rice, dal, khichuri, milk. It was a question of asking not for alms as charity, in terms of what others could spare, but demanding the basic resources for health that was due to any human being. It was a question not just of ensuring their mere survival, but taking responsibility for their *well-being*,

Amartya Sen (1980) attributes the death of 3 million people during the famine to a political lack, a lack of 'entitlement', to a system of power so deep rooted that the poor, subject to it, have no chance of justice, as Manik Bandyopadhyay (2011) too records in his fictionalized account of the famine. Nussbaum's (1992) account of human capabilities, that human beings need the help of others in realizing their capacities, and her emphasis on the fundamental importance of enabling all people to develop their capacities, points to the notion of needs as an objective standard by which we can identify the deprivations and suffering that deserve attention. Identifying human needs, thus, becomes a way of addressing the question of entitlements. Yet, such conceptual identification of needs still remains vulnerable to systems of power, for as Tronto (2009:140) points out, 'Part of the privilege enjoyed by the powerful is their ability to define needs in a way that suits them.' As Chaudhuri (2012) rightly asserts, moral economies of well-being must contend with the concrete ground realities, 'with the problem of who eats and who starves'. She elaborates:

> The moral economy is not simply an account of the moral principles of our actions, the ends that we judge to be necessary to our wellbeing, and the economic structures that we endorse. It is finally, in my view, a critical account of *power* and its exercise, of capabilities and entitlement in the most basic terms. It has to be articulated in terms of those whose power we have taken away, those whose claims we have ignored.

It was from the most basic level of life-saving work, from a 'receptive and affectively induced engrossment' (Dalmiya 2007:300) in the famine victims' reality, and the responsibility the women took on to procure the resources for their continued survival, that they succeeded in exposing the workings of power. Involvement in the concrete *processes* by which life is sustained demands that the notions of entitlements and human capabilities be translated into human practices. The ethic of justice and rights, grounded in universal, abstract principles, does not engage with the specific ways in which power may be exposed or justice implemented in particular contexts. The ethic of care, rooted in addressing concrete human needs, cannot but do so. Women's responses to the famine were grounded in intimate, affective and intersubjective practices of life-saving work that compelled them to take on the responsibility of ensuring the survival of the human beings to whom they had extended their care. This responsibility entailed developing effective political strategies for procuring resources for the victims' survival. It was this internal logic of care work that compelled them to step out in massive hunger marches, to begin to hold the government and traders accountable, to demand and procure food and cloth for those rendered destitute. Thus, this political activity was part of a logical trajectory of an ethic of care. And it brought into sharp focus the concrete imperatives for the ethic of justice and rights to be realized, and the practical, material ways in which this had to be done.

The women's responses to hunger clearly went beyond standard notions of duty or moral responsibility by virtue of their direct affective human involvement in care work. They were also clearly distanced from any form of religious practice or any concept of charity in their critical, political impulse. They transcended any notions of altruism because while the activists may have reached out to care for the famine victims in selfless concern, what they gained from this process was tremendous. This is evident in their profound enjoyment of their emergent yet powerful political consciousness, their own abilities to transform the social sphere, and their newfound solidarities. A unique politics had taken shape that was not hitched to an abstract notion of rights and justice—it was rooted in concrete intersubjective experiences and the responsibilities of the process of caring for another that embodied and concretized the ethic of justice and the claiming of rights.

Care is often discussed and described as if it is related only to the domestic sphere and is about limited personal concerns rather than larger ethical issues and those of rights. This neglect of issues of care in the sociopolitical sphere is also evident in the concerns of philosophy, for while there are some notable exceptions, 'for the most part questions of natality, mortality, and the needs of humans to be cared for as they grow up, live and die, have not informed the central question of philosophers' (Tronto 2009:3). Care is also gendered and privatized into domestic relations, which in turn are privatized in society as a mode of controlling women's power. Thus, the processes that ensure the survival and health of human beings, and their well-being as well as reproduction, are marginalized and almost invisibilized in the public sphere. However, while care is not the only principle for modern moral life, it is an important practice for establishing a moral society. This is so in at least two ways:

> First, care serves as a critical standard. Given the centrality of care activities for human (and other) survival, how well or how badly care is accomplished in any given society will stand as a measure of how well that society is able to adhere to other virtues as well... Second, care puts moral ideals into action. (ibid.:154)

The first has a political dimension. From the standpoint of care, its standards available in a particular polity become a measure of that society's investment in the well-being of all sections of the populace, specially those more deprived. They are also a measure of people's access to rights and of the functioning of democracy itself. Inadequacy of care becomes a concrete launching pad for political demands for rights. And, second, by virtue of being a practice, care does not remain at the conceptual level; it involves actual implementation of ethical values that go into the making of a moral society. Care is, therefore, one of the most challenging—and maybe, thus, one of the most elided—constituents of democracy in practice. In the anti-imperialist context of the 1940s, and especially in the face of the devastation wreaked by the famine, the moral arguments foregrounded by the women of MARS and the CP did find ready ground, and were immediately taken up by the CP and huge sections of the populace.

The multiple practices of the imperial market economy of World War II, of the feudal system and of the middle-class hoarders that resulted in over 3 million deaths were clearly immoral. Yet, what is significant about this period is the emergence of a uniquely moral political culture, which developed as much in response to the extensive starvation caused by the famine, as in a challenge to the workings of the market economy driven by the economy of the jotedar, hoarder and empire. A new and powerful ethic of care became an integral aspect of the left public sphere of Bengal. It was new in that it went deeper than conventional political modes of comradeship in its mutual enrichment of the famine-stricken peasant and the social or political activist, and thus facilitated affective ontological attachments that provided the impetus for a heady politics of solidarity. The influence of this political mobilization too was considerable: not only did it draw over 43,000 women into MARS, it also affected large sections of civil society, ranging from ordinary households to doctors, tram workers and government guards, and finally it impinged upon government officials too. Ultimately, it did shape considerably the response of the government to the famine-stricken population, and simultaneously led to a sharpening of the anti-imperialist critique across all districts where urban and rural activists came together in famine and post-famine work. In the process, the relief work of women created the grounds for a new and unique quality of political bonding based on personal intersubjective relations that transformed unobtrusively, yet significantly, the ethical fibre of political culture and collective struggle in the 1940s. It was a quality of political bonding that also foreshadowed the powerful modes of comradeship evident a few years later in the Tebhaga movement.

The central questions, however, are about this politics of care: at what point did the *ethic* of care change to a *politics* of care, not just in practical terms of taking on the responsibility to procure resources to keep another human being alive, but in terms of a *subjective* shift?[7] And what constituted the undeniable force, the compelling power, of this politics of care?

The moral outrage against the injustice of the famine found an outlet in the care extended to the famine victims and in the taking on of responsibility for them to ensure their survival. Yet, this practice could constitute charity too. Somewhere, a critical shift had taken place, from the ethic of care to a politics of care, and while in concrete practice it can be located in the act of taking up responsibility for the famine victims and demanding resources for their survival, this too could be seen as an extension of the practical logic of care. The women, however, ranging from the CP leader Renu Chakravartty to the reputed Congress Party member Sarojini Naidu, all clearly saw this as a political act, and Manikuntala Sen even called it a 'revolution'. There had clearly been a transformation of subjectivity.

[7] I am grateful to Tridip Suhrud for putting this question to me.

The critical shift from the ethic of care to a politics of care seems to have balanced on the knife edge, where the ethic of care confronts an abyss and the only recourse is politics. This abyss was the fearsome loss of dignity of those devastated by the famine. Words failed Manikuntala Sen, Bina Guha, Ila Mitra and others when they talked about the 'terrible' loss of dignity they encountered in the unclothed women who withdrew into themselves, mothers who consumed milk meant for their dead children or even snatched food from the mouths of living ones, husbands who sold their wives, mothers who traded their daughters, and starving women who sold their bodies for food. That the loss of human dignity became a haunting force of the time is reflected in the slogans of the MARS women too. Bina Guha remembered:

> There was hunger and distress everywhere. The dark shadow of the famine was so terrifying—you had to see it to understand its impact—the same conditions prevailed in the rural as well as in the urban areas. Large numbers were rendered homeless. Black marketeers, hoarders, thrived from that time.... Our slogan was '*Bangla bachao*' [save Bengal], 'Save the dignity of women' ... and 'Give us milk for our children', 'Give us food'—this was our slogan.

And one of the central thrusts of the second conference of MARS, held in Barisal in May 1944, by which time its membership had exploded, had to do with the question of women's dignity and stringent punishment for those who traded in women's flesh. It stated categorically:

> To stop the rot in society and to re-establish the shelterless and destitute women in social life is one of the prime tasks in defence of the dignity of the women of Bengal. (Chakravartty 1980:55)

At its highest, even abstract, end, dignity signifies nobility or elevation of character, worthiness, dignity of sentiments, fulfilment of the highest of ideals or values. But at the other extreme loss of dignity entails loss of volition—the volition to love, live, eat, communicate; it entails a withdrawal into a void 'below meaning', beyond signification. Pain *seeks* acknowledgement, so one could reach out in care and address the pain of hunger and disease that the famine spawned.[8] But loss of dignity results in withdrawal; it creates a chasm. Loss of dignity, as experienced during the famine, thus marked a dead end for practices of care, as did thousands of deaths that the urban women and men witnessed. Moral outrage such as this could not find solace in practices of care; it was compelled to seek other avenues of redressal. The cause in this case was not 'natural' or 'God' given, it was 'man-made', so the outrage was directed against the men responsible for the famine. Redressal had to take the form of politics directed against human beings. In this 'man-made' famine, Chakravartty (1980:69) reports, Manikuntala Sen had charged human beings for destroying social morality too. 'The famine had not only killed 35 lakhs of men and women ... it had also killed the ideas of social morality.'[9] The search for redressal metamorphosed into demands for redressal. Born out of an outraged morality that could find no other outlet, the moral compulsion to demand redressal for destroying human dignity became the catalytic force of the politics of care.

It was a morality that went beyond the relativity of values perceived from different locations and touched the very core of what is human. It was the starkness of right and wrong stripped down to a nakedness that could neither be avoided, nor be borne. Systematic and continued deprivation had emptied human beings of their dignity, destroyed their volition, rendered them non-human, beyond representation. If dignity is also the name for the quality of humanity that is capable of morality, for the ability of human beings to choose their own actions, then this was a naked reality that also demanded choice on the part of those who witnessed it.[10] And it demanded a choice that went beyond any relative value, a choice between what was clearly, radically, human or inhuman. The

[8] See *The Blue Book* (Wittgenstein 1958).

[9] At a meeting organized by MARS, the Nari Seva Sangh, the Vigilance Associaton and ten other organizations on 6 January 1945 at the Calcutta University Insititute Hall, where they decided to launch a widespread campaign to stop the prostitution of women due to famine conditions (Chakravartty 1980:69).

[10] See Kant (2010): 'Morality, and humanity as capable of it, is that which alone has dignity; "free will" is essential; human dignity is related to human agency, the ability of humans to choose their own actions.'

dignity of the perceiver lay in making that choice. Not to make the appropriate choice would be to render oneself non-human. Thus, witnessing the non-humanity of the other, her inability to be human, impinged on one's own implication in being human. The opposition between who eats and who starves translated into who can be human and who cannot. To deny the other the possibility of dignity, that is, of being human, would be to empty oneself of that dignity. The moral force of this politics was such that it posed a radical challenge of choice: between a response made in the preservation of one's own human dignity and the annihilation of it.

# 4

# *'Meyera Andolane Antarikata Aanlo'* Women Brought an Inwardness to the Movement

## Redefining Political Agency, Forging Affective Comradeships*

When asked what was the most significant way in which women had shaped the Tebhaga movement, Bina Guha, the leader from Dinajpur, replied thoughtfully, '*Meyera andolane antarikata aanlo*', indicating that women had infused the movement with a sense of inwardness, a sincerity, a quality of investment that stemmed from within the self. This was, certainly, not meant as a critique of the male activists, to imply that their participation was insincere or inauthentic; yet, there is a clearly distinguished gendered thrust in the emphasis on the processes of interiority in the quality of women's participation. It seemed to be a distinction between the men's focus on the exterior workings of politics in terms of specific

* I thank Arindam Chakravarty, Tridip Suhrud and Vrinda Dalmiya for the involved discussion from which evolved Arindam's wonderfully apt translation of the word 'antarikata'.

political goals and the strategies required to achieve them, and the *shared* importance of the reasons from within that had motivated the women to act. What was very telling for me in writing about this was that the sections on gendered transformations in politics and gendered transformations in the family pushed their ways into each other till they finally fused completely, echoing Bina Guha's insight across various Tebhaga areas. Given that Guha was herself a seasoned activist, her emphasis on the sense of inwardness women brought to the movement would have been made in full cognizance of the intertwined nature of interiority and exteriority, of the intimate internal motivations in personal life, and the external practices and effects of politics.

Processes of interiority are inherently subjective and it is only to be expected that the deeply unsettling impact of the multiple crises of this historical period, ranging from World War II, to the famine, to the intensified economic exploitation and rampant sexual abuse by the zamindars and jotedars, as well as their engagement with what was, for most peasant women at least, the radically new ideology of communism, also triggered deeply their responses and transformations of subjectivity. Women's entry into Tebhaga in massive numbers threw up new challenges as well, of new ways of being, of being acted upon, and of relating to and acting upon the world. All this must have made it imperative for them to constantly renew and reinvent themselves and their actions while in struggle. Their participation was marked by a powerful sense of action and solidarity, and Bina Guha's reflection, as well as that of other activists, indicate that it was this force of interiority, of recently wrought and profound subjective transformations experienced by the women, that became the driving and shaping force of an emergent yet compelling political agency and comradeship. What I try to grasp, then, is not the gendered differences between the men and women's relation to the movement, or how they shaped it differently, but the connections between the deeply felt needs articulated by the women and the movement's response to them, and the nature of the inwardness that it brought to the movement. I attempt also to engage with the workings of new subjective experiences as revealed in the women's expressions and actions in the struggle, and how these informed their sense of political agency and comradeship across social divides.

The women's politics of care that took shape during the famine years translated into other forms in the villages when the Tebhaga movement was finally launched in 1946. One set of work, underlined by practices of care, comprised literacy training and political education that urban women imparted to their rural comrades in the mahila samitis and in makeshift centres set up in homes and fields in the villages. Another widely pervasive activity related to rural women opening up their homes to provide food and shelter to travelling and fleeing activists. In this, they sustained the travelling of activists across the villages of Bengal, facilitating the spread of the movement; and in the caring acts of cooking, serving and sheltering activists from all social backgrounds, they also knit solidarities across regions, castes and ethnicities. Ranging from married women like Jannat-un-nisa in Narail, to widows like the legendary Burima of Dinajpur, thousands of homemakers transformed their homes into intimate political bases, thus extending domestic affects of nurture and care into the political struggle.[1]

Bina Guha also referred to the widespread material base that the movement found in the infrastructure women provided for the activists travelling from village to village, including those on the run from the police. Had women not opened up their homes as bases for the movement, the considerable degree of mobility between them, which also facilitated the spread of the movement, would not have been possible.

> If the women did not come forward? The movement would not have had such a wide base. That it assumed the nature of a massive movement was due to the participation of women in such huge numbers. This, according to me, would not have happened had women not thronged to join it.

However, while men emphasized the need for the infrastructure women provided, Guha's underlined the number of women involved and the massive spread of the movement due to them. What she

[1]Bina Guha's narrative recounts the intimate maternal relationships she forged with the activists she sheltered.

indicated, then, was: one, that there were transformations of an inward quality that led women to 'throng' to join the movement; and two, that huge numbers of women came together to infuse the movement with this attribute, which indicates that this experience of meaningful subjective transformation was widespread amongst them.

A third point about how women transformed the movement qualitatively was made, curiously enough, only by men, and as an instinctive first response that: 'Women knit the movement into one big family.' This in some ways reinforces what Bina Guha said about women bringing antarikata to the movement.

Indispensable, thus, to the forging of political solidarity across villages, women also shaped the Tebhaga movement *strategically*, creating not only an efficient infrastructure and network of political bases in their homes, but also an elaborate spy system right across the Tebhaga areas. Abani Lahiri said that women formed the most effective intelligence wing of the underground CP and the krishak sabha in the days of state terror during the Tebhaga movement. MARS, the mahila samiti of the CP and the krishak sabhas, as well as the zamindars and jotedars' fields, became centres of intense struggle. Women began to play other roles in the movement too, forming *gaynbahinis* or battalions carrying *gayns* (used for pounding rice) and chilli powder for attacks, carrying the grain from the fields to their own threshing floors in defiance of the landlords' orders, and marching to the zamindar or jotedar's house in protest against sexual exploitation (Chattopadhyay 1987; Cooper 1988; Custers 1987; Ganguly 1992; Majumdar 1993; and others).

In addition, they also took on leadership of the movement, both on a daily basis and specially when the men were arrested or forced to flee, often themselves being the ones hunted by the police and in need of shelter, as evinced in the narratives of peasant women like Bimala Majhi of Mednipur and Phuli Goldar of Narail, and urban women like Rani Dasgupta of Dinajpur and Ila Mitra of Narail. Without such qualitative political participation of women, Tebhaga would have been scarcely more than a series of sporadic attacks. The women, it becomes clear from the oral narratives of activists across the two Bengals, did not merely play additive or supportive roles, but qualitative and strategic ones. They actually gave the movement a sustained, organized and widespread form, proving the indispensability of women's contribution to peasant struggle.

Ila Mitra testified that one of the successes of Tebhaga was that it marked an awakening amongst peasant women:

> Anyway, as I've told you, the Tebhaga struggle assumed the shape of a mass uprising and I want to say something about the role of women here. There were some aspects of both success and failure in the Tebhaga movement, because in the fight against zamindars and jotedars—I'll come to the question of Santals later—peasants were swept away in a flood of blood … they lost everything. But there are some aspects of success too. One of the most remarkable successes is the courage and fight of the peasant women in this struggle … the bravery of those peasant women will remain unparalleled in history. They'd done a lot both directly and indirectly for the Tebhaga movement. On the one hand, they would protect the crops while men were busy fighting the police or the goons sent by zamindars or jotedars. Or, they would be guarding houses and protecting comrades who used to live with them—they've protected us all in a lot of ways—also giving shelter to party leaders. But on the other hand, in cases of warding off the police, they had fought shoulder to shoulder with men.... It is to be noted that it was through the Tebhaga movement that women's awakening started here—I believe that.

She also drew attention emphatically to the courage of the peasant women and their impact, on not just women but 'anyone in struggle', in their readiness to even lay down their lives:

> Women had come out, as they would also have to starve if the crops couldn't be protected. It was this consciousness that had compelled then to come out to stand beside the men … and of the peasant women who'd played a major role, I'm recounting just some names: Deepeshwari of the Atawari *thana* of Dinajpur district—she was a martyr in the struggle—Joymoni of Baliadangi, Bhandani of Rani Sankail, Phuleshwari of Beerganj, Bhuteshwari of Setabganj, Madhumani and Jamuna of Phulbari, Burima of Debiganj, Saraladi of Jessore, then Ahalya Devi of Chandanpidi here in the Sunderbans.... These are all names to be remembered as they were all martyrs of the struggle; they gave up their lives fighting and their lives can be inspirations to anybody in any kind of struggle.

> One of the most remarkable aspects of the Tebhaga movement is this unprecedented bravery of peasant women. There are many histories—different incidents in different areas. It's not necessary to recount all those histories here. I just wanted to point this out.

All this could happen only on the strength of a powerful propelling force of political agency and comradeship. One such history, now legend in Narail, Jessore, is that of Sarala Singha's physical courage, her daring and strategic intelligence, in hoodwinking the police. Her friends Phuli Goldar, Anima Biswas and Amal Sen, all recalled her exploits with glee. According to Phuli Goldar, Sarala could climb trees, swim under water, and pull from land into water heavy boats like the *donga* (a long, thin boat made from the bark of date palm trees), that even men found difficult to handle. She said:

> In that Bakri school, there were many people. The police came. She was there. They wanted to catch her. She went and hid under water. Our people then went out [secretly] with a boat to help her out of the water. They helped her escape. On this side, everyone [the police] got into the water to look for her. They found some wet clothes and thought that they were hers. But Sarala Singha couldn't be found.

Amal Sen had a similar story to tell about Singha hiding among the hyacinths under water till rescued by her comrades in a boat. Anima Biswas's story was the most evocative, partly because this was one of the rare moments of joy in her narrative of disillusionment that will be discussed later, and partly because of her celebration of her comrade's humorous daredevilry:

> She was afraid of no one. One day she was surrounded at Bakri. She went down and hid under the water and nobody could trace her. She took refuge inside a boat that was sailing past.... Then she went ashore to the other side and watched their activities from there ... as they continued to search a bed of hyacinths for Sarala Singha.

The courage to challenge the police came from the sense of being in collective struggle together and fighting shared dangers; and the triumphant sense of fun in actually managing to undermine the power of the police reinforced the women's solidarities across community and caste. Hence, shared political experiences of plotting, planning and subverting served not only to bridge social divides, but also enhanced women's sense of collective political agency in the very midst of the dangers they confronted. Bimala Majhi of Mednipur narrated one such incident with the Bagdi women of Mednipur thus:

> I had gone to a place towards the sea—what's the place—Bishal Lakhki—somewhere near there—I had gone by boat to conduct a meeting there. It was a village with ten to twelve homes but there's no land route—you have to go by boat. When we were at the meeting, suddenly it was declared that the police were coming.... What could we do then? I told a woman, 'You lie down and scream with pain like you would if you were delivering a baby.' And what did I do? I got the other women in the house to put *mol* on my feet—they had to cut them and forcibly put them on for me.... That's what they wear on their feet, mol. It's a silver bangle-like ornament—they put those on my feet. Then I turned to three four other women and gave each one of them a basket.... So far the police had not been allowed to enter. I told two elderly women to tell the police that this woman [referring to herself] is in labour, since morning she has been in labour pain. Whenever there was such a case, women from all around congregated. So if the police asked why there were so many women there [that would be the ready answer]. By then fifty to sixty women had gathered there! I continued, 'You tell them that the woman is in pain, she's having trouble delivering the baby, that's why we are all here, to help. If things don't work out then we will send her to the hospital in Nandigram.' I had worn the mol because all the women there wear them [so that her feet, the only part of her body visible from the door, could look like theirs].
>
> Yes, so this is what they told the police, who of course were disbelieving. They said, 'Really, is this what's happened?' I had pushed forward the two old women and the daroga was having a massive argument with them. There were twenty to twenty-five armed policemen. We then took up baskets in our hands and started to slip out through the crowd ... in the fields there is something called *rari dhan*—very sparse-yielding paddy [that] many poor people go to the fields to get—they would collect a kilogram or two of this dhan at a time. So we tried to leave, pretending to be women armed with baskets for dhan picking.... The police said, 'No, none can pass through.' The old women retorted, saying,

'If you dare touch any of them we will cut you to pieces with the *hesha* [sickle].'

As those women started arguing with the police, the old man ... the owner of the house ... he was shaking. He felt vulnerable about a woman getting caught in his house. He quickly said, 'Take her out to the field, she is asthmatic and needs to get out. Just take her out.' And this how I got out. It was eight in the night.

[I slipped out] with a basket and with my sari tucked around my waist. I was wearing the thick rough sari that the village women wear, high above the knee, with my head covered like the other women; basket in hand, I joined the other women. That night the police checked 500 women—they went to each house and examined the face of every woman of the house with torchlights to check for this mark on my forehead. They said a 'hammer and sickle activist' has the sickle inscribed upon her forehead! This was what they spread around!

The women's responses regarding their experiences of participation in the movement ranged from those of tribal women like Poko Oraoni of Odlabari in North Bengal saying '*mazaa tha*' (those were charged times), referring to the excitement of taking the world on together as women, to urban leaders like Manikuntala Sen recollecting the 'magic' of the times in relation to the dream of socialism; peasant women like Phuli of Narail talking about the 'ananda' or joy of being united in struggle with friends such as Anima Biswas and Sarala Singha; and Anima recalling the 'shanti' or peace that came from 'talking things out with women and male comrades too'. It seems to have been the affective power of the subjective transformations that women experienced, and with which they shaped the movement, that they treasured most; and the nostalgia, affection and wistfulness, or even sudden spark in their tones testified to this. Yet, while these subjective shifts took place within individual women, they were all clearly grounded in the intersubjective joy of camaraderie—of socialism, with other women, with friends and also with male comrades. What, then, was the nature of these inward processes that shaped the political agency and comradeship of women, and what was the quality of these that enabled the women to forge unique, often unshakeable, bonds across gender, class, caste and other social divides?

Taking charge with Marxism's inadequate theorizing of political collectivity, Benhabib and Cornell (1987) have said that mere identical positioning in the class hierarchy is insufficient for ensuring collective identity, and production relations alone cannot define a collective consciousness. They highlight the disjunction between the 'structural model of class' and the 'political concept of class'. The former follows from the primacy of production relations and the location of a person in the class hierarchy (from the place a person occupies in the class structure) and the latter denotes the collective agency of social transformation, that which facilitates bonding and inspires sustained, united action across various differences of identity (caste, community etc.) across the particular class. Underlining that the structural model of class has been privileged at the cost of the 'political concept of class', they stress upon the importance of women's consciousness, agency and historical experiences in developing and sustaining the collectivity critical for unified political struggle:

> Also, what these formulations miss is the more radical challenge posed to Marxist theory by the very presence of women not only as an oppressed group but as collective actors in the historical scene: when collective actors emerge on the historical scene is it the memory and consciousness of production alone that moves them to act? What about forms of collective identity and memory rooted in aspects of communal and public life? (ibid.:3)

Tebahga complicates this question even further by raising issues of cross-class solidarity in peasant struggle, with the urban middle-class CP members playing a catalytic role in the movement. How does one theorize political solidarity when the location of the activists may *not* be identical in the production process?

As Benhabib and Cornell say, neither the positioning of a social group in the production process, nor the positing of production relations are in themselves sufficient for either defining collective identity or consciousness, or for conceptualizing how nurturing, caring, expressive and non-repressive social relations may develop. They draw attention thus to the political imperative of forging a 'minimal utopia of social life characterized by nurturant, caring, expressive and non-repressive relations between self and other' (ibid.:4). All these characteristics that they see as the grounds for developing a collective agency for social transformation are based in subjective awareness and thoughtful intersubjective relations. If an ethic of care became the basis of political agency of women during the famine, then what shape did it take in the Tebhaga movement? And what was the nature of the other subjective and intersubjective experiences that fashioned women's political agency during this movement, that forged such powerful camaraderie and enriched the movement? It would be too premature to make claims to theorizing women's collectivity in movements such as Tebhaga here. But what I do wish to embark on is the attempt to at least understand the bases of women's solidarity and political agency in light of their transforming subjectivities in the course of this movement. And while all of them may not necessarily be gendered, but common to women's and men's activism, what follows represents the reflection and processes that comprised the Tebhaga women's political experience of negotiating social divides.

## Comradeship and Gendered Transformations: Work, Sexual Politics and New Forms of Love

### ♦ *Work and Politics* ♦

The Tebhaga women's movement was a landmark in terms of the articulation of gendered demands for rights relating to work, economic control and sexual oppression. The nature of the gendered negotiations was such that it enabled the flourishing of hitherto underrated personal values, related to the logic of both political and human desire. As the two began to be experienced as intertwined, the movement acquired a unique sense of comradeship underlined by affective values.

It is significant that the peasant women were far more perceptive about inequities, and active about demanding shifts in the quality of gender relations, especially concerning issues of economic and sexual exploitation, than the urban CP women. They were already well honed in the egalitarian values of the party in terms of class equality. Yet, the strategic intelligence they extended to gender relations is an indication of the levels of sophistication they reached in areas with a strong record of women's organization, in tackling issues of political participation and comradeship. The nature of their claims also reveals the changes that were taking place in their perceptions of self and abilities in relation to the world.

The largely professional town of Dinajpur was the hub of Dinajpur district. There was a liberal environment supportive of women's activism and a tremendous amount of urban–rural interaction. A local branch of MARS already existed there, led by urban women activists like Rani Mitra and Bina Guha, when Tebhaga was launched. For women, then, this became a time to step out of homes. The poor peasants were mainly Rajbangshis, and some were from the Oraon and Munda tribes too, all bound to the jotedari system. Their women were subjected to far fewer restrictions than middle-class or -caste women, and they participated in all the activities that men did, apart from ploughing.[2] Yet, the lives of these Rajbangshi, Oraon and Munda women in these communities were even more oppressive as they were exploited both economically and sexually by the jotedars. Thus, it was logical that peasant women should focus on work and sexuality in their negotiations with the krishak samitis and the mahila samitis.

Expressing a critical instance of how the sense of self-worth derived from the peasant woman's work both in the home and the field evolved into the confidence to demand equal rights with men, Bina Guha observed about Dinajpur:

> We [middle-class urban women] didn't consider the issue of women as equal workers. But the peasant women did. They said that we do the same kind of work as men do, so we also have to have the same rights. We work at home and in the fields, so we have to get our rights.

It is significant that they raised radical questions of equality that had not yet become issues for the progressive urban middle-class activist women. Abani Lahiri cited instances of peasant women in Dinajpur who began to assert their basic economic rights. These women,

[2] See Nandy and Raman (1997:454) for the relatively egalitarian sexual and gender relations between Rajbangshi men and women.

who were engaged in poultry farming, declared that they were the ones responsible for all the work right up to the marketing stage. Hence, they, and not their husbands, should have the control over the produce and its consumption or sale. Rani Dasgupta also talked of other peasant women who insisted on retaining the income from the sale of produce at the *haat* (market) rather than handing it over to their husbands, for they too were producers. This issue, of control of domestic income, was alien to the middle-class activists and emerged from peasant women's newfound understanding of their work as economically productive labour, as well as of the relation between the control of domestic economy and gender hierarchies in the family.

The claiming of rights as workers, as labouring peasants, was in turn mobilized into a claiming of place in the political movement to secure freedom from exploitation as workers. Bina Guha recounted Joymoni Barmani and other peasant women's demands to join Tebhaga on the strength of their identity as workers:

> A krishak samiti meeting was going on. There were no women there when Joymoni Barmani, an extremely assertive and powerful peasant woman, entered the meeting with a large number of peasant women, and said, 'Hey, don't we do Tebhaga? Don't the zamindars/jotedars drain our blood too? Don't we work in the fields? We will join the Tebhaga movement, we will be volunteers.' Then one of our leaders said, 'Sure you are also volunteers,' and from then on they became part of the movement. There were long lines of women wanting to be volunteers.

Tebhaga probably witnessed the earliest instances of peasant women in India claiming equal rights as agricultural labourers, and then claiming their place in the movement alongside the men on the strength of these rights. What is interesting here is the complex intertwining of gender and class issues. Women were establishing their identities as equal workers within the home and in the field, not just for equal control over domestic finances, but also to demand their just rights as workers on the broader political canvas of an exploitative economic system.

Demanding entry into politics, however, was no guarantee of acceptance, for patriarchal forces in the left too would have to be negotiated. Heleketu Singha, a Rajbangshi peasant leader of Uttarparia village in Dinajpur, narrated a story of his late wife Jaya Barmani choosing anti-imperialist politics as her launching pad, which sheds some light on the nature of such negotiations. He spoke of the transformations of consciousness that motivated Jaya to launch into a subversion of empire to justify women's activism:

> These women [of the mahila samiti] were smart. They participated in discussions, heard about books and news. Like they learnt that in England, the queen walked first and the king followed her, get it? So they would say, 'There a queen can run a whole country, and we Bengali women can't?' That's how they'd developed a certain point of view.

As other peasant women had earlier cited their investment in swadeshi to argue for the need for mahila samitis in the villages, these women too used the platform of anti-imperialist politics strategically as a springboard to open up new spaces of political activity. And in envisaging both the anti-imperialist imperative and women's activism as mutually reinforcing, they simultaneously created a scenario within left politics in which their political activism could be welcomed as anti-imperialist politics rather than be perceived as a threat to patriarchal interests. Jaya Barmani, thus, cast political agency along powerful contours, with the anti-imperialist imperative lending weight to the feminist one.

## ♦ *Sexual Politics* ♦

Combined with the factor of economic exploitation was the need for women to protect themselves from the sexual exploitation perpetrated by the jotedars and zamindars. In Narail, Phuli Goldar said that peasant women repeatedly demanded that rape be taken up as an issue, but met with no success in the face of the CP's reluctance to get involved in the matter. In Dinajpur, however, where the women's movement had a longer history and already seemed to have reached a point of some maturity, the women were determined not to take no for an answer. The jotedar not only ruled all aspects of their lives, it was also the system that a girl from the village had to be sent to the *baro khoda* (the senior jotedar) each night to sleep with him. Bina

Guha narrated an account of Joymoni demanding that the mahila samiti and the party make a rule about women not being sent to the jotedars, and the exhilaration when the CP made it a law and the jotedars and zamindars were forced to obey:

> The jotedars were so powerful that they controlled the lives of the peasants under them, including deciding on their marriage, matchmaking, which woman was going to spend the night with them, festivals, rituals—everything was decided by the jotedars, all aspects of their lives.... It had become a convention.
>
> I had been to a meeting. I saw a girl of about twenty-two or twenty-three crying non-stop.... I asked them, 'Why is she crying?' She was called Hirala.... An older woman named Joymoni said, 'Why, you don't know? She'll have to spend the night in the jotedar's house. She has a small baby at home. But she'll have to go to the jotedar's house. That is why she's crying.' Then and there, they tapped the ground with a staff and said, 'Comrade, you make a law... that we won't go to the jotedar's house any further. We will not remain bonded labourers.' So it was made into a law. Once it became a law, it had to be passed. The resolution had to be passed to make it a law. We did it in the [mahila] samiti's meeting. But there were the krishak samiti and Communist Party. So we said, 'Okay, send a copy of the resolution to them. Send them a copy, saying that we have formulated this law.' They did that [and] we wrote down the resolution. They [the krishak samiti and the CP] said, 'Okay, fine then. You don't have to go. You don't go.' They called the big jotedars, bodo khoda, and the small jotedars, *chhoto* khoda. Chhoto khoda and bodo khoda were distressed.
>
> The Communist Party was the supreme board. The girls stopped going. Absolutely. Stopped completely.... The jotedars... could not do anything. Tebhaga was in full swing. All the villages were red. The jotedars and zamindars fled. They fled from the villages. All the villages—Thakurgaon, Balurghat, Raniganj—wherever you went, there was the red wave. Even little boys and girls used to paste it [red flags] on sticks and shout slogans—'Adhi nai, tebhag chai' [not half, we want two-thirds].... It was a tumultuous festival. It seemed like a red wave.

It was a moment of great historical import. Women had convinced a political party to take an official stand against exploitative sexual politics for the first time in agrarian politics in Bengal. They had not only won the official support of the mahila samiti, but also of the krishak samiti and the CP. Later, when women also began to be exploited by the police, who collaborated with the landlords in intimidating and arresting peasants to prevent them from taking the crop to their own threshing floors, the issue was taken up beyond the local level, and at least one committee went around to Dinajpur to investigate charges of rape (Majumdar 1993:109).

Moreover, even though issues of caste and ethnicity were indeed subsumed by the class perspective of the movement, the fact remains that steps like the banning of the sexual exploitation of women by the jotedars affected the under-caste and tribal families the most. For there was clearly a dimension of caste and ethnicity to such feudal practices of sexual exploitation: lower caste and tribal women were the poorest and most subject to the jotedars' lust. The fact that the krishak sabha and then the CP too engaged seriously with matters that most concerned the lowest of castes and tribes, and even took steps to redress the injustices that had violated their deepest sense of intimacy and integrity, would of course have played a critical role in strengthening the bonds across the divides of not just class, but caste and ethnicity too. So even if caste and ethnicity did not feature theoretically on the political agenda of the CP, the actual political moves made and small battles won did affect in positive ways the lives of the under-caste and tribal populations, creating the ground for sincere, committed comradeship across these divides too.

Bina Guha spoke from her experience of Dinajpur, the district best organized and most politically advanced in relation to women's participation, specially due to extensive work done there by MARS right since the famine years. The attempts to ban jotedars from exploiting peasant women sexually or husbands from beating wives were the most successful here. Even if such transformations may have taken place only in Dinajpur, they remain a powerful example of the deep comradeship, layered with a powerfully enriching sense of the inseparability of the personal and the political, that can be forged in political movements.

As early as the 1940s, then, at least in one area of Tebhaga, the familiar communist ideology of egalitarianism was harnessed by women for asserting their rights as producers for equal control of the domestic economy, as workers for an equal role in the movement against economic exploitation, and as comrades to put an end to the sexual exploitation by the jotedars and domestic violence at home.

Principles of class equality, pervasive in the struggle spearheaded by the CP, were also brought to bear on reinforcing notions of gender equality in comradeship. Rani Dasgupta and Bina Guha narrate the story of Bhandoni who stood up at a krishak samiti meeting and, pointing to her husband, questioned loudly, '*Amar comrader ki odhikaar amar opor haath tulbe*?' (What right does my comrade have to raise his hand against me?). Had she brought this complaint to the samiti more conventionally, as a question of domestic violence, the likely response would have been that the party did not want to interfere in family matters. But Bhandoni's move harnessed the egalitarian ideology of the left to bring domestic issues into the political arena. The result was that wife beating was banned and offenders violating the ban thereafter were punished.

This logical mobilizing of the value of equality in both the political and the private sphere carried the potential of transforming the quality of both comradeship and conjugality. Gender equality in conjugality was accepted by the krishak samiti as a principle to be upheld, and the fact that it had been done on the grounds of a political ideal inevitably reinforced the notion of equality in comradeship, which had been the springboard for this move. Even as women claimed their place in the movement through a logical positioning of themselves in relation to the intersectionality of their identities as women, homemakers and workers, they now launched out from the intersection of their multiple identities as women, wives and comrades to claim equality and respect both in the home and within the movement. This incident was no exception during Tebhaga. Rani Dasgupta and Abani Lahiri both said that such issues would come up everywhere that masses of peasant women got involved.

Tebhaga also witnessed strategic negotiations of issues of chastity in the interests of political struggle and the active recruiting of women by women. One of the most interesting narratives was that of Phuli Goldar, the 'licentious' child widow of Hatiara, Narail, who was looked upon askance by the people of her village. Amal Sen narrates that one of the peasant activists, Anima Biswas, had decided that her friend Phuli Goldar had the makings of a fiery activist, and had thus persuaded her to give up her 'wayward activities' and join the movement. She had not set eyes on Phuli Goldar for fifty years when I met her. A completely disillusioned woman by then, Anima Biswas had refused to talk to me on her first visit, and agreed to do so on the second only when moved by a photograph I had taken a month ago of her friend Phuli. She chuckled in a rare moment of indulgent humour:

> Oh, she was nothing ... she used to follow us around ... she used to just follow us around.... She did not know to read and write, she only could repeat whatever she heard us saying. She knew nothing more.... There was many a girl like her.

While Goldar agreed readily, it was quite another matter for Biswas to persuade their older comrade, Sarala Singha, to enrol her in the movement. Singha had also been widowed in childhood but had, in stark contrast to Goldar, gained fame for a strange combination of 'chaste' modes of political daring. The latter, as discussed earlier, she had demonstrated especially in hoodwinking the police. It was Amal Sen, the much loved and highly respected leader of Narail, who narrated the whole story to me. Talking of Phuli Goldar, especially in a context where widow remarriage was not allowed, as a 'militant and brave' woman, he told the story of these three women:

> Sarala Singha was a puritan. Phuli was a young widow. When she was widowed, her parents were already dead and her brothers were very young. She was pretty yet she was militant. She could not control her sexual desire, but she was a militant when protecting her young brothers. The whole region knew that Phuli was sexually 'corrupt'. Anima contacted Phuli because she saw the militant potential in her, and convinced her to give up her wayward behaviour.
>
> [When] Sarala came to the meeting for the first time, there were around forty, fifty women there. Phuli was there too. Sarala asked, 'I see Phuli here, is she a member of your *samiti* too?' Anima answered, '*Mashi* [aunt], Phuli has left all that.' Sarala said, 'You think that Phuli is not corrupt anymore? You continue your samiti with Phuli. I am leaving.' But Anima did not give up trying to convince her. She even asked, 'Whose fault is it?'

> Sarala was concerned about Phuli bringing a bad name to the samiti. Then she made a plan of her own. Her village was Hatiara and Phuli's village was Barinda. In the rainy season, Sarala decided to complete all her household chores and walk all the way to Phuli's house at night. She would sleep with Phuli on the same bed.... She did not disbelieve Anima, but she wanted to prevent any further gossip about Phuli [implying that when people learnt that a self-respecting chaste woman like Sarala had slept the whole night next to Phuli, then the latter's reputation would be cleansed].
>
> Sarala later challenged people in public saying: 'If anybody dares to malign Phuli anymore, I will tear him to bits. I Sarala Singha, am beside her.' Within a few days, it was seen that nobody challenged or gossiped about Phuli anymore. Phuli always stayed with Sarala Singha.

To read this 'purifying process' as merely a veiled reinforcement of conventional notions of chastity would be to miss its deeper significance. Sarala Singha's actions and declaration mark a radical shift in the semantics of a widow's dignity, from sexual 'purity' to political loyalty. They harness the value of political commitment to facilitate shifts in the notion of a woman's 'honour'—if a widow had been rendered an outcaste for her unchaste behaviour, she could still be restored to a place of respect in society on grounds of her political credentials. In the strategic stand that Singha takes, political sincerity is invested with greater value than sexual chastity, and even if this incident is read as one that ultimately reinforces conventional notions of chastity, it still demonstrates a new willingness to accept 'unchaste' women as political leaders. It also stands testimony to the ways in which peasant women developed modes of empowering their female comrades. As Anima Biswas, Sarala Singha and Phuli Goldar triumphantly reinforced their comradeship in daring acts of hoodwinking the jotedars and the police over the next few years, Goldar, the outcaste widow, became one of the most celebrated and powerful activists of Narail.

Such incidents also take on a deeper significance in light of Namasudra history of the 'Brahminical' transformation of sexuality and curbing of Namasudra peasant women's autonomy that had taken place in the late nineteenth century. According to Sekhar Bandyopadhyay (2004:154):

> When the Namasudras lived an almost amphibious life in boats in the marshy tracts of Bakarganj and Faridpur, the very physical environment of their social existence subverted the stricter rules of sexual discipline, marriage and structures of kinship, and this was stereotyped by genteel society as amorous or sinful sexual habits. So when in the late nineteenth century, they emerged as a settled peasant community, they moved from their boats to homesteads, acquired land, started looking for status, felt the necessity of having legal heirs to inherit property, and invented a Brahmanical genealogy. First on their agenda of social reform was the streamlining of marriage rules and the family structure, thus establishing stricter control over female sexuality and reproductive power following the orthodox norms of Hindu society. Before their social reforms began, their women participated in agricultural production and visited markets to sell their merchandise. But a meeting of their community leaders in 1872 prohibited such practices, as the freedom of their women was considered to be a reason why the larger Hindu society held them in disrespect. In other words, as we have argued in the first chapter, in order to command respect from Hindu society, acceptance of its behavioural norms became mandatory, and this had the unfortunate result of curbing the relative autonomy that the Namasudra women had previously enjoyed.

The topography, habitat and livelihood patterns of a community shape its gendered norms and relations, as is implicit in Bandyopadhyay's observation too, but these were then transformed in the face of social pressures of sanskritization in the Namasudra community's transition from amphibian to settler status. What is interesting is that in this situation of insurgency in which activists were challenging their opponents on their own terrain, earlier sedimentations of gendering originally related to this amphibian existence reappear, earlier forms of women's autonomy are asserted again. Sarala Singha, amphibian and expert at negotiating deep waters and tall trees alike, had a direct experiential vantage point from which to challenge the conservative sexual norms that had developed within the community; and her act of supporting Phuli Goldar was simultaneously an act of reclaiming the authority of women in her community, even if she herself may not have seen it as a reclamation.

The assertion of a woman's identity either as a worker claiming her rights or as a sexual being compelled to protect her own body from hunger as well as sexual exploitation was relatively new. Yet, in the actual claiming of the rights, the peasant women of Dinajpur had already evolved sophisticated strategies that made full use of the intersectionality of identities. Thus, for women like Joymoni Barmani, it was a complex and *conscious* interplay of their multiple identities as equal workers and women that underlined their involvement in the Tebhaga movement. For others like Jaya Barmani, political agency was posited at the intersectionality of the resisting colonial subject and the emerging feminist one. For yet others like Bhandoni, it involved harnessing the egalitarian ideology of the CP, as comrades and wives, for transforming violent conjugal relations. While Sarala Singha drew upon the value of political commitment to yoke the power of rebellious women like Phuli Goldar to the cause of the movement, transforming in the process the hitherto unshakeable strictures on the chastity of widows.

Gendered political demands arose from within the needs of personal life. Personal issues were indeed viewed by the krishak samiti in light of political issues of class exploitation and the nature of comradeship respectively, for the jotedar could claim proprietorship of the poorest of peasant women's bodies by virtue of his class power, and men and women who were husband and wife were also comrades in struggle. What we have, then, is a translation of deeply private and intimately experienced deprivations and injustices into the political discourse of the movement, articulated in terms of rights, equality, anti-imperialist ideals and the value of political commitment. Thus, as a result of women's participation and demands, political activity in the movement was experienced not just as a struggle for the realization of economic demands for Tebhaga; it was far more richly nuanced, as collective activity also began to transform intimate experiences of activists' lives at the core These transformations included freedom from sexual exploitation, the happiness of equal partnership in conjugality, the unprecedented joys of finding acknowledgement of their labour as workers, the fulfilment of personal needs and political desires in the public sphere of the movement, and, of course, the thrill of camaraderie both amongst women and across the divides of gender. The experience of political activism comprised simultaneously the experiences of such dimensions of interiority, bringing a sense of inwardness to the movement for both women and men.

### ♦ *Eros and Politics: New Forms of Love, New Modes of Comradeship* ♦

The fact that peasant women worked in the home as well as with men in the fields had also created a sense of mutual bonding that emerges in the actual process of sharing work side by side, doing work together. This bonding as workers became the ready ground in which political notions of comradeship too could take root. The comradeship of work shared evolved into the comradeship of politics shared; it prepared both men and women for a joint participation of mutual respect in political struggle. Abani Lahiri stated:

> [In the movement,] both men and women took part in the processions—not that women walked 3 miles and men 10 miles. This sense of a common bond—both men and women facing the enemy was a big factor in pulling women into the movement.

This sense of political camaraderie and shared commitment to the cause of an exploited populace had not only begun to unsettle conventional gendered norms of women's passivity; it had also expanded the field of love and added unique dimensions to men and women's relationships. Kalyani Dasgupta, an urban schoolteacher of Jalpaiguri, recalling what she loved about her activist husband Sachin Dasgupta and the way in which they related to each other, said:

> He was nine years older than me. He was a very quiet man. I suppose I married him rather than him marrying me. At least, it seemed like that at that time. He was a person with a difference ... I loved him. Today, my life could have been like my sister Uma's; she is rich. But I didn't want a life like that. My mother didn't really oppose our marriage, all that she said was he should work because he was very, very poor. He refused, saying, 'I will not become a doctor.' My father wanted to pay for his studies to become an MD. But he said, 'I shall not work, nor shall I study further. I shall continue to do what I am doing.' He was very friendly with Uma. Uma would say to him, 'You wear two different socks.' And he would reply, 'I shall keep on wearing two different socks.' He wore whatever people gave him....

> [A]nd we never uttered a word about our love. On a rare day or two he [Sachin] would say, 'There are some things that one does not have to articulate, they reside in the mind....' Our love was of a different kind. We were never restricted to the home; our love developed working together out on the roads and fields.

In Dakkhinparia village of Dinajpur on the other hand, the Rajbangshi peasant Heleketu Singha talked of his late wife Jaya's passionate investment in women's equality with a pride that indicated how much he treasured the camaraderie that they had shared in their marriage:

> Her demand was equal rights. 'Women in our society are neglected. But women are half of humanity, so why should they be shut indoors? We also demand the rights to education, to work, to speak out. We are reprimanded if we go out to work....' These were her views. She was very vocal about the fact that even though women did a lot of work, men still thought that they could keep them under their thumbs.

That Heleketu Singha's recollections were narrated with a joyous, wholesome pride in the context of the political ideals of the movement indicated a recognition that the same principle of equality that was the font of the Tebhaga movement was also the grounding force for Jaya's feminist politics, and of their love for each other. And the love for Jaya that shone in Heleketu's eyes as he talked about her rendered home to me the realization that the antarikata Bina Guha had spoken of, that women had brought to the movement, had infused men's sense of the intimate connection between personal relations and political ideals too. Heleketu Singha still stands tall in my imagination as a rare, beautiful man embodying a wisdom that bespoke an unthreatened, celebratory understanding of the deep connections between love and politics that the value of equality can forge.

The coming together of sexual desire and political desire on the terrain of this political struggle has been captured by Manik Bandyopadhyay in his fiction too. Referring to his story 'Mangala', named after the single, childless, activist peasant woman who is its protagonist, Malini Bhattacharya (1987:55–56) observes that it represents a new possibility in associating an 'astonishing vitality, political and sexual' with Mangala and her militant peasant lover, Golok. The crucial point that she makes in this analysis is that the peasant woman's 'conscious struggle against her class enemies and her struggle to fulfil her sexuality are part of the same system of values'. This intertwining is what facilitates such a radical shift in gender roles, both political and sexual, and layers the political experience with the richness of the experiences of self-fulfilment.

This fusion of eros and politics in the fields of Tebhaga finds perhaps its most profound articulation in the life of Anima Biswas, the peasant activist of Narail. Amal Sen, one of the most enlightened and respected leaders of the Tebhaga movement, talked admiringly of her as a spirited leader, marrying Karuna Kishore, the man she had grown to love, and facilitating the transformation of her husband from a wealthy arrogant farmer into an efficient peasant activist through a rich and nurturing relationship. Of her activism, he said that her role in the *mahila samiti* constituted but one aspect of her role in the movement because, 'from within this heroic struggle, her contribution towards cleansing, purifying and reforming the distorted views that were prevalent then is amazing'. One such effort was in relation to initiating the liberation of her feisty friend Phuli Goldar from puritanical social mores; the other was clearly in relation to her vision of love and political liberation.

He observed that even as she fought for a democratic society, she worked at establishing a democratic vision in her love for Karuna Kishore, the comrade she married. Biswas's political activity and her personal life were part of the same system of values, and the new man–woman relationship that she and her husband forged was possible only on the terrain of their love for their people and their political commitment. For Sen, this love took root in the ground of love, 'premer jomi': this ground was of the ideals they valued in politics, and on this ground their love for each other, their love for their people and their political commitment became extensions of each other. Amal Sen also indicated that the fact that Biswas not only understood this but valued it deeply is reflected in the fact that she wanted to write a book called *Premer Jomir Khoje* (In Search of the Terrain of Love). Theirs was a new family, created in a space of new historical aspirations, and shaped by a new egalitarian relationship of mutual love, respect and camaraderie.

That the connections between private life and political life were acknowledged, that personal issues were seriously taken up thus as political issues, and that political moves to redress the injustices highlighted by the women did transform the quality of personal life too—all this would have brought that sense of interiority to the movement that Bina Guha highlighted as women's unique contribution. For both women and men, then, political struggle began to be layered with the experiences of transformation of one's very sense of being—in relation to integrity of body and self (for the woman her own and for the man that of his wife or daughter), to the inviolability of conjugal intimacy by a powerful outsider, to the equality of partnership in marriage, to the enjoyment of political comradeship even after the loneliness of social rejection, and even in some cases to the expansive thrill of experiencing the fusion of eros and politics. The experience of political struggle, thus, achieved a quality of inwardness; it became a palimpsest of transformations experienced at the level of intimate, personal, everyday relations too.

## Comradeship Across Social Divides

Given that one of the unique features of the Tebhaga movement relates to the linkages that were forged between the urban CP women and the rural peasant women, which also led to the political awareness and massive participation of peasant women, the bridging of differences of class and location became a central issue. Urban male leaders of the CP, as indicated earlier, had begun to have experiences of living with peasants from 1941 onwards, and this had initiated within the party a culture of sensitivity to the peasants' needs and respect for their perspectives. Abani Lahiri (2001:41–42) says:

> When we set out to analyse our experiences of this period, we felt we had learnt two valuable lessons from this phase of living in hiding. One of these was the sense of intimacy with the peasants and being able to see the problems of their lives at very close quarters; and the

> other was learning to look at the problems of their villages through their eyes. This was something we couldn't do before.

Rani Dasgupta had a moving account of male activists in Dinajpur, who even shared the hunger of the peasants during the famine; this rendered home the degree of sincerity that had gone into the formation of one of the most powerful bases of the movement:

> In Dinajpur where the Communist Party had been able to acquire such a huge mass base, the reason for it was some of our leaders, communist leaders ... they all came from decent families, all educated, they went and stayed among the peasants. Their entire life, I mean their entire political life had been spent living among the peasants in the villages, staying in their houses, eating and sleeping with them. For example, I can mention a few such names. One of them is still alive, Basanta Chatterjee. Itahar. Have I told you about Itahar?
>
> Itahar, a police station, it's in Thakurgaon province. During [those] days ... it included Dinajpur proper, Thakurgaon, Balurghat ... and ... Raiganj. These were the four provinces. Itahar was one of the police stations ... of Thakurgaon. Basanta used to stay in the area which fell under Itahar police station.... I first started going into the rural areas from the year [19]43.... Why? I'll tell you that. It was from then on that the lines of his ribcage began showing through his body ... because of inadequate nourishment during the time of famine. It was because of malnourishment. Everybody called Basantada 'Chatujje'. The people of that region recognized him a 'Chatujje *thakur*'. So that was how, by integrating themselves completely into the peasant community, they built up the kisan sabha and the base of the Communist Party among the peasants. They even taught them how to read and write. Some places were—Dinajpur was one—those places where the Christian missionaries had propagated literacy.... The Santals, Kohls, Virs, etcetera, occupied a large part of Dinajpur. That was in the Balurghat province.... In the entire Tebhaga movement, the first martyrs were ... there were two of them ... in a place called Chiribandar.

Then she went on to narrate the strength of the solidarity such sacrifices had wrought. In districts such as Dinajpur, where jotedars had tried to bring in Muslim *lathials* (hired men with sticks), not only had the krishak sabha resisted such communal incitement firmly, but

Muslims had also risked their lives for the movement. The first major clash took place between the police and peasants in Chiribandar on 4 January 1947. The jotedars had lodged a number of charges of looting against peasant activists who had carried the harvest to their own threshing floors as per the '*Nij khamare dhan tolo*' (take the paddy to your own threshing floor) programme. When the police came to arrest the peasant leaders, the Santals came out with bows and arrows, and the Rajbangshis with sticks to stop the police, but the latter opened fire on the peasants (Majumdar 1993:194). Rani Dasgupta recounted:

> Chiribandar ... 14 miles from Dinajpur town. There, on the fourth of January 1947, after the harvest had begun, a Santal named Shibram, a sharecropper, and Samiruddin who was a bonded labourer—bonded labourer means one who has no land of his own but cultivates another's land for a certain wage—they were shot dead by the police. One policeman got injured by their arrows, the arrows of the Santals. He died later in the hospital. This was one incident. The first martyrs of the Tebhaga movement were a Hindu and Muslim together. The Communist Party integrated with the peasants in all these places.

Urban women of the CP, however, did not interact at such close quarters with the peasant women in their homes until much later. Referring to the CP leader PC Joshi's now well-known hard-hitting critique, articulated publicly at the April 1944 All India Peasants' Conference held in Netrakona, Mymensingh, about urban women not having reached out enough to the peasant women in the villages, Abani Lahiri stated:

> I think that it is correct that a good relation was not established. Individually Monidi [Manikuntala Sen] attended many meetings of the peasants' organization. But our party workers were unable to develop a women's movement or generate effective solidarity except with women from the slums. Working with peasants was restricted to attending and addressing meetings, but they did not stay with the peasants.

Then he went on to explain that this was the case because the prospect of long-term stay in the villages was a difficult one for urban women, both practically and because of a lack of psychological acceptance of their presence in the villages by peasant society:

> It was a problem for them to stay in the villages because even when we men stayed, we had to face a lot of problems which were difficult for women to bear. They mainly went, say, to Burnpur [a small town near Asansol] and stayed in middle-class households and worked from there. But in Dinajpur, the strongest centre of the Tebhaga movement, there was no other place to stay except in kitchens and cowsheds. One has to accept that. In the beginning, this was a problem for women. They went maybe for three days for campaigning or to address a rally.... Previously it was impossible to arrange for a place to stay for women even for three days.... But during Tebhaga they went to villages. By then, a support base had been created that enabled the women to go to the villages. This support base was created through the movement. The peasants too were in a psychological frame of mind by then to receive urban women.

Thus, the full-time political activity of urban women in the villages was preceded by a slow process of acculturation both on the part of the urban women and the rural population.

## ♦ *Ghare–Baire: Domestic to Political, Political to 'Familial'* ♦

Tebhaga facilitated a slow but sure maturing of political vision for women. The experience of hunger within the family, and economic and sexual exploitation, had led to the desire for political participation. On the one hand, this generated a need in women to step out of domestic confines towards education, greater political awareness and active struggle. On the other hand, women's participation gave a unique shape to the movement itself, as they began infusing the political arena with domestic modes of interaction and familial patterns of caring, bonding and loyalty, infusing the entire movement into with what many activists called the sense of being 'one large family'.

Both urban and rural men repeated, and with great nostalgia, that the entire movement had become like an extended family. Implicit in their nostalgia and emphasis of was, of course, a sense of the uniqueness of this relationship amongst comrades. That women opened up their homes to activists, providing food, shelter and nursing, was not usually a matter of compulsion, but one of choice. It wasn't just wives acting at the instance of their husbands. Often, women would secretly start sheltering activists till such time as they could win their husbands over, and in many cases, it was widowed women living alone with their children who would chose to transform their homes into secret party bases. As hundreds of women in Dinajpur, Narail, and every other area of Tebhaga, began to feed and shelter activists in transit, fleeing the police or living underground, the activists became family, and these familial relations were gradually extended to larger sections of the party. Domestic boundaries were expanded to encompass the political arena. These were quiet transformations of women's domestic roles, but their political ramifications were immense. Whole families participated and the village participated as a family in turn. Prominent leaders such as Amal Sen and Abani Lahiri asserted that the massive character of the movement developed only because women were involved so extensively. Yet, the transformation of values that this involved, leading both to the political empowerment of women themselves, and a powerful enrichment of left culture, has never been discussed.

This transition involved a considered harnessing of modes of intimacy and care—to be found in forms of familial bonding and domestic interactions—into relations of political bonding. It eventually marked a significant shift in subjectivity, and formed the basis of a powerful solidarity that spread from village to village as women opened their homes to shelter activists, both urban and rural, who travelled across Bengal forging the networks of the movement. Such processes of weaving solidarity, that, in the words of the activists, bound the entire movement into an 'extended family' and sustained it, deserve to be understood better. For even Marxist thought, as Benhabib and Cornell (1987) point out, though rich in theorizations of class, is lacking in theorizations of solidarity across divides of class, ethnicity, religion and language.

The home is a critical site for the reproduction of social and cultural processes that form the basis of social life. As peasant women opened up their homes right across Bengal to itinerant activists, the domestic modes and values of sharing food and caring began to form an important manner of interaction between activism. An ethics of care, which prevails at home and emphasizes the value of relationships (Gilligan 1982), became the basis for solidarities across regional and social differences. Burima, literally 'old mother', an impoverished widow of Sundardighi, Dinajpur, had only one old *photua* to wrap around her body, but her house became the home and shelter of activists first from her own village and then from right across the area. Kalyani Dasgupta of Jalpaiguri talked about her close acquaintance with Punneswary Barman, affectionately called Burima, a leader of Rajbangshi women, who had initiated the first Tebhaga protest in Jalpaiguri, following up on the harvesting of paddy with the slogan 'Nij khamare dhan tolo', and organized hundreds of women to gherao a police camp during harvest time (Majumdar 1993:110). Revealing the personal side to this fiery leader Kalyani Dasgupta said: 'She was an amazing human being, a soul full of incredible compassion, love for the young men of the party—she had protected the activists, and helped them through thousands of difficulties.' She looked after party workers like her own children. The familial relationships she developed with these young activists became, veritably, the relations of comradeship between her and them, and between them. As more and more women opened up their homes, and such relations multiplied, a familial sense of intimacy began to mark the nature of comradeship within the movement. Dasgupta recalled this sense of belonging with each other across the villages of Bengal: 'But this was not only a characteristic of Burima. I cannot explain how it was, I went to those areas frequently, though I did not stay there for long. I felt whenever I went there that I had a right—that is, I and my party workers have a right in those households.' Her assertion that it was not possible to explain what that experience was like indicated that this was a unique transformation in the nature of comradeship during Tebhaga, and that the experience of belonging with each other, to the point where one began to feel one had a right over the other's household, could not be captured in words.

A transformed understanding of political relationships, in terms of responses to another fellow activist according to her or his needs, began to shape the subjectivity of the times, as became evident in a range of relationships, from the ones such as Burima forged to others such as the comradeship between Ila Mitra and the Santals of Narail, where both she and Harek risked their lives for each other, as I will show later.

As with the urban famine workers, so for the Burimas of Tebhaga it was a conscious and political evolution from motherhood to social motherhood and an extension of domestic values into the political sphere. What goes into their actions is the personal gendered investment of women as mothers within families, that which creates bonding. And such bonding is the very basis of solidarity about which most theorizing on class struggles is silent. However, there are also historical silences that have pushed into oblivion the indispensable contribution of hundreds of homemaker-activists. This includes a large number of Muslim women, many of whom, given the greater restraints on women in their community, did not have access to political activity in the public arena, but were political activists operating within their homes. Riziya Khatun of Narail talks about her mother Jannat-un-Nisa's silent suffering. Jannat-un-Nisa participated from within the house, as a provider of food and shelter to activists amidst severe economic constraints, and she managed the whole household and farm administration, leaving her husband free to pursue his activism. The public sphere invaded and took over her home, but for her and for thousands of invisible activists like her, their resourcefulness and managerial skills, as well as the sense of collectivity that they infused into the movement, were never acknowledged publicly.

Widows like Burima of Jalpaiguri were legendary for having opened up their homes, and others like Sarala Singha and Phuli Goldar of Narail for their dynamic leadership in the Tebhaga movement. The standard explanation is that widows had fewer responsibilities than married women did, and were often back in their natal homes outside of the restrictive purview of their in-laws. Bimala Majhi, who had also joined the movement in Mednipur as a widow, before she married again, this time a fellow comrade, cast another light on the experience of widowhood in relation to activism. When asked why she came to join the class struggle despite being so well off, she replied: 'Well … after I became a widow, there was a change in my thinking against all injustice in the society. I found injustice against women both in homes and outside. So I thought work such as this would give me the opportunity to express my own thoughts and opinions.'

Thus, there was also a sense of expansion taking place from the understanding of gender injustice to caste and class injustice. Women 'enjoyed' the epistemic privilege of the exploited, and the knowledge and understanding of the modes of oppression they suffered most intimately as women became a natural launching pad for relating to other modes of exploitation across class, caste, ethnicity and community. And the fact that the majority of rural women were not only impoverished but also under-caste or tribal, would also have led to an experiential understanding of intersectionality as women shaped at the intersection of their identities of gender, class and caste, tribe or community.

In fact, Kalyani Dasgupta also indicated that while urban women's analysis of the injustices of life came from communism, rural women did not have to be 'taught' communism; their analysis of exploitation came from their own experiences of life, and was often more sophisticated than that of the urban women:

> In Pachagarh, we had a party worker, Tilaktarini Nandy. She was a widow and had a daughter. We called her Didi. Somehow they landed up in Pachagarh. They came during a riot—[her daughter] Buri and she came.... We did not teach them what communism is, what wages are. But they learnt it, how we do not know. They learnt it from the oppression and exploitation in their own lives. Didi learnt to read and write. We often say that we love the party and we can give our lives for the party. But actually, only a few of us could do that. One can jump into it spontaneously—that is one kind of sacrifice. The other is suffering each day—knowing the police can come, anytime, and if the police comes, the women will have to face tremendous disrespect and insult, will be beaten up in jails. They knew all this and yet worked for the party and faced everything—there is a difference between the two. I really do not know from where they learnt all this—it is from them that I learnt how to work for and love the party. Maybe they learnt it from their own life experiences. We had only said that the cause of all our sufferings is foreign imperialism. At that time we did not see the Congress capitalists, only imperialism was prominent and we highlighted it.

It is indeed telling that while urban women were pressing the anti-imperialist agenda of the party, the rural women had already seen the connections, as Dasgupta implied, between the oppressions of imperialism and of indigenous capital. Yet, the peasant women clearly saw their own analyses reflected in the CP—this is what Dasgupta suggested made them 'love' the party and in turn induced similar feelings in the urban women. What, then, was the nature of the transformations that the rural women experienced in their lives that elicited such 'love'? For the party could not have been an abstraction for those who were compelled to understand the world through their own experiences—it comprised one's comrades, one's work, as well as a sense of collective resistance—and 'love', then, would apply to all of these rather than to a mere political structure. The reasons for the use of such an intimate term being for a political collective has to lie in processes of interiority that the peasant women found fulfilled in the concrete political work and negotiations in the movement led by the CP.

## ♦ *Literacy and Education* ♦

If the care work of urban women during the famine related to saving lives, then during Tebhaga it focused on developing the abilities of the village activists. Education became important as a means of political communication. The urban activists now began to extend their care to the village women to develop the latter's abilities to read. They began to impart to them some knowledge of what was happening in the world to enable them to develop their perspectives and locate themselves in relation to world politics, and they started to teach them how to write. This became important as a means of recording one's own history as it evolved and of reaching out to the world through communication. Given the face-to-face, one-to-one work that teaching involves, it also became the ground for the forging of relationships across the rural–urban divide. Bonds of camaraderie were formed through the intimate, often startling and humorous, processes of teaching and learning that in themselves were rewarding for urban women. For such teaching was not unidirectional; in the process, the urban women and men too began to appreciate diverse forms of expressive intelligence and learn about other modes of communication, such as through drawings, signs and colour codes. Bina Guha talked about the confounding experience of training the village women in literacy:

> We had to continue simultaneously with the work of the Mahila Atmaraksha Samiti and Tebhaga. In the villages, when we got back the books [that we had distributed to the women] and opened the pages, we found there were only pictures. Pictures of trees, leaves, roots - only pictures and nothing else.... Pictures in lieu of names.... Say, somebody was called Phuleshwari, but was unable to write that, she had drawn pictures instead, spelling out her name.... They had drawn pictures. The names of villages had been drawn—which village had which mahila samiti—everything had been illustrated. They decorate their huts, doors and windows with beautiful paintings, they are skilled artists. They are also very neat and clean.
>
> Whatever it was, I was startled when I saw those books. 'My God! What will I do? Not a single name has been written,' I told Rani. Those girls burst out laughing, 'Comrades, you are educated, we are illiterate, this is our way of writing.' They started 'reading' one by one—this is this name, this is that village—they went on continuously without stopping—they 'read' the pictures.... The names were all there in the form of pictures.... The pictures were unbelievably good—drawn in different inks, red, green—the names of villages were written in red ink, the names of the girls in green ink. It went on page after page.... They had their own code.

Abani Lahiri spoke about the movement generating a desire in Joymoni Barmani and her husband to educate themselves and others, and the initiative they took:

> For the uneducated, illiterate peasants, a renaissance takes place when they join struggle and new perspectives open up. Certain questions arise in their minds. For example, Joymoni was a young peasant woman whose husband, Spashtaram, was a poor illiterate peasant. In the peasant and workers' meetings, some members handed in written reports. Joymoni and Spashtaram then started a literacy programme. They learnt to write and started submitting written reports within three months. They worked hard, nearly

> taking the entire day to write one report on the number of women they had mobilized in their area.

Rani Dasgupta, who had taught Joymoni how to read and write, also recollected with pride the latter's painful striving for literacy, and how she learnt to communicate their history to the outside world by writing reports of meetings on bamboo mats.

A sense of universality began to develop across and beyond the villages of Tebhaga. Even though one of the limitations of the period was the failure to link up the peasant struggles of Tebhaga with movements of workers, students and others in the cities, Lahiri recounted in one of his interviews the role of the newspaper, and the enthusiasm with which peasants would gather around one of the literate activists every evening who would read out the daily newspaper to them:

> In the evenings, men and women sat together to listen to and read the various nationalist magazines. This was training. For women, it generated consciousness about the strikes and the upheavals. People carried the *Swadhinata* [the CP newspaper] and read it out, [the women would say] tell us what the news is today, and, standing on the road, they would listen. This period was one of a great awakening and a very important dimension of that awakening was the participation of women.

Thus began their identification with what Partha Chatterjee (2004:5), drawing upon Benedict Anderson (1998), refers to as 'the unbound seriality of the everyday universals of modern social thought: nations, citizens, revolutionaries ... workers, intellectuals, and so on'. He further explains:

> Unbound serialities are typically imagined and narrated by means of the classic instruments of print-capitalism, namely the newspaper and the novel. They afford the opportunity for individuals to imagine themselves as members of larger than face-to-face solidarities, of choosing to act on behalf of those solidarities, of transcending by an act of political imagination the limits imposed by traditional practices. Unbound serialities are potentially liberating. (ibid.)

That education would become politically significant for peasant women as they began to gain more confidence in representing themselves was something the urban women clearly realized. Various nurturing relationships, such as between Rani Dasgupta and Joymoni Barmani, began to develop between urban and rural women, which not only yielded tremendous satisfaction to the former, but also resulted in the creation of what the urban-educated Rani Mukherjee of Rangpur would later tell me was a force of 'trained activists' in the villages. The literacy that the urban women imparted to their rural comrades thus played a significant role in their joint liberation by nurturing a sense of universality and solidarities that transcended the fields of Tebhaga.

In fact, Bimala Majhi, the peasant woman who had studied only till class IV, yet went on to become a leader of Tebhaga in Mednipur, attributed her growth to the urban leader Manikuntala Sen, with whom she developed a close friendship:

> Whenever Monidi took me [to the villages], she'd bring along books on *ka kha ga gha* [the Bangla alphabet]. She'd teach me more of writing, she would say you have some knowledge of the alphabets, you have forgotten them, so I'm giving you so many days, you must write letters to me.... She'd buy postcards, envelopes, pens for me wherever we stayed. She'd teach me till late in the night.

Manikuntala Sen (2001:129) also writes about Bimala Majhi's transformation:

> Another district conference was planned in Tamluk.... The Bimala of the village would now have to work among the middle class people of the towns. That was why we had been called here. I dressed her up in one of my saris, draping it on just as the city women did, and she went out with Bina [Das]. She got over her fears after listening to the women and she joined in the campaigning and the fund-raising. She did not find it difficult to sit at the table and have her meals with everyone in the lodgings, nor did she find it difficult to adjust. It was a pleasure to see how well she managed. This was the young Bimala who once did not know how to write. She got the young men to prepare the samiti's reports and sent them to Calcutta. Once I wrote to her angrily, 'Learn how to write. I will read the reports only if you prepare them yourself.' After a few months I received a letter and a report written out in clear unbroken letters. How happy we all were! The letter and the report

> were published in the party journal and held up as an example so that everybody would be inspired.

This was clearly a mutually rewarding friendship. Manikuntala Sen's sense of intimacy with Majhi is evident in the way she dresses her in one of her own sarees. Her noticing small transformations such as Majhi getting over her fears at campaigning and fundraising amongst middle-class women, or having learnt to sit at the table for meals with them shows an understanding of her efforts, and that these were not easy transitions for a peasant woman to make. The 'angry' letter threatening not to read reports unless she wrote them herself represents a mode of encouragement that rests on easy familiarity, and her happiness—and that of her comrades—is clearly one of pride at Majhi's response. The care that Sen had put into teaching her had clearly become a source of much joy for both women, across the urban–rural divide.

Bimala Majhi went on to write in party newspapers and magazines—*Janajuddha* and *Kalantar*—and even sit at the negotiating table with the government. Such educational care work of urban women thus empowered their rural comrades, who in turn strengthened their forces and also gained the ability to represent their own perspectives as peasant women. Manikuntala Sen writes of the public meetings against the repression of peasants by the police, the media coverage, the growth of public opinion in favour of the peasants, and the meeting held during Suhrawardy's tenure as prime minister of Bengal a year after Tebhaga had been launched:

> Suhrawardy Saheb realized he had lost the battle and agreed to a settlement with the peasant leaders. There was a huge gathering of peasants from the Tebhaga and other areas at the Maidan and the working class and middle class came forward in support. Bimala Majhi was present with other peasant leaders at the negotiating table: she had led the Tebhaga movement in Midnapore. Her presence underlined the fact that peasant women were equal partners with men in the struggle. (2001:163)

## ♦ *Across Community, Caste, Ethnicity and Class* ♦

A significant feature of Tebhaga was the realization that in order for class struggle to be successful it was imperative that the divides between religious communities and between castes be addressed, some of the existing hostilities and hierarchies be transformed, and women be drawn into the movement from all backgrounds; otherwise class solidarity, if achieved at all, would at best be a fragile structure, vulnerable to easy collapse. Conscious work went into building bridges across communities and castes, and women's work was indispensable to this deeper social structuring of political solidarity in Tebhaga,

In some areas like Narail and Dinajpur the ground had to be prepared very strategically for Hindu–Muslim solidarity before Tebhaga could be launched. Bandyopadhyay's research (2004:187) based on journals of the 1920s onwards, shows that there held sway amongst the Rajbangshis 'the modern Hindu masculinist discourse of "abduction" in the 1920s, based on the stereotype of feminine victimisation necessitating male protection'. It foregrounds that the Rajbangshi publication *Kshatriya* from 1923 onwards, and the reports of the Kshatriya Samiti in 1925, reported hundreds of cases of the 'abuse of Hindu women' (ibid.), of 'Hindu women being abducted by hypersexual Muslims in east Bengal and organised efforts to protect them' (ibid). Bandyopadhyay observes that though this subsided in the 1930s, following the 'rupture in their [Rajbangshis'] relationship with the Hindu Mahasabha and their joining the Depressed Classes movement that provided a different cementing ideology', yet, the effect of this discourse of abduction had continued to affect community relations: 'But the communal suspicions that these sentiments generated lingered on, and as late as 1946, during the Tebhaga movement, this mutual mistrust often tore apart the class solidarity between the Rajbansi and Muslim sharecroppers' (ibid.:215).

What is extremely interesting is that this very discourse of 'abduction' was deployed strategically by activists in Narail to stem a chain of retaliatory 'abductions' and consequent riots, engineered by the powerful Hindu zamindar of Tularampur. Veteran activist Nurul Akbar of Dumurtala village in Narail recounted a series of incidents, that he recalled had taken place in 1945–46:

> All the powerful Hindus were with the zamindars. We didn't get to know what decisions were taken that night at the [Hindu] zamindar's

> house [in Tularampur]. But that night, in a neighbouring village, Naralgram, the wife of a doctor named Abdul Qadar was abducted by the Hindus. As a result of this, our efforts to unite the people to fight communalism met with a blow. This happened before the Tebhaga movement. Now the Mussalmans said, the Hindus have taken a Mussalman's wife away, the they can't get away with this. The next night, the Muslims abducted a Hindu woman in Tularampur. This happened as a result of the conspiracy of the zamindars. Their Muslim jotedars, *gaatdars* abducted this Hindu woman.... The zamindars had Hindu and Muslim supporters. They were all affluent subjects. Then, everyone was ready to get into battle—the communal riots were about to erupt. It couldn't be prevented. Communal riots started in Abhaynagar thana, Keshubpur thana, Manirampur thana, Narail thana, Shalka thana, etc.The entire belt that our organization had been declaring as independent was affected. Hindus were a majority in this area.... This happened in the beginning of 1946.

At a meeting of the Tularampur Union Board that comprised largely Muslims and was led by its president Abdul Haq of Baroligram, a resolution had been taken to attack the nearby Hindu villages and ransack them. Nurul Akbar explained how elders amongst the peasant activists strategically harnessed the discourse of abduction to prevent the abductions that could have inflamed communal tensions beyond repair:

> We saw that the situation was grave. Our collective fight against the British wouldn't be possible if this took place. Amongst us, there was an elderly person named Lal Miyan. He used to live right here. Lal Miyan then said, 'We have something to say.' In the beginning, when we arrived, they had been angry with us, 'Why did you come so late, we have already made the resolution? Go home now!' He said, 'We have something to say. That is, we need two days' time. Does this thing have to carried out tomorrow itself? We support the resolution. But we want two days.' 'Why do you want two days?' 'See, all the Mussalman villages will not be able to defeat all the Hindu villages. These are small Mussalman villages beside large Hindu villages. These are less powerful, they will not be able to overpower the Hindus. We were planning this [abduction] because they have abducted one woman. We are doing this because

> one woman has been dishonoured. But in the villages that will be defeated by the Hindus... all the women there will be taken away by the Hindus. We need two days so that we can transfer our women to the more powerful villages. We can't do that tonight, so we need two days to leave reach our women to such villages so that our honour remains secure.' At this, one old man at the meeting got up and said, 'Yes, let's wait. We can't begin the work tomorrow.' 'Why?' 'Because the women have to be transferred. All the villages are not equally powerful. We can begin our mission only when the women have been cleared out.'
>
> Another elderly person now got up. He was quite old, must have been about eighty or eighty-five at that time. 'We won't be able to carry out our plan,' he said. 'Why?' 'We will leave our women in other villages, but will the men in those villages ensure that our women remain untouched? So, the work cannot be done. We have to reconsider everything carefully before we can begin our mission.' That's how we were saved. Our workers were in Mailot too. They were wondering what the result of this meeting would be, and we were wondering what the result of that meeting would be. Then we sent news of this meeting there. And both meetings ended with a decision not to begin the riot.
>
> We had our people there [amongst the Hindus] too. We sent this message to them. There too it was stopped. We were there to stop it. The party's objective was to prevent it from happening. They [the Hindus] also realised that there were weak Hindu villages that would be overpowered by the Muslims, their women would be abducted, and so on. It was explained to them in this manner. This was a strategy that was adopted and explained in this manner.

It was this history of strife, Nurul Akbar explained, that compelled them to delay the launching of Tebhaga in Narail for six months till they had put in enough work to unite Hindus and Muslims, and prepare the ground for a movement that could hold together in the face of the zamindar's and/or jotedar's exploitation:

> After that we had to postpone the movement. We had wanted to begin earlier in 1946, but we had to postpone it. Because of this excitement and tension, this Hindu–Muslim factor, we knew that if they got divided, we wouldn't succeed. It took us another six months to get the Hindu–Muslims together and united once again. That's

why we started the Tebhaga movement at the end of 1946. This is how they tried to break us up—the supporters of the British.

This strategy of deploying the discourse of abduction to prevent communal riots however also seems to have been deployed by Muslim patriarchy in these villages to keep their women at home, and was, according to Nurul Akbar, a major reason for the low levels of participation of Muslim women in the struggle in Narail. He said:

> Because of this reason, our women couldn't step out. Very few of them stepped out. That was a very strict and rigid society fifty years ago. Even now, our fundamentalists rave and rant if our women step out.

The participation of Muslim women from peasant families not only varied from one area to another, but also from family to family within a village. In many places their role was confined to staying indoors and arranging for the infrastructure in terms of food and shelter. Nurul Akbar also cited religious and social taboo in the face of atheism as a reason for the dearth of Muslim women in the movement:

> We held small meetings in different areas and it was unanimously decided that in order to strengthen the movement, women had to be brought in. The movement wouldn't be a success without the help of the women.... But we couldn't draw many women into our movement because of the social taboos.... Of course, we tried but the Hindu families proved to be comparatively more successful as far as the participation of the women was concerned than the Muslims ... it was the social taboo ... the name communist itself.... Overall, we failed to draw in Muslim girls. Only a few of them participated. For example, I was a political activist, so women from my house took part and also women from other activist homes....
>
> Actually ... in our house, say, for example, I am the only party member. Now I have to leave the house, society and risk social taboos in order to wage the movement. Now if the woman also goes out ... you know what I mean [laughs].... At that point of time being a member of the Communist Party was considered to be a sin in religion as well as society.

There is, however, clearly need for caution against the danger of stereotyping all Muslim women's participation as confined to the home, even in areas such as Narail. Riziya Begum recalled that young unmarried women and girls like her would be brought together from different households to enact plays and chant slogans, some of which came back to her from childhood as she spoke to me, of which she performed the following with great gusto: 'British *samrajyabad dhangsho hok*' (Down with British imperialism); '*Tebhaga pratha chalu karo*' (Start the practice of tebhaga); '*Langol jaar, jomi taar*' (The land belongs to the tiller); '*Lal jhanda ki jai*' (Hail the red flag); and 'Nij khamare dhan tolo' (Bring the paddy to your own yard).

Anwara Begum's account from the neighbouring village of Dumurtala too testified to a range of roles Muslim women did play in the movement. An activist herself from the time the Tebhaga movement started, just after her marriage at the age of about 16, she pointed out how there would often be stark contrasts even within the same family:

> My sister-in-law was very religious and conservative. She used to read the namaz, so she didn't step out in front of men.... Of course, I read (the namaz too), but my sister-in-law was extremely staunch, never in her life did she appear in front of another man (outside the family) and never spoke to one. Oh ... but my other sister-in-law was dangerous. She used to lead and we followed her. She even used to throw things at the police to stop them from entering the house.

At this point, another woman in Dumurtala joined in enthusiastically to reinforce, 'She used to go from one place to another and urge other women to come with us, how to deal with the police and how to stop them from entering our homes.'

In fact, it is significant that even in villages that did not have women's organizations Muslim women had become politically conscious to a degree that motivated them into courageous resistance in the face of the police. Anwara Begum narrates:

> One day the police, that is the SP [superintendent of police] came to arrest our men. He sat in our sitting room. Her [pointing to her daughter] father was at home, so he ran away to another house. The woman of that house held a cutter in her hands and promised to kill the SP with one stroke [if he dared to touch anyone]. All the villagers had gathered there by then ... they worked under the leadership of

her father, so made the SP rub his nose on the floor and promise not to come to Dumurtala again.... We didn't have one [a women's committee]. May be the other villages had, I am not sure.

In other areas like Mednipur where 100 to 150 Muslim women joined from one village alone, it was a question of fighting ingrained gendered norms. Humour played an important role in getting Muslim women to shed their inhibitions and join the movement in Nandigram. The assertion of a common peasant identity across the Hindu–Muslim divide had already been successful in bringing the two communities together in the area. Bimala Majhi indicated that gentle humour and gradual urging worked to draw in Muslim women into the movement:

> A banana tree had been planted and some bamboo trees, and amidst them a lantern had been lit. Otherwise the zamindar's henchmen would know of the Tebhaga meeting! That was my first [experience] in Nandigram. Then whatever I said, the women would just nod their covered heads—only the long cloth over their heads would shake [laughs].... I said, 'My god, how am I going to get them to fight along with me? [We have to fight] the police... the goondas... how will I fight?' I thought I'd return home the very next day.
>
> But they [the other comrades] tried to convince me all night, and said, 'Why don't you attend a meeting tomorrow night and see how you feel.' When the women got up to go, twenty, twenty-five of them came up and they said to me, "You have to give us the dust of your feet, "*payer dhula*".' The dust of my feet! They thought I was a Brahmin—with my feet so fair! I said, 'No, no, and unless you uncover your heads, you will not be able to see my feet—so how will you touch my feet anyway? I don't accept anyone's *pranam*, so don't do that.' The next day I found there were fifty or sixty of them.
>
> Yes, it was again in the darkness that the meeting was held so that the zamindar's people don't get to know. Gradually, I found that at some meetings about 100 to 150 women—Hindu, Muslim put together—had started attending.
>
> Yes, yes, Muslims were members of the Communist Party. They were farmers and knew if they fought for their rights, they would get land. This is what [enabled the women to come]. We had a slogan, 'Hindu Muslim *bhai bhai* ... [brothers]'. This slogan really worked

in the case of Nandigram. About fifty to sixty of the purdah-clad Muslim women joined us. They fought in the fields....

I was to organize my first protest march—we had to show zamindar that we had so many fighters—otherwise how could we fight? I asked them, 'Will you be able to chant slogans?' And they reacted fearfully, saying, 'God, we have never ever dared even to walk past the zamindar's house. What shall we say?' I said, 'You will have to say:

Hindu Muslim bhai bhai
*Sab krishaker ek ladai*
*Dhan chhara rashid nai*
*Tebhaga pura rashid chai*

Hindus and Muslims are brothers
For all peasants it's the same struggle
No paddy without receipt
We want a full receipt for one-third of the share.

Her encouragement worked, and within five or six weeks she'd succeeded in getting the women to uncover their heads and set out on their first protest march, even chanting slogans:

There were about 200 to 250 women in the procession and the way the slogans sounded they rocked the fields, the village.... Yes, they came, ready, complete with [the ends of their] cloths secured around their waists! They chanted slogans—and with that I felt brave and confident, that I would be able to do what I wanted to do with them.

The term Bimala Majhi used to describe the way they came is the idiomatic *ekebare komore kapad bendhe*, which literally means with the loose ends of their cloths or sarees secured around their waists, ready for action, but also has a powerful metaphorical connotation of unshakeable determination. Underlying her gentle humour was a joyous pride in the women's newly acquired political commitment, for she had made them aware of the possibilities of their own collective strength:

Now, if you were to rebel and were successful, then how many zamindars are there? They will run away and hide themselves somewhere and then you will see you are the ones who will bring home three parts of the yield. They said, 'Will that happen, can there be such a law?' I said, 'Laws don't happen by themselves—you have to create them. How can laws happen by themselves? We will make the laws and that's how the government will agree to them and pass them, and that's how the laws will get implemented. You are the ones who will make the laws.' That's when they found a lot of courage and confidence.

What is significant is that, once the ground work had been done in drawing the Muslim community into the struggle, the resistance to the women stepping out had become weaker. After that, getting Muslim women to join the movement was no different than with women of any other community; it was not a matter of cultural difference so much as one of creating political awareness and confidence.

How radically courageous Muslim women had become in Mednipur became clear in Bimala Majhi's testimony of the time when she was fleeing the police and taking refuge in Muslim villages:

> These women from the Muslim parts [Nandigram] were so brave you cannot imagine, watching them would make shivers run down your spine. I am inside the mosquito net, the police have surrounded the net and they are shining their torches and asking, "Hey! Is Bimala Majhi here?" And they say, 'Look here, you swine, we shall not tell you whether Bimala Majhi is here or not. But if you dare lift the mosquito net with your guns then we will just chop you up with our heshua. You know, how the juice of trees is tapped with the heshua—we will do just that to you … let's see how you touch the net, just try and lift the mosquito net—if you are brave enough.' Three four of these women just pounced on them, I sat inside dead scared, not quite sure whether I would get caught or not. How much room is there to hide inside a mosquito net? But those four women! That comrade, he was a sincere party worker, his name was Nasiruddin, he has died, when I went to Nandigram later he was no more.… His wife, his brother's wife, his mother and his aunt [*kaki*]—just the four of them, and they had the police dead scared, their sickles were shining brightly.… They said to the police, 'You just lift the mosquito net with your guns and we will see to you! Just you lift it once! We don't know if Bimala Majhi is here or not. Who is Bimala Majhi? … So, I was saved that day. The police just left in sheer fear. These women would have chopped them up. So brave they were!

In Dinajpur, an affective emphasis on the experiences of motherhood common to Hindu and Muslim women had also been mobilized to prevent riots that communal *maulvis* were trying to initiate in 1946. Bina Guha explained of the Muslim women:

> They did not understand the impact of riots. They had experienced only the famine. They had not the knowledge that Calcutta was reeling under heavy bloodshed or that Noakhali and other districts were in a terrible state—they were unaware of these. They did not even know what riots were. So, the communal maulvis sent their henchmen to start off riots in their area. That's when they came to know of all this—that Calcutta was drenched in blood. It was at the same time that Tebhaga had started. It was only in Dinajpur that there was no incident of communal riots whatsoever.
>
> [The Hindu women told the Muslim women]: 'When your son's blood flows, so will that of mine.... Yes, your son and my son are the same. Tears will trickle down your eyes if your son is hurt, I am also a mother, the same will happen to me. Do we want this? You also pray to Allah. Then who is responsible for our miserable lot? We do not have enough to eat or to wear, our children have nothing at all. You do not get enough, I also do not get enough. You are deprived and so am I. There are so many restrictions imposed on us women.

In Mednipur, Hindus and Muslims had been mobilized together in their shared identity as peasants. For women in Dinajpur, it was the knowledge of the sufferings already caused in Noakhali and the fate both Hindu and Muslim women would have to face as mothers if they did not resist the riots that finally led them to prevent communal bloodshed in Dinajpur. Ultimately, said Bina Guha, though Muslim women were not allowed to come out of their homes easily, many did join the mahila samiti in Adhiar.

Even the seemingly innocuous practice of rural women opening up their homes to activists not only sustained the Tebhaga movement, it also helped to knit solidarities across regions, castes and ethnicities, and religious communities too. While food continued largely to remain a marker of divides between castes and between Hindus and Muslims, the activists' need for it, as well as for refuge as they travelled through villages and homes in East and West Bengal, did help wear away at least some of the divides of caste and community, as did the need to forge solidarities across these divides in the interests of building a more effective movement against feudal exploitation.

In Mednipur Bimala Majhi talked of finding shelter with the Muslims of Muhammadpur, and also spending a year being sheltered by Muslim families, eating everything cooked by them, including beef:

> I never bothered about who was a sweeper, or about this Hindu–Muslim divide. Though I belonged to an affluent family and was brought up in considerable segregation, I didn't bother about Muslims and Hindus. In Nandigram I lived mostly with Muslim families for a year. They would barbecue beef, mix it with garlic and coriander leaves and eat it—I too was offered the same, and I never bothered as long as things were clean. Never had prejudices like I wouldn't eat stuff touched by them and all of that.

From the Muslim perspective, Riziya Khatun, daughter of the famous peasant leader Nur Jalal and his wife Jennat-Un-Nisa, claimed a total lack of awareness of social divides amongst the activists in Narail in those days. Surmising that she would have been 8 or 9 years old at the time, she said:

> At that time, during the Tebhaga movement, we were quite young, but we never had a notion that Hindu and Muslims or Kayasthas and Brahmins were different people, of different caste, or different from one another.... Even at our house, as I said, Amal Sen, Hemanta Sarkar, Karuna Kishore Biswas ... then Adhir Ghosh, Adhir Dhar, Bamacharan ... many of them used to come to our house, conduct meetings, or have their meals while returning from [other] meetings ... we never thought that they were distant from us.

In fact, Riziya Khatun claimed that even in houses that were not those of prominent activists there was free mixing amongst people of different social backgrounds.

Her account not only detailed how women who remained within the home, like her mother, could often play a critical role in sustaining the movement at the cost of much suffering; it also showed that feeding could become a community affair, with an entire neighbourhood rallying together to provide food for the activists:

> Well, my mother helped in all this ... she herself was from quite a well-to-do family, she had grown up in comfort. But when my father was in [the movement], I also used to see her suffer a lot. I have seen the extent to which my father could be so busy with party affairs and be completely unconcerned about domestic problems of our house. He would suddenly come home with ten people asking mother to cook for them. It could be that there were no rations [at home] ... who would fetch them, how would one arrange for [a meal for so many]—he was uninterested in all that. 'I've left everything, the farm, the land, everything upto you; you have to be prepared always, like I may come home with ten, twenty or thirty people and you have to entertain them' ... he would say, and we would have do it.
>
> So mother would send someone to other houses to get enough rations for cooking a meal for so many people. Sometimes someone would bring in a chicken ... or something. At times there would be fish, cultivated in certain village households, and then eggs.... So maybe my cousins or uncles would go around [informing households] about the number of activists that had come [and need to be fed] ... and they would give them whatever they had. In that situation mother would cook and serve them as late as ten or eleven at night. I've even seen rain falling through our torn roof making it impossible to sit in there ... mother would cover up the torn portion with a tin and then continue preparing the meals.

While the strictures against Hindus eating food touched by Muslims weakened significantly in the Tebhaga areas, they could not be completely done away with. Such taboos across caste lines, however, seem to have been largely erased amongst activists during the movement and this played a big role in forging cross-caste solidarities.

Bonding across castes was facilitated by the dismantling of divisive and hierarchical upper-caste practices of segregated eating and living; and it was further intensified across divides by determined efforts to transform hierarchies of caste into relationships of equality and comradeship. Bimala Majhi narrated an incident illustrating an instance of this when she was arrested from the home of lower-caste Kior fisherfolk who had given her shelter while she was fleeing from the police:

> [The policeman said:] 'You've been caught now. Let me ask you something—how can someone from a good family eat at a fisherman's house?' I said, 'Should there be a difference in the rice just because it's in a fisherman's house? Rice is rice in everyone's house—like blood is always red. How can there be a difference?' The policeman said that they would also be taken in with me because they had dared to shelter a person like me. They should not just be imprisoned. They should be hanged. I said, 'If they must, then let the court decide that, but you cannot hit them.' Then they told the three young men and old lady to go with us and ordered them to pick up my bedding and suitcase and carry them. I said, 'This is your job. These people have committed a great crime by giving me shelter, so the court will try them, but why should they carry my suitcase? You ask someone else to do that, you could take it, or all these people who are your followers can. Why should these poor people carry my luggage all the way to the police van?' Then two village *chowkidar*s [watchmen] were called, one carried my suitcase, the other took my bedding.

So, when cultural hierarchies were evoked by the police, when attempts were made to 'shame' activists for violating social taboos of caste, then honouring comrades from lower castes as equals and shaming policemen instead on grounds of violating laws would become a mode of intensifying the sense of belonging across castes. Social dignity became a powerful component of comradeship for the lower castes as age-old humiliations began to give way to new relationships of mutual respect.

Forging comradeships across ethnic divides, such as those between upper-caste Hindus and the Santal Adivasis of Nachole or the Oraons of Jalpaiguri, also required thoughtful, painstaking work. Urban women, who had begun by travelling to the villages for week-long trips to work with the peasants, started to stay for longer periods. There were also rare ones like Ila Mitra, who, as the daughter-in-law of a wealthy zamindar in Nachole, left the homestead to go and live with the Santals of her area in their bare, impoverished homes for over a year.

Ila Mitra singled out lack of trust as the biggest hurdle in working with the Santals: 'They were so deprived and exploited that they didn't trust any gentlefolk.' She also indicated that compared to the upper-class men of the zamindari who chose to become CP activists, it was far more difficult for a woman married into the family from outside to gain acceptance amongst the Santals. The men, on the other hand, had two advantages—feudal leverage and a history of local organization as CP and krishak sabha members.

> My father-in-law was dead, but Matla Majhi had some connections with him as his family sharecropped our land, and using that connection, my husband got direct access to them. But I had no such advantage and that's why I had to go through a lot of tests to earn their trust. He had been working among them for quite some time by then to have earned their trust. They were leaders in both the krishak sabha and they were Communist Party members also. So they'd been moving around there and working with the peasants for quite some time. That was an advantage they had, which made it easier for the Santals to trust them, but I didn't have any such thing in my favour.

Women who wished to bridge the distances of class and ethnicity to gain even preliminary acceptance in such circumstances required a preparedness for much physical hardship and psychological endurance. Ila Mitra recalls her sustained efforts to win the Santals' trust before she could even begin communicating with them on matters political during the period she lived in the Santal leader Matla Majhi's home:

> My husband [Ranen Mitra], Brindavan Saha, Animesh Lahiri, Azahar Hossain—he was from Ramchandrapur itself—these four were the ones mainly responsible for organizing the peasants in Nachole, and then I landed up there. Since I was the daughter-in-law of a zamindar family, no one [amongst the Santals] talked to me and neither did they believe that I could do anything good for them. Anyway, I continued to sleep with them on the same bed, eating the same stuff with them, wearing the same kind of clothes—dirty clothes as they did—and gradually started to talk about my organization. I managed to earn their trust and they started listening to me. But for one whole year they hadn't trusted me, and sleeping on their dirty beds, sleeping and eating in the same room where they spat also—just like them—I had to earn their trust and it was only then that they started relying on me. However, it was not just

> the Santals—Hindu, Muslim, Santal, Rajbangshi—all the peasants were becoming united against jotedars and zamindars.

It was not, however, a one-way process. This comradeship developed into a sense of mutual understanding and loyalty that crossed epistemic borders and forged a sense of comradeship so deeply ontological that more than twenty-four Santals chose to be brutally murdered by the police rather than betray Ila Mitra. On her part, she refused to succumb to the most painful and humiliating sexual torture rather than give up on her loyalty to them. While there was a residual feudal respect for her as 'Rani Ma', the wife of the young zamindar 'Raja Babu', and for her renunciation of social privilege and hardships endured in living with them, the experience of sharing everyday lives had also enabled a deeper seepage of perspective and mutual belonging between communities that were socially as poles apart as of the rural Santals and the urban communists, resulting in an interweaving of the histories, as I will show in the next chapter. Such identification, epistemic, ontological and historical, formed the basis of unshakeable loyalties in comradeship.

Other urban middle-class women too talked about physical adjustments they made in terms of giving up soap, toothpaste and toothbrush, as use of such 'luxuries' would have reinforced a sense of divide between them as the 'haves' and the peasants as the 'have-nots', rendering the middle-class women 'outsiders' in the eyes of the latter. Manikuntala Sen says:

> After spending a month in the Tamluk sub-division, I came to Midnapore town. Gopenda was at that time the leader of the district committee. The minute he saw me he said, 'What have you done to yourself? Your clothes have turned red in the dust and your hair too. Go and quickly take a bath.' I had not realized that this was the state I was in. I had stopped using soap and toothpaste and toothbrush. This was because boys and girls who stood by the side of the pond observed these little luxuries which would embarrass me. I felt that they might consider me to be an outsider and had thus given them up. Besides, where would I find enough soap to wash clothes with? Even my dusty clothes seemed cleaner than theirs. After a few days we were no longer bothered by the state of our clothes. (2001:93)

These changes signal a restructuring of consciousness, for the urban women had begun to see themselves through the eyes of the peasants too, and realizing that what urban middle-class folks took for granted as necessities may seem luxuries for impoverished peasants. What is also interesting is that such reconstruction of consciousness was not seen as a mere local phenomenon—there were international referents to such processes of negotiating solidarity, especially in the socialist world. This is revealed by the fact that immediately after narrating the previous incident that related to Midnapore, she spontaneously turns, in the very same paragraph, to accounts from China:

> I heard stories about party workers of China from a woman member whose name was Luth-Sui and whose husband was the political advisor of the Red Army. I was told that when Mao Zedong had sent the students to the villages to work with the farmers they were told: 'You should not hang curtains across your windows. If you do a barrier will be created between you and them that will never be removed.' (ibid.:94)

Neither does Sen claim such experiences to be uniquely hers. On the contrary, she stresses such to be the experience of her other middle-class comrades too:

> When she [Luth-Sui] returned home after three years, her mother broke down in tears the moment she saw her. Luth-Sui had to have her head shaved to get rid of the lice. And it took her a couple of months to get rid of the skin disease she had contracted.

And then adds:

> Our middle class women workers had similar experiences while they were working in the villages. I met Gita Mukherjee often when we worked together in Midnapore. She had lost so much weight that she was down to half her size when she was touring the district. (ibid.)

If the village women were to change their mindsets and begin thinking about class politics, then it became incumbent upon the city women to first learn to give up their privileges of class to establish some sense of solidarity. Basic everyday practices had to be renegotiated on the basis of intersubjective reflection about ways in which middle-class urban histories and privileges were implicated in the peasants' histories of impoverishment. If connections were to be made between middle-class urban and impoverished rural women on the grounds of a shared anti-imperialist and class politics, then their own disconnections or differences could not be glossed over as mere 'diversity'; they would have to be negotiated as histories that are co-implicated. Solidarity, thus, was not an easy 'romantic sisterhood'—it was built on practices that showed a relational, historically aware understanding of differences of location, and it was based in an intersubjective, 'self-reflexive and comparative praxis'.[3]

Sen also narrates another instance of a poignant realization of differences of perception across class, revealing that what may be aesthetically pleasing to a middle-class urban woman could well spell disaster to a rural woman:

> Luth-Sui spoke of how she had seen the blood-red sunset sky and said: 'Oh, what a beautiful red sun,' but the peasant woman had not responded. After a while one of them said, 'It won't rain tomorrow too, the fields and farms will be so dry and will burn.' Luth-Sui realized that these people did not have the time to appreciate such beauty. She felt very ashamed thinking of her inability to share their worries. (ibid.)

Manikuntala Sen narrates this in clear identification with Luth-Sui and her experience. And her relating to this acknowledgement of ignorance and shame at the inability to understand another's problems reveals a humility and a desire within Sen too to learn from the peasant woman's experiences, to learn to understand reality from her standpoint, to share her problems.[4] Such critically self-reflexive intentionality, and the readiness to shed the exclusivity of one's privileged middle-class perspectives and share another's burdens, shows a desire for an extension of self in solidarity with the peasant woman.

Even more powerful a sense of bonding was forged through

[3] See Mohanty (2003) for a theorization of cross-cultural and cross-class feminist solidarity, and Dalmiya (2007) for an illuminating discussion of this.

[4] See Dalmiya (2007) for an elaboration of the notion of relational humility and its critical importance for forging feminist solidarities across hierarchical social divides.

experiences of the peasant women's commitment to the movement that had translated into deep respect and love for the activists. Rani Dasgupta recalled an incident that took place in the house of a peasant woman of Dinajpur who was sheltering her and Gurudas Talukdar:

> Let me tell you about an incident of a certain day. They were not giving me anything to eat. It was well past the scheduled time. I could see no signs of their cooking, even their children were roaming around naked. I was wondering what was going on. Then they served Gurudasda and me. Gurudasda said, 'Hey ...'—he used to stay there ... so he called the woman by her name and said—'Hey, bring your cooking pot here. Let me have a look at it.' She said, 'Oh don't bother ... you eat'.... He said, 'No, bring the urn.' It was found that the urn had nothing left. Even the children wouldn't eat. Then Gurudasda and I gave back our meal.
>
> Yes, somehow, they managed our food. Somehow, they managed to get a little rice so that we could eat. Such love and affection drew me to them.

If the urban women had once found food for the famine-stricken rural women to keep them alive, now it was the latter often going without, and depriving their children too, to keep their urban comrades fed and active. These were changes wrought in inward reflective processes that had laid the foundations of a genuine, deeply felt, *antarik* solidarity across the divides of class and privilege. Such dynamics of solidarity, as well as the experience of political activism—of layers of processes of much desired personal transformations in relation to dignity, equality, sexuality and conjugality in the movement—brought to it the genuine, inward quality that antarikata represents, and it buttresses the massive and qualitative political transformation that took place in the fields of Tebhaga that Abani Lahiri called the 'political renaissance of Bengal'.

## Conclusion: The Nature of Political Agency and Comradeship

Abani Lahiri, speaking from a broad political canvas, stated: 'It was the democratic character of the movement that inspired women to participate. It dealt with *every aspect of their lives*, extending beyond simple partisan lines' (emphasis added).

The 'magic' of the times, thus, lay not only in the women's experiences of personal, subjective growth and self-fulfilment, or peace, expressed in terms such as ananda and shanti.[5] At the subjective level, the participation of many must have stemmed from a memory of concrete and profound experiences of hunger and shame, and loss of children and family during the famine, and the recognition that these were 'man-made', due to the role of the jotedar, hoarder and empire. The fact that three years later the root causes of the hunger and sexual exploitation had not been addressed fed into the sense of political outrage that fuelled the Tebhaga movement. Yet, the peasant women's disposition to extend care to travelling or fleeing activists, urban women's impetus to nurture peasant women through practices of teaching and sharing knowledge and political perspectives, and women's propensity to forge relationships of various kinds across gendered and other social divides, were all sustained, along with the outrage, by the political institutions of the krishak sabha, MARS and the CP.[6] The prevalence of these subjective dispositions of women were critical for the development of a peasant movement, as also the fact that they were sustained by the three critical political institutions functioning in the villages, which created the grounds for hopes of a significant sociopolitical transformation that drew both urban and rural people to the movement. For most, then, political activism also related to the sense of personal, subjective transformations, and for women especially to the sense of political agency that they acquired.

The extraordinary transformations of subjectivity that shaped both women's lives and the sense of comradeship in the movement call for a redefining of the very notions of political agency. Political movements are usually theorized in terms of conflicting social and economic forces, contestations of power, strategies deployed and the nature of domination or resistance. The Tebhaga women's narratives

[5] The first two articulated by Poko Oraoni and Bina Guha, and the last two by Phuli Goldar.

[6] See Dalmiya (1997:316): 'Dispositions needed for social justice—not virtues or character types in the abstract, but as they are sustained by material practices—need structural configurations, political institutions that can keep them in place.'

add a valuable dimension to such theorizations by foregrounding the importance of *processes* of forging solidarities between political subjects across social divides; processes that are crucial to any democratic movement in which communities of people chose to come together and fight together, but are seldom discussed.

As Mohanty (2003:8) asserts, 'History, memory, emotion, and affectional ties are significant cognitive elements of the construction of critical, self-reflective, feminist selves... and towards envisioning democracy and democratic collective practice.' She adds that such democratic practice also involves 'the recognition that experience of the self, which is often discontinuous and fragmented, must be historicized before it can be generalized into a collective vision' (ibid.:122). The political agency of the Tebhaga women, expressed in these very terms, was variously layered, comprising subjective dispositions such as outrage at injustice, sensitivity to loss of dignity, caring, nurturing and readiness to endure hardships, and renounce social privilege. It also involved the cultivation of intersubjective skills of relating and caring for another across social divides, and an 'inter-historical grasp of particular social locations' (Dalmiya 1997:317), as is evident in the narratives and actions of Manikuntala Sen, Ila Mitra and others. Such solidarity also comprised a self-reflexive and comparative praxis across differences of location and social hierarchy. The Tebhaga women, thus, went beyond any notions 'romantic sisterhood' to forging solidarities that were sensitive to historical differences and comprised both 'a political and an ethical goal' (Mohanty 2003:3).

The ethic of care of the famine period continued to inform the relationships between urban and rural women in the work of educating and reinforcing the political consciousness of the latter in thousands of rural homes across Bengal. Other new modes of comradeship also developed, in terms of inward, self-reflexive processes of relating across social divides. When urban and rural women came together, it was through cognitive struggles to understand the other not merely as individuals, but as historically constituted women. The nature of their intersubjectivity was grounded in their histories of privilege and oppression. What was unique also was the acknowledgement of the place of intimate personal needs and desires not only in conjugality but also in comradeship. Such dynamics of interiority, that facilitate the forging of cross-cultural and intimate solidarities, that in turn can issue radical challenges to oppressive forms of power, rarely find place in notions of political agency.

Central to their experience, then, was a rare sense of collectivity, of intersubjectivity, expressed in terms such as 'magic' and 'mazaa'. This magical sense of fusion alluded to unique interpersonal, social and inter-historical experiences of relating across class, caste and religion, underlying the coming together of the urban and rural women, of the camaraderie of Mondal, Haldar and Namasudra women with Muslim women in Mednipur, Kakdwip and Narail respectively, the absolute commitment of Ila Mitra to the Santals in Nachole, and the radical openness of Rani Dasgupta to the Rajbangshis of Dinajpur and Kalyani Dasgupta to the Oraons in Jalpaiguri.

This 'magic' was not limited to a phenomenological perception—it had referents in concrete political processes that were simultaneously deepening and expanding the interiority of its subjects, across the historical divides of urban and rural, and with growing knowledge of the relation of international events to their lives too. Such intersubjective joys and expansion of interiority as these women experienced went beyond the personal to an inter-historical level. It was a solidarity structured around sincere engagement with the differences of social location and history.

Oral narratives of the Tebhaga women allow us to access that source of comradeship or universality or ontological identification across class, caste and community which enabled women from diverse contexts to own up to a difficult struggle that ended in brutality for some, loss for others and yet enabled some others to live on to essay political roles. In this sense, this is about the conditions for an expansive comradeship that women could own up to, and ways of bringing together the personal and the political that is not usually found in the conventional ways, individual and collective, in which we access the public and remake it to be ours.[7]

These relationships and the transformations they catalysed invested the political consciousness of collective identity with an

[7] This observation was worked out in a conversation with V. Geetha.

ontological sense of solidarity, which sustained the movement's belief in itself. And that women consciously and repeatedly chose to emphasize these intersubjective values of nurturing, caring and expressive relations in a world of political struggle has also to be acknowledged and understood as a privileging of ethical feminist values and choice. There was, thus, an epoch-making transformation: from a limited logos of masculinist revolutionary politics, and its suppression of the natural logic of human desire and relationships, as evident in Telengana and later the Naxalite movement too, to a conscious liberation of hitherto underrated psychological values, validated by the 'feminine' aspects of culture.[8] Political comradeship in the movement had acquired a uniquely layered sense of antarikata, and an ontological sense of bonding, underlined by ethical and liberating affective values.

[8] See Bandyopadhyay's (2008) feminist critique of the Naxalite movement and Stree Shakti Sangathana (1989) for a powerful indictment of the masculinist suppression of personal and sexual desire in these two movements.

# 5

## '*Atiter Jed*' The Persistence of the Past The Santals and the Times of Revolution*

Something curious happened in Nachole, Bangladesh, on 5 November 1996. The borders across India and Bangladesh, Santal tribal and upper-caste Hindu, rural and urban, impoverished and middle class, became irrelevant as over 100,000 Santals, men and women, turned up from across the country, to welcome a 71-year-old woman from India. She was an urban communist of upper-caste Hindu origins, and none of them had ever set eyes on her before. Yet, she was their leader. The occasion was the fiftieth anniversary of the Tebhaga movement, and Fazle Hussein Badshah, a prominent left leader of the area, described it thus:

> Tribal women had dressed in their best clothes. They had decked up with flowers in their hair—they looked upon it like a festival, and they had come to pay homage to Rani Ma, whom they looked up to as the goddess of their dreams.[1] When she went to the stage,

[1] 'Rani Ma' literally means queen-mother, that is, one who has the interests of her protectorate at heart.

* An earlier version of this chapter appeared in the *Economic & Political Weekly*, 14(33):53–59.

everyone stood up with *ulu-dhvani.*[2] Even the men—they came in their best dresses, in their traditional costumes with their traditional things like *dhol* [double-headed drum], bow and arrow, spears. We saw great emotion in these people. They were waiting for the orders of Rani Ma. They wanted to relive the days of the revolt.[3]

The woman was Ila Mitra, a CP leader of the Santals in the Nachole revolt during the Tebhaga peasants' movement from 1947 to 1950.[4]

[2] A cry of welcome, a traditional form of greeting amongst the Santals and other communities in Bengal, specially during festive occasions. It is noteworthy that *ulu-dhvani* is also a Santal warcry.

[3] The Nachole revolt, of which Ila Mitra had been a leader.

[4] Ila Sen was born into the upper-caste Hindu family of a middle-class government officer in Calcutta in 1925. She graduated with a B.A. degree in Bangla literature, with honours, in 1944 from Bethune College, Calcutta. While this was not unusual for middle-class urban women of her time, what was extraordinary was that she was also an accomplished swimmer, basketball player and junior champion athlete of Bangla presidency from 1935 to 1938. A star in the world of sports in the 1930s, Ila was the first Bengali woman to be selected to represent India in athletics for the 1940 Olympics in Japan. However, the Games were never held because of World War II.

In 1941 she joined a girl students' committee that was set up for the first time within the students' federation and become a member of their study group. Later, after seeing hundreds of people dying in the famine of 1943, she started to work in the public food kitchens of MARS and eventually joined the Communist Party in 1944, recommended by two of its women members, Manikuntala Sen and Kamala Mukherjee. Ila did not come from a communist background and her involvement in politics ran counter to the wishes of her family. In 1945, her wedding was arranged with Ramendranath Mitra who belonged to a zamindar family of Ramchandrapurhat in Nawabganj district, but was, quite providentially, also an organizer of the communist movement in Maldah and a district president of the krishak sabha.

It was a typically conservative aristocratic household and, as a daughter-in-law, Ila found her mobility severely restrained. However, within six months of marriage, she had found her way out, first by starting a school in the home of Altaf Mia, a Muslim friend of her husband's, in a Muslim majority area of the region. The sudden arrest of her husband's comrade Sitangshu Moitra, in 1946, caterpaulted her into organizing the people of the area, and ultimately going underground to escape the police. Fleeing to avoid arrest, and staying over at people's houses during the nights, Ila ultimately found her way to Nachole, and joined her husband who had been actively organizing peasants there. Nachole was a predominantly tribal belt. Most of the peasants here were Santals and one of them, Matla Majhi, was their leader.

The year 1947 had marked the emergence of the nation-states of

---

Being Ramen Mitra's wife, however, did not guarantee acceptance for Ila. Living in Matla Majhi's home, with his wife and family, she had to work hard at winning the confidence of the Santals on her own grounds.

Ila Mitra took on leadership of the Santals in the Nachole revolt against the state, at the forefront of a movement spearheaded by the CP in an armed struggle. As a Hindu fighting the Muslim League government in a Muslim majority nation of East Pakistan, and a woman daring to challenge a heavily patriarchal establishment, she was an exceptional figure. As an activist who commanded the loyalty of an entire tribe and a movement, she embodied a concrete political force to contend with.

The yet undivided CP, which had virtually withdrawn the Tebhaga movement in November 1947 (Umar 2003:37) in order to extend its support to the Congress and Muslim League regimes in India and Pakistan, had, by March 1948, launched an armed revolutionary struggle against the two nation-states (Surjeet 1984:ii; Umar 2003:43). The Tebhaga movement in Nachole too turned militant, and the violence of the Nachole revolt was exercised under clear instructions.

On 5 January 1950, the officer in charge (OC) of Nachole police station and his constables attacked Chandipur, which was the strongest base of the Tebhaga movement in that district. The local Santals issued the customary warning signals—a red flag atop a pole and the sound of drums (*madal*), heeding which hundreds of villagers arrived at the spot. This was the phase of the armed rebellion, when the CP was following the Ranadive line, and there were standing instructions to kill any policemen if they should attack. The OC and five constables were captured and consequently killed by the armed Santals after having opened fire on them.

On 7 January, nearly 2,000 soldiers headed for Nachole from Amnura, setting fire to twelve villages on the way. This initiated a mass exodus, and Ila Mitra, one of the last to leave, finally fled with the last 300 to 400 Santals of Chandipur village, dressed as a Santal woman herself. When they reached a spot near Rohanpur—there were police camps everywhere—a group of police surrounded and arrested her and Brindaban Saha, along with sixty to seventy of her companions. Many other Santals, and leaders like Azhar Hossain and Animesh Lahiri were arrested from other fleeing groups. The Nachole revolt marked a massive exodus of the Santal population from the district across the border to Gajol and Habibpur in Malda district of West Bengal, already inhabited by other Santal communities. Those arrested were subject to brutal torture, and it is estimated that approximately 70 to 100 of them were killed over the next few days, but not one state witness could be found amongst them who was ready to identify Ila Mitra. Subject to repeated gang-rape and torture, Ila Mitra later presented her testimony in court, which was not printed in any newspaper, but widely circulated in the form of leaflets. Her case was covered by the media both in East Pakistan and West Bengal. She was ultimately released on parole for treatment in 1951 and crossed the border into West Bengal, where after a long recovery period, she worked for an M.A. degree in Bangla, became a college lecturer, and renewed

India and Pakistan, and the division of Bengal by an international border. It had also ushered in an era of escalating violence between the contesting forces of the nation-state and the armed revolution of the left. For large numbers of poor peasants, independence meant little more than a transfer of power from the British to the new government of India. The betrayal of the promises of independence for peasants and workers began to resonate in the left's slogan '*Yeh azaadi jhuthi hai*' (This freedom is a farce) right across India and led the still undivided Communist Party to launch an armed revolution in 1948 under the leadership of Ranadive right across the borders of India and Pakistan.[5] The Tebhaga peasants' movement, which had earlier had an anti-feudal and anti-imperialist thrust, now developed an anti-state dimension too. It began targeting jotedars, zamindars and state personnel such as the police, adopting the violent tactics of armed struggle in the places where it continued. At the same time, the newly emergent states of India and Pakistan unleashed blatant state violence in determined moves to contain the groundswell of peasant movements. The politics of class, caste and ethnicity, which had so far been camouflaged by communalism, became manifest in official police and military violence. The violence of the armed struggle and the crackdown of the state on the CP together succeeded in ensuring that the Tebhaga movement had virtually petered out by 1950.

This was Ila Mitra's first visit back to Nachole, and she had not been in touch with any of the Santals in the years that had intervened when she had made her home across the border, in Calcutta. While the upcoming fiftieth anniversary celebrations of the Tebhaga movement had been much publicized both in Bangladesh and West Bengal, there had been no special efforts made to rally the Santals to

---

her political activity as a member of the Pashchimbanga Mahila Samiti and the CP, eventually also becoming a Member of the Legislative Assembly. She died in Kolkata in October 2002.

[5] In Bengal, the common form of the slogan was 'Yeh azaadi jhutha hai', with 'azaadi' sliding, clearly unintendedly, into the masculine gender. This inattentiveness reflected, tangentially, the absence of any gendered distinctions in the Bengali language.

attend this gathering. Narrating her own efforts to locate the reason for this massive turnout, Ila Mitra said:

> I asked the organizers too, but they told me, 'We don't have much contact [with the Santals] in Nachole any more.' The national committee was formed with seven different parties together, and they all said, 'We have no contacts in Nachole any more. We've just distributed a leaflet; we've not even been able to go inside'.... The organizers themselves were surprised [at the turnout]; they said: 'We hadn't done any publicity at all.' When we have a party meeting, we go to the people repeatedly to ask them to come, and then we bring people over ourselves. Here, no one had gone to bring anyone over, but they were all there. Not just the Santals of Nachole, but from adjacent areas also—they'd all come.

The air was rent with cries of 'Rani Ma has arrived!' as the intensity of jubilation and the size of this gathering, the largest ever in history of the disinherited and oft-dislocated Santals, left government officials, political activists and ordinary citizens from both India and Bangladesh stunned. What was even more inexplicable was this appearance of a new generation of Santals, the one following those whom Ila Mitra had fought with almost half a century ago, 'reliving' the days of a revolt as if time had collapsed unto itself. Far less the revolt, they had not even participated in the Tebhaga movement, yet they were waiting to be led by Rani Ma 'again'.

Ila Mitra's own perception of this event was as follows:

> I was very anxious before going to Nachole. Nobody is left there. Everybody has only heard the story. I went with all these apprehensions in my heart. But the day I went there, there was a strike. In spite of that there were over 100,000 people.... They had circulated some leaflets stating that I was coming. Many Santals came after hearing the news of my arrival. Women dressed specially for the occasion, thousands of women came. There were lakhs of people everywhere. It was a peculiar feeling. When others delivered their speech, nobody listened. There were a number of policemen who controlled the crowd otherwise there would have been a stampede. But when I stood up to deliver my speech, there was pin-drop silence....
>
> My husband had told me, 'Don't go to Nachole if you find that

> difficult.' That's because the memories of Nachole are not good at all—we lost everything we had, the Santals had their houses burnt down, were evicted and lost everything—so we were a little apprehensive about what'd happen in Nachole.... Anyway, there was some strike in that area that day, yet these trucks were all lined up and there were people streaming in from every corner—you can see from this snapshot and you'll be able to understand even more clearly if you see the [video] cassette. When I say a lakh, I'm actually making an understatement—there were more than a lakh.... Santal women probably comprised more than half the people there. Normally, they wear dirty clothes, but that day they were all dressed in clean clothes, had flowers in their hair.... Why it happened this way is a question even I have.

Ila Mitra's leadership of the Santals in Nachole during the Tebhaga movement, and her arrest and resistance to state violence in East Pakistan have become legendary on both sides of the border. Disseminated in historical and biographical accounts, testimonies, essays, pamphlets, fiction, poetry and songs, these narratives comprise images of a woman's body repeatedly brutalized and torn into in the war waged by a newly emergent nation-state against its communists and tribal peasants.[6] They are simultaneously eulogistic accounts of Ila Mitra's resistance and her refusal to betray her comrades, including the Santals. These popular political and literary constructions thematize her life in the context of heroic communist leaders, feminist resistance and the political sexual torture of women activists. Building up on the resistance of a Bengali woman to the dominant West Pakistani government, some also depict her as an icon of the *bhasa andolan* or language movement, waged by the Bangla-speaking majority of East Pakistan against the imposition of Urdu as the official and national language by West Pakistan. The other significant dimension of these tracts comprises an extraordinary narrative of recovery wrought by

[6] See Kamal (1996) for a historical account of Ila Mitra's role in the Nachole revolt, and Begum (1987) for a biographical account of her life. See *Aparajeya* (1996), *Samaj Chetana* (1997) and *Chalar Pathe* (1997) for testimonial essays by Ila Mitra; *Samaj Chetana* (1996), and Telengana Tebhaga Subarnajayanti Publication (1997); and books by Das (1996), Dutta (1985) and Isma (1996) for heroic and hagiographical accounts and poems dedicated to her. For a fictional account, see Selina Hossain's 1989 novel.

the collective therapy of writers, poets, singers and comrades who brought her back to an active life again through renditions of poetry, song and a shared political commitment. And across fifty years, these give way to a contemporary deification of this leader ranging from hagiographic narratives to postage stamps.[7]

The most widely circulated and violent narratives relating to the Tebhaga movement are of the sexual torture of Mitra by the new East Pakistani state. She is the most written about leader of the Tebhaga movement; yet, paradoxically, no historical account has been able to offer an adequate explanation for this unprecedented event of 1996, or for the deep-rooted historical and political loyalties at work between her and the Santals, literally bracketing almost half a century of no contact. There are many extraordinary facets of this history that are still beyond comprehension and the need to find some way of understanding them initially formed the motivation of this analysis. Why did over sixty Santals succumb to police torture and death rather than betray their leader's identity? How and why did Ila Mitra find the strength to survive sexual torture and renew her commitment to active politics? Why was there such an unprecedented turnout of Santals to welcome her back half a century later with a combined fervour of past histories and future imperatives?

Ila Mitra and the peasants' commitment to the ideals of the CP and the hold of the passion that characterized the latter in the late 1940s and very early 1950s is one of the most obvious reasons for the first two. However, it clearly does not explain the third, the massive turnout of Santals to welcome her back after half a century, because the communist parties of Bangladesh themselves admit that they did not have a strong base amongst the Santals at this time. Since these three facets of this history are integrally connected, commitment to the CP, however intense, falls short of providing a satisfactory

[7] A postage stamp was issued by the government of Bangladesh, during her visit on the fiftieth anniversary celebrations of Tebhaga. Maleka Begum's biographical narrative, *Ila Mitra* (1987), a documentation of Mitra's activism and letters, as well as of poems and fiction centring around her, takes on hagiographic dimensions too in its framing of her resistance as sacrifice and referring to her home in Kolkata as a pilgrimage centre for Bangladeshis. The same is characteristic of innumerable essays and pamphlets on her.

explanation. It was evident that some other powerful rationale was at work, and it was one that had to be located in Santal history. This chapter is a cross-reading of Mitra's own narratives with those of other activists, and with the history of Santal movements. It explores the relation between the Santals' sense of temporality, memory and history, and suggests that the lack of explanation of these events is due to their rooting in processes of memory and history in ways that lie beyond the ken of mainstream historiography. What this analysis ultimately arrives at is an understanding of an extraordinary process of political *and* subjective identification, across urban left and rural Santal historical imperatives, that took place in a rare conjuncture of Santal temporality and communist teleology in the Nachole revolt.

On another level, while discerning the multiple layers of the gendered self of a left leader in a time of immense transition and combat, this chapter also explores the impact of the 'frameworks of repressive subjectivity' that were put in place during this period of extreme violence.[8] The pervasive violence and intense conflicts of class, caste and caste, that continued to mark the consolidation of nation-states after partition, also cast people within frames of repressive subjectivity, structured both by the nation-state from above and by the armed struggle from below. How these frames were broken (or not), and what these acts signify, not just in the past but also in the very act of narration, carry deep implications for both the past and the present—and these historical and cultural implications go beyond the agency of Ila Mitra as an individual activist.

## Sexual Violence and Resistance: Engraving and Rupturing the Boundaries of the Nation-State

Comprehending the political rationale for the imposition of such suffering as Ila Mitra was subject to is important for understanding

[8] I draw upon Dori Laub's approach to narratives of the holocaust, specifically his analysis of testimonies in relation to the functioning of 'frameworks of repressive subjectivity'. See Laub (1992:62) for a discussion of how Auschwitz survivor testimonies of resistance and affirmation of survival actually break the frames of death and repression.

the ways in which the new nation-state constructed its boundaries, and for mapping the precise hierarchies and subjectivity that it reinforced and that ultimately defined it. It is equally important to take into account this political rationale in order to comprehend the significance of Mitra's own response to the workings of state power, specially in terms of its rupturing of these very boundaries.

Since the army succeeded in razing to the ground virtually all the villages of Tebhaga activists in the area, and it was followed by a mass exodus of Santals to India, the revolt had been crushed. The threat of the CP as well as the Santals had virtually been controlled. The Hindu woman who had transgressed all norms to actively lead a militant left tribal movement against a Muslim-dominated state too had been arrested, and her ability to jeopardize the state had also been contained. The crisis was over. *After* this, the police turned on Ila Mitra herself. There were no immediate concrete threats or fears that can explain the brutality with which she was abused through the weeks that followed her arrest. The reasons for this seem to lie in the realms of anxiety and hatred that formed the subconscious of the new nation and defined it. Thus, sexual violence became a privileged mode for inscribing the boundaries of the nation-state both within and without. Ila Mitra's body became the ground for the newly emergent nation-state's confrontation with multiple forces, communist, Santal and Hindu, all of which extended across the borders of the nation and were perceived simultaneously as an internal as well as an external threat to its 'integrity.'

Although the Santal uprising had been crushed in Nachole by the time of Mitra's arrest, yet the threat for the Bengali upper and middle classes ran much deeper than the immediate political level. As Banerjee (2002:244) has argued, in her readings of Bankimchandra and Bhudev Mukhopadhyay, the Santal as 'primitive' became the necessary figure that explained the decline and *disunity* of the colonized nation:

> Santals seemed indispensable as the best agricultural and forest-clearing labour.... Santals also rebelled time and again against the Bengal moneylenders and the colonial state.... The so called 'primitive' and non-historical Santal thus represented a perpetual threat to the Bengali middle class certainty that the 'primitive' was

> always already suppressed at the originary moment of the nation's history in the foundational battle between the enlightened *arya* and the dark *anarya*.

The Santal was perceived not just as the primitive other, and thus a threat to the homogeneity of the nation; s/he was also a potential threat to its unity and integrity.

In addition, there was the Hindu dimension. Pakistan had been constitutionally envisaged as a secular state, but as a Hindu woman, Ila Mitra was squarely located in the realm of symbolic anxieties of the new nation. Communal polarization in Bengal had been sharpening since the 1920s and 1930s. Also, the violent history of the communal riots of 1946 was too recent a memory for any secularism to succeed overnight. The fact that East Pakistan was a Muslim majority nation could not quell the powerful residual fear and hostilities of the preceding decades. And Mitra's own narration confirms this:

> Two things I must say here. On that side, there was a great effort to spread communal tension. There was a great attempt at projecting our case as communal also as many of us were Hindus and the police persons killed were Muslims. So there was quite an attempt to present it as a communal case. This is a very important aspect of the case—they had tried to buy many Muslims with money to give false witness and say that Rani Ma was the one who'd given the order to kill the police, and that she had done it because she was a Hindu. What's striking is that they couldn't get a single Muslim witness. Not a single Muslim witness had come, despite all these temptations—they were poor after all. But not a single Muslim witness had come. That's why they couldn't dub it communal. Communal tensions were high and there were riots somewhere or the other everyday. Noakhali had such a big riot. If they had managed to represent it as communal, it would have created a burning inferno of riots. But they didn't manage to get a single witness. The other thing they'd tried was to get from among the Santals—they must have thought that they were so poor and illiterate, so simple-minded that it would be easy to buy them off—was to get a *rajsakshi* [an official witness who gives false statements in favour of the state]. You must know that in many big cases rajsakshis are procured, but for this one they couldn't get even one. This also was something unprecedented—

> there was no rajsakshi and no Muslim witness either. This was because Hindus and Muslims had fought together. In the Nachole area, that is what the strength of the Tebhaga movement was—what the zamindars and jotedars were really afraid of was this unity of Hindus and Muslims.

The repeated torture of Ila Mitra thus carries valence at multiple symbolic levels, all condensed into the figure of one woman. Assertion of any one of the identities, Santal, communist, Hindu and woman, would jeopardize the homogeneity of a patriarchal Muslim majority state, and Mitra represented all combined in one, either by political affiliation or by origin. The power of this figure was also different from the earlier symbolic linkages of woman with nation and oppositional community, because she was not just the enemy *without*—in her converged all the multiple threats to the new nation, and she stood for the condensation of all the enemy forces *within* too that must be purged to ensure the homogeneity, integrity and stability of the nation. The relentless, repetitive nature of the torture she was subject to is an index of the intensity of the obsessive fear, the 'primitive' challenge to middle-class certainty, the threat of class warfare, as well as of the paranoia of the communal other. In such a situation, Ila Mitra's articulations and determined resistance were extraordinary in that they signified a 'breaking of boundaries' that not only unsettled established constraints of gender and sexuality, but also revealed the workings of not merely ideological solidarity, but a deep *ontological identification* with the Adivasi that has rarely found place in our political culture.

## Memory and the Structuring of Self and History

### ♦ *Contradictory Layering of Self* ♦

Complex layers of self and memory interweave in Ila Mitra's narrative; and readings of these allow for a more nuanced understanding to emerge, both of the historicity of her past, as well as of the time of her narration. The understanding of oral historians, that collective memory highlights what *can* be said, while individual memory becomes significant because it often indicates what *cannot* be said easily in particular times, is of considerable import here. The dynamics of Ila Mitra's own narration—the silences, ambivalence, the renewed wonderment, as well as the paradoxes inherent in her narrative—all contribute to an understanding of the texture and impact of that period.

One version of herself that Mitra recounted was clearly that of an upper-class, upper-caste urban woman who laboured with sincerity as a communist to win the trust of peasants. Yet, her narrative of declassification was simultaneously punctuated with an underlying squeamishness about the Santal's lack of cleanliness that echoed an upper-caste Hindu discourse of purity and pollution, upon which rests the edifice of the caste system. Her unapologetic upper-caste distaste of the Santals' lack of cleanliness, repeated at various times in her narrative, was further underlined by a hierarchical assumption of knowledge that is extremely Brahminical, and may also imply an assumed unidirectional hegemony of the CP in her structuring of political hierarchy, for she clearly saw herself as imparter of political knowledge and the Santals as the listeners. It is evident that the unity that was forged between her and them was not under any illusion of Mitra being a declassed subject to the point of assuming the identity of a poor Santal peasant. She clearly continued to be, for them, an upper-class zamindar family's daughter-in-law. As Ramen Mitra pointed out in our interview with him too, as a zamindar, he was to them Raja Babu and she Rani Ma.[9]

This indicates that the social hierarchy, of residual feudal structures of relationships of parent and child that had been prevalent between the more benign zamindar families and their peasants, played a role in securing for Ramen Mitra, and specially for Ila Mitra, the unique place of confidence she finally acquired as an upper-class urban woman amongst the tribals. It is clear, however, that this could not have happened but for their genuine economic declassification, and a sharing of hardships and common political goal with the Santals.

[9] Narrated to me by Ila Mitra and confirmed by Ramen Mitra. Mesbah Kamal (1996:47) is of the opposing view that Ramen Mitra was not addressed as Raja Babu. Even if this is the case, it still holds that Ila Mitra would be referred to as Rani Ma by virtue of being a daughter-in-law of the zamindar's family. The parental connotation of ma is inbuilt into the form of address used for her.

Yet, the Santals' mode of referring to them as Raja Babu and Rani Ma suggests that a relationship of a protectorate with its zamindar and his wife continued to be operative. Discernible here are the workings of a feudal paradigm paradoxically reinforcing, in its own demolition, the new egalitarian forms of political solidarity being forged by the Communist Party in the region.

When asked whether she had gained acceptance with them because she was from the zamindar's family or because she had become part of their struggle, she nodded her acquiescence to both, and in a matter-of-fact manner added yet another dimension—that of being trained for armed struggle herself:

> Yes, they considered that important.... I'd taken this training too, and I could also shoot then.... Tebhaga was a reality there in the Nachole area. What to do in case of direct confrontation—the peasants there, and we too, received training in that—all of us, including me. If the police came with guns, how to snatch guns, how to lie flat on the ground to escape firing, how to shoot—we had training in all that.... We had different names then.... When they finally came to trust me, they accepted me as their Rani Ma and loved me very much. Otherwise, would I ever be have been able to make them listen to me?

Her earlier narration of how she had felt imprisoned in her in-laws' home is a reminder that training in arms was unthinkable for upper-class, upper-caste Hindu women, a large number of whom still remained confined to the *andar mahal* (inner quarters ) of their homes. Yet, the un-self-conscious manner in which she cited her training in armed struggle as another factor of leadership reinforced the sense that accrued through the interviews of many women activists that this had been a period of unprecedented openings for women: rapid transformations in self had been facilitated through their allegiance to the movement and its ideals.

That the violence of armed struggle could be ethically problematic, however, is not something Ila Mitra questioned. She merely explained it as the fervour of the period: In response to a query regarding her role in organizing action against the jotedars, she was outright direct and said, 'Yes. You have to kill them, I told them [the Santals]'.

And to another query as to whether such killings would have been under instructions from the party, she was equally unambiguous and asserted, 'It was the Kakdwip line.'

When asked whether she had speculated on the near certainty of violent retribution and the cycles of violence that one act can initiate, she responded, 'We did not consider things that way ... it was an obsession then. No, we didn't consider things that way.' Violence simultaneously constituted the primary language of political activity, as well as the ideology of the period. In a context where procuring the rights of the disinherited was articulated in terms of a takeover through a violent revolution, violence also constituted the dominant framework of subjectivity, standing in symbolically for the very ideals of the CP. To question the violence was perceived as a questioning of the basic allegiance to the movement itself.

Mitra's sense of the political status she acquired later in electoral politics in West Bengal also demonstrated a continuity between her privileged position as Rani Ma during the Nachole revolt and fifty years later. The first time she returned my call, she left a message saying, 'The MLA [Member of Legislative Assembly] had called.'

Yet, such incongruity does not take away from her commitment. She had suffered determinedly the hardships of declassification and she had refused to be released at the cost of abandoning her political activity despite being subject to the severest forms of torture in prison; she conveyed this conditional offer of release to us with a continuing touch of indignation:

> By the time the United Front ministry was formed, many including Fazlul Haq himself, came over to visit me and then Fazlul Haq told me: 'Go wherever you want to get treated. I'll arrange for money, whether you want to go to London or to America or just to Calcutta—you go for treatment.' The government told me that if I gave them an undertaking that I'd never be involved in politics again, then they would release me unconditionally and also give me back all that they had confiscated—the house and all the property had been confiscated, of course, I was in jail, my husband they couldn't catch, my mother-in-law was there in the house with my infant son, but she was ousted. Our house and everything else had been confiscated. Anyway, I refused to give any such undertaking.

After she set up home in Kolkata, it often served as a shelter for the freedom fighters of Bangladesh in 1970–71 as well as later; and she remained a communist and an activist of the Paschimbanga Mahila Samiti, working with marginalized women till her last days.

The Tebhaga movement had made it possible for thousands of women to step out into the fields of struggle. It had opened up a world of freedom and facilitated radical transformations in their sense of themselves. It had harnessed their potential to shape the political sphere. In fact, one of the recurrent themes of Ila Mitra's narrative is about 'the taste of freedom'. What her narrative also reveals, though, is that these rapid transformations, and women's exposure to the intensely conflict-ridden world of politics, had yet to be negotiated within the self; and maybe even then paradoxes would abound.

It is also precisely because of this extremely contradictory layering of self that I felt compelled to explore the motivations for her solidarity with the Santal peasants, her commitment to the ideals of the Tebhaga movement, and her continued political activity even after a hard-won recovery from the complete psychological breakdown that was a result of the torture.

## ♦ *The Interweaving of Experience and Identity: Ila Mitra, the Santals and the Muslims* ♦

There were various factors that linked this complex subjectivity of the past with that of the present in Ila Mitra's narration. One was her very *uncertainty, about owning her court testimony*, expressed to her biographer Maleka Begum, who in turn conveyed this to me in an interview in Dhaka. Another was her uneasy ambivalence regarding the mode in which to communicate to me her experiences of sexual torture. The third was in relation to Harek, the Santal comrade who had been loyal to her through severe torture and unto death. There was a distinct interweaving of her torture and Harek's when she recalled the experience afresh to me—this was new and had found no that representation in the much circulated and reprinted court testimony.

Maleka Begum's first question when I met her in Bangladesh was whether Ila Mitra had owned her testimony that was reprinted in the former's biography. She said that when she had first taken a copy of the testimony to Ila Mitra in Calcutta in the mid-1980s, she had read it in complete confusion and asked if it was really hers, whether this was what she had said in court. By the time I went to meet Ila Mitra, almost ten years later, she had clearly acknowledged her authorship of this document. This inability to recognize her own testimony earlier could clearly be a consequence of the mental breakdown that she had suffered after the torture. It could have been a natural process of blocking out a painful experience in the interests of survival. However, the confusion could also signify, across this chasm between an earlier self and the present one, a certain anxiety regarding the sexual explicitness of the testimony. For when she narrated to us the hesitation she had had in writing it, she emphasized the difficulty of taking such a step as a married upper-caste Hindu woman, and she did so with an unconcealed awkwardness that continued to unsettle her owning up to it even in the late 1990s. Unease surfaced yet again in her constant vacillation about the mode in which to share her experience of custodial violence—should she recall it afresh, read out her testimony or just hand out a copy of it? Despite her acceptance of it as her own testimony, which she finally decided to read out aloud, her relationship with it continued to be one of unease, not just with the pain of the experience but also the explicitness of it.[10] It was as if

[10] Her testimony goes thus:

I was arrested at Rohanpur on 7 January 1950 and taken to Nachole. When I reached there I was beaten up by the police, and then I was taken to a cell. The SI [sub-inspector] threatened to strip me naked unless I confessed everything about my role in the murder. Since I had nothing to confess, they took away all my clothes and I was kept locked up in the cell completely nude. I wasn't given any food, not even a drop of water. That evening, in the presence of the SI, the constables started hitting me on the head with the butts of their guns. My nose started bleeding. After this, my clothes were returned to me and around 12 at night, I was taken, probably to the SI's [Sub-Inspector's] quarters, but I wasn't very sure of that. There they continued torturing me in different, inhuman, ways in the attempt to extract a confession. My legs were placed between two sticks and pressed hard. Those standing around me were saying that I was being given the Pakistani injection. While this torture continued, I was gagged with a handkerchief. When they failed to get me to say anything, they also began pulling my hair out. After that torture, the constables had to carry me back to my cell as I couldn't stand up any more.

the radical historical rupture of the 1940s and very early 1950s had

---

Inside the cell, the SI ordered the constables to bring four boiled eggs and declared, 'She'll speak now.' After that four to five constables forced me to lie on the ground, flat on my back, and one constable forced a warm boiled egg inside my vagina. I felt as if I was being burnt. I lost my consciousness after this. When I regained consciousness on 9 January 1950 morning, that same SI and some constables came into my cell and started kicking me on my stomach with their boots. Then a nail was driven into my right heel. At this time, in my state of half consciousness, I could hear the SI saying that, 'We're coming back at night and unless you confess, the constables will rape you one by one.' Late at night, the SI and the constables came back and uttered the same threat again. When I refused to say anything, three or four constables held me down forcibly, and one constable really started raping me. Soon after this, I lost my consciousness again. When I regained consciousness on 10 January 1950 morning, I discovered that I was bleeding profusely all over. All my clothes were completely drenched in blood. In that very state I was taken to Nawabganj from Nachole, and at the Nawabganj police station the constables welcomed me with hard blows on my face. I was in a completely bed-ridden state then. So the court inspector and some constables carried me into a cell. I was still bleeding and had a very high temperature. It was most probably a doctor from the Nawabganj government hospital who checked my temperature and found it to be 105 degrees. When he heard about my bleeding, he assured me that I'd be treated with the help of a female nurse. I was also given some medicines and a couple of blankets. On 11 January 1950, a nurse from the government hospital came to check me. I don't know what kind of report she submitted about me, but after she left, my blood-smeared clothes were changed for a fresh sari. This entire period I spent in a cell in the Nawabganj police station, under the treatment of one doctor. I was running a very high temperature, experiencing a lot of bleeding, and also losing consciousness from time to time. On 16 January 1950 evening, a stretcher was brought to my cell and I was told that I had to go somewhere else for treatment. When I said that I could hardly move, I was hit with a stick and forced to get on the stretcher. I was then taken to a different house, where too I confessed nothing, but the constables forced me to sign on a sheet of white paper. At this point, I was running a very high fever and was only half conscious. Since my condition was steadily deteriorating, I was shifted to the government hospital in Nawabganj the next day. But my condition became more critical, and on 21 January 1950, I was brought to the Central Jail in Rajshahi and admitted to the district hospital. At no point of time had I said anything to the police, and I have nothing more to say than whatever I've said in this statement. (Translation of the testimony read out to us by Ila Mitra from Maleka Begum's biography of her.)

enabled a sexual frankness in political discourse that the relatively conservative ethos of the 1990s had again disallowed.

It is also significant that even more than her commitment to the CP, she emphasized the sacrifices of the Santals as motivation for continuing to play an active political role. Harek, the Santal, returned as a symbol and recurring presence in her narrative whenever she reflected upon the source of the strength that had enabled her to maintain her commitment to activism. In the process of exploring the symbolic valence of Harek, one realized that the most striking aspect of her narration lay in the marked interweaving of the torture he had been subject to in her presence, and her own experience of sexual violence.

> They [the peasants] were being beaten up and so was I. I was kept… oh, no, I couldn't see them then. Anyway, this continued—we were beaten up very thoroughly…. I can't tell you the kind of torture that went on [with] these Santals. There was one Santal with us called Harek—this is mentioned in the book [Maleka Begum's biography of her]. When we worked, Harek used to be a habitual latecomer—whatever it be, a meeting or something else—he was always late. So we used to get very angry, and I used to tell him that I wouldn't keep him in the Communist Party any more, that it was just not right to be late when important activities were on. He used to say: 'You'll see that I'll be right there with you whenever any real activity occurs.' I could see … this is one of the things that caused my nervous breakdown … this Harek was being beaten up, and they were only being asked about the guns and to 'admit that your Rani Ma had given you the order and that's why you killed'. Repeatedly. But what was most surprising was that these illiterate, poor Santals—they were being beaten to death, but never said anything other than, 'We don't know her.' I really don't know how this was possible. They were saying, 'We don't know anything; we don't know who she is. Who is she?' It continued like this.

The interweaving of her torture with that of Harek and the other peasants started at this point in her narrative, and was completely new. This had not been part of either her testimony in court or of the various interviews and pieces published. She continued, with her account of the incidents marking a continual shift from him to her and back.

> Harek was down on the ground … the beating he got…. Then, right in front of my eyes, I saw that one came running and kicked hard on his chest just as one kicks a football and Harek died panting. But he never once said that I was Rani Ma and that I was involved in such and such activities. Not one word—I can't tell you what a terrible history this is! This is what … how old was I then—25, 26 … this changed the entire course of my life. I might have broken down or something, but seeing this, this made such an impact on my consciousness… this silent viewing of the whole incident…. Then at night, there was even more severe torture on me. Beating me up, stripping me and then beating up, bringing in my son—he was an infant then…. I saw Harek being thus beaten to death…. Then, at night, I was stripped nude and beaten up severely … raped by the police … the details are here [Maleka Begum's biography of her], I can't tell you all that…. Then my clothes … they call it Pakistani injection—two bamboo poles are tied together like a [pair of] tongs and the legs are pressed with that … then blanket thrashing [beating up severely with cudgels, after wrapping the victim up in blankets so that there are no marks]…. That's why all my limbs are weak…. Anyway, the other peasants and Santals who were picked up were also tortured equally severely…. Their [the oppressors'] demand was that I had to confess to being the mastermind behind the murders … Unless I confessed, they wouldn't stop…. They did not give me even a drop of water…. The torture continued—they kept hitting me with the butts of their guns—I started bleeding…. All my clothes were taken away … Should I read it out? No.

It is significant that this braided narrative followed the broken sentences that had consciously emphasized the impact of witnessing Harek's torture: 'This is what… how old was I then—25, 26 … this changed the entire course of my life. I might have broken down or something, but seeing this, this made such an impact on my consciousness.' While the interweaving itself seems to have been completely unconscious, what it reveals is a restructuring of self after torture in which the torture of the Santals, specially Harek, and her own take on an identical significance. Another level of bonding is created that has the potential to enable her to deal with the survivor's guilt too: the others were tortured because they would not tell; she too was tortured because she would not tell.

What would have been unbearable guilt about them being tortured to death for not betraying her can be lived with only and precisely because she too did not give in to torture. Very shortly thereafter, she also wove into the narrative her own resistance in terms of her refusal to confess despite severe torture and thirst: 'Their demand was that I had to confess to being the mastermind behind the murders... Unless I confessed, they wouldn't stop.... They did not give me even a drop of water.'

In addition to involvement in a joint political praxis, this shared experience of acute suffering inflicted by a common torturer created a bond of identification that surpassed all other barriers of identity and forged an ontological identification between rural Santal and urban upper-caste woman. It also enabled Ila Mitra to deal with the traumatic guilt of the survivor, but what was significant is that this guilt was then transformed into a sense of responsibility in her:

> I don't understand how I got the strength. Earlier I had this jed [stubbornness/determination]. Then I had been very sick for three to four years. In 1958, I joined the college job and then again got involved with a different movement. Because the past stubbornly continued to pervade my heart. This gave me the strength. Atiter jed [the stubbornness of the past]. The way the peasants had struggled for freedom from exploitation, this continues to be my inspiration. It's because of this that I can continue to fight for them, continue to think of human beings [*manush*], despite being in poor health. I had imparted political training to them, but I had learnt a lot from them too. They increased my will power and continue to inspire me. I have told you about Harek. He was beaten to death but did not utter a single word. All this still inspires me.

This incident, which, in her own words, changed the entire course of her life, and created an intimate sense of identification with the peasants, clearly lived on within her as atiter jed. Ila Mitra also referred to the Muslim peasants who were tortured before her but did not betray her, to those Muslims who later kept her alive by either looking after her, like Rahman Saheb, the officer in charge of Nawabganj police station, and Dr Alam, who cared for her after her torture, brought her to India and was consequently demoted for that reason, and also those Muslims who donated blood:

> Because he [Dr Alam] took such good care of me, including bringing me over himself, he had to face demotion. I used to need blood regularly; blood in my body was constantly on the decrease. It was my Muslim brothers who'd then given me blood. That's why I'd once said that I don't know if I still retain any religion, because Muslim blood flows in my body—I'd said this in a speech. After this, I got better, but I still couldn't walk properly. So after nine months in the hospital, I spent some months in Ghatshila. Then when I could walk again, I came back to Calcutta.

Yet, it is the Santals around whom her entire narrative was structured. And the leitmotif of atiter jed punctuated her analysis of her own history. The question that arises next is, what did this past mean to the Santals of the end of the twentieth century, who had not even witnessed this incident, and was there any commonality between their notion of the past and Ila Mitra's that had continued to shape future history even after the Tebhaga movement had died out?

## ♦ *Atiter Jed: The Persistence of the Past* ♦

The term 'jed' actually has wider connotations in Bangla than the English 'stubbornness' or 'obstinacy'. Ila Mitra's use of it was unambiguously positive, more in the sense of the momentum of a persistent force. And the term 'atit' or past was not merely evoked in nostalgic mode; in Ila Mitra's usage, it referred to concrete practices based on certain historical beliefs that inspire commitment and energy. Thus, she indicated that her activism, far from marking a beginning, was a part of an already existing continuum, and was driven by its force.

The continuum she narrated, however, was not, as would be expected, that of communist history. She categorically stated that: 'What happened in Nachole was that the Tebhaga movement or the revolt there was a continuation of Santal revolts.' Her entire account of the Nachole revolt was framed by her account of Santal rebellions. She chose to locate it not within a CP trajectory that traversed both the Bengals, but within a far more localized Santal 'history'—a history that was an ever-returning past that constituted the very *stoff* of the present:[11]

> As I've told you, this was known as the Nachole revolt. Even before the Sepoy revolt, the first serious Santal revolt that occurred in the last century was in 1855—the Sepoy revolt was in 1857—this was two years before that. On 7 April 1855. In 1857, was the Sepoy revolt. The British government had swept this Santal revolt in blood, and thousands of peasants lost their lives. The Nachole revolt faced the same fate. This uprising in Nachole—who were the ones involved? Hindus, Muslims, tribals and Santals were all there, but mainly the Santals. The failure of the revolt in the last century made the Santals leave their homes and migrate to different parts of the country—like Bankura, Birbhum, Malda—they spread to different regions. Though they spread out like that, the terrible atrocities that they had to face in 1855, memories of that continued through oral traditions from generation to generation. The father would tell his son, who would tell his son in turn, and they'd composed songs about that too. Through all this, the memories had travelled down generations and there was always a slow fire burning in their hearts because of the torture back then. And no wonder, because literally thousands of peasants had been killed.
>
> [In] 1932, Santal peasants revolted in demand of an independent Santal province. Though they'd spread out to Malda, Birbhum, etc., the memories of that revolt and the atrocities afterwards were stored in their minds from generation to generation. A fire of revolt always burnt in their hearts. There were songs also, and all this contributed towards keeping the memories alive in their hearts. Then what happened was that the Santal peasants of Malda district revolted in 1932 in demand of an independent Santal province. Let me tell you why that happened. Once upon a time, Santals lived independently in the region where they were born. Then, at some point of time, the jotedars and zamindars came with some papers and claimed that all the land there belonged to them. Santals had been living there for years independently, but these people said that they had the papers to prove that those lands were theirs. The Santals were asked to show papers, which they didn't have. Then they were told that the law was that those who had the papers owned the land and they were

[11] Indicating both substance of history and subject matter of narrative.

threatened that if they refused to accept that, then they would be killed or forcibly evicted as that was the law. The Santals wondered what kind of law that was and they didn't accept this easily. Conflicts continued to occur between representatives of the government or of jotedars and zamindars on the one hand, and the Santals on the other. They used to wonder what sort of people the *bhadralok* were, that they always played with the fate of the Santals.[12] Plots of land that were dense jungles once but were producing golden crops then, those plots were supposed not to belong to them, though they were the ones who'd fought with wild beasts to change these jungles into cultivable land. But all that land then belonged to bhadralok, and the Santal peasants became landless. They were evicted. Naturally, their discontent was constantly on the rise. How were they to live?

What happened in 1930–32 was that the whole of India was swept by waves of freedom struggle and those waves touched them also. They were not conscious enough to understand that freedom meant freedom for the whole country from the British. They thought that they could also agitate for an independent Santal province where they'd rule themselves and regain their land rights.

There was one Santal called Jitu Sardar—I remember this name—he was here and this Jitu Sardar issued a call to all the Santal peasants of Malda district to come together to establish an independent Santal province. They were so strongly mobilized that ... there's a Madina mosque some 8 miles away from Malda town—I was supposed to go there too for a meeting; meetings were being held in many different places, but I couldn't go as I broke my leg before that.... Anyway, they went to that mosque and hoisted a flag of independence there, proclaiming the birth of a free Santal province.

India's freedom struggle was very strong then and Jitu Sardar invited all Santal peasants to join the struggle for freedom. Freedom to them meant an independent Santal province where they'd get back their land rights, and they united and revolted and hoisted the flag of independence in Madina mosque there. But so what if they'd hoisted that flag? They didn't understand the issues of violence or non-violence; they were fighting with sticks and spears, and the police came with rifles, and that was the end of their freedom struggle. They were again drenched in their own blood.

[12] Bhadralok refers to a privileged social class that was historically a product of the British land reforms, trade policies and early colonial education.

> Then again in 1947–48—the source was that movement, which is why I recounted that. This was a long time later, quite a few years, 1932 to [19]48, but the memories were alive. How they had been exploited, how their fathers had been shot dead—all these memories were alive. That's why in 1948 the peasant struggle started once again in Nachole. Sixteen years had passed in the meantime, but the struggling peasants hadn't forgotten anything, and the link between the two struggles was provided by Jitu Sardar. Jitu Sardar was there in this struggle too, and Jitu Sardar's right-hand man, Ramu Sardar, he also played a very big role in this struggle. As in Rangpur and other areas of north Bengal, here too there were jotedars with huge landholdings. Most of them owned some thousands of acres of land. Peasants were peasants in name only. They were allowed to cultivate if it suited the mood of the jotedars, refused if they so pleased. Not only the Santal peasants, Hindu or Muslim peasants too fared no better. Their communities differed, but there was no difference in their class character; they were all equally ruthlessly exploited by the jotedars. The revolt in Nachole started because they remembered their earlier struggle for independence and the way they were mobilized in 1932.

It is significant that Ila Mitra not only located the Tebhaga movement in Nachole as part of the continuum of a Santal past, but also that she slid into a typical 'once upon a time' formula of narration of oral cultures: 'Once upon a time, Santals lived independently in the region where they were born. Then, at some point of time, the jotedars and zamindars came with some papers and claimed that all the land there belonged to them.' Further, she narrated it not from the CP, but from the Santals' point of view: 'The Santals wondered what kind of law that was and they didn't accept this easily.... They thought that they could also agitate for an independent Santal province where they'd rule themselves and regain their land rights.' And in the context of their history of repeated disinheritance, she emphasized the powerful role of oral culture in connecting the Santal insurrection of 1855, the movement of 1932 led by Jitu Sardar and the Tebhaga movement in Nachole in 1948, as well as the importance of Jitu Sardar as a living link between 1932 and 1948: 'Sixteen years had passed in the meantime, but the struggling peasants hadn't forgotten anything, and the link between the two struggles was provided by Jitu Sardar.'

As Jitu Sardar had been the link between 1932 and 1948, she herself was the link between 1948 and 1996. The memory of 1948 was still alive amongst the Santals as inspiration for the return of the past, and of the leader, even as the earlier memories had been kept alive and stoked the 'fire of revolt' that 'always burnt in their hearts'. Her own explanation to herself of the phenomenal turnout of an entirely new generation of Santals fifty years later too took up a place in this Santal history, in identification with them:

> That I'd said myself, that they must have been hearing about it from generation to generation and that's how it's been preserved. The other thing is that I was with them throughout their struggle, I never left; when they were tortured, I was tortured too.

The Santals' relation to the past and history, however, is not one of causal connections, but of the urgency of an unfinished and unresolved past:

> When Santals sang songs of the *hul*, the Santal insurrection of 1855, it was not only because memories of the revolt were a crucial inheritance, but also because the rebellion was not yet completely past.... Invoking the *hul* therefore was not as much of a mobilization of a past for the present—as nationalist history writing was—as it was the question of the unfinished nature of the past. (Banerjee 2002:11–12)

Memories articulated the nature of the present, rather than that of a past, and further:

> Every Santal invocation of the past and practice for the future had also to be a creation of a temporality. Time itself appeared as a practice, and as the product of that practice. Rather, pasts and futures had to be forcibly *made present* through practices of temporalization, for the present was ordinarily inhospitable to Santal pasts, and Santal pasts 'unnatural' to the colonial present. (ibid.:6)

Ila Mitra's own insistence on atiter jed echoed these very notions of the past as a practice, as well as a product of that practice, and was underlined by the sense of *time as an agent*, forcing its way into her present to create other temporalities. Even as she had been propelled by this atiter jed across the decades, for the Santals too one dimension of this temporal imperative was 'the formulation of time itself as a supreme agent, who dispensed justice with the ruthlessness of the sovereign ruler, and before whom all were equal' (ibid.:7). The hul of 1855 had been one instance of time acting in favour of the Santals, who articulated as reason for their revolt simply the fact that 'the time to rise had arrived' (ibid.).

This 'unexpected' turnout of over 100,000 Santals takes its place in this punctuated history from the hul to the present as another such act of temporalization. The hope invested in Ila Mitra's return that was expressed through the ritualized festivity and welcome, and the demand that she come back again to lead them, all indicates that once again, it seemed that 'the time had come to rise'.

The years 1948 to 1950 had marked a powerful conjuncture between the CP's sense of historical necessity and the Santals' temporal imperative, which cannot be explained in the causal sense. For the Santals, the Nachole revolt had happened because, as with the hul, they had believed it could happen then—it was a coming together of two different relations to the past, one of an urban left culture, the other of a rural Santal one. The force of the events of 1996 too can only be explained in terms of the sanctity of such temporalizations for the Santals, which goes beyond the conceptual explanation of a cause-and-effect analysis. Those memories were being rearticulated in 1996, to welcome back a leader to deal with a still unfinished past.

Amongst others, the hul, Jitu Sardar's movement and then the Nachole revolt had given them an imperative to act irrespective of the possibilities of success, imbued with the force of unflinching loyalty and rebellion. In fact, Ila Mitra's apparently insignificant detail about Harek's sense of time takes on much deeper significance in the context of this sense of the temporal imperative. She recalled:

> We used to get very angry, and I used to tell him that I wouldn't keep him in the Communist Party any more, that it was just not right to be late when important activities were on. He used to say:

> 'You'll see that I'll be right there with you whenever any real activity occurs.' I could see.... This is one of the things that caused my nervous breakdown.

Could it be that she was struggling to understand the full force of the Santal sense of temporality and the loyalties it could elicit?

It is in the context of her experience of this atiter jed of the Santals that one can begin to understand Ila Mitra's own fierce commitment to her past, which, it becomes evident, was as much of the Santals as of the Communist Party.

## Commemoration Across Borders

> I don't know if there is any other instance of a memorial trust being formed in the name of a person who is alive, but there is one in Nachole—the Ila Mitra Smriti Samsad. This shows that Ila Mitra is a memory for the people of Nachole.
>
> – Fazle Hussein Badshah

If memorials commemorate only the dead, then what is the meaning of the 'deaths'—virtual or real—that are remembered in these transactions of memory across borders? The commemoration of a living Ila Mitra through a memorial trust implies to us the assumption of a virtual death—of the loss of a person to another nation-state. It seems to seal the borders through this intensely experienced finality of absence, even as it defies them through the symbolic act of owning her despite the power of borders. A paradoxical trope characterizes the memories and communications of most populations dislocated and divided by partition: it comprises a forced acceptance of dislocation, loss and finality at an everyday pragmatic level and a treasured continuity across borders at a deep symbolic level, embodied in the realities that live on in their memories. As Manas Ray (2000–2001:158) has observed, they talk of 'events, people and places *determinedly lost*' (emphasis added). To visualize pasts, rendered politically 'other' and inaccessible, as continuing into the present as one's own, would be to jeopardize one's future as a citizen of the nation of one's current location. The demands of citizenship and national boundaries slice through the beings of refugees, disallowing ontological continuities of time and space.[13]

Yet, can one attribute this intrinsically paradoxical phenomenological perspective of simultaneous loss and continuity to the Santals too? Did the memorial to Ila Mitra imply an acceptance of 'death', even if only in terms of loss? And was it this same sense of continuity in memory, which defies modern political borders, that compelled over 100,000 Santals to claim her as their own? Do the Santals, whose very identity is constituted by a history of dislocations forced first by British colonial forces and then by the independent Pakistani state, also relate to their pasts as 'determinedly lost'? And what is the significance of borders in constituting the identities of those who continue to be marginalized by the modern nation-state too? It is crucial to interrogate this notion of 'death' implied in the Santals' commemoration to understand the place of borders and the modern political state in Santal life.

The Judaeo-Christian tradition attributes to death a finality unfamiliar to many cultures, including that of the Santals, which seals off all entry points for comprehending the significance of the their commemoration of a living Ila Mitra other than in terms of a sense of permanent loss across borders. This, in turn, would signify their deference to borders and a power of partitioning equivalent to that of life and death. That their actual relationship to these borders is in fact the opposite is what I argue.

Death is not imbued with finality or with a sense of permanent loss in Hindu and other notions of death and rebirth. In fact, this difference between the Judaeo-Christian sense of finality and the Santals' had also been a bone of contention for missionaries converting tribals in the nineteenth century, for it had also

[13] It is significant that only in those rare cases when borders are recrossed back to the 'absent horizons' that the unities of time and space can be restored, as happened in the case of Bir Bahadur Singh who went back to his village in Saintha, Pakistan, and forged a reconciliation with the Muslim friends who had been rejected by his family during partition (see Butalia 2001). Also refer to my narrative, *Old Maps and New*, where I describe how these boundaries of 'eternal loss' vanished into the air of my parents' hometown the moment I entered Shikarpur, in Sindh, Pakistan, to explore the topography of their 'lost pasts' (Panjabi 2005:66).

involved a conversion of Santals to a new and rational time of linear succession. The missionaries insisted that rather than merely add Jesus to their repertoire of spirits, they give up their beliefs in their own *bongas*. For the Santals, belief in ghostly spirits was the result of an 'inability to grasp the fundamental temporal act—that the dead were inexorably and fully past, and that the present was a pure present, successive to the death and obsolescence of ancestors'. (Banerjee 2002:3)

One can find a key to this commemoration in other tribal notions of the continued life of a leader or loved one even after death. For the Mundas of the Chhotanagpur plateau, Birsa Munda, the legendary leader of the Ulgulan, continues to be alive, even though he died in 1900:

> Birsa came of Ulihatu…
> He will rock this country,
> His death will make it tremble,
> They say, he is still alive.
> Sometimes he is black, at times white, still at others red.
> Let us go and see him.
> They say he is still alive.
> Sometimes he is seen, at others he hides himself, still at others he speaks out.
> Let us go and see him.
>
> (Singh 1966:105)

The faith in a past leader as a future saviour and 'chosen one' too infuses the songs of Birsa Munda:

> Let us hurry to him and see him.
> Let us visit him.
> Let us, carrying our possessions, lodge there (near him).
> We shall stay there.
> We had been there.
> We heard his words.
> We listened to him.
> His words are true, our hearts brimmed with joy.
> We listened to him, we were filled with happiness.
> He was chosen for our land.
> A shepherd in the forest.

There is no more sorrow in our heart.
Our troubles will end shortly.

(ibid.:107)

Santal songs too allude to the extraordinary hold that the insurrection of 1855, and its leaders, Sidhu and Kanu, continued to have in their life, and the conviction that they will return each time to lead the people.[14] Thus, tribal culture right across eastern India disrupts this notion of death as permanent loss; rather, it invests the death of a leader with a continued living presence, a haunting power of return and hope of future victory—and Ila Mitra was only dislocated across the border. Considering whether her memories were revived upon her return to Nachole, she responded as follows:

IM: No, it was not so. My feelings became numb both in Nachole and there [Nawabganj police station and Rajshahi jail]. I did not feel anything. It was as if my senses, my capacity to feel, had been somewhat destroyed.
KP: But the enthusiasm of the Santals moved you?
IM: Some women gave me some papers, some showed me false *patta*s, their lands had been snatched from them. I handed them over to my party members. There is not a single peasant movement now and no party is organizing the peasants. Everybody has a tremendous yearning to get me back there. They think if I go back, there will be a movement again. Actually, the situation is not like that.
KP: Do you want to go back ?
IM: At this age, can I do anything? Everybody reiterated the same thing: 'Please come back again .'

Read in this context, the memorial trust in Ila Mitra's name could only be a commemoration of a living reality and an indication of hope for the Santals. As death does not mean finality, absence does not mean loss. More significantly, what this implies is that despite the prolonged absence, the direct line of connection between the Santals and Ila Mitra had not been disrupted by the borders of the nation-state. States that continue to marginalize Santals seem to have been powerless in shaping their identities as citizens in rendering the other side of the border as politically 'other' and inaccessible. Hence,

[14] See Suhrid Kumar Bhowmick's collection of Santal songs in Bhowmick (1996).

the past continued into the present, but as a discontinuous present, punctuated by a long absence. In the final run, Ila Mitra was not just a 'lost' past commemorated in the memorial trust; she was a living presence for them. The demands of citizenship and national boundaries had not succeeded in robbing them of a sense of their past as their own; neither had it ruptured their ontological sense of space and time as it had done with other refugees who had been interpellated as 'citizens'.

Prathama Banerjee's insightful work on the Santals' sense of time and history helps us understand better their relationship with borders and territoriality. She observes:

> Effective memories could exist even of a past which could not be quite remembered or recovered. Memories, in other words, acted as the articulation of the nature of the present—rather than as an impression or residue of the past.... [T]he present could not even claim to happen in the same location as the past. Repeated invocations of the old land of Champa, which could never be located on any map nor discovered by travelers and ethnologists, only acted as a reminder that even territoriality did not necessarily assume the form of a permanent and incontrovertible foundation of a people's history. While to the nineteenth century Bengali historian, the nation seemed identifiable as always already present because of its permanent location, its pre-existing territoriality, Santals articulated their past of continuous displacement from lands in order to demonstrate how lands could be lost forever just as pasts were. (2002:5)

The Santals' history of repeated dislocation had enabled them to forge identities in which territoriality did not assume foundational signification in the construction of identities, as it does in modern nation-states, which in turn imbues borders with the power to separate peoples, and peoples with the rationale for wars across these borders. Thus, far from inculcating a deference for the borders, Santal oral history created the conditions for challenging these borders instead. The Santals' massive expression of allegiance to Ila Mitra from across the border between Bangladesh and India is testimony to that.

This commemoration also compels us to explore the reverse:

that is, the significance for us of her memory of those Santals who were lost to her forever, be it by death or dislocation. In her context, a forced acceptance of loss seems to be the dominant paradigm primarily because of her complete incomprehension and surprise at the phenomenal turnout to felicitate her. Ila Mitra and the Santals clearly seemed to be functioning on two different axes of time, borders and belief. The Santals did not need to see Mitra physically to keep her alive in their history, and political borders had no power to destroy their ownership of her; she was simply a leader who had returned as expected. Her existence, on the other hand, had been shaped by the borders of the nation-state. She had remained in India, unable to return to East Pakistan because of the cases against her, and the uncertainty of her legal status was a matter of concern as late as the 1970s when she had returned for the first time after the emergence of Bangladesh. She seems to have lost the Nachole revolt to the past too, as she immersed herself in urban left politics in West Bengal. Matla Majhi, the leader of the Santals whose house she inhabited, had migrated to India with his fellow Santals, and, in fact, they lived in the same state, a few hundred miles from her. Even though she travelled widely through the state for her subsequent political work, she never joined the Santals in struggle again on this side of the border—physical proximity did not mitigate dislocation and conceptual loss.

Yet, it was more than a shared memory that bound Mitra and the Santals together at that historic meeting in 1996. That magic time had persisted in the lives of both. For her, the Santals were part of a dislocated past, both in terms of landscape and memory; yet, they had continued to inspire her sense of political mission. The Santals had, in their own characteristic ways, reimagined that time, with her leadership and its possibilities, and it had recurred once again in the fiftieth anniversary celebration of Tebhaga. 'It is that time, however ritualized for the Santal, and epiphanic for Ila Mitra, that seems central to the political trajectories of both.'[15]

## Conclusion

[15] V. Geetha, in conversation.

These accounts are, thus, ultimately about the *breaking of frameworks*, the crossing of boundaries, the intensity of commitment, which are now forgotten hallmarks of the Tebhaga movement. Yet, it is precisely in their haunting sense of loss that they are simultaneously a resource for the present, providing the impetus to 'detach human memory from all forms of totalitarianism, in politics as well as in culture, and to help it play its part in the forming of a democratic consciousness' (Passerini 1992:18).

Implicit in the critique of left historiography, in that it subsumes issues of caste and tribe into those of class, is the left's negligence of caste concerns. While the widespread participation of under-caste and tribal populations is widely acknowledged in this historiography, it is also marked by a complete absence of any discussion on the historical conditions of such interaction or about the problematics of actually negotiating difference across social boundaries. In this context, narratives of activists like Ila Mitra become a valuable resource for both.

There was not only an intense relationship that developed between these inhabitants of Santal culture on one hand and Ila Mitra rooted in a communist commitment on the other. In fact, there seems to have developed a unique historical conjuncture between the Santal temporality and communist teleology—between the former's allegiance to the past and the CP's commitment to the future—that calls for further understanding. The narratives reveal that the CP's—and specially Ila Mitra's—political engagement with the Santals facilitated transformations in social terrain, and a significant convergence of varied politico-cultural investments in history. Historical memory and conscious political choice intersected in complex ways wherein one nurtured the other through the belief in a recurrent temporality—the moment has arrived—and future victory; and contemporary political activism reinforced historical memory with practices of comradeship and political choice.

What is significant for us today is that the intensity of this powerful engagement that took place between the urban left and rural Santal culture during the Tebhaga movement was not the result of a chance conjuncture. There were others too, with the

Mondals and Majhis in Kakdwip and Mednipur, the Rajbangshis in Rangpur and Dinajpur, the Namasudras in Narail and the Oraons in Jalpaiguri. This history also indicates that the immersion of self was not necessarily in the logos of the CP movement only—that there were alternative solidarities and collectives too with which activists could and did identify. Even if Ila Mitra was an exception, her radical openness to Santal culture and its historical imperatives, and the conditions of possibility of this engagement, derived from an investment in class transformation and social justice that transcended divisions of caste and community, and went beyond political stakes for power. It was a quality of investment that enabled a deep transformation in the subjectivity of activists and created the potential for ontological identification with the dispossessed in the very realms of interiority. The material gains of Tebhaga in Nachole were soon lost to the violence of the state, but knowledge of the ways in which left politics had once been a compelling force for both channelling and shaping the finest ideals of societal life may still mean something to us.

In fact, the mutual life-endangering loyalty between Ila Mitra and the Santals in Nachole stands witness to a politics of comradeship forged through deep ontological identification. It goes beyond declassing and has to do with a dynamics of interiority that takes over one's consciousness. Mitra's invocation of Harek the Santal's sacrifice as inspiration for her continued resistance, even in the face of severe sexual torture, marks a genuine crossing over across cultures in mutual identification of political and existential belief through comradeship. Such ontological identification includes the political notion of comradeship, but goes beyond it—it is another way of understanding the intoxicated state of shared commitment to the transformation of a world. The uniqueness of the activists' perception of Tebhaga was that 'its significance condensed in a manner in which its agents would not betray it'.[16] Yet, it was short lived. What were the impasses when do they become visible, and why and what do they tell us?

[16] This is from V. Geetha's insightful response to these narratives. This concluding set of arguments was worked out in conversation with her.

The contemporary political situation is witness to an extreme and insidious relativism that 'marginalizes' and facilitates the 'demonization' of disinherited caste and tribal populations even as it claims to create special provisions for them. One of the critical concerns today has to be about the relation of political parties with the people, whether in struggle together or engaged in modes of governmentality. While the struggles on the ground seem to be lacking in processes that nurture and build solidarities across difference, the actions of the state demonstrate only too clearly an unwillingness to even engage in any dialogue with the perspectives of the disenfranchised. Narratives such as Ila Mitra's provide an alternate account of negotiating difference, an account that is a lived history of a shared *process*, and not the characteristic set of epistemological theorizations about difference that pre-empt dialogue and reinforce the isolation of the already marginalized. Actual political engagement across caste and tribe calls for some understanding of committed and affective processes of negotiating difference and the risks it involves, as well as of the complex yet powerful solidarities that are possible.

# 6

# '*Premer Jomir Khoje*'
## In Search of the Terrain of Love
## Alienation in a Politics of Violence*

You have called me here.[1] How did I participate in the struggle, why did I do it, what was the aim, what happened later—what have you done about it? What did the party do? Whether the aims and ideals of the party were reflected [in its actions], you have not cared to see....

Bring the past to the forefront. Without [an understanding of] the past, how can the present find its stepping stones? The past has become like a canal, like a trench. You are modern, you [think you] know everything. So you don't bother to look around. You are sure to fall. If we are to save ourselves from this situation we have to tell our children, 'Look, here there's a pit.' But they [the party leaders] did not bother to show them [the younger generation] the pits.

– Sibarani Dikshit, Tebhaga activist of Mednipur

[1] Sibarani Dikshit refers to the CP as 'you' at an event organized by the party in the late 1990s (actual date, place and time not stipulated).

* Some of the material in this chapter has been published in an earlier article: 'Women's Subjectivity and the "Political" in Oral Narratives of the Tebhaga Movement: Alienation in a Politics of Liberation' (Panjabi 2012).

When I first met Amal Sen, a much loved leader of the Tebhaga movement in Narail and president of the Workers' Party in Bangladesh in the late 1990s, he said to me: 'If you really want to learn something about the women in the Tebhaga movement, go find Anima [Biswas] and try to understand why such a dynamic activist as her went completely underground. She had been in search of the terrain of love.'[2] What exactly was this terrain of love? What were the impasses that had forced Anima Biswas, an unsung Namasudra peasant activist of Narail, to retire into quiet oblivion? Were they connected to the historical reasons for the end of this powerful political culture that had also transformed the personal lives of the Tebhaga women and men? Did they have to do with the violence of the state or of the armed struggle? Were the reasons for withdrawal into silence political, existential, gendered?

Anima Biswas had been forced to flee across the border from East Pakistan to West Bengal after she and her husband opposed the 'Ranadive line' of 1948 and the violence of the armed revolution. She continued to remain underground even after the ban on the CP was lifted, having 'chosen' a life of silent self-exile in Barasat, just outside of Kolkata, where I finally met her.

While the upper-caste urban leader Ila Mitra's resistance to state violence is now the stuff of legend, silence clouds the torture of over sixty Santals, and killings of twenty-four of them imprisoned with her as well as the massive forced exodus of the Santals from Nachole to Maldah not just across one district but also across the border from East Pakistan to India. Similarly, the least circulated perspectives were those of the impact of the CP's violent politics on rural under-caste women like Anima Biswas, and they are now shrouded in deep silence. It is a silence relating to the impact of the violence of the state and of the left on lower-caste and tribal populations, of the armed revolution on the hitherto democratic nature of the movement, as well as of the consequences of partition and subsequent dislocations for women's lives and political participation.

After I finally met Biswas, the process of unravelling her silences

[2] The Workers' Party (WP) is one of the two most important political parties to have emerged out of the split in the old Communist Party in Bangladesh, the other being the Communist Party of Bangladesh (CPB).

also alerted me to the significance of other silences, including those of Ila Mitra, and together they began to represent a body of the gendered and under-caste critiques of the violence of the CP. The violence that marked the armed struggle was further revealed to be not an exception, but, in fact, a prismatic index, a condensation during crisis, of far more pervasive practices endemic to the political culture of the CP. Finally, a critical question that remained, and seemed to point to the persisting force of the lived past in contemporary history was: what had prompted Amal Sen, one of the most important leaders of the Tebhaga movement, and still politically revered in the late 1990s, to direct me to one who inhabited the underbelly of a glorified left revolutionary culture?

In his *Theses on the Philosophy of History*, Walter Benjamin (1969b:254) asserts that 'only for a redeemed mankind has its past become citable in all its moments'. What, then, is it that has not yet become citeable? The impact of the violence of those times, that clearly continued to plague Amal Sen, continues to haunt the present with its repression and its erasure of the transformations that are now forgotten hallmarks of the Tebhaga movement. The silences that mark Anima Biswas, Ila Mitra and other women's lives, and Biswas's total withdrawal from the world of politics, draw attention to lacunae resulting from the suppression and elision of certain histories in the world of politics, especially those related to ideological critiques, as well as the 'unspeakable' critiques of violence and sexual politics. Learning to understand silences such as these became a process of learning to locate, and then reinstate, that which was buried under, or deliberately excluded from, the passage of history. It also became a process of drawing upon 'recalcitrant events' to 'call into… crisis the easy way in which the mainstream story gets told, has been told.' (Amin 2002:1)[3]

The Tebhaga movement had continued from 1948 to 1950 in the form of an armed struggle, and remained largely concentrated in

[3] See Amin (2002:1): 'New history, I shall be suggesting, requires not just old and "new sources" and newer interpretations, but new ways of narrating what I call recalcitrant events: you can spawn them as tellable tales by calling into major crisis the easy way in which the mainstream story gets told, has been told.'

some areas, such as Nachole, Narail, Khulna and Mymensingh in East Pakistan, and South 24 Parganas, Midnapore and Hooghly in West Bengal (Cooper 1988; Dasgupta 1995; Lahiri 2001; Majumdar 1993; Mukerjee 2010; Rasul 1982, 1989; Umar 1984, 2003). On 25 March 1948, soon after the Second Congress of the Communist Party of India in February 1948, the West Bengal government decided to ban the party in the state and proceeded to institute 'a regime of repression and anti-Communist witch-hunting' (Bandyopadhyay 2006:8–9).

The CP intensified the Tebhaga movement in the aforementioned areas and, under its leadership, urban and specially peasant activists, including women such as Ila Mitra and Anima Biswas, began to receive training in arms and orders to kill. The killings became rampant. Jotedars, zamindars, the police and villagers who became agents of the police were all targets. However, internal repression within the CP became an integral feature of the party too at this time. All dissent was squashed. Dissenters had to flee or risk being killed at the hands of their own comrades. At the same time, the newly emergent nation-states of both India and East Pakistan exerted blatant violence in their determination to contain the groundswell of violent peasant movements. The crackdown on the Telengana people's struggle in Hyderabad in 1948 was followed by violent onslaughts on peasants and communist leaders of the Tebhaga movement in various places, including Kakdwip in the south of West Bengal in India and in Nachole in East Pakistan in the early 1950s. Leaders and activists were arrested, imprisoned and tortured, homes were burnt down and sometimes, as in Nachole, entire villages were razed to the ground.

While the armed struggle in Nachole was centred around a few Santal villages and petered out after the severe crackdown of the police in the aftermath of Ila Mitra's arrest, the movement in Kakdwip in 24 Parganas covered a wide sweep of areas and became the chief locus of the violent revolution.[4] In Kakdwip Tebhaga became a battle for political power. There was a radical change in strategy to one of direct confrontation with the jotedars and the state, with

[4] See Majumdar (1993) for a substantial account of the armed struggle in South 24 Parganas.

the police harnessed in the interests of the jotedars and *lotdars*. The demand now was for the abolition of the zamindari system without compensation (Bandyopadhyay 2006:9). The slogans changed to 'Langol jaar jomi taar' (Land to the tiller) and a demand for not two-thirds but '*purobhag*' (the whole crop). Others, like 'Jaan debo toh dhaan debo na' (I'll give my life but not paddy) convey the state of intensification of the poor peasant's passion in the area.

The peasants' militancy intensified to a point such that by 1949 they also declared certain areas, such as, Layalganj or Lalganj (red market) and Haripur, to be liberated zones or *muktanchals*, taking over the harvested crop of thousands of *bighas*, forcing the lotdars to flee, and also abolishing the zamindari system, declaring that the land would belong to the tiller after proper distribution. On 10 August 1949, a people's government was established in Layalganj. *Gana adalats* (people's courts) were set up a month later for the trial of enemy jotedars and spies, and a veritable *mazdur–chasi raj* (workers'–peasants' rule) took root (Majumdar 1993:238–40).

The Adivasi Santal peasants used bows and arrows, while other peasants had been trained in the use of arms and were well equipped with them. They indicated that these were sent in from some foreign country, and were secretive about the source. Amulya Kamilya of Layalganj wondered aloud: 'The Sten guns weren't produced in our country. I am not sure [where they came from].' Bijoya Mondal communicated his acquiescence with this policy of secrecy:

> It was not necessary for us to know where the party was getting these from.... I knew, but knowing everything was not necessary.'

This cover of secrecy also extended to party representatives sent in for training in militancy, and it sometimes became cause for much consternation amongst the peasants when they were confronted with having to cater to the needs of a completely alien figure, a north Indian army man. Bijoy Mondal said:

> For example, the party sent a representative. I knew.... But he was a commander, a military man ... didn't come out in the day time ... stayed in a dark room ... needed at least 5 kg flour [for chapati]. If we could give uncooked things, it was best ... fish, meat or eggs.

For peasants who lived on semi-starvation diets, it must have been no mean task coming to terms with the difference in both the nature and the quantity of the diet, and then procuring it too. This was Major Jaipal Singh, who had been despatched to Kakdwip after a daring jailbreak from Fort William, but found the facilities there too limited to impart proper training (Majumdar 1993:245).[5]

Police firing on peasants who went to demand paddy from the lotdars, who were hoarding it for sale in the black market, or others who went en masse to remove the paddy they had harvested from the jotedars' fields to their own, became the norm of the day. The fact that peasants began to fire back, or even burn down cutcheries, attack police posts and kill jotedars and their agents led the state to further intensify its violence against them. Significantly, the Congress, which had been working with middle and rich farmers and landlords, now organized them into a movement, the Congress Seva Dal, against the poor peasants (ibid.:232–38).

Kakdwip also became a bastion of women's militancy, with an estimated one-third of the activists being female, and in fact, more women dying of police firing here than men (ibid.:246–48). In some areas, their estimate of their own participation seemed to be much greater, with women such as Tulsi Samanta of Budhakhali asserting that, 'Women comprised three parts [of the movement], men, one part,' and Lakkhi Saotia, a Mahisya woman also of Budhakhali, asking indignantly, 'What would have happened if women had not gone [to join the men]? Women *were* the majority!' The women had a categorical sense of life changing before their very eyes. Basanti Das, another Namasudra woman of Chandanpidhi, said, referring to the way peasants set out collectively in processions to claim the land from the zamindars: 'There was the eviction of zamindars and … some had to give up 10 bigha, some 50 bigha, some 800 bigha…. When the procession started moving, the world started to move.'

Women characteristically led the processions against the police and the jotedars to protest the killings of peasants who had gone to harvest or collect paddy together, only to be shot down point blank by the police. The first two women to be killed thus, in November

[5] See also Singh (1984).

1948, were Ahalya and Batasi of Chandanpidhi. They have now become the stuff of song and legend in the annals of Tebhaga. In Budhakhali, the most poignant history is that of Mandakini, also known as Paki Bala Sinha, who was pregnant at the time and lost her child as a result of merciless police beatings. Several women were killed, others lost an eye, an arm, a leg, but what is striking is the continued confidence of the women, and the men too, in the power of women.

Lakkhi Saotia, sister of the legendary martyr, Neelkantha, and an activist in her own right, who had been pregnant and shot in the leg, declared her own belief in the power of women even as she questioned me about mine:

> Women are the real source of power. You must be knowing that they are the real source of power? Don't you believe this? Mother is Shakti [Kali]. And we all are her offspring. Hence, we must provide the power and energy.

And Jamuna Das, a Namasudra activist of Tebhaga in Chandanpidhi, invested this association of women with Kali, who is one of the most prominent deities worshipped in the Sunderbans area of 24 Parganas, with an ethical impulse too. In her emphatic articulation of the complete name by which she was known there—Adyashakti Mahamaya, which means *adi-shakti* or the primal force, also simultaneously the principle of *maha-maya* or great *karuna* (empathy or pity), with both combining in the figure of Kali to symbolize her destructive power over evil and protection of the good—she echoed what other women had said, that the jotedars and police had killed so many of them, caused such great sorrow, that is why women had come to the fore:

> When women joined the men, they gathered some courage.... Men do not have so much power as women.... You are a woman. You don't know?.... Women have Adyashakti Mahamaya—she is mother. We have a power like that—like Adyashakti Mahamaya can suppress a demon, we have a power like that. The womenfolk have power like that. That is our strength.... Women like Ahalya, Batashi went ahead.... At that time, they had no fear.... At that time, we became fearless figures like Adyasakti Bhagavati [Goddess Kali]—because

> we saw our men were being tortured and they did not let them cut paddy—women became fearless.... The women would lead. Men would follow.... We carried the red flags in the time of meetings and processions. Men followed. It is not a question of helping [to pre-empt police attacks]. We go first.... Ahalya... was five months pregnant. That was like being empowered by Adyashakti.

This sense of the capabilities of women must have been reinforced even in the example of some of the city women who came to Kakdwip to serve with the People's Relief Committee. Bijoy Mandal, one of the commanders of the liberated area of Layalganj, confirmed that there was also a medically trained person amongst them (another woman by the name of Ila Mitra, from Kolkata), who was affectionately called Ranga Didimoni or Ranga Boudi by the people of the area. Ranga Didimoni 'was a member of the People's Relief Committee. She saved many people. She could take out bullets.... [She went around and] stayed in different camps.'[6]

What is interesting is that the women's own sense of their superior power also seems to find echoes in men's perceptions of them. Bijoy Mandal, who was one of the most feared revolutionaries in the area, while considering the importance of the role his mother and other women played in the movement, said:

> Of course ... we couldn't have done anything if women weren't there. Collecting food, communicating to us the whereabouts of the police. If necessary, they could prevent the loot of our paddy by the owner.... We had become vagabonds. Who would have protected us?

In Narail, the character of the armed struggle took on other contours, with a focus on killing the *dalals* or local villagers who had become agents or spies of the police. In 1948, the Bengal Provincial Committee adopted a resolution '*Dalal halal koro*' (kill all the agents [of the police]). Nur Jalal, a peasant leader of Narail, writes in his memoirs, of how he participated in the very first killing of a dalal in Bengal in compliance with this resolution. He begins his account of

[6] Ila Mitra's son, Rahul Bose, who runs a farm and educational centre for local Adivasi children just outside of Santiniketan, later confirmed that Ranga Didimoni was his mother, and she was a medical student doing her internship in Kakdwip at that time.

this incident by saying: 'A list of dalals was drawn up in every area. The person who found first place in the list prepared for our area was my elder brother, Nurul Huda by name' (1995:49).

Nur Jalal was in hiding in Chandpur village, the home of a CP leader called Munshi Modachcher, when the police came a second time to look for him, and what ensued was as follows:

> After a few days, in the beginning of December 1948, the police launched another search in Chandpur in order to capture me. With them was my elder brother [as their agent]. The police arrested Munshi's paternal cousin Momonuddin and one more person and took them to the thana [police station]. After the attack was over, news came that my elder brother had been seen walking, alone, towards the town. Immediately the Chandpur party workers, Nurul Huda (this one being another paternal cousin of Munshi), Abdul Azziz and I, and a few other party workers rushed off in that direction. We saw that he was busy walking, to the west of Nayanpur, on the road to the town. We apprehended him, took him to a desolate structure in Chandpur, and the first dalal halal in all of Bengal was committed here, in keeping with the party resolution. (ibid.)

The fact that the police agent he helped kill was his own brother is narrated with a cold-blooded composure and pride that indicate a quality of ideological submission to party diktat beyond all human considerations. In fact, it was after this incident that Anima Biswas's husband, Karuna Kishore, had spoken up, voicing his categorical objection to such violence, even as this first murder set off a spate of others:

> The next day we reached Bhakri village before dawn. At night there was a meeting of the local committee. Comrade Karuna Kishore strongly criticized such blatant murder. However, everybody else expressed satisfaction at this first instance, across all of Bengal, of the realization of the Party resolution. Following our example, yet another dalal was killed in Egarokhan village. In Khulna too, an enlisted dalal was killed under the leadership of Comrade Bishtu Chatterjee. (ibid.:49–50)

Conscientious objectors began to find themselves trapped in the crossfire between the violence of the state (for being members of an armed insurrection) and of the CP (for challenging this very insurrection), and finally fell out of history, either into oblivion like Karuna Kishore and Anima Biswas, or killed by the state or even by their own party. The armed insurrection of 1948–40 was ultimately written off simply as a 'mistake'; the experience of this violent phase was never subject to the critical and genuinely self-reflexive examination by the CP that it deserved. It remained as a deep gash in a uniquely humane history, suppurating into recurrent violence with a persistence that still calls for close attention and remedy.

In the course of the armed revolution, there developed ironic similarities and connections between the violent contesting forces of the nation-state and the left. The state had refused to address the reasons for the dissent of the CP, and the CP, under Ranadive, refused to engage with the reasons for the internal dissent of its own members. Both had chosen to respond to dissent with authoritarianism and violence, and the impact of the repression and brutality of both converged to impact most critically the lower-caste and tribal peasants who were the most vulnerable, with not even the negotiating power that the urban leaders had. The ground realities of the armed struggle reveal deep tensions, ranging from an unquestioned internalization of the violent ideology to profoundly troubled questioning and rejection of the violent line.

The CP's rationale for the armed struggle was ostensibly one of liberation for under-caste and tribal peasants and workers, while that for the violence unleashed by the state was 'national security'. Yet, the ideology, absolutism and repressive control inherent in both marked commonalities of subjectivity and impact that constitute one of the most difficult and least discussed themes of post-independence South Asia.

## In Search of the Terrain of Love: Violence And the Betrayal of the Ideal

Anima Biswas, the peasant woman of Narail, had wanted to write a book called *Premer Jomir Khoje* (In Search of the Terrain of Love). It was to be her vision of love, of a unique fusion of eros and politics that she and her husband Karuna Kishore had actually achieved on the fields of Tebhaga. Yet, said Amal Sen, 'she never managed to write it.... their whole outlook on life had changed.' What was it about the Tebhaga armed struggle that destroyed this vision? What was it that completely changed Anima Biswas and Karuna Kishore's relationship to life, to each other and to themselves?

Given Biswas's withdrawal into herself, the only way one had of approaching this history was through a cross-reading of her silences with Amal Sen's narratives. He understood her life, decisions and actions from a uniquely mature perspective of a gender-sensitive male friend, mentor, comrade and theoretician.

Sen began his story by signalling shifts initiated in practices of love and conjugality during the Tebhaga movement, exemplified in the relationship between Anima Biswas and Karuna Kishore:

> There, in their times, in the peasants' area, love marriage was an unknown concept.... But they were the first to do this.... Anima and Karuna Kishore. Karuna Kishore was her husband. Yes, now, they had a love marriage. They were the proverbial love birds.

It is from the vantage point of a close mentor to the couple that Sen explained how his own example had played a critical role in enabling Karuna Kishore, also a Namasudra like Anima Biswas, but a relatively well-off peasant, to shed his class privilege and come into his own as an activist in the movement:

> Yes. [I knew them] both. Anyhow, because I [took on the leadership], or for whatever reason ... they slowly got involved [in the work]. Very soon, their capabilities started showing. Karuna gave up his rudeness, his haughtiness as a result of this. I worked as a factor in their development. I am the son of a reputed family, I am of a higher caste.... That such a person as I could fight side by side with the farmers for their rights became an important example for Karuna. It was a catalytic factor that enabled him to mature to his full ability as an individual.... He had to change himself a lot. But after that he became a very good organizer. And in this, Anima was always beside him.

Sen also indicated that their work together for the liberation of their people became the ground on which their love flourished: 'After that, at last, after doing a lot of thankless work together, they finally found the soil of real love.' And the reason he saw this as 'real love' is to be found in its realization of the self in society:

> The awareness of my being. Who am I? The awareness... yes, I am an individual all right... but certainly at the same time I am a part of the whole, of society.

Anima Biswas understood the fusion of her love and her politics. Amal Sen recollects that when she was filling up her membership form for the CP:

> There was a little space left blank. She had to respond to the question, 'Why do you want to join the Communist Party?' I told her to write whatever she wanted to. She said, 'Whatever I want to write?' I had answered, 'Yes, that is what you will write, why should you write what I think?' She filled up the form and came to show it to me, joking that it [the fact that theirs' was a love marriage] had become international news. She had married for love, and she wrote: 'My husband was like a wild, insane bull. In front of my very eyes, I saw this savage bull change into a beautiful human being. Now I realize that a party that can transform a savage into such a beautiful person may also change this man-made society and make it beautiful. This is why I want to join the party.'

According to Sen, she had reached out to Karuna Kishore in the context of their work, grown to love him, and chosen to marry him. Their love had grown on the ground of their love for their land and their people, and in their dreams of a better world. The terrain of their love of their people was the same as that of their love for each other. It was a camaraderie layered with the experience of personal desires fired by political desires for one's people. Even Faiz, with his powerful rendering of the transmutation of eros into politics in the epoch-making ghazal '*Mujhse pehli si mohabbat mere mehboob na maang*' (Do not ask of me, my love, the love that I once had for you), had not imagined how compelling the *fusion* of eros and politics could be when the woman would no longer remain the beloved at home, when woman and man would realize their love together in the fields of struggle. Of the attractive force of this couple, Amal Sen said: 'I was really drawn to them. If I stayed with them even for a day, I loved it.'

Amal Sen also said that the fact that Anima Biswas not only understood this but valued it deeply is reflected in the fact that she wanted to write a book called *Premer Jomir Khoje.*

The armed struggle in 1948 changed everything. Sen was posted in Narail at that time, and he recalls his unease with this shift, indicating the beginning of a cycle of violence, in which each atrocity gave birth to others, that emerged presumably in retaliation:

> At that time, the slogan 'This freedom is false' resonated everywhere, through hundreds of ups and downs.... The destructive consequences of the [Ranadive] line became clear to us in Pakistan. I understood what it meant because of my experience [in the Tebhaga area]. Nothing remained [because the police razed everything to the ground]. This gave rise to other atrocities.

His own stand was clear, but he had been torn between his own conviction and his party loyalties that allowed him only to voice his dissent internally. The result was not favourable; instead of agreeing to any kind of dialogue with him, the party insisted that he continue as secretary:

> I sent notes to many communists. I came to the district committee and said that I thought that it was wrong, it was destructive. But that was inside the committee, no one outside knew.... They disregarded my objections telling me I could take them to the headquarters, the district headquarters; instead, they insisted I would have to be the secretary. They placed the whole responsibility on me.... Yes. I told them that the post of the secretary should be given to someone else. In spite of having a difference of opinion, I tried my utmost [to do my best by them]. They told me that they too would think it over, and then they decided that I should come back.

Party loyalties won, but when Sen was on his way back to take up the leadership of the armed struggle in his area, he was suddenly arrested: 'On my way back, I was unwell... and before I could return I was arrested.... I did try to give my best to this line, but then I got arrested.'

Though Sen had objected strongly, it was clear that he had made the decision to follow the party diktat, and fifty years later too testified to his loyalty. Yet, the sense of distress about the devastation the violence had caused persisted, and found expression especially in his concern for the comrades close to him.

Shortly after Sen's arrest, mass warrants were issued:

> Three, four hundred people had warrants on them. Murder charge warrants were on seventy people including Anima, Karuna Kishore, Rishikesh's wife, countless. I used to stay in their house often.... [with] Anima and her little daughter.

Sen's association with Anima and Karuna's home and daughter, in the moment of recalling the warrants issued against them, tells of a concern born of intimacy with them.

Karuna Kishore too had voiced his objection to the violent line; the difference was that he did so openly. Sen emphasized the difference in the party's treatment of him and them. He reiterated his position in relation to the CP: 'I had told the district committee that this was a dangerous line. Only the district committee knew, nobody else knew.... I was arrested by that time. After that I was asked to leave the secretaryship.' Having been ordered to continue with leadership despite his unease, Sen was merely relieved of the post of secretary after he was arrested, when in any case he could not have led the party. He spoke of Anima Biswas and her husband's predicament as a contrast to his own:

> Whereas they were suspended from the party ... they [Karuna and Anima] declared to the party in all the areas that they were against the party line. They were suspended, not expelled. Now, where could they go with a small child? Going against the party line meant they wouldn't get shelter anywhere ... but they had murder charge warrants against them, where should they go? In spite of that, for four, five months they tried to stay here. When it became impossible.... The party—they received no shelter from the party ... with a small child. After that, they crossed the border and went across.

Anima Biswas narrated, haltingly, the experience of being caught in the crossfire between the violence of the police, aided by secret agents on one hand, and the threat of being killed by the very CP they had fought for right through the movement on the other:

> At that time there was a surfeit of dalals.... Whenever we entered the locality the news would spread everywhere. There used to be the agents who would go one by one to every area.... A couple of murders took place.... Then they tried to torture us.... The dalals ... and along with them the police. The police and the agents.... When the police looted our house and the people had gathered to stop them, then he [Karuna] said not to stop them. If stopped, they would burn down the entire village. Yes, by then, along with our house, a couple of other houses had also been looted. They couldn't be stopped then. Were we to have objected, they would have destroyed our entire neighbourhood.
>
> Well, after that, we were asked by the party as well to leave. One could well have been killed [by the party] and such a plan had even been hatched. Seriously, there had been such a plan.
>
> Thereafter, when everything became intolerable, we came over to this country. Well, he [Karuna] came first, through Khulna ... while I came over later, with my brother-in-law's son, to Calcutta.

For those who had objected openly to the violent line, it had become a matter of choice between life and death—to stay on would have meant a sure death, either at the hands of the state or their own party; the only chance of life lay in fleeing across the border.

Biswas responded with a vehement 'No!' to the question of whether the CP would pay any heed to what women had to say. In fact, her reason for disillusionment lay much deeper, for she narrated an incident when CP activists had killed one of their own members when he'd sat down to eat—and killed him in front of his parents. Her only grim comment on this was, 'After all, one is entitled to have one's own views.' It was no insignificant critique of a party that had once, in its catholicity, campaigned even for the release of Congress leaders, and had reached out in genuine openness and willingness to learn and engage across divides of class, caste and community.

Her faith in the CP had been destroyed, and it eventually came to rest on an individual—Amal Sen, whom she referred to as Basuda, whose advice had saved their lives: 'Then Basuda told him [Karuna] to leave, or else the same could happen to him.'

When asked about how she thought about the movement now, after her involvement in it in its early stages, Biswas withdrew into her shell, with the bare words: 'I do not think anything about it now.' After that, all I got was staccato, fragmented responses from her. Asked if she and her husband had maintained any contact with the party, the response was a terse: 'No, we left it.' And later she burst out: '*Ghenna dhore gelo* [we were seized with repugnance]. We had worked for it all our lives, but at the end we had to face such torment.' Yet her final sentence again indicated that the trust in the party had been transferred to an individual who was still humane: 'But Basuda used to come and meet us.'

Anima had consequently withdrawn into a shell of tortured silence. The betrayal by the party had led to the loss of the terrain of love and land, both personal and political, and deep disillusionment. Yet, the memory of Tebhaga continued to haunt her as a utopic force, as she hovered on the knife-edge between nostalgia and the sundering of relations—between love and betrayal, equality and authoritarianism, desh (nation) and *deshbhaag* (partition).

Anima Biswas had escaped while their home was being ransacked by the East Pakistani police. With Karuna Kishore, she fled to West Bengal, and once there, they contacted the CP. But, Amal Sen recalled, by then the party congress of 1948 had taken a decision that there would be two parties for two countries.[7] Thus, the couple received

[7] See also Umar (2004:46–47):

> At the second congress in 1948, the Pakistan Committee was formed with Sajjad Zaheer as general secretary. This committee, however, could never meet, and for all practical purposes remained only on paper. The East Pakistan Committee was constituted on 6th March 1948... with Khoka Ray as the general secretary...., At the time the East Pakistan Party was facing a serious crisis, owing to large scale migration of party members, members and active workers of mass organizations. Out of about 12,000 members of the Communist Party in East Bengal, the vast majority came from Hindu families, and because of family considerations they had to migrate.... [T]he initial migration was on quite a large scale and this created a big shortage of workers making it difficult for the district committees to function.... Also, except for some stray cases, there was practically no migration of party members belonging to Muslim families from India. In view of these difficulties, it was decided that a few leading party members like Abdullah Rasul and Mansur Habibullah, who belonged to West Bengal, would be transferred to East Pakistan.... Abdullah Rasul returned to West Bengal

no response from the CP in West Bengal. Rani Mukherjee, a leader of women in Rangpur, East Pakistan, who came away to West Bengal and finally settled in Debananadapur near Calcutta, also talked of her bitter disappointment with the CP after partition. She did not know anyone in the party on this side of the border, and when she contacted the local unit in the hope of doing activist work in West Bengal too, she said her entire experience of activism was discounted, her claims to having fought in the Tebhaga movement questioned. It was a sense of waste both for her and, in her perception, for the party, whose work would have benefited from the experience and expertise of leaders like her. 'We were trained activists,' she said, but were not welcome in the party when they came to West Bengal.

Sen was still imprisoned when Anima Biswas and Karuna Kishore fled to West Bengal, so he was helpless, but he voiced a powerful critique of the party for not having shouldered the responsibility for all the activists, including a large number of peasants like Karuna Kishore and Anima Biswas, whom it had drawn into the movement to strengthen it:

> Yes, [I was still in jail] I couldn't be a part of this. This *gundaraaj* [rule of thugs] was going on everywhere. So many activists had struggled during the movement. So many peasants had become Communist Party members. Everything was getting destroyed at one go. But I couldn't do anything. What could I do? Then Anima and Karuna were left feeling very hurt. They were party workers. The party had a lot of workers. The party should have taken all the responsibility. He [Karuna] went there as a representative of the party. He said that the party did not want them anymore. They had to go away.... There the party declined to put them up anywhere. So where could they go then? They had been with the party all along.... They became

---

soon afterwards, but Mansur Habibllah decided to continue work in East Pakistan was subsequently elected member of the East Pakistan Committee of the Party.... [A] short congress of the East Pakistan Committee was held immediately after the second congress on 6th March, and a thesis, very much in line with that of Ranadive, was adopted for East Pakistan.... [T]he new strategy notwithstanding the Communist Party was not formally banned until 1954. But in view of the radical changes in the party line and policy, it was decided that except for a few party members others would not work openly and remain underground.

> emotional. They would say that 'The party has done this to us... [we faced a] murder charge, warrant, police custody—they [the party] took our shelter away from us.' It was a terrible time of tremendous strain. Where could they go? They faced ultimate humiliation. They had chosen not go to relatives, even though they had relatives.

Amal Sen talked of their continued commitment to a now unresponsive party, their despair at not being able to continue their work in West Bengal, and how the reliance on the party that distanced them ruthlessly was then transferred on to him as an individual. He said Biswas used to keep saying, 'Basuda will not stay in jail forever. If he were to come and to stay near us, we would have more strength. We could work with him.' But his terse comment on his own decision was: 'I didn't go back to them.'

He then elaborated upon how those who had fled to India remained completely alienated from the party, yet made concerted efforts to get him across from East Pakistan to become their leader in West Bengal:

> Then, in the year 1956... the day I came out of jail, I heard that my father was on his deathbed and my brothers had taken him to India.... I got hold of my passport and visa and came to India. As soon as they heard that I had come, in spite of the fact that they were in Midnapore, both [Karuna and Anima] came to see me.... They took leave and came.... Generally speaking, they were trying to figure out what my decision was. They understood that if I went back, I would have to go to jail. They wanted to know my decision. After talking to me, they realized that I would not stay. Then and there, both of them tried to think of a plan to keep me back. They were sure that if Basuda went, he would immediately be arrested.... Then they both planned a meeting and decided to call the communists who had gone from here [East Pakistan].... I did not know. My father was serious and on his deathbed. Almost 150 of them from that side [West Bengal] met. A majority of them had a warrant on them, hence, they had not contacted the party. They had a meeting.
>
> At the meeting both of them said, 'Both of us used to work for the party there. Now we don't do any party work.... Now Basuda has come. He wants to go back. If he goes back he will immediately be arrested. He will not be able to do any work for the movement

> there. If he comes here, he will have a lot of work here.... His returning there [to East Pakistan] will cause so much damage to our revolutionary work. Should he be allowed to go?' The rest said, 'No, it would be good if he stays.' Then they said: 'It is not the question of good or bad, tell us whether it is right for him to go or not. If it is not right, then he should not go.' So the decision was made.

What seems evident is that it was the strength of the camaraderie between activists and their trust in the local leaders that had carried the movement forward; that there was no access that peasants had to the party in the absence of these leaders; that the party, far from taking on responsibility for their dislocated members, had not even set up any channels for communication. Respected local leaders seemed to have been the only face of the party for the peasants, and the sense of bonding with ones like Amal Sen was so strong, that they felt they had the right to make decisions regarding his choice of location in the interests of the party to which they still felt a powerful allegiance. It was a tragic situation in which the political desires that had been the propelling force for the Tebhaga movement, uprooted from their original terrain, could not find any ground again. It was too soon for Amal Sen also to comprehend the deep consequences of this political uprooting in the lives of the activists, to understand that such uprooting, from a movement that had given meaning to their lives at the political and personal levels, would ultimately have an impact on personal relationships too. He continued:

> I told them that I had left behind fourteen peasants, who had been with me, still imprisoned in the Pakistan jail. I was the only one who had been released. Should I have left them in that situation and come here?
>
> I beat about the bush and said that I would like to leave. I still didn't understand. The fact that Karuna was actually distressed deep inside—for the love that they had found inside them, they had begun to understand that they were about to lose that love. I did not understand this. I was thinking of something else then, I didn't understand this dilemma.
>
> I did not understand their problem. I did not understand that the vital thing that was affecting them the most was that along with the loss of the revolution, they were also losing love.

What I'm trying to say is that they felt that the ground under their feet was getting weaker. How long could they carry on like this?... It meant that they could not breathe and were suffering from agonizing pain. It felt as if everything was coming to an end. So they had hoped that if I went and started work there....

They were losing their hold on their lives and I did not understand this. After that, around the time the United Front took charge in Bangladesh ... they got separated.[8] After the marriage of their daughter they got separated and [Anima] went to Gaya, she stayed in an orphanage and found work there.

Alienated from the terrain of their politics, which was also the terrain of their love, Karuna Kishore and Anima Biswas gradually drifted apart from each other and eventually their marriage ended. Yet, the desperate hope of regaining at least her political ground still haunted Biswas, so when she heard that Amal Sen had come to the border to organize refugees, she went there in frantic search of him:

Yes. Then... [in 1971]... she took time off from Gaya. Anima took leave from the orphanage in Gaya and she went all around the borders where the refugees had formed camps.... Roaming about looking for me. 'Basuda has come, Basuda has come.' We were there making suggestions about how to do party work there and what to do. Anima came there.... She nurtured a hope inside her that 'this time when Basuda goes back, he will take me with him'. It is not that I didn't understand. But, by that time, all had been divided.... There was no way she could have made it. If I could have taken the initiative on behalf of the party and told her that she was wanted, then it would have been different. Till the very end she was hoping that Basuda would take her with him.

By 1971, the borders of the nation-state had sealed the borders of the parties and identities too. Anima Biswas had found no place in the West Bengal CP; neither did the CP of the newly formed Bangladesh have any place for her. She had become a non-entity lost in the chasm of a 'mistake' and then deeper in that of the partition of a nation, a party and a people. Yet the conversation I was having with Amal Sen seemed to mark his moment of stock taking too, for he

[8] This was in 1954 (Umar 2004:270).

emphasized repeatedly the ethical responsibility of a political party to its cadres who had pledged their lives to it. He stated categorically that it was not the fact of having made the mistake of adopting the wrong line, but the refusal to shoulder any responsibility for the consequences of that mistake that had laid to waste the lives of thousands of committed activists like Anima Biswas and Karuna Kishore.

> It shouldn't have happened. It happened because, if the party had been responsible this wouldn't have happened.... If they [the CP] had wanted to, they could have done something.... It is not the question of a wrong line. It is the question of basic responsibility.

After 1971, Biswas took up the job of a superintendent of an orphanage in Shyambazar. Karuna Kishore got married again, had more children, lived in dire poverty and then fell ill. Yet it was Biswas he turned to again in that condition. Amal Sen went on:

> In the meantime ... Karuna Kishore came to Shyambazar. He was in very bad shape ... yet, in that condition, Karuna went to the orphanage where Anima worked.... Anima saw that he was very sick. She realized that he did not even have enough money to go to a doctor. They never spoke to each other. She would just go, give him money for treatment and leave. After this, every month she would give him money for further treatment. They never talked to each other.

Living together had become impossible for them. Yet, living apart too was unbearable. The chasm Biswas found herself sucked into was of unfathomable alienation—from politics and from love. Ultimately, when their daughter, Jhunu, got her father home to look after him in his last days, Biswas too moved in there, in silence.

Amal Sen was the only one who understood what Anima Biswas had fought for and what she had lost. He was the only living trace of a wrecked past and it was only his presence that could bring feeling back into her alienated self, as it did when he went to meet her after Karuna Kishore's death:

> After that, when I went there, I heard Karuna Kishore had died. Then, very apprehensively I went to Shyambazar. I went to the

> office. They said that she [Biswas] was unwell, but upon hearing that I had come, they sent her word and I was asked to sit and wait. She was the superintendent. There were a lot of girls there. She was still upstairs. I was downstairs. She came, stood in front of me and held on to the chair—she was the superintendent. But, in spite of that, she couldn't resist her feelings. She held me and broke down crying, 'What happened?'...
>
> Her attachment to him had remained.... Anima was the superintendent.... Yet, she couldn't restrain herself, couldn't restrain herself after seeing me. She just broke down in front of me.

This meeting had obviously continued to haunt Amal Sen because he felt compelled to go back to it in yet another conversation with me months later. This time, he said that twenty days after Karuna Kishore died, he had gone to the orphanage, and as soon as Biswas saw him, she had put her head on his lap and broken down uncontrollably, howling, '*Dada*, dada [elder brother]'. He says, 'I was older than her, and I too found myself on the verge of crying. What could I tell her?'

It was a pain unbearable for Amal Sen; of a personal trauma that was rooted in political despair, and of political despair that could find voice only in personal trauma. There are no narratives, no scripts for a tragedy such as this, neither in the realm of the personal nor of the political histories that are our legacy. The affective power of this tragedy had compelled Amal Sen to grope for its cause with ruthless honesty, and in the process, he articulated a critique of the nature of comradeship that strikes at the core of hierarchical party relations. Earlier, he had held the CP culpable for shirking its responsibility; now he took the entire blame upon himself. His own role, that he had described earlier, as an inspiring force in their lives, and thus of the movement too, transformed paradoxically, in this moment of desperate self-criticism, into that of a culprit:

> I feel like a culprit, they were dependent on me and that I didn't understand. And by making them dependent on me, I have made a very big mistake. I should have behaved with them in such a way that it would not have mattered whether Amal Sen stayed or not—if they could have started a movement with the 150 people he had chosen, that would have been enough. My biggest mistake was that I made them dependent on me, I did not make them independent.

The force of this repetition and the strange tone mixed with regret and rage in which he conveyed it stayed with me for years, and yielded meaning only with my own affective immersion in this history. Exploring the unsettling power of this apparently contradictory response of regret combined with rage led me, years later, to the cognition that they were on two sides of the same coin—with the regret about the devastation of Anima Biswas and Karuna Kishore's lives that he held himself responsible for on one side; and rage at his own uncritical internalization and perpetuation of a hierarchical party culture, albeit in a humane paternal mode, on the other. What seemed to have been merely a self-critique of his almost paternal role in terms of leadership and guidance yielded another layer of meaning: the activists were not encouraged to develop their own qualities of leadership to a point where they could take up the mantle of the movement side by side with seasoned leaders like him. The hierarchies remained in place, as did the dependency of the activists on the leaders. Because of the deference in which they held the party (the male leaders) that had given birth to them as activists, the women did not develop a critique of patriarchy. In the case of Anima Biswas, Karuna Kishore and their comrades, their dependence on and deference to Amal Sen hindered their own learning of how to launch a movement. In holding himself personally culpable, Amal Sen was also holding the party politically culpable for perpetuating a hierarchical structure, for it was this culture of paternalism that he had internalized. It was a hierarchy that Manikuntala Sen too had questioned, but only in retrospect, that served to keep power relations strictly in place and ideologies virtually unquestioned, but crippled the potential of activists and their ability to forge new political visions in the face of ruptures and crises.

Admitting his own culpability and that of the party in reducing a dynamic Anima Biswas to a mere cipher, Sen seemed to be clutching at the last hope of restoring her sense of self-worth, and of the worth of the history that she had shaped in Narail, as he turned to me and the oral history of the Tebhaga movement that I was writing, and said:

> You will go and meet Anima. After telling her what you have seen and heard, if you could convince her that whatever she had done has made a mark, has had some influence, she will not feel so hopeless.

Earlier too, when he had narrated their story, he had ended on a similar note:

> At that juncture, I couldn't give her the place she wanted. Even now, as you are beginning to write about the Tebhaga movement—if she could be involved [in your work], then she would feel some consolation—that her contribution was not all for nothing. Then, she would feel less sad.

It was unsettling to be drawn into this history thus—the burden of restoring the self-worth of an agent of history was being placed, half a century later, on one unearthing that buried history. It was a burden that I was not equipped to shoulder. Biswas's alienation from her own past ran too deep for the present to touch her.

## Militancy and Obsession: Ila Mitra's Perspective on the Ranadive Line

Given that Anima Biswas's entire life had been devastated by the violence not just of the state, but also the party, and given her fierce critique of both, the non-committal matter-of-fact tone in which she indicated that she herself had received training in arms was striking. When her daughter Jhunu recalled that on some nights she had seen her mother and other women on the banks of the river, attired in white shirts and trousers, practising using guns, all Biswas said in response was, 'Yes.'

Wielding guns and training in violence had become part of the political experience of Tebhaga during the armed struggle launched in 1948, as had the intensified violence of the state both in East Pakistan and India. The ground realities of this period were fraught with ambiguities that reveal, at the very least, the disorienting impact of violence. Certain kinds of 'knowledge' of the violence of the period is available to us, but whatever knowledge we have of 'facts' remains 'dead' unless we make attempts to understand them (Koch 1997:395). What Friedlander (1976:37) had said about the holocaust echoes in the context of the period in the Indian subcontinent too: 'Decades have increased our knowledge of the events as such, but not our understanding of them.'

Violence and repression went hand in hand. There are various strands of history relating to both that we do have access to in some contexts, but these are usually approached in isolation from each other, as unconnected parts of a 'master narrative' of the violence of the period that included the fraught relationships between the state and the CP, as well as within the CP. A wider focus on history is required that takes into account the representations from below too, of the various narratives of brutal violence as well as repression, and how they are inflected by each other, if we are to come to some understanding of them.

In the context of Ila Mitra and the Santals, three critical 'known' strands that are now operative are: the responses of the CP's ground-level leaders to its armed struggle, which included training in weapons and diktats to its members to kill, responses which ranged from unquestioning obedience to deep unease and even rejection of the violent line; the heroic narrative spun around Ila Mitra for her staunch refusal to give in to the sexual torture inflicted on her by the state; and the relative public silence on the torture of over sixty Santals who were in the same prison but refused to betray her, as well as the killing of at least twenty-four of them, including Harek, who was tortured to death before her (Begum 1989; Umar 2004:138–44). An exploration, of how these strands developed in relation to each other, which takes into account 'a wider range of emotions, affects and aesthetically induced expressive reactions' (Koch 1997:405) that go beyond a focus on moral feelings such as pity, righteousness, loyalty and so forth, calls for engagement with emotions and attitudes much undervalued in left historiography—and for that matter in any historiography. Attention to such emotions as pain, rage, guilt, unease, confusions, as well as telling elisions and blind spots can lead us to comprehend the fraught impact and reception of violence. It can also enable us to understand the motivations intrinsic to the choices of heroization or erasure that together underlie the grand narratives of violence. Addressing these dimensions of political experience, which are available to us in oral narratives, enables one to 'avoid sinking into a morality tale and express the more complex subjectivity contained in aesthetic representation' (ibid). Subjectivity, thus, offers itself as a prism that may enable us to begin understanding the complexities of the CP's 'mistake' as well as the consequences of the violence of the state in relation to each other.[9]

Ila Mitra described, also in a non-committal, matter-of fact tone, the training she and other activists received in arms:

> Tebhaga was a reality there in the Nachole area then. What were we to do in case of direct confrontation—the peasants were there and we too received training— I did too. If the police came with guns, how to snatch guns, how to lie flat on the ground to escape firing, how to shoot—we had training in all that.... Someone had come from a different area [to train us]. This struggle was raging across all of Bengal ... [he'd been trained in the army], yes. He used to train us and we had taken on different names then.... We also had bows and arrows. The krishak sabha and the party had then organized the training—many men and women had participated and I did too.... Many were trained and I was also one of them.... Because too many Santals had died already—many of them had died before they could be organized.

And she openly admitted to having given orders to kill the jotedars:

> There were arrest warrants in our name. We had to hide ourselves, fleeing from one village to another. I had to organise them [the Santals]. Yes. 'You have to kill them [the jotedars],' I told them.

Even when she talked about it having been the 'wrong line' or the fact that she had to 'pay a lot' for the violence, it was not in terms of the ethicality of violence, but of a mistaken strategy of targeting small jotedars too who could actually have become their allies:

> Then our party leader was Ranadive. He introduced this line which was, 'Murder all of them.' Later this line was changed. It was proven to have been the wrong one to have taken. After we went to jail, the news came to us that it was the wrong line because many jotedars were small, all of them were not big. Above them were the big zamindars. In order to attack big enemies we have to join forces with the smaller ones and move with them. First it had been decided that we would murder these small jotedars; later we were told it was the wrong line. I had to pay a lot for this.

[9] See Koch (1997:405). Here, I have drawn upon her analysis of Art Spiegelman's method of representing the violence of the holocaust in *Maus*.

Ila Mitra indicated that initially there was widespread acceptance of the violent strategy, but later, when dissenters were actually murdered by the CP, the matter of the killings was hushed up:

> Ultimately in our area … the Tebhaga movement was quite successful. Almost everybody accepted this … once they sensed the unity of the force. But later on in these … matters … it wasn't the case that they would always have to be murdered, but … we don't talk about such things in the open, like the death of Sankar Sen…. We had deliberately murdered them. It was as per the Ranadive line.

Upon further questioning, however, she revealed that there had been dissenters she herself knew, and that it was only because of the pressure to obey that many had accepted the violent line:

> Yes. Wajid Mondal. He did not join. Another was, his name I forget … he died a few days back, his name was perhaps Rasik. They had dissented, they kept saying the line is incorrect, look, the line is incorrect. So many had refused to join while many did join. There was … since at that time there was tremendous pressure, many had acquiesced because of that … almost everybody.

I also questioned her about whether she had thought about the possibility of violence inviting retribution, of her being tortured and killed by the police in retaliation for the incident of the murder of the police inspector that had finally led to her arrest. Her response was: 'We didn't consider things that way … *we were seized by obsession then*. No, we didn't consider things that way.'

Not only did Ila Mitra seem to be uncritical of the violence that she and the Santals had been trained to exercise, and did, against the jotedars and the police, she also narrated violence in extremely simplified ways. It is all too easy, and in fact contradictory, to explain away the violence of the times as a 'mere' obsession, specially after having admitted to both, a significant number of dissenters as well as the pressure from the leadership of the CP to adhere to the violent line. And given the complex strategies that must have been required in the planning of killings, Mitra's narrative clearly excluded the complexities and nuances of the event. There seems to be a considerable lack of fit between the actual experience of exercising violence and the narration of it later. Was it a mechanical, unreflective recall, a reflex action that pre-empted evaluation of that which had induced and perpetuated violence? Or was it her internalization of the violent ideology that resulted in such flattened out, uncritical and simplified narrations that camouflage both the complexities as well as the unethicality of violence?

As Young (1997:53) has observed, 'The silences that come with incomprehension were part of the events as they unfolded then and part of memory as it unfolds now.' Despite having suffered sexual torture so severe that it led her to a serious nervous breakdown, the fact that Ila Mitra could still continue to be uncritical about her own complicity in perpetuating violence from below signals telling blind spots and confusions in the activists' understanding of it. Her narration, even fifty years later, indicated the silences and simplifications in the discourse of violence that evaded issues of ethicality and pointed to representations that would allow for an unquestioning perpetuation of violence. In fact, her unquestioning loyalty to the party clearly took precedence over whatever unease she may have felt about perpetuating violence herself. She made this point categorically in the case of Azhar Hossain, who had been given instructions to kill a food inspector and probably a constable too, but who, in the last instance, left them alive and absconded. Of Hossain she said: 'Yes. Wrong line or not, whatever they'd been told to do they should have paid heed to.'

In the overwhelming influence of the period, violence could not be questioned—both Ila Mitra and Anima Biswas testified to this in significantly different ways. That the violence of armed struggle could be ethically problematic was not something Mitra questioned; rather, she had given explicit instructions to kill, and she merely explained it as the 'party line' of the time. The premium on obedience was such that instructions could not be questioned; hence neither could the ideology underlying the instructions be debated, nor, in turn, could the ethicality of the activists' own actions become matters for reflection. The armed struggle was marked by a structuring of political consciousness that disallowed all ethical consideration.

Ila Mitra's mode of narrating violence, thus, gives us some insight into the reasons why the survivors, as well as victims, responded to the events as they did, 'and to ignore this is to ignore the highly contingent reasons why events actually unfolded as they did' (Young 1997:55). Yet, despite the straitjacketing of political consciousness, it is indeed puzzling that she was not critical of her own violence, and of the CP, especially given the degree of torture she herself had suffered. For at a deep level, the violence of the state had made a definite impact on her. While she was certainly celebrated in her heroism in a multitude of ways, as indicated in the previous chapter, yet, as Langer (1991:2) observes, 'Accolades do not honour the painful complexities of the victim's narratives, any more than they reflect the ambivalence of their trials.' 'Tributes are cheering, memorials sad' (ibid.:4). In the midst of these cheering tributes, and in the midst of the historical silence on the equally grim torture and killings of the Santals in the same prison as her, Ila Mitra carried within her the memorial of Harek, who had chosen to be tortured to death rather than betray her. In fact, it was the continuing presence of Harek and the Santals in her consciousness that had compelled her to continue her political work for justice for the marginalized. But was it the continued and overwhelming presence of the shroud cast over the 'mistake' that prevented her from even examining her own violence and that of the CP?

## Sexual 'Propriety' and the Shifting Sands of Political Contingency

The force of interiority, of residual modes of internalization of party loyalties, serves as a revealing prism for bringing to light the silences of this history, specially in relation to sexuality and violence. In all was evident a central paradox between a heroic memorialization and nostalgic memory of the enjoyment of political activism, and articulated critiques of party violence or a telling silence that sat in uneasy contradiction with each other.

The degree of sexual freedom permissible varied across caste and tribe. Poko of the Oraon tribe laughed mischievously as she narrated her account of her growing dissatisfaction with her husband, and her relationship with and consequent remarriage to another man, reassuring us that this had gained full social acceptance. The story was rather different in relation to the young Namasudra widow Phuli Goldar's promiscuity, that Amal Sen had communicated to me. Anima Biswas, who had been responsible for drawing Goldar into politics, after having once let it slip out that she 'had a roving eye... there was... in her, the desire to do something', had slipped back into a complete silence on her 'licentious' behaviour, and carefully avoided all questions regarding this that I asked her. She talked indulgently about Goldar and acknowledged her transformation, even while skirting the reasons for the stigma from which her friend had been 'rescued'. Her only comment was, 'Well she was bound to change in our association,' but in response to my urging that she could now talk about it candidly, all Biswas would say was, 'I do not remember it properly... I cannot tell.'

This uneasy ambiguity relating to her friend's sexuality fifty years later and the final decisive recourse to silence reveals an internalization of sexual repression across the years. Amal Sen talked proudly of the women overcoming social taboos and transforming an outcaste widow into a dynamic activist as an example of a transformation of consciousness:

> They [these peasant women] proved themselves again. This actually happened in this region. What I feel bad about is that [it's not recognized that] what Tebhaga achieved, in terms of meeting its demand, is not the most important question; more important is the more developed consciousness and changed attitude of the working class. They had been deprived in terms of their own consciousness.

Read in conjunction with Amal Sen's narrative, Anima Biswas's silence indicates a sad regression. If Tebhaga had wrought liberating changes in consciousness in relation to attitudes to sexuality, her refusal to talk about it marks an internalization of a repressive sexual politics in later years. In Biswas's narrative, then, Sarala Singha's public initiation of Phuli Goldar takes on the character of a 'purifying process' that reinforces conventional notions of chastity, and fits with the conservative left discourse on sexuality—or rather the silence on it.

In the urban and largely upper-caste context, women testified that as men and women were thrown together in intense struggle, relationships naturally developed, but they had to face layers of 'disapproval' from the party and from society at large. One middle-class urban woman leader of a town in West Bengal recounted that because of the intimacies that did develop, the CP used to be referred to derogatorily as the 'Projapati Party' (Butterfly Party) by conservatives, leading the CP to adopt puritanical standards of sexuality in order to ensure larger acceptability in society. Talking strictly on conditions of confidentiality, she voiced her own critique of the party for expelling two comrades for the relationship that had developed between them. She asserted, instead, the need to address the role of human, sexual desire in the movement. Referring to the man expelled for such involvement, she said: 'No. He was already quite aged. I don't blame him [for the relationship]. One is a human being first, then a communist, or a woman.' Yet, she too maintained strict secrecy regarding this relationship in the interests of party loyalty and the activist's 'honour':

> It was a question of my honour. Actually, none of us talks about it. We are very close to his family—we stayed with them, ate at their place—we are indebted to them. Only a few of us came to know about this incident, but we did not disclose anything to the cadres. There was some gossip, but we did not fan it—rather, we tried to keep it a secret. Otherwise, the party would have suffered. People had begun to refer to the party by a special name, the Projapati Party.

Party loyalties and social propriety constituted honour. One's own beliefs, however deep rooted, logical or far-sighted, had to be suppressed in the face of this 'honour'—and this is something she had clearly internalized. Her final comment on this, then, was in complete contrast to the earlier one that argued for a need to recognize the place of human desire in the fields of politics too. It reveals, as in Anima Biswas's case, a closing in on her own more radical view, and a deep ambiguity that prevailed regarding sexuality in the face of such pressures. She ended with: 'Thank heavens, I was already married when I came into the party—well, not exactly married then [but soon thereafter].' It was evident that the culture of disapproval had marked sensibilities so strongly that even fifty years later, she would share her account of certain relationships only on condition of confidentiality. The party's puritanical, repressive stand on sexuality continued to remain in conflict with the imperatives of human desire and sexuality, and this tension continued to mark the subjectivity of activists half a century later.

There was also a deep tension between Mitra's subjectivity and the CP's political strategy. Her narrative, while predominantly one of heroic survival, was nevertheless also underlined by certain silences and distortions of memory that signal ambiguities, revealing the impact of both state violence and the repressive frameworks of the CP. In her own words, delivering her testimony in court of sexual violence done unto her by the East Pakistani authorities after her arrest was not easy. 'After all', she was 'a Hindu wife', indicating that a certain degree of privacy regarding sexual matters was integral to her being.

In the face of the political imperative to have Ila Mitra deliver a candid testimony of her torture, all the sexual taboos of the CP had suddenly disappeared. Her sense of dignity and privacy were clearly being violated in the act, but this is a fact brushed under the carpet in the heroic narrative of Ila Mitra in official left historiography. Badruddin Umar (2004:141), for example, says:

> At the Rajshahi central jail, Ila Mitra was kept in a solitary cell and a case was instituted against her and all the Santal prisoners.... Ila Mitra was considering what she would state in her deposition before the court, because it was a really delicate and difficult mater to state in detail of what actually happened to her, and the kind of torture that the police inflicted on her Nachole and then at the Nawabgunj and Rahshahi jails. At that time she unexpectedly received a secret letter from Manorama Basu of Barisal and Bhanu Devi of Khulna, both of whom were detained at the Rajshahi central jail at the time. They urged her to state everything that had happened to her and asked her not to feel shy. The letter was helpful to Ila Mitra who finally rose above all inhibitions and stated in very clear language the inhuman torture and outrage on her honour that was committed by the brute policemen of the ... government of Pakistan.

Despite the sensitivity of approach, this version too toes an official masculinist line in its interpretation that the letter was 'helpful' to

Ila Mitra. That it was certainly 'helpful' to the party is evident in the fact that she did ultimately deliver the explicit and powerfully indicting testimony. What the cost of this second round of violation of personal dignity—the first one in actual endurance of such sexual torture, the second in having to narrate it in a public court—might have been for her was never considered.

Her own version, narrated haltingly, painfully, had a different thrust:

> Fifteen days later, the other Santals and I were taken to Rajshahi jail. There I was kept in solitary confinement for eleven months. The case hadn't yet started; it couldn't be started as I wasn't well. As soon as I was somewhat back on my feet … the first day I was brought to court.… After all, I was a Hindu woman, not very old, I wasn't sure if I should talk about the rape and all that.… I had a lot of reservations.… I kept thinking about all this. All the other women who were there as political prisoners, they were all known to me—some seventeen, eighteen of them were there. There was someone called Bhanu Devi from Khulna. She somehow managed to slip a chit to my cell with a message scribbled on it.… She had written—they all knew what kind of torture I'd had to face—so she'd written: 'The first statement you make in court, you must tell us everything you've faced. You mustn't leave anything out. *Unless you can do it, we won't have anything to do with you any more and nor will you have your party membership any longer.*' (Emphasis added)

Thus, she had to deliver the testimony on threat of banishment from the CP. Manorama and Bhanu had clearly privileged the political gains that the CP would derive from such an explicit testimony over the loss of dignity it would mean for an already traumatized woman comrade. Yet, it was the time of the armed revolution; the party diktat was inviolable.

When we first began talking about her testimony, Ila Mitra started, in awkward fragmentary phrases, to recall it all over again. Then, stopping almost as soon as she had started, she went and fetched Maleka Begum's biography of her that carried the full text of the testimony.[10] She handed the book to me, saying I could read

[10] See Chapter 5 for the full text of her testimony.

it for myself. Then, she took it back, saying she would lend it to me in any case, and began to read aloud the entire text in a curiously deadpan, distanced tone. It was only a few months later, when I met Maleka Begum in Dhaka, that the import of this deep vacillation began to hit me. When she heard that Ila Mitra had read out the testimony to me from the biography, she asked me repeatedly, 'Did Iladi say it was *her* testimony? Did she own up to it, did she claim it as hers?' The testimony had been suppressed; it had never been published in the Pakistani newspapers, only distributed in the form of leaflets, and had thus gone out of public circulation across the next five decades. When Maleka Begum finally procured a copy of it, and took it to Mitra in Calcutta, a few years before I first met both of them, the latter had looked at it in bewilderment and said, 'Is this my testimony? Did I really say all this in court?' That it was indeed the testimony she had delivered in court is verified by the Bangladesh Home Department records.[11]

Why had Mitra lost all memory of this testimony? After her release on parole in 1954 on grounds of severe ill health, she came to Calcutta for treatment. Once back in West Bengal, she ultimately gave way to a complete nervous breakdown, from which it took a few years to recover. To attribute the loss of memory of this testimony to the nervous breakdown would be rather simplistic for a resilient woman who remembered the rest of the struggle in full detail. Was it the unbearable nature of the torture itself that could be lived with only by blocking it out, or was it the trauma of a complete loss of dignity while narrating it in court? Or both? The answer lies in the fact that Mitra never asked, 'Did I really endure all this?' Her question was, 'Did I really say all this in court?' In recent years, the Truth Commissions in Latin America have recognized the toll it takes on victims of severe and sexual torture to recall, retell and thus relive all over again the terrifying indignity of such violations. The political gains of such public testimonies have to be weighed against the personal costs to the victims.

Ironically, party notions of appropriate political subjectivity

[11] See Government of East Bengal (1955). I am deeply grateful to Wilhelm van Schendel for sending me a copy of this document, which he procured from the National Archives of Bangaldesh.

for that historical moment had eroded its sexually conservative stance and opened up the space for an explicit public discourse on sexuality. Later, when I met her in 1996, Mitra's disquiet with her own testimony and its explicitness, which made for uneasy reading, seemed to have undergone yet another shift. Her changed sense of herself, from the radical leadership of those days to that of an MLA, now seemed inflected with the more conservative contemporary party notions of 'proper' political subjectivity underlining the fact that once the crisis was over, the vocabulary for expressions of sexual experience had been purged out of its political discourse.

The realms of interiority, thus, remain marked by the tension between the repressed standpoint of women and the residual modes of affective internalization of party loyalties. This force of interiority, then, serves as a revealing prism for bringing to light the silences of this history, especially in relation to sexuality and violence. Unease and silences reigned in the narrations of sexuality and violence, punctuating the political confidence of activists decades after the events. The interweaving of affirmation and of inferiority, that processes of female emancipation have visibly included in recent decades, underlay the continuing relationship of women with themselves across half a century. The modes of narration of Anima Biswas and Ila Mitra all reveal the tension between the obligation to the 'collective' demands of the CP on one hand and the imperatives of personal values and individual probing on the other; between the constant presence at samitis, sabhas and courtrooms, and a growing suffering.[12]

## Conclusion: The Limits of the Political?

In tandem with issues of subjectivity, then, 'the political' is that which permeates, in symbolic mode, the everyday reality of political subjects, and which is possible to grasp in representation. Additionally, and in contrast, it also signifies a lacuna in the conceptualization of the world of politics. This is in relation to the argument that politics is 'constituted' by a fundamental lack—that of the radically

[12] V. Geetha's observation.

'political' 'on whose "repression" reality [politics] itself is founded' (Zizek 1997:21).[13] It is by excluding 'the political' that the matrix of politics is constituted (ibid).

The Tebhaga women's narratives point to lacunae resulting from the suppression and elision of certain histories in the world of politics, specially those related to gendered critiques from the standpoint of women, as well as the 'unspeakable' critiques of sexual politics. The critical question that needs to be addressed, then, is: how does one identify, locate and then reinstate this repressed, absent or deliberately excluded 'political'?

A central question that the women's narratives pose implicitly and urge us to ask is: does violence mark the limits of the political, the point where the political impetus gives way to the obscuring power of violence? The history of the Tebhaga women demonstrates that feudal forms of violence began to be layered by the violence of the state and the CP. In this 'reformulation of patriarchies' (Sangari 2008:3), while new forms of violence appeared, such as state torture, some things did not change. Ila Mitra's narratives as a leader of Santals, and of the under-caste Namasudra and Mahisya women of Narail and Kakdwip, draw attention to the fact that the violence of the state and the repression of the CP both converged on the bodies and selves of women, especially lower-caste and tribal women, as had feudal violence earlier. Sexual violence, of upper-caste/-class men against lower-caste women, accepted, naturalized and even overdetermined as 'caste privilege' (Chakravarti 2003:156), had been 'de-naturalized' and challenged by the CP at the behest of Tebhaga women. But what about the omission of the CP's own violence and that of the state?

In the context of the sexual violence of the state against women, Ila Mitra's history is located at the intersection of the tribal politics of the Santals and the sexual politics of the state. While she was an upper-middle-class urban woman herself, she was, nevertheless, arrested and tortured as a leader of Santals. Her experience has still to be viewed in the context of the pervasive sexual exploitation of lower-

[13] 'The political' is used here in parallel to Zizek's use of the term 'spectre', 'the irrepresentable X' (in this case, the radically political that has been repressed).

caste and tribal women in Tebhaga, and also of the mature political consciousness of the movement in relation to sexual exploitation that was reflected in the gendered demands within it for the abolition of the same. Sexual exploitation by the feudal jotedars may have been banned in at least one of the Tebhaga areas, but women's bodies continued to remain the battlegrounds of the newly emergent nation-states against dissenting marginalized populations.

Namasudra and Mahishya women in Kakdwip too testify to the rape of women by the police, as well as other forms of torture that were clearly casteist in nature, such as the police knocking men down and then urinating in their mouths. Lakkhi Saotia of Budhakhali, who was shot herself, narrated the humiliation in death of her cousin Samanta, a martyr of Budhakhali, and others too:

> I couldn't understand that I had been hit by a bullet. My clothes felt different, as if I had just had my bath. Blood was dripping from it just like drops of water. A man fell down just in front of me and I thought that it was his blood. I couldn't make out that I had been injured too. I didn't even lose consciousness. Everybody had fled by that time. Neelkantha was being dragged by his feet. Sudhir was alive and his mother was giving him water [to drink]. Then the police killed his mother and took him away. Neelkantha had been shot. He too had asked the police for some water. They urinated in his mouth.

In his study of humiliation, Gopal Guru observes how the stigmatization of the human body is one of the grounds for the politics of untouchability:

> The ideology of purity-pollution ... primarily aids the politics of cultural metamorphosis that involves the conversion of the walking body into ... the carrion body which thus becomes repulsive. Walking carrion is the concentrated expression of repulsion.... It is in this sense that the untouchable's body is perceived and treated as a 'sociological danger'. (2008:14)

The bodies of untouchables are stigmatized by relegating them to the job of disposing excreta; in this case, even though Neelkantha was not an untouchable, he was from a lower caste, and his body was stigmatized not as a scavenger but as the very repository of excreta/

urine, in the most extreme expression of abjection. The corporeal language of the worst form of caste humiliation was harnessed in symbolically eliminating the resistant lower caste peasant from the social field.

In contrast, even when the peasants did have the upper hand in some instances during the armed revolution they had refrained from such social humiliation. Riziya Khatun narrated an account of one such incident in Baghbari village of Narail when the gun-wielding police had been surrounded and outnumbered by armed villagers:

> All were prepared with *ramda, sarki, dhal,* swords; determined that if they [the police] fired one single shot none could save them, they [the villagers] would kill them.... In fear of them they [the police] did nothing that day, such was the situation.... One of them wanted to drink water, someone from among the daroga, police guards, and when he asked for a drink of water, someone said, forget water, make them drink urine.... In the end that was not done.... I heard that somebody else said such cruelty ... could not be permissible ... we could not be so barbaric.

In addition to such violation of human dignity, the mass exodus of Santals after the police razed to the ground entire villages in Nachole, as well as the demolition of Namasudra homes and villages in Narail to which Anima Biswas had testified, all map the casteist, anti-tribal and sexualized nature of state violence, hitherto buried under questions of class conflict and 'national security'. As scholars such as Rege (2006), Chakravarti (2003) and V. Geetha (2012, 2013) have asserted repeatedly, any critical, reflexive, anti-caste analysis in the Indian context 'cannot and must not easily disentangle caste from gender' (Geetha 2013:35). For violence premised on the intersectionality of caste and gender runs the greatest risk of being invisibilized in the scheme of politics.

The openly declared violence in the Tebhaga movement was that of the armed struggle. And to have written it off as merely a 'mistake', as was done by the CP, is deeply problematic for any notion of radical politics. For the impact of the violence of the CP, though directed against the jotedars and the state, hit the supposed beneficiaries of the revolution—the lower-caste and tribal populations—the worst.

The Santals of Nachole, who were forced to flee across the border, too survived because of the support of their kinsfolk in Malda. When I went there and managed to meet a few Santals, the common refrain there too was that once they fell out of the armed struggle, the CP did not take up responsibility for them either. Ila Mitra's tension too, between internalization of ideology in the past and assertion in the present of the 'mistake that cost me a lot', highlights the importance of the death of the Santals and the trauma of the memory of their torture in her life. Her lived memory connects the past with the present though a renewed commitment to the ideals she and the Santals had fought for together, except that the Santals no longer remained in the orbit of CP work, and, hence, remained distant from her work too.

In Kakdwip, where the armed struggle was at its strongest, with the CP having set up 'liberated zones' such as Layalganj and held public trials of jotedars, women's militancy had also been the strongest. Kakdwip women such as Ahalya of Chandanpidi and Batashi, who had led protests, dared the gunfire of the police and died in battle, are now enshrined as martyrs in songs, local histories and public memory. Yet, fifty years later, the women's perspective was one of disillusionment. 'What gains and what losses are you talking about?' would be their cynical response as they talked about the sense of betrayal by the CP. A fusion of personal and political desire had mobilized amazing energies and force in the liberation of political charge in Tebhaga. Then why was the movement subject to such internal repression? There was clearly a lack of fit between the violent strategies of the leadership and the will of the activists at the ground level, especially in the case of women.

At first, it seemed contradictory that the very women who had initially lauded the power of women and glorified courageous leaders like Ahalya in their accounts later revealed their reluctance to join the armed struggle. Lakkhi Saotia of Budhakhali, who had talked proudly about women being the majority and deriving their power from Shakti/Kali, later admitted quietly: 'I did not want to take part in it… my brother Neelkantha, who was shot dead [later], he was my uncle's son. He did all this [implying that he drew her into the movement too].' Basanti Das of Chandanpidhi, in response to a question about whether men had readily accepted women's active participation, replied, in a matter of fact manner: 'No, laws were different at that time. One had to go. If they called, everyone had to run, leaving their cooking.' Sushila Maity, a Mahishya woman of Chandanpidhi who also used to be singled out as one of the courageous revolutionaries of the area for having faced the police firing and also losing an eye in the process, said, 'The party people took me from my house.... They forced me to go. I went, I was called.'

Admitting that they had joined the violent phase of the struggle because of peer pressure in the villages, the women pointed to the internal contradictions in the playing out of the armed struggle at the ground level too. They had waged the strongest battle in Kakdwip, sacrificed so many lives, yet after 1950, they were ignored by the CP. The historical eulogizing of these peasants, largely Namasudra and Mahishya, in left historiography was rendered hollow by the decades of practical neglect.

Their narratives were marked by a self-contradictory quality. There was an underlying tension to them, and it could be possible that, given that these interviews were conducted when the leaders who had worked in the area during Tebhaga, were in power in West Bengal, like Jyoti Basu, they were wary of being critical of even the violent phase of the movement. Yet, if one stayed in conversation with each person for more than an hour, the stories of reluctance and forced participation would surface.

The reason for the repeated emphasis on associating the power of women with the Adyashakti Mahamaya form of Kali began to dawn on me in this fraught context—the one way in which women could come to terms with their role in the violence was by justifying it in ethical terms as their fight against evil, and not as a battle for power that Tebhaga did become in its last stages in Kakdwip. Budhakhali's Tulsi Samanta's comment on her reason for joining the movement too had been that it was 'out of hunger. I cultivate paddy and the mahajan reaps the profit.' This was the main reason given by most of the Kakdwip women, as in other Tebhaga areas; not a single woman perceived the armed struggle in terms of a takeover of power—their sense of politics still centred around a fight against hunger and exploitation, not towards appropriation of power, which was the direction in which the CP had taken the movement under the leadership of Ranadive.

Ramachandra Guha (2011) describes Ranadive in a nutshell, and very aptly, when he says: 'In 1948, he thought he would become the Indian Mao and come to power via the barrel of a gun.... [He] disregarded the social history of his own country.' What is significant is that even an enlightened leader of peasants like Abani Lahiri is unaware of the blind spots of the middle-class urban leadership when he admits to the rift that developed in the years 1948–50, and continued later too, between 'the backward sections of the peasantry who constituted the majority, and didn't join hands with the advanced sections in their confrontation with the state apparatus' (2001:101). The very value-loaded official party terminology used to refer to the two sections ignores the possibility of the 'backward' peasants having sound reasons for not joining a violent revolution. Lahiri suggests that the reason for the rift was that 'the strategy adopted was beyond the consciousness of the mass of the peasantry' (ibid.). At another point, he says, 'We called for the overthrow of the Congress government without waiting for the people to come to that conclusion' (ibid.:128), as if there was only a temporal lag in the understanding of the peasants. The fact that they may actually have held a different point of view from their locations on the ground was not even considered to be a possibility.

It was telling that Bijoy Mondal, the commander of Layalganj, who continued to be in acquiescence about the need for loyalty to party dictates, was also critical of the CP's lack of understanding of the ground realities of the time and its complete lack of vision:

> Now, if the party could have seen to it that the organization or the movement was carried on nationwide, then the desired independence or socialism could have been achieved long ago. Because it didn't happen across the whole of India... India is a vast country... [it happened in just] two states within it, and in two places within these two states. If they thought that could free the country, then it was a [mere] dream.

Satish Sahu, one of the prominent peasant leaders of the movement in Budhakhali, who had been expelled from the Action

Committee, had a more focused critique of the armed struggle as a 'revolution' imposed from above. Sahu's account also challenges all the claims of the movement in Kakdwip having been organized essentially from below.[14] For, even if that may have been the case in the early stages of Tebhaga, it certainly was not the situation during the armed struggle. Sahu, in response to a query regarding whether he had ever thought the revolution could succeed, replied in a clearly agitated tone, starting pointedly with a reference to Ashok Bose, a middle-class militant leader who had been sent to Kakdwip in 1948 to assist the peasant leaders, and by the harvesting season of the year had become the most militant in the area:

> Listen, Ashok Bose [and] Kangasari Haldar were moving under the directions of Bhavani Sen or P.C. Joshi,[15] when they said all this [launched the armed struggle]. It did not happen here because I said so—this revolution you are talking about. We did not have the background for such a movement here, it could not happen here, it could not have happened anywhere because neither did we have the type of organization required for it, nor had we built ourselves up for it. Then they expelled me from the Action Committee.

Sekhar Bandyopadhyay introduces his analysis of the 'second Tebhaga', written after the belated release of the Intelligence Branch (IB) records at the West Bengal State Archives, with admirable astuteness by highlighting 'the dangers of trying to write the history of insurgency from the texts of counter-insurgency' (2006:1):

> The grand communist scheme of bringing about a 'People's Democratic Revolution' had little meaning for the peasant volunteers, who were motivated mostly by local grievances. The initial leadership and the initiative for mobilisation of course came from the educated *bhadrolok* leaders coming from outside and performing their supposed 'pedagogic' role. (ibid.:11)

Yet, he ends with the assertion that: 'This was not a movement

[14] See Majumdar (1993:218) who recounts the version narrated to him by Jatin Maity and Kangsari Haldar, other leaders of Kakdwip; see also Sunil Sen (1982, 1993).

[15] It is telling of the distance between the central committee and peasant leaders in 24-Parganas that Sahu was not even aware that P.C. Joshi had fiercely opposed the launching of the armed struggle.

entirely mobilised from above, as in every area the local leadership from among the peasantry emerged and seized the initiative' (ibid.). The perspectives of Bijoy Mondal, Satish Sahu and the women of Kakdwip cited earlier, Azhar Hossein, who had chosen to abscond rather than kill the food inspector and constable in Nachole, and in Narail Amal Sen, Karuna Kishore, and, most poignantly, Anima Biswas's experience of painfully thwarted desire, all represent deep unease with violent insurgency for those involved in it. They would call for a nuancing of the claim that in every area the local leadership seized the initiative for armed struggle. In most areas of the armed struggle, the local leadership also faced dissent from within, was fraught with conflict, compromise, violence, dislocation and the murder of comrades.

The political desires of societal groups based on caste and tribal affiliations were thus displaced by the focus on radical class politics of Tebhaga, suppressed by the CP and in turn by the new nation-states of India and Pakistan, as Bandyopadhyay has observed in other contexts:

> Questions have been raised about the nature of the Indian nation, which claims to speak for everyone, but the processes of construction of which are supposed to have involved a series of exclusions, closures and erasures. So when that national identity is celebrated by the postcolonial state, it underscores at once the stifling of several voices and the marginalisation of certain identities—such as non-Brahman, dalit and gender identities. (2004:40–41)

There was also a communal dimension to this in some areas, such as Nachole and Narail. In Nachole, Azhar Hossein had fled from prospect of killing officers in the employ of the state, but there were Muslim officials who had been killed by other Tebhaga activists. As discussed earlier, Ila Mitra had recalled the Pakistani state's attempt to communalize the issue to disrupt the class solidarities of Tebhaga, in keeping with the narratives of the newly emergent states of India and Pakistan. The fact that the attempt failed is another matter, and is also testimony to the bonds forged across differences of not just tribe and class, but also the Hindu and Muslim communities of Nachole.

In relation to the role of the CP, Amal Sen, president of the

Workers' Party of Bangladesh, further pointed out important issues of political responsibility and hierarchy that had destroyed the movement, and that, in the absence of any serious self-critique, also continue as some of the most debilitating features of left organization today. The deep sense of betrayal, as was felt by the Kakdwip women and the Namasudras of Narail, had also brought on the complete collapse of the quality of antarikata and comradeship that women had brought to the movement. Anima Biswas, in one of her rare articulations, voiced the powerful regret and rage of the activists who worked at the ground level:

> The party let us down—they would follow what the big leaders above had to say—why would they listen to what we had to say? Basuda too did not agree with what the leaders had to say about the Ranadive line.... When Ranadive came into power... all the orders used to come from above.... [They] wouldn't listen to us. As soon as they rise in the ranks their views change.... *Kono din era sachetan hobe na* [they will never become aware of the problem inherent in this].

Her critique of the functioning of power in the CP, and of Ranadive and other leaders of the armed struggle, echoes in uncanny ways in the critique Manikuntala Sen made retrospectively in the 1980s of P.C. Joshi's treatment of women in the Netrakona conference.

The fact that critiques of women subject to violence stemming from completely opposite ends of the political spectrum—Ila Mitra's of state violence, and Anima Biswas and Manikuntala Sen's of the CP—can come together to create a common ground for understanding the impact of the violent and repressive subjectivity of this period is in itself telling. On the one hand, the parallel themes in their narratives, of dislocation, of repression, as well as of the significance of that which was lost due to the political violence of the period, all point to the insidious power of violence to 'equalize' ensuing histories in its devastation, even when it is used as a 'means' for completely contrary political 'ends'. On the other hand, when the tremendous political liberation of women that Tebhaga certainly facilitated is weighed in relation to the degree of their emotional and sexual liberation, what is revealed is a carefully repressed and thorny area of the relationship between the CP and the Tebhaga women.

While the movement represented a political birth for women, yet, in different ways, their narratives also reveal their partial alienation from it, especially in relation to desire and sexuality, violence and repression.

The armed struggle of the CP and the crackdown of the near-absolutist state were ideologically in opposition to each other. Yet, ironically, what they shared in common was a violent ideology that structured both and that functioned through frameworks of repressive subjectivity. The violence of the period continues to haunt the present. The frameworks of repressive subjectivity imposed by the nation-state from above fix firmly in place certain pre-existing hierarchies of caste, class and gender; yet, other frameworks of repression, which had characterized the armed struggle from below, continue to pre-empt engagement with alternative perspectives that need serious consideration if redressal of inequities, or even effective unity of the marginalized, is a goal.

What happened during the armed struggle was not just a chance 'mistake' in terms of the devastating impact on lower-caste and tribal populations, but had become a pervasive aspect of political culture even in left politics. The CP, especially because it was the only party that worked with poor peasants and sharecroppers, and actually created a powerful culture of egalitarian politics too, does need to assess the costs of this 'mistake' seriously. It needs to address the rift between the perspective from which the armed revolution was launched by the leaders at the second congress and the realities at the ground level. It also needs to take into account the continuing impact of the repression of its own members. What the discourse of the 'mistake' camouflages may yet be significant for the success of left politics.

Narratives of the first phase of Tebhaga are marked by an unforgettable public liberation of private feelings in the women's narratives. And in sharp contrast to these are the ambiguities, silences and ruptures observed in the narratives of Ila Mitra, Anima Biswas and the Kakdwip women in the later phase of both state violence and the armed struggle. They stand testimony to what Luisa Passerini (1992:13) has observed in other repressive, authoritarian contexts: 'Violence accentuates the gap between the political sphere and daily private life, creating wounds in the tissue of memory which cannot easily recompense what has been forcefully separated.' This critical insight also becomes relevant to the life of the nation. Passerini's incisive observation drives home the fact that in forcefully separating the political and personal spheres, violence posits a considerable threat to the making of feminist perspectives, and of national ones too, as both are built on the bridging of the two spheres. How we may confront and even find a language to express or comprehend the power of such violence across cultures that are fractured and perpetually in conflict is of central concern.

Questions of violence, thus, continue to loom large: what was the right line and what wrong? The party and the activists were unable to work through its implications. What reigns in this underbelly of a culture of submission to party diktat? Despite the admission of a 'historic blunder', what could this violence mean for the individual conscience? An important aspect of memory is 'its capacity to be subsumed and thus have its force lie repressed in society in many ways' (Passerini 1996:8). How did this violence sit with those who stayed on with the party as Ila Mitra did, or with others like Amal Sen who acknowledged the violence as a betrayal and yet continued to lead the party? Did this violence, and its memory, remain largely unquestioned, accepted as an aspect of revolutionary culture reinforced by the unquestioned 'magic' of the times, only to surface again in later years such as the present? Is it because Amal Sen understood so well the costs of such violence as well as his own silence that he directed me to Anima Biswas in the first place?

# RETROSPECTION

Anima Biswas, Narail

Phuli Goldar, Narail

Amal Sen, Narail

Anwara Begum, Narail

Nurul Akbar, Narail

Sushila and Pramila Maity, Kakdwip

Asha Chakravarty, Rangpur.

# 7

# *'Bhije Matir Gandhe Naach Kori Anande'*
# In the Fragrance of the Wet Earth We Dance in Joy
## From the Aesthetics of Liberation to the Wreckage of History

*Langal chalai, mora kodal chalai*
*Nacher taley taley, phasal phaley phaley*
*Mora sona phalai, bhije matir gandhe*
*Nach kari anande, sakal thekey sandhye.*[1]

[We till our land with plough and hoe
The crop grows to our dance beats, we grow gold
In the fragrance of the wet earth
We dance in joy, morning to evening.]

Yes, women sang this song. They also danced to it in circles.... We taught the younger girls how to dance.

– Asha Chakravarty, Kurigram, Rangpur

[1] This song was written by Hemanga Biswas, singer, songwriter and reputed exponent of Bangla folk music. He was one of the most important cultural figures of the left movement in Bengal.

> A Klee painting named 'Angelus Novus' shows an angel looking as though he is about to move away from something he is fixedly contemplating. His eyes are staring, his mouth is open, his wings are spread. This is how one pictures the angel of history. His face is turned towards the past. Where we perceive a chain of events, he sees one single catastrophe, which keeps piling wreckage upon wreckage and hurls it in front of his feet. The angel would like to stay, awaken the dead, and make whole what has been smashed. But a storm is blowing from Paradise; it has got caught in his wings with such violence that the angel can no longer close them. The storm irresistibly propels him into the future to which his back is turned, while the pile of debris before him grows skyward. This storm is what we call progress. (Benjamin 1969b:267–68)

Coming to the end of 'Langal chalai, mora kodal chalai', a lively Tebhaga song, Asha Chakravarty mused wistfully, 'I never thought these would be needed again.' It was a paradoxical moment. Even as the retroactive joy of a collective past pushed its way into the present through her songs, the sadness of a sense of their irrelevance for all time to come simultaneously overcame her. The times had changed. The wreckage of history was all that was left of that charged sense of collectivity. A certain storm of progress had forced them, back turned, into a future—the present—that they were condemned to inhabit with faces turned towards the debris of the past. This storm of progress still rages, still continues to turn history into wreckage and hurl it at our feet, but we have not grappled with it yet.

'Langal chalai' was one of the many songs that the women of the Kurigram mahila samiti would dance to in circles of solidarity. They would teach younger girls how to dance to it too, and they would go from village to village singing and dancing these songs in ever widening circles when other local mahila samitis called upon them to do so. These were not the characteristic 'protest' songs of a political movement and this was not the traditional language of politics. Some songs they would create themselves; others about peasant life, like this one, they would adopt, and mobilize them into the forging of deeply bonded collectivities. For these songs touched upon the core of their lives, the core that was threatened, and this was an affective mode of weaving solidarities—through songs of celebration, evoking, in full sensuousness, the dance of crops and the love of the earth they tilled.[2]

It is significant that it was this song that became one of the favourites of the women in the mahila samitis, for its vocabulary too describes their experience of being in the movement—of ananda (joy), mazaa (enjoyment), nasha (intoxication), shanti (peace)—indicating a powerful affective experience of liberation. These expressions mark linguistic shifts in the conventional vocabulary of political struggle, as do terms such as '*antarikata o andolan*' (inwardness and the movement) or 'premer jomir khoj' (a search for the terrain of love). All these are expressive of linguistic innovations in the making of new political subjectivities.[3] And the joyous, creative dimensions of these expressions point towards an 'aesthetics of existence' (Bowie 1990:13).[4] For them, it was an aesthetic of subjects constituted through practices of liberation. The most significant insights that emerge here are that of Tebhaga as a utopic force, of the universality it forged in the very core of desire for a beloved, and for the land and people.

As narratives of political subjects, the women's accounts largely elided discussion of the ways in which they may have determined the course of the movement. Rather, their experiences found articulation in far more affective terms. They related much more to their celebration or valuation of aspects of the culture of the movement, in the context of a newfound liberation, in relation to their senses

[2] Aesthetics, conceived as a science of sensitive cognition, has as its purpose the perfection of sensitive cognition—this perfection is beauty. The basic experience in the aesthetic dimension is not of sensuality (appetitive), but of sensuousness (sensitive cognition), 'the nature of which is "receptivity", of cognition through being affected by given objects' (Marcuse 1987:176).

[3] See Bowie (1990:12) on subjectivity and the workings of aesthetics: 'The aesthetic object affects the subject without the subject wishing to determine the object. Neither are the subjects slaves to language: the capacity for situated linguistic innovation will be fundamental to the subject.'

[4] Foucault 1988:50 (cited in Bowie 1990:12–13). Bowie further relates aesthetics to the subject constituted by liberation thus: 'If the subject can be constituted by "liberation", there must be some way in which one can conceive what a free subject is. This is one of the tasks of aesthetic theory from Kant onwards, which, like Foucault, did not always regard the subject as sovereign.'

of political agency. While men would generally deploy conventional political vocabularies of oppression, organizing and strategizing, or victory and defeat, women would emphasize the pleasures of not just the kind of solidarity inherent in the words, actions and rhythms mentioned earlier, but also of new forms of creativity; and occasionally, or with difficulty, some owned up to the unease of sorrows that continued to haunt them. The new forms of creativity were manifest in the sense of interiority they brought to the collective struggle, as well as in the new knowledges of other standpoints of historical awareness, such as garnered from the Santals, and in the new visions of liberation. In these forms of creativity, we encounter the heart of these memories of a collective, their raison d'être—the connection between the collective and the individual, between the other and the self. In this, the shift from the external to the internal emerges.[5] The sorrows, on the other hand, lead one to a sense of meaninglessness, of having fallen out of history after the euphoria of being able to shape it, and of grim disillusionments after the experience of liberation.

There was a gendered difference in the perception of peasant women, but their standpoint was far from an isolated one. It was shared by urban women, and had in fact been enriched by the rich history of sharing between peasant and urban women; and it was also one respected by the few extraordinary men who had the will and the capacity to grasp the wisdom of the transformations the women had enacted in politics. Amal Sen, filling in for Anima Biswas's deep silence, had articulated her innovative quest for the terrain of love. Sen had also won the affection (and clearly more!) of the women, and no wonder, for not only could he theorize gendered critiques of Marxist practice with passionate insight, he was as acutely sensitive to the women's experiences of elation and disillusionment as he was to the intelligence of the thoughtful transformations they wrought. In some ways, he was also a powerful example of the 'new man' that the conditions of this period had made possible, as they had made possible the liberated woman activist.

For the rare urban man who had learnt to transcend the

[5] This draws partly from Passerini (1968:31–32).

straitjackets of ideology and dominant discourses, as Amal Sen had, the experience of a shared struggle with the peasants had given rise to a new aesthetic sensibility. This is evinced in a unique poetic idiom, infused with the desires of the rural peasants, communicated in the words of the city folk. Amal Sen had spent much of his time in prison reflecting upon the aesthetic worldview of the peasants he had grown to know so intimately, and upon his own sadness about their distance from the dominant discourses of poetry. He shared his own theorizing about folk culture:

> Those who control production control language too, and, thus, it is their social consciousness that finds pride of place in society. On the one hand, the distance between production and nature has distanced peasants from a creative access to language; on the other, the dominant social consciousness works as a mode of censorship preventing expressions of their own feelings and passions. As a result, the most significant areas of life cannot be enriched by them. It is in moments of historical crises, when the peasant is involved in passionate struggle, that this social censorship breaks down. Yet, they do not have access to poetic language to express the feelings that erupt then. Such feelings can still find poetic expression if the peasant has a comrade in struggle who can sense these feelings, who can place an ear close to the peasant's heart [and listen hard]. Then what form literature can take!

Amal Sen had tried to forge a new idiom to give voice to the peasants' desires. One of his poems is about what he would like to become, if granted the choice of a willed birth, *ichchhajanam*:

> The paddy seeds have long played like golden anklets
> At the feet of the peasant woman.
> As if trapped in the play of light
> They fall crashing and turning, rolling waves
> Now, in the hearts of the paddy seeds awakens a dream
> A dream tangled in the golden sun
> A dream of tiny seedlings like little infant boys.
> My mind had wanted to be born as its twin.
>
> In the grace of the setting sun all the paddy seeds have been sold
> He returns, vacant, wandering eyes
> roving the lanes and bylanes of the market

Suddenly, his gaze is transfixed upon a saree hanging in a shop,
The noises of transactions in the market place subside, give way
To the sound of the saree rustling in his wife's steps
—And what a rain!
The evening star that's shining in his heart
In its soft light and distant dream
I found the goal of my seeking
Without a doubt, that is where I took birth.

Just before this, Amal Sen had quoted Rabindranath Tagore's lines:

*Krishaker jibaner shareek jejon*
*Je aachhe jomir kaachha kachhi*
*She kobir lagi ami kaan petey aachhi.*

(One who is a part of a peasant's life
Who lives close to the earth
It's that poet's voice I long to hear.)

And then built up Rabindranath's idea of peasant poetry thus:

> I beg Rabindranath's pardon and seek to introduce an amendment in the poem—it is not enough to be a part of a peasant's life; it is only when you share the perspective of the peasant, become a comrade in struggle and place your ear to his heart that you can hear the peasant's voice, his real words.

These new forms of subjectivity were clearly not 'effects' of the discourses and texts that governed their lives. And the peasant women themselves were, quite un-self-consciously, creating new texts of struggle and new discourses of politics based on their own experiences in the fields of struggle. This was not just a consequence of a newfound liberation, but also a historical compulsion. For the ruptures of history had been such that often there were no scripts, no prescriptions that existed for such unprecedented events in modern times. They had to be written anew by the actors of history, both men and women.

For peasant women, this historical moment was one of political birth, and it was also a moment of radical political innovation. A critical point of difference in the peasant women's experience of struggle was that they had not yet been indoctrinated into the ideology of the CP even to the extent that their men had been. While there had been other peasant movements earlier, none had been marked by such a pervasive and influential participation of women. Tebhaga was a political birth for peasant women, and they responded from their own experiences of injustice, exploitation and the endangering of all that was dear to them in their lives. Kalyani Dasgupta had also said of them, 'We did not teach them what communism is, what wages are. But they learnt it, how we do not know. They learnt it from the oppression and exploitation in their own lives.' And she indicated that the women were drawn to the CP because they saw their own analyses reflected in it. The women were far from naïve about the modes of exploitation prevalent in their lives. They were located in a moment in history where they were fully aware of the need to struggle against such exploitation, but were unfettered by ideological baggage. While a unique urban leader like Amal Sen had the wisdom to transcend the limitations of conventional political ideology and forge new modes of intersubjectivity, as is evident in his thinking about the interface between urban and folk cultures, the peasant women were located in a moment in history that was certainly one of political activism, but one still not conceptualized in terms of the ideological discourse and political strategies of the CP. This was also the case because the CP did not have any scripts for women's strategies of participation in the first place; the women had to forge these themselves.

These were subjects constituted not just by 'subjectification' to the current forces of inequity and oppression, or a party ideology, but also by actual 'practices of liberation' (Foucault 1988:50). It is indeed striking that, in a period bracketed by cataclysmic tragedies, women should emphasize an aesthetics of joy. Or maybe it is purely logical that the experience of human life and potential laid to tragic waste gives rise to a determined privileging of human value and cohesion, of a renewed valuation of joy. The sustained emphasis on the aesthetic dimension of their experiences is what distinguishes the women's narratives from that of the men's. This marks a significant difference in gendered standpoints in the approach to politics, because one of the attributes of the aesthetic is that what makes an object beautiful 'has nothing to do with its usefulness or its exchange value' (Bowie 1990:4). While men were focusing on the usefulness of their analytical projections, the efficacy of their political strategies and the economic goal of the Tebhaga movement implicit in its very name, the women were unobtrusively structuring social relations of bonding, pleasure and caregiving amidst the extreme hardships and violence that governed their lives. While the caregiving must have evolved naturally out of women's traditional domestic roles, yet, as their self-transformations in the context of the famine show, and as the emphasis on antarikata as the quality of inwardness women brought to the movement demonstrates, they had clearly forged modes of caregiving and bonding that transcended the boundaries of tradition and were infused with new meanings.

Central to this process of making new meaning was the extension from subjectivity into a culture and politics of intersubjectivity. A culture of intersubjective communication was, of course, not new to the Tebhaga women. What was new was the field of such communication. Stepping out from their homes into the langarkhanas of the famine and then the fields of Tebhaga, the women extended the ways of relating they knew within the family and village community to their comrades in struggle. Several of the experiences narrated speak of the power of intersubjectivity underlining the force of the political culture women forged at that time: experiences of joy in solidarity; of functioning at levels of interiority with comrades; of integration into the worldview of marginalized Santals to the point of life-endangering commitment; and of conceiving and forging a world in which the love of the beloved fused with the love of one's land and people. It is simultaneously a sense of intersubjectivity located in an understanding of history—one's own and that of the other.

The knowledge that women had garnered from the exposure in the fields of politics had been harnessed to the transformation of the self and society, and the joy of these transformations too, at both subjective and intersubjective levels, was no less an aesthetic experience.[6] In fact, it became the vibrant ground for yet more transformations. The narratives thus render home in no uncertain

[6] See Foucault (1983 interview cited in Bowie 1990:13): 'The transformation of one's self by one's own knowledge is, I think, something rather close to the aesthetic experience.'

way the centrality of aesthetics in women's shaping of the movement: it was the aesthetic, affective impact of the 'man-made' devastation and political upheavals of the times that had initially mobilized them into transforming themselves and their worlds, and these transformations in turn were of an order of aesthetic experience that shaped the Tebhaga movement in qualitatively unique ways.

The victories or defeats of the movement itself, in confrontation with the feudal or state powers, were not the central focus of the women's accounts. Nor were they directly focused on questions of political efficacy, even though that clearly would have also been a consequence of the strengthening of solidarities. It was pride in their transformations of self and society that fuelled the 'retroactive force' of their narratives, still challenging, more than half a century later, the exploitative character of the rich landowners or the state, still asserting the values of care, bonding and love with which they had made an alternative society possible in the fields of struggle.

Also, given the modern investment of the activists in a rationalist class politics, the aesthetic pleasures articulated so forcefully by most of the women take on considerable political significance.[7] For this acknowledgement of the undeniable power of the individual's affective and sensuous relationship to the world, which limited conceptions of reason repress, enables one to play a significant role in the larger universe of politics. The headiness of solidarity, and the joys of interiority and intimacy, the compelling force of the past and the mobilizing power of the search for a terrain of love, all modes of sensitive cognition, translated into meaningful modes of intensifying the movement. The aesthetic of liberation, thus, also entailed for the women a liberation of desire in the world of the political.

An aesthetic in itself, though, however transgressive or revolutionary, cannot validate a reality principle (Marcuse 1987:172). Yet, the aesthetic, in its bringing together of sensuousness and intellect, desire and cognition, and practical and theoretical reason, can be suggestive of possibilities in lived reality—as is the case with Kabir's

[7] Under the predominance of rationalism, the cognitive function of sensuousness has been constantly minimized. In line with the repressive concept of reason, cognition became the ultimate concern of the 'higher' non-sensuous faculties of the mind (Marcuse 1987:180).

notion of love. Moving beyond the poetic aesthetic to the realms of the social, and from self to other, such love offers the possibility of cognitive action, on the basis of which 'a theoretical discourse of love as a force for social change' may yet be forged. Sufism and Bhakti celebrate 'an order of sensuousness (sensitive cognition)' (ibid.:183) that is integral to their aesthetics, and that compensates for the passive cognition of the rational faculties. Introduced into culture, this notion of sensitive cognition 'far from destroying civilization would give it a firmer basis' (ibid.:181) in its radical potential to liberate the senses from forces of repression (Panjabi 2011:48).

What women were giving voice to in their narratives were their perceptions of their 'life-worlds.' These perceptions—of their everyday experiences—comprised an integral part of the truth of their relationship to the world, and also a challenge to the scientific rationalism of the CP. This everyday world is usually the chief site of tension in women's lives. Dorothy Smith (1987) terms women's traditional experience of the everyday world as 'problematic' in terms of the conflict between the sociopolitical 'relations of ruling' that govern women's lives, and their everyday experiences and desires. In Tebhaga, this characteristic conflict gave way to a rare fusion, of the CP's nurturing of women as activists and the women's fulfilment of their own desires, at least in some areas, and at least for a while, even if it was short lived.

The pleasure of self-fulfilment and the moves towards political liberation slowly but surely began to find meaning in the larger whole. The women used a secular modernity as a launching pad to paradoxically transcend the repressive limitations of this modernity, and in doing so created a world unique in modern times. The aesthetics of joy formed the bedrock of the political ground on which the sensuous and the rational, and the personal and the political, became integral to each other; as a result, the particular became meaningfully integral to the whole in ways such that existential fulfilment became a distinct possibility for an entire collective, albeit for but a moment, in the modern history of the Indian subcontinent.[8]

[8] 'To Kant the aesthetic dimension is the medium in which the senses and the intellect meet.... [T]his mediation is necessitated by the pervasive conflict between the lower and the higher faculties of man generated by the progress of civilization—

Power had taken on a new meaning in the early stages of the movement. It was a power of the people capable of bringing 'peace' to every individual; radically different from a politics of seizing power. It had enabled a realization of the sensuous and the rational, of the ethical in the political. All aspects of life seemed linked by one's ethical and political commitments. This sense of these intrinsic connections had been a collective historical experience even though the loss of it is manifestly different in different individuals. The 'magic' of the time was also infused with the experience of such power; it was a 'way of recognizing transcendence in the secular sense', in the sense of being able to influence the march of history. What Passerini (1996) observes about the 1960s across the world had already manifest itself earlier in the Tebhaga movement in the 1940s in Bengal: 'That power could be addressed in daily life as well as in formal politics meant that one made a constant effort to participate in reality and to understand it.'[9]

A critical revelation in all of this was the extent to which it indicated the immersion of self in the logos of the movement, which was articulated alternately by various women, rural and urban, as the magic of the times, the nasha, mazaa, ananda or the 'dream of socialism that was in the air'. On one hand, politics was 'feminized' by an ethic of care and women shaping subjectivities; on the other, it was almost as if the individual had disappeared—the efforts required of an individual in order to assert her standpoint, and to make a unique and inimitable contribution to a shared subjectivity, were overshadowed by 'the collective elaboration in which the instant of fusion prevailed' (Passerini 1996:68). It was an all-encompassing

progress achieved through the subjugation of the sensuous faculties to reason, and through their repressive utilization for social needs' (Marcuse 1987:179).

[9] There is a certain resonance between the sense of the magic of the 1940s that Manikuntala Sen holds on to and the power of the 1960s as Passerini describes it. The latter observes: 'It is precisely the demise of the question of power [of the 1960s] that is the central grief hanging over the entire seventies and casting its long shadow on us still.' The question of power then, as she explains it, 'was a way of recognizing transcendence in the secular sense… in the sense of being able to influence the march of history. That power could be addressed in daily life as well as in formal politics meant that one made a constant effort to participate in reality and to understand it' (1996:132).

universe in which the public and the private were fused. This attitude went beyond the claim of a critical knowledge; the question was always more emphatically of a political and existential nature, where these two aspects tended to mesh.

Was the power of the secular transcendence and universality of the 1940s such that even as it empowered women, it ironically prevented them from articulating their critiques of the repressive ideologies of sexuality and violence? Was it that despite the enmeshing of the political and the existential, the force of the political actually repressed certain crucial existential dimensions of women's experience, which those like Anima Biswas and Ila Mitra, then, hid even from themselves, and refused to process as memory? The political is where we work through cognition. The Tebhaga women's narratives reveal that the movement's 'magical' subsuming of the personal in the universalist imperative, even as it was marked by a radical fusion of eros and politics, pre-empted the possibility of an anti-patriarchal feminist politics for the women who *revelled in its intoxication.*

The demise of the question of such power to transform one's own life and transform history is the central grief hanging over the 1940s, and that which destroyed it casts its long shadow on us still. Equally significant, then, about this sense of 'magic' are the factors that mark its limits and bring it to an end. The central question has to do with what takes away the intoxication, what challenges such ontological identification—and the answers begin with the questions of violence and partition, but do not end there. For one, what continues to punctuate the activist's sense of self is deep unease with the party's discourse on sexuality—or the lack thereof. Also, with Ila Mitra's account, there is the question of what is lost when ontological identification loses its physical and social anchoring, on account of state violence and of partition, and the history of affective bonding that ensures a continuing commitment to the struggle for justice. Equally pressing is the understanding of a politics based on love, and the impact of violence on such a politics. With Anima Biswas's narrative, there is the problematic of how love could be retained when the nurturing context is destroyed, specially by the violence of one's own comrades. The thwarted search for the terrain of love and the ontological experience of affective bonding both persisted, in their own ways, haunting the lives and narratives of the Animas and Ilas of Tebhaga as 'retroactive' forces shaping future histories.

It is not enough to write off a violent turn as a 'mistake' and then live with a narrative of the fall, of a productive, creative movement degenerating into excesses as is often the case in left historiography. Rememory of movements such as Tebhaga, of their constitutive histories, suggest that the possibilities of the past did not have to degenerate, but given the pressure of events, state violence and partition, on the one hand, and perhaps the exhaustion and sadness of cadres on the other, how do we theorize historical choices?[10] As permanently foreclosing all options? As flattening out all differences? Does the internal repression of the armed struggle that brought that 'magic' time to an end continue in the repression of the memory of those times? It may be relevant to the present to understand this demise, and the continued silence on it, in relation to the dilemmas posed by the violent movements from below today. And, indeed, in relation to the continued impact of such repression on other movements too that have hastily elided their histories of violence.

The darkest silence that looms large in the history of Tebhaga, then, is that of violence. All the indications of forced, self-imposed silence point to a complex culture of internalized repression that had become an integral part of the armed revolution. Ila Mitra's deep trauma, revealed in her momentary rupturing of her silence on the CP, despite her endorsement of revolutionary violence and her stoical endurance of it; Anima Biswas's grim silence and her withdrawal into an abyss of disillusionment; Amal Sen's acknowledgement of the treachery of the repression and the tortured silence in which he continued to live with it; all of these people haunted by the internal violence of the party, and still reluctant to break their silence on it fifty years after Tebhaga, stand testimony to the continuance of a culture of repression set in place during the armed revolution.

Manikuntala Sen (2001:206) articulates, with a brutally honest self-reflexivity, her complicity in such a culture of silence and its consequences:

[10] Many thanks to V. Geetha for this vital question.

> Women, who had just been brought in [to prison] after their arrests, also had many startling stories and news which would at times make us tremble. Village women, especially, would tell us how the peasants and the jotedars were fighting each other. One woman said that a jotedar had been cut to pieces, put inside a clay pot and sunk in the river. As I listened to this gruesome report, I felt like throwing up. I was nervous, and tried to get a grip on myself but failed. One day the question was asked: If our children and jotedars were in the same place would we hurl a bomb at the jotedars? I did not have much to say during these sessions. I could not find the words. *If I had been made to speak I would have said yes, for fear that expressing any other views would mark me out as one who was less revolutionary. What is the point of blaming the Naxalites? We created them.* (emphasis added)

It would do well to remember that the politics of the CP was primarily based on a culture of compassion. The Congress, of course, had not even managed to organize amongst the poor and under-caste peasants, and they were certainly not a cause for concern for right-wing parties either. As Arendt (1955:236) too points out, in implied agreement with Brecht, it was the 'passion of compassion' that had initially fuelled revolutionary movements:

> Brecht discovered by instinct what the historians of revolution have persistently failed to see: namely that the modern revolutions, from Robespierre to Lenin, were driven by the passion of compassion.... 'The classics', Marx, Engels and Lenin, in Brecht's coded language, were the most compassionate of all men.

The CP's basis in compassion is a fact that we cannot afford to forget, and its descent into a culture of fear is a reality we cannot afford to ignore.

Yet, the question of violence in left politics also seems to hang on a curious relationship between compassion and shame. There is, in fact, an international revolutionary culture of the concealment of such compassison, which Arendt points to, that calls for attention, especially in relation to an analysis of the reasons for its internalization in the Indian context:

> Ever since the French Revolution... there have been many among the revolutionists who, like Brecht, acted out of compassion and

> concealed their compassion, under the cover of scientific theories and hardboiled rhetoric, out of shame. (ibid.:237–38)

If a revelation of the ethical impulse of compassion is cause for shame, then it indicates a clear privileging of scientific rationalism over ethicality. What, in any case, is the nature of this shame? And if the scientific rationalist concealment of compassion can lead to an actual obscuring of compassion, as Arendt implies, and if it can open up ways of justifying the violation of good, even if in the interests of a long-term good, then the very nature of such adherence to rationalism is ethically in question. This erasure of ethicality, as Arendt has shown in the case of Brecht's poetic death, also signifies the destruction of the aesthetic possibilities of the human being.

The Tebhaga women's movement was unique in that it signalled the power of affective, aesthetic and ethical fulfilment of being in politics. The first phase of Tebhaga compels us to see that central to the question of revolutionary movements are concerns underlined by these very impulses, as evinced in the politics of care, the power of the layered antarikata of the movement, the forging of deep comradeship across social divides, and the fusion of eros and politics in a comradeship of love. The second phase urges us to confront what happens if these are substituted or taken over by an overriding rationalist logic of fighting power or wanting power, and its associated culture of repression. A logic of violence that destroys the conditions for genuinely liberatory politics, such as the Tebhaga women had shown was possible to forge, may then find itself caught forever in its own trap. It may indeed be condemned to repeat itself in an ever-recurring cycle.

# Interviews Conducted

## Areas Now in Bangladesh

### ♦ *Dinajpur Area* ♦

- Abani Lahiri (in Calcutta): 17 November 1996, 2 January 1997 and 5 July 1998.
- Rani Dasgupta (in Calcutta): 7 Novemer 1996, 16 November 1996, 17 December 1996, 7 January 1997, 26 April 1997; (with husband Ajoy Dasgupta 12 July 1997), 12 September 1997.
- Bina Guha (in Calcutta): 25 August 1997, 18 September 1997.
- Dipti Bagchi (in Calcutta) (from Dinajpur and Rangpur): 26 April 1996, 4 May 1996, 5 June 1996.

***Thakurgaon***

- Uttar Paria village
    - Paranshari Barmani, wife of Kamparam Singha who was imprisoned and killed during the Tebhaga movement, and was herself directly involved in the movement: 16 June 1997.
    - Digendranath Singha (m), Tebhaga activist: 16 June 1997.

- Dakkhin Paria village
  - Heleketu Singha (m), Tebhaga leader and activist, local CP leader: 24 October 1997.
  - Chunilal Singha (m), Tebhaga activist: 16 June 1997.
- Morolpara village
  - Shaheban Barmani, possible activist: 16 June 1997.

*Ranisainkel*

- Bajebaxar village
  - Poharkiram (m), possible activist: 25 October 1997
  - Sajala, possible activist: 25 October 1997.
  - Balendra Barman (m), possible activist: 25 October 1997.
- Baro Sundarpara village
  - Godo Barmani, possible activist: 25 October 1997.
- Bachoo village, Gondipara
  - Hemanta Bewa, possible activist: 25 October 1997.
  - Bokuler Ma, Tebhaga activist: 25 October 1997.

### ♦ *Narail Area* ♦

- Amal Sen (m) (in Dhaka): 9 June 1997, 20 June 1997, 26 October 1997.
- Anima Biswas (in Barasat, near Calcutta): 25 November 1997.
- Narail town
  - Riziya Khatun: 19 October 1997.
- Hatiara village
  - Phuli Goldar and Dhirendranath Biswas: 18 June 1997, 19 October 1997.
  - Manik Biswas (m), Phuli's brother and Tebhaga activist: 18 June 1997.
- Dumurtala village:
  - Anwara Begum, activist: 19 October 1997.
  - Nurul Akbar (m), activist: 19 October 1997.
- Ujirpur village
  - Abdul Majid Mullah (m), activist, leader Chandpur Village: 20 October 1997.

  - Mohammed Mominuddin Mullah (m), activist: 20 October 1997.
  - Rupbanu, related to activist: 20 October 1997.
  - Rabeya, related to activist: 20 October 1997.
  - Abdus Samal Munshi (m), related to activist: 20 October 1997.

### ♦ *Rangpur Area* ♦

- Abani Lahiri (m) (in Calcutta): 17 October 1996, 2 January 1997, 11 March 1998, 5 July 1998.
- Rani Mukherjee (in Debanandapur, near Calcutta), activist and leader of Rangpur: 4 October 1997, 14 December 1997.
- Shobha Lahiri (in Calcutta): 23 March 1996, 18 April 1996.
- Rekha Pandey (in Calcutta) from Rangpur: 20 June 1996, 7 July 1996.
- Dipti Bagchi (in Calcutta) from Dinajpur and Rangpur: 26 April 1996, 4 May 1996, 25 June 1996.

*Neelphamari*

- Dimla town (earlier Greater Rangpur District),
  - Ghulam Rabbani Bulbul (m): 13 June 1997, 14 June 1997.
  - Ganeshchandra Singha Roy (m): 13 June 1997, 14 June 1997.
  - Abdur Rahim: 13 June 1997, 14 June 1997.
- Dholpara village, Dimla
  - Sarodini Barmani: 13 June 1997, 14 June 1997.
- Dakkhin Kharibari village, Dimla village
  - Sukhomoni Roy, from daughter of Tan Narayan, martyr of the Tebhaga movement, was 10 or 12 while active in the Tebhaga movement: 13 June 1997, 14 June 1997.
- Dimla thana
  - Kartikchandra Roy: 13 June 1997, 14 June 1997.
- Interviewed in Siliguri, W. Bengal
  - Asha Chakravarty of Kurigram, activist and singer, 1 sitting: 24 January 1998.

*Kurigram 23/10/97*

- Kurigram town
  - Harun-al-Rashid 'Lal' (m), contemporary left activist cum lawyer, 1 sitting: 23 October 1997.
  - Samsunnehar Chowdhury (Sa) (m), contemporary left activist: 23 October 1997.
- Baidyer Bazar village
  - Birendranath Ray (m), activist: 23 October 1997.
  - Gyanoda Barmani, activist: 23 October 1997.
  - Indu Bhushan Ray (m), activist's son: 23 October 1997.
  - Nirmala Rai (Baidyer Bazar) : 23 October 1997.
- Kanchipara village, Kurigram
  - Kaminibala Ray, young girl during the movement: 23 October 1997.
- Ulipur village, Madhyapara
  - 'Dr' Kalipada Barman (m), activist: 23 October 1997.

## ♦ *Nachole Area* ♦

- Ila Mitra (in Calcutta), important leader of Nachole, CP member: 12 December 1997, 11 March 1997, 17 September 1997.
- Ramen Mitra (in Calcutta), veteran CP leader, important leader of Nachole and husband of Ila Mitra: 17 September 1997.
- Maleka Begum (in Dhaka): between 8 June 1997 and 12 June 1997.
- Rajshahi
  - Fazle Hussain Badshah (m), 6 pages: between 8 June 1997 and 12 June 1997.
- Kusmadanga village*
  - Pani Kisku, Santal tribal, activist: between 8 June 1997 and 12 June 1997.
  - Puni Birsa, Santal tribal, activist: between 8 June 1997 and 12 June 1997.
  - Kanna Moral (m) husband of Puni Birsa, Santal tribal, activist: between 8 June 1997 and 12 June 1997.
- Kendua village*
  - Paanchu Daktar (m): between 8 June 1997 and 12 June 1997.

  - Satian Murmu: between 8 June 1997 and 12 June 1997.
- Pirpur village*
  - Khuda Baksh (m): between 8 June 1997 and 12 June 1997.
- West Nizampur village
  - Mangalchandra Barman (m): between 8 June 1997 and 12 June 1997.
- Kadipara village, Amnura
  - Shokhor (m): between 8 June 1997 and 12 June 1997.
- Champai Nawabganj village
- Ranjitkumar Bagchi (m): between 8 June 1997 and 12 June 1997.

### ♦ *Malda Area (Now in West Bengal)* ♦

- Malda town
  - Naren Das (m), activist: between 1 February 1998 and 2 February 1998.
- Bhabanikotha village, Gajol
  - Narayani Mondol (Sarkar) activist: between 1 February 1998 and 2 February 1998.
  - Bhoto (m), activist: between 1 February 1998 and 2 February 1998.
- Sholakuri village, Gajol
  - Kando, activist Roghu Desi's first wife: between 1 February 1998 and 2 February 1998.
  - Activist Roghu Desi's second wife: between 1 February 1998 and 2 February 1998.
- Sholadanga village, Habibpur
  - Jhoru Das (m), Bhupesh Chandra Singha (m), old men: between 1 February 1998 and 2 February 1998.

## Areas In West Bengal, India

### ♦ *Jalpaiguri Area* ♦

- Abani Lahiri (m), interviewed in Calcutta, veteran CP leader, in charge of all areas in north Bengal where movement was at its peak: 17 November 1996, 2 January 1997, 11 March 1998, 5 July 1998

- Jalpaiguri town
    - Kalyani Dasgupta, activist, important leader: between 21 January 1998 and 23 January 1998.
- Odlabari, Malbazar
    - Poko Oraoni important tribal activist: between 21 January 1998 and 23 January 1998.
- Mangalbari, Chalsa, originally Mathachulka
    - Sukra Oraon, tribal activist, singer: between 21 January 1998 and 23 January 1998.

### ♦ *Medinipur Area* ♦

- Medinipur town
    - Bimala Majhi, activist, important leader: 24 January 1999, 25 January 1999.
    - Ananta Majhi (m), activist leader and Bimala's husband: 24 January 1999, 25 January 1999.
- Amonpur village
    - Sibarani Mitra (nee Dikshit), activist, important leader: 24 January 1999, 25 January 1999.

### ♦ *Kakdwip* ♦

- Budhakhali
    - Satyabhama Maity: 26 December 1997.
    - Satish Sahu: 26 December 1997.
    - Tulsi Samanta and Basanti Mondal: 26 December 1997.
    - Basanti Mondal: 26 December 1997.
    - Tulsi, Swarnadhar Samanta and Madhab Mondal: 26 December 1997.
    - Kanan Das and Dhanapati Das: 26 December 1997.
    - Lakkhi Saotia: 26 December 1997.
- Chandanpiri
    - Janaki Bala Pradhan: 27 December 1997.
    - Jamuna Bala Das: 27 December 1997.
    - Snehlata Das: 27 December 1997.
    - Basanti Das: 27 December 1997.
    - Sushila Das: 27 December 1997.

  - Pramila Maity: 27 December 1997.
  - Sushila Maity: 27 December 1997.
- Layalgunge
  - Bijoy Mondal: 28 December 1997.
  - Amulya Kamilya: 28 December 1997.
- Barujjye-mahal, Nishchintapur
  - Mandakini Haldar: 8 April 1998.

## Miscellaneous

- Somenath Hore (m), interviewed in Calcutta, painter and sculptor, observer and documentator of Tebhaga movement as CPI member in Tebhaga areas: 5 July 1996.
- Kamala Mukherjee (Calcutta), urban activist, in Calcutta during Tebhaga: 30 December 1997.
- Kanak Mukherjee (Calcutta), urban activist, in Calcutta during Tebhaga: 31 December 1997.
- Maleka Begum (Dhaka): 8 July 1997.
- Dr Abdur Rahim (m), activist from Khulna, interviewed in Aramghata, Daulatpur, Bangladesh: 21 October 1997.
- Henna Das (interviewed in Dhaka), activist and important leader of Tebhaga in Mymensingh, Bangladesh: 28 October 1997.

# Appendix

## Literary Representations of Tebhaga*

### Fiction


1. Das, Susnat. 1998. *Tebhagar Galpo*. Kolkata: Nakshatra Prakashan.
2. Fuyad, Afif (ed.). 1998. *Diba Ratrir Kavya*, July–September (special issue on the art, literature and culture on the Tebhaga movement).
3. Elias, Akhtaruzzaman. 1996. *Khwabnama*. Kolkata: Naya Udyog.
4. Hossein, Selina. 1989. *Kaanta Taare Projapati*. Dhaka: Jatioya Sahitya Prakashani.
5. Patri, Purnendu. 1998. *Anyagram, Anyapran*. Kolkata: Thema.
6. Roy, Sabitri. 1986. *Paka Dhaner Gaan*. Kolkata: Suprakashini (Eng translation *Harvest Song*, translated by Chandrima Bhattacharya and Adrita Mukherjee, Kolkata: Stree, 2005).


* This is by no means an exhaustive list. More stories and poems are also to be found in the main bibliography, in the Special Tebhaga Centenary Publications and special issues of journals, in which they have been published along with memoirs and analytical essays. Only issues of journals that focus exclusively on literature are included here, in addition to anthologies and works by individual authors.

7. Sen, Kamalesh (ed.). 1987. *Gram Banglar Galpa*. Calcutta: Deepayan. 1995. The following stories in this book are directly related to the Tebhaga movement:
i. Swarnakamal Bhattacharya, 'Mantrashakti'.
ii. Sushil Jana, 'Bou'.
iii. Narayan Gangopadhyay, 'Banduk'.
iv. Nani Bhowmik, 'Agantuk'.
v. Golam Kuddush, 'Laakhe Na Milaye'.
vi. Umanath Bhattacharya, 'Shaada Kurta'.
vii. Alauddin Al Azaad, 'Sundari'.
viii. Mihir Acharya, 'Dalaal'.
ix. Mihir Sen, 'Haaush'.
x. Arun Choudhuri, 'Halaal'.
xi. Aba Oshaq, 'Jonk'.
xii. Souri Ghatak, 'Aranyer Swapna'.
xiii. Kirankumar Roy, 'Ider Chaand'.

## Drama

1. Mukhopadhyay, Harimadhav. Year not available. 'Mantrashakti: A Play', in *Sharadiya Basumati*.

# Bibliography


Anderson, Benedict. 1998. *Spectre of Comparisons: Nationalism, Southeast Asia and the World.* London: Verso

Amin, Shahid. 2002. 'Writing the Recalcitrant Event', http://www.transforming.cultures.uts.edu.au/pdfs/recalcitrant_amim.pdf (accessed 25 February 2015).

Arendt, Hannah. 1955. 'Bertolt Brecht (1898–1956)', in *Men in Dark Times*, pp. 207–50. New York: Harvest.

Bahuguna, Sunderlal. Treading the Gandhian Path. URL: http://gandhifoundation.org/2008/09/14/treading-the-gandhian-path-by-sunderlal-bahuguna/ (accessed 9 April 2015) (first published in *Gandhi and the Contemporary World*, edited by Antony Copley and George Paxton, Indo-British Historical Society, 1997).

Bandyopadhyay, Krishna. 2008. 'Naxalbari Politics: A Feminist Narrative', *Economic and Political Weekly*, 43(14): 52–59.

Bandyopadhyay, Manik. 1946. 'Mangala', in *Granthabali,* Vol. 6, pp. 292–96.

———. 1980 (1386). '*Haraner Naatjamai*', in Jugantar Chakrabarty (ed.), *Manik Bandyopadhyayer Sreshtho Galpa*, pp. 160–71. Calcutta: Bengal Publishers.

———. 2011. 'Chhiniye Khai Ni Keno?' (Why Did They Not Snatch and Eat), in Abdul Mannan Sayyed (ed.), Shreshttha Galpo, pp. 172–78. Dhaka: Abosar.

Bandyopadhyay, Nripen. 1981. 'Operation Barga and Land Reforms Perspective in West Bengal: A Discursive Review', *Economic and Political Weekly*, 16(25/26): A38–39, A41–42.

Bandyopadhyay, Sekhar. 1989. 'Social Protest of Politics of Backwardness? The Namasudra Movement in Bengal, 1872–1911', in Basudeb Chattopadhyay, Hari Vasudevan and Rajat Kanta Ray (eds), *Dissent and Consensus: Protest in Pre-Industrial Societies*, pp. 170–232. Calcutta: K.P. Bagchi.

———. 1995. 'Popular Religion and Social Mobility in Colonial Bengal: The Matua Sect and the Namasudras', in Rajat Kanta Ray (ed.), *Mind Body and Society Life and Mentality in Colonial Bengal*, pp. 152-192. Calcutta: Oxford University Press.

———. 1998. 'Changing Borders, Shifting Loyalties: Religion, Caste and the Partition of Bengal in 1947'. Asian Studies Institute Working Paper 2,: Asian Studies Institute, Victoria University of Wellington, Wellington, pp. 1–10.

———. 2003. 'Freedom and its Enemies: Politics of Transition in West Bengal, 1947–1949'. Victoria University of Wellington, Wellington. http://researcharchive.vuw.ac.nz/bitstream/handle/10063/720/article.pdf?sequence=3 (accessed 9 April 2015).

———. 2004. *Caste, Culture And Hegemony: Social Domination In Colonial Bengal*. New Delhi: Sage.

———. 2006. 'The Communists in Post-Colonial Bengal, 1948–52: The Untold Story of "Second" Tebhaga'. Victoria University of Wellington, Wellington. http://hdl.handle.net/10063/646 (accessed 15 April 2015).

Banerjee, Prathama. 2002. 'Re-Presenting Pasts: Santals in Nineteenth-century Bengal', in Partha Chatterjee and Anjan Ghosh (eds), *History and the Present*, pp. 1–19). New Delhi: Permanent Black.

Barrios de Chungara, Domitila. 1978. *Let Me Speak! Testimony of Domitila, a Woman of the Bolivian Mines*. New York: Monthly Review Press.

Bartika. 1997. *Bangladesher Jatiya Adivasi Parisater Tebhaga Andolaner Ponchash Bachhor Purti Sankhya*. January–June.

Barman, Santosh Kumar. 1997. *Lalbagane Shishu Telengana: Kakdweep Tebhaga Andolaner Itibritta; 1950 Shaler January Porjontya* (A Short Historical Story of Kakdweep Tebhaga Andolan up to January 1950). Kakdwip, South 24 Parganas: Barma Pustakalay.

Basu, Jyoti. 2009. *Memoirs*. http://www.jyotibasu.net/?q=node/255 (accessed 9 April 2015).

Begum, Maleka. 1989. *Banglar Nari Andolan* (Bengal's Women's Movement). Dhaka: University Press.

———. 1987. *Ila Mitra*. Dhaka: Gyan Prakashani.

Benhabib, Seyla and Drucilla Cornell. 1987. *Feminism as Critique: On the Politics of Gender*. Minneapolis: University of Minnesota Press.

Benjamin, Walter. 1969a. 'The Storyteller', in *Illuminations* (translated by Harry Zohn, edited with an introduction by Hannah Arendt), pp. 83–110. New York: Schocken Books.

———. 1969b. 'Theses on the Philosophy of History', in in *Illuminations* (translated by Harry Zohn, edited with an introduction by Hannah Arendt), pp. 253–64. New York: Schocken Books.

Bhadra, Mita. 1987. 'Cha-Shilper Mahila Sramik', *Madhuparni, Bishesh Jalpaiguri Jela Sankhya*, December: 229–32.

Bhattacharya, Malini. 1987. 'The Class Character of Sexuality: Peasant Women in Manik Bandyopadhyay', *Social Scientist*, 15(1): 46–59.

Bhowmick, Suhrid Kumar. 1996. *Santali Gan o Kavita Sankalan* (Santal Songs and Poetry Collection). New Delhi: Sahitya Akademi.

Bowie, Andrew. 1990. *Aesthetics and Subjectivity from Kant to Nietzsche*. New York: Manchester University Press.

Butalia, Urvashi. 1998. *The Other Side of Silence: Voices from the Partition of India*. New Delhi: Viking.

———. 2001. 'The Persistence of Memory', *Civil Lines: New Writing from India*, No. 5, pp 169–98.

Chakravartty, Renu. 1980. *Communists in the Indian Women's Movement*. New Delhi: People's Publishing House.

Chakravarti, Uma. 2003. *Gendering Caste: Through a Feminist Lens*. Kolkata: Stree.

Chatterjee, Srilata. 2003. *Congress Politics in Bengal, 1919–1939*. Delhi: Anthem South Asian Studies.

Chattopadhyay, Kunal. 1987. *Tebhaga Andolaner Itihas* (History of the Tebhaga Movement). Calcutta: Progressive Publishers.

Chaudhuri, Supriya. 2011. 'Hunger: Some Representations of the 1943 Bengal Famine', in Supriya Chaudhuri and Rimi B. Chatterjee (eds), *The Writer's Feast: Food and the Politics of Representation*, pp. 223–36. New Delhi: Orient Blackswan.

———. 2012. 'Moral Economies of Wellbeing'. http://humanitiesunderground.org/the-moral-economics-of-wellbeing/ (accessed 9 April 2015).

Chauduri, Tripti. 2006. 'Mahila Atmaraksha Samity'. http://www.banglapedia.org/HT/M_0064.HTM (accessed 9 April 2015).

Cooper, Adrienne. 1979. 'Herstory: When Peasant Women Rose', *Manushi*, July/August.

———. 1988. *Sharecropping and Sharecroppers' Struggles in Bengal: 1930–1950*. Calcutta: K.P. Bagchi.

Custers, Peter. 1987. *Women in the Tebhaga Uprising: Rural Poor Women and Revolutionary Leadership (1946–47)*. Calcutta; Naya Prakash.

Dalmiya, Vrinda. 2007. 'Unravelling Leadership: "Relational Humility" and the Search for Ignorance', in Peter D. Hershock, Mark Mason and John N. Hawkins (eds), *Changing Education: Leadership, Innovation and Development in a Globalizing Asia Pacific*. Dordecht: Springer, pp. 297–322.

*Dainik Sonali Sangbad*. 1996. Various issues.

Das, Ajit Kumar (ed.). 1996. *Nachole Ila Mitra*. Nababganj: Tebhaga Kriskak Andolaner Ponchash Bachhor Purti Udjapan Committee.

Das Gupta, Ranajit. 1983. 'Krishak O Rajniti: Jalpaiguri 1938–1940' (Farmers and Politics: Jalpaiguri 1938–1940), *Parichay*, November: 39–79.

———. 1992. *Economy, Society and Politics in Bengal: Jalpaiguri 1869–1947*. New Delhi: Oxford University Press.

Dasgupta, Atish. 1995. *Groundswell in Bengal in the 1940s*. Calcutta: National Book Agency.

Dasgupta, Kalyani. 1997. 'Tebhaga Jelar Meyera', in *Paschimbanga: Tebhaga Sankhya, 140, Tathya o Sangskriti Bivagh, Paschimbanga Sarkar*, No. 30, pp. 42–46.

Dasgupta, Rani. 1973. 'Tebhaga Sangrame Krishak Meyeder Bhumika' (The Role of Women Farmers in the Tebhaga Struggle), in *Tebhaga Sangram Rajat Jayanti Smarak Grantha*, pp. 107–113.

———. 1989. *Abibhakta Banglar Tebhaga Andolan*. Calcutta: Jayashri Prakashan.

Dreze, Jean and Amartya Sen. 1993. *Hunger and Public Action*. New Delhi: Oxford University Press.

Dutta, Shekhar. 1985. *Tebhaga Andolan*. Dhaka: Bangla Akademi.

———. 1988. 'Anaanyasadharan Tebhaga Sangram' in Bangladesh Krishak Samiti (ed.), *Tebhaga Sangram: 40 Barshik Smarakgatha* Dhaka: Bangladesh Krishak Samiti.

Eagleton, Terry. 1995. *Heathcliff and the Great Hunger: Studies in Irish Culture*. London: Verso.

Elias, Akhtaruzzaman. 1996. *Khwabnama*. Kolkata: Naya Udyog.

Fernandez-Armesto, Felipe. 2001. *Food: A History*. London: Macmillan.

Foucault, Michel. 1988. *Politics, Philosophy, Culture: Interviews and Other Writings 1977–84*. New York: Routledge.

Friedlander, Saul. 1997. *Nazi Germany and the Jews: Volume 1*. New York: Harper Collins.

———. 1992. 'Trauma, Transference and "Working through" in Writing the History of the "Shoah"'. *History and Memory*, Vol. 4, No. 1. (Spring-Summer, 1991), pp. 39–59.

———. 1984. *Reflections of Nazism: An Essay on Kitch and Death* (translated by Thomas Weyr). New York: Harper and Row.

———. 1976. 'Some aspects of the historical significance of the holocaust'. *Jerusalem Quarterly*, No. 1, fall, pp. 36–59.

Gandhi, Nandita and Nandita Shah. 1992. *The Issues at Stake: Theory and Practice in the Contemporary Women's Movement in India*. New Delhi: Kali for Women.

Ganguly, Arati. 1992. *Banglar Itihase Narir Bhumika O Sangram*. Calcutta: Gana Unnayan Parishad.

Geiger, Susan. 1990. 'Dialogue: What's So Feminist About Women's Oral History?' *Journal of Women's History*, 2(1): 169–81.

Ghatak, Maitreya. 1984. 'Peasant Mobilization in Bengal', *Translations*, 3(1): pp. 13–142.

——— and Boudhayan Chattopadhyay. 1986. 'Share-Croppers of West Bengal: A New Deal', in Amit Kumar Gupta (ed.), *Agrarian Structure and Peasant Revolt in India*. New Delhi: Criterion Publications.

Ghosh, Purnendu. 1987. *Tebhagar Smriti*. Bilaspur, Madhya Pradesh: Setu Sahitya Parishad.

Gilligan, Carol. 1982. *In a Different Voice: Psychological Theory and Women's Development*. Cambridge: Harvard University Press.

Greenough, Paul. 1982. Prosperity *and Misery in Modern Bengal: The Famine of 1943–44*. New York and London: Oxford University Press.

Guha, Bina. 1996. 'Nari Samaj o Krishak Andolan', in Mahasveta Devi (ed.), *Aparajeya*. Calcutta: National Publishers.

Guha, Ramachandra. 2011. 'After the Fall'.
http://caravanmagazine.in/essay/after-fall?page=0,1 (accessed 9 April 2015).

Gupta, Ashoka. 2008. *In the Path of Service: Memories of a Changing Century* (translated by Sipra Bhattacharya with Ranjana Dasgupta). Kolkata: Stree.

Guru, Gopal. 2011. *Humiliation—Claims and Context*. Delhi: Oxford University Press.

Haoldar, Sekander Ali. 1996. 'Tebhaga Sangramer Aitihijya o Itihas', *Samvaad*, 4 November.

Harding, Sandra 1991. *Whose Science? Whose Knowledge? Thinking from Women's Lives*. Ithaca: Cornell University Press.

Hossain, Selina. 1989. *Kaanta Taare Projapati*. Dhaka: Jatiya Sahitya Prakashani.

Isma, Shahidul. 1996. 'Ranima Ashchhen', *Samvaad*, 13 November.

Jatiya Udjapan Committee (ed.). 1997. *Tebhaga Andolaner Ponchash Bachhor* (on the occasion of the golden jubilee celebrations of the Tebhaga movement). Dhaka: Jatiya Udjapan Committee.

Kamal, Mesbah. 1996. 'Post-Partition Peasant Movements in East Bengal: A Case Study on Nachole Uprising'. Chapter 6 of unpublished Ph.D. dissertation, Department of History, Dhaka University, Dhaka.

Kamble, Baby. 2008. *The Prisons We Broke* (translated by Maya Pandit). New Delhi: Orient Longman (originally published as *Jina Amucha* in Marathi).

Kant, Immanuel. 2010 'Transition from Popular Moral Philosophy to the Metaphysic of Morals', in *Fundamental Principles of the Metaphysic of Morals* (translated by Thomas Kingsmill Abbott). http://creativecommons.org/licenses/by-nc-sa/2.5/au/ (accessed 23 February 2012).

Koch, Gertrud. 1997. '"Against All Odds" or the Will to Survive: Moral Conclusions from Narrative Closure', *History and Memory*, 9(1/2): 393–408.

Lahiri, Abani. 1985. 'Last Battle of Bengal Peasants under British Rule', in *Challenge: A Saga of Indian's Struggle for Freedom*. Calcutta.

———. 1996. 'Tebhaga Struggle and After', in *50th Anniversary of the Tebhaga Struggle: The Mightiest Upsurge in Post-War India*.

———. 2001. *Postwar Revolt of the Rural Poor in Bengal: Memoirs of a Communist Activist* (interviewed by Ranajit Dasgupta, translated by Subrata Banerjee). Calcutta: Seagull Books.

Laub, Dori. 1992. 'Bearing Witness, or the Viccissitudes of Listening', in Shoshana Felman and Dori Laub, *Testimony: Crises of Witnessing in Literature, Psychoanalysis and History*, pp. 57–74. New York: Routledge.

Langer, Lawrence 1991. *Holocaust Testimonies: Ruins of Memory*. New Haven and Albany: Yale University Press and State University of New York Press.

Lifton, Robert J. and Eric Markusen (eds). 1990. *The Genocidal Mentality: Nazi Holocaust and Nuclear Threat*. New York: Basic Books.

Lowenthal, David. 1985. *The Past is a Foreign Country*. Cambridge: Cambridge University Press.

Lyotard, Jean-Francoise. 1988. *The Differend: Phrases in Dispute* (translated by Georges Van Den Abeele). Minneapolis,: University of Minnesota Press.

Majhi, Bimala. 1986. 'Women's Role in the Tebhaga Movement' (interviewed by Peter Custers), *Manushi*, 32 (January/February): 28–33.

Majhi, Biplab. 2002. *Tebhagaye Ma Baba*. Mednipur: Prakashana.

Majumdar, Asok. 1993. *Peasant Protest in Indian Politics: Tebhaga Movement in Bengal.* New Delhi: NIB Publishers.

Marcuse, Herbert. 1987. *Eros and Civilization: A Philosophical Inquiry into Freud*. London: Ark Paperbacks.

Menchu, Rigoberta. 1984. *I Rigoberta Menchu : An Indian Woman in Guatemala* (edited by Elizabeth Burgos-Debray, translated by Ann Wright). London: Verso.

Menon, Ritu and Kamla Bhasin. 1998. *Borders and Boundaries: Women in India's Partition*. New Delhi: Kali for Women.

Mir, Ali Husain and Raza Mir. 2006. *Anthems of Resistance: A Celebration of Progressive Urdu Poetry*. New Delhi: IndiaInk.

Mitra, Ila. 1996. 'Amar Jeebane Swadhinatar Swad', in Mahasveta Devi (ed.), *Aparajeya*, pp. 41–43. Calcutta: National Publishers.

———. 1997. 'Ila Mitrer Nachol Baktita', *Samaj Chetana*, January/February: 12–13 (Ila Mitra's lecture delivered on the occasion of the fiftieth anniversary celebrations in Nachole, Bangladesh, November 1996).

Mitra, Jaya. 2010. Calcutta: Anyadhara, 1989. Transl. Rinita Mazumdar: *Hannaman: One Who is in the Process of Being Killed* (Prison Memoirs of Indian Women). Kolkata: Towards Freedom, 2010.

Mohanty, Chandra Talpade. 2003. *Feminism without Borders: Decolonizing Theory, Practising Solidarity*. Durham: Duke University Press.

Mohanty, Satya P. 1998. *Literary Theory and the Claims of History: Postmodernism, Objectivity, Multicultural Politics*. New Delhi: Oxford University Press.

Mukerjee, Madhushree. 2010. *Churchill's Secret War: The British Empire and the Ravaging of India during World War II*. New Delhi: Tranquebar Press.

Mukherjee, Janam. 2011. 'Hungry Bengal: War, Famine, Riots, and the End of Empire, 1939–1946'. Ph.D. dissertation, Department Anthropology and History, University of Michigan, Ann Arbor.

Mukherjee, Kanak. 1989. *Women's Emancipation Movement in India*. Delhi: National Book Centre.

Nandy, Vaskar and Vasanthi Raman. 1997. 'The Long Transition: The Koch Rajbangshis of North_Eastern India', in Dev Nathan (ed.), *From Tribe to Caste*, pp. 46–60. Simla: Indian Institute of Advanced Study.

Niyogi, Robi. 1996. 'Tebhagar Larai', *Samvaad*, 4 November.

Nora, Pierre. 1989. 'Between Memory and History', *Representations*, 26 (Spring): 7–24.

Nur Jalal. 1995. *Krishakneta Nur Jalaler Atmakatha.* Dhaka: Ganaprakashani.

Nussbaum, Martha C. 1992. 'Human Functioning as Social Justice: In Defence of Aristotelian Essentialism', *Political Theory,* 20(2): 202–46.

Omvedt, Gail. 1992. *Reinventing Revolution: New Social Movements and the Socialist Tradition in India.* New York: M.E. Sharpe.

———. 1975. 'Rural Origins of Women's Liberation in India.' *Social Scientist* v. 4, no 4/5, pp. 40–54.

Panjabi, Kavita. 2016. 'The "Man-made" Famine and Women's Responses to Hunger: The Pivotal Dynamics of Food in the Tebhaga Movement.' in Uma Chakravarti (ed.) *Thinking Gender, Doing Gender: Feminist Scholarship and Practice Today*, New Delhi: Orient Blackswan, pp. 132–43.

———. 2012. 'Women's Subjectivity and the "Political" in Oral Narratives of the Tebhaga Movement: Alienation in a Politics of Liberation', in Kavita Panjabi and Paromita Chakravarti (eds), *Women Contesting Culture: Changing Frames of Gender Politics in India*, pp. 304–23. Kolkata: Stree Publishers.

———. 2011. 'Introduction', in *Poetics and Politics of Sufism and Bhakti in South Asia: Love, Loss and Liberation*, pp. 1–52. New Delhi: Orient Blackswan.

———. 2010. 'Otiter Jed or Times of Revolution: Ila Mitra, the Santals and Tebhaga Movement.' *Economic and Political Weekly* 14(33): 53–59.

———. 2005. *Old Maps and New: Legacies of the Partition*. Kolkata: Seagull Books.

Partnoy, Alicia. 1986. *The Little School: Tales of Disappearance and Survival in Argentina* (translated by Alicia Partnoy with Lois Althey and Sandra Braunstein). San Francisco: Cleis Press.

Passerini, Luisa. 1989. 'Women's Personal Narratives: Myths, Experiences and Emotions', in the Personal Narratives Group (ed.), *Interpreting Women's Lives: Feminist Theory and Personal Narratives*, pp. 189–200. Bloomington and Indianapolis: Indiana University Press.

——— (special ed.). 1992. 'Introduction', *International Yearbook of Oral History and Life stories*, Vol. 1.

———.1996. *Autobiography of a Generation: Italy 1968* (translated by Lisa Erdberg). Hanover and London: Weslyan University Press.

———. 1998. 'Work, Ideology and Consensus under Italian Fascism', in Robert Perks and Alistair Thomson (eds), *The Oral History Reader*, pp. 53–63. New York: Routledge.

Pawar, Urmila. 2009. *The Weave of My Life: A Dalit Woman's Memoirs* (translated by Maya Pandit). New York: Columbia University (first published as *Aaydan* in Marathi).

Pawar, Urmila and Meenakshi Moon. 2004. *We Also Made History: Women in the Ambedkarite Movement* (translated by Wandana Sonalkar). New Delhi: Zubaan Books.

Portelli, Alessandro. 1991. *The Death of Luigi Trastulli and Other Stories: Form and Meaning in Oral History*. Albany: State University of New York Press.

Pradeshik Krishak Sabha (ed.). 1996. *Tebhaga Subarna Jayanti*.

Randall, Margaret. 1981. *Sandino's Daughters: Testimonios of Nicaraguan Women in Struggle*. London: Zed Press.

Rasul, Abdullah. 1982. *Krishak Sabhar Itihas*. Calcutta: Nabajatak Prakashan.

Rasul, M.A. 1989. *A History of the All India Kisan Sabha*. Calcutta: National Book Agency.

Ray, Manas. 2000–2001. 'On Growing up Refugee', *Hindi: Language Discourse, Writing*, 1(3/4): 148–98.

Ray, Sabitri. 2005. *Harvest Song* (translated by Chandrima Bhattacharya and Adrita Mukherjee). Kolkata: Stree (originally published as *Paka Dhaner Gaan*, Kolkata: Suprakashini, 1986).

Rege, Sharmila. 1998. 'Dalit Women Talk Differently: A Critique of "Difference" and towards a Dalit Feminist Standpoint Position', *Economic and Political Weekly*, 33(44): WS39–46.

———. 2006. *Writing Caste/Writing Gender: Reading Dalit Women's Testimonios*. New Delhi: Zubaan Books.

Roy, Srila. 2012. *Remembering Revolution: Gender, Violence, and Subjectivity in India's Naxalbari Movement*. New Delhi: Oxford University Press.

*Samaj Chetana*. 1996. 'Tebhaga Andolaner Ponchas Bachhor Ebang Ajker Bhumiproshna: Swadinatar Rajatjayanti', December (special issue on the occasion of the golden jubilee of independence, with essays on the Tebhaga movement by Abani Lahiri, Fakhre Alam, Anwar Hossain Fakir, Imran Sayyed Chandan, Abdush Shaheed, Molla Akhtar Ahmed, Mahmud Jamal Kaderi, Altaf Parvez, Nurul Anwar and Mizzanur Rahman Chandan).

Sangari, Kumkum. 2008. 'Gendered Violence National Boundaries and Culture', in Radhika Coomaraswamy and Nimanthi Perera-Rajasingham (eds), *Constellations of Violence: Feminist Interventions in South Asia*, pp. 1–33. New Delhi: Women Unlimited.

Sarkar, Sumit. 2001. In Abani Lahiri, *Postwar Revolt of the Rural Poor in Bengal: Memoirs of a Communist Activist* (interviewed by Ranajit

Dasgupta, translated by Subrata Banerjee), pp. xli–l. Calcutta: Seagull Books.
———. 1983. *Modern India: 1885–1947*. New Delhi: Macmillan.
Sarkar, Tanika. 1984. 'Politics and Women in Bengal: The Conditions and Meaning of Participation.' *The Indian Economic and Social History Review*, 21.1, pp. 91–101.
Sen, Amal. Undated. Unpublished poems.
———. 1984. *Bibidha Prasange*. New Barrackpore, North 24 Parganas: Subhanudhyayi.
Sen, Amartya. 1980. *Poverty and Famines: An Essay on Entitlement and Deprivations*. New Delhi: Oxford University Press.
Sen, Ilina (ed.). 1990. *A Space Within the Struggle: Women's Participation in People's Movements*. New Delhi India: Kali for Women.
Sen, Manikuntala. 2001. *In Search of Freedom* (translation of *Sediner Katha*). Calcutta: Stree Publishers.
———. 1982. *Sediner Katha*. Calcutta: Nabapatra Prakashan.
Sen, Meenakshi. 1993. *Jailer Bhetor Jail: Pagolbari Parba*. Calcutta: Spandan.
Sen, Sunil. 1993. *Banglar Tebhaga Sangram, 1946–47* (Agrarian Struggle in Bengal, 1946–47). Calcutta: Chatterjee Publishers.
———. 1987. 'Peasant Movements and Decolonisation in India, 1885-1948', in Rajeshwari Ghose (ed.), *Protest Movements in South and South-East Asia: Traditional and Modern Idioms of Expression*, pp. 37–70.. Hong Kong: Centre of Asian Studies, University of Hong Kong.
———. 1985. *The Working Women and Popular Movements in Bengal*. Calcutta: K.P. Bagchi.
———. 1982. *Peasant Movements in India: Mid-Nineteenth and Twentieth Centuries*. Calcutta: K.P. Bagchi.
———. 1979. '*Tebhaga Chai*', in A.R. Desai (ed.), *Peasant Struggles in India*, pp. 442–452. New Delhi: Oxford University Press.
Siddiqui Kamaluddin. 1987. 'The Nature of Peasant Resistance During the Tebhaga Movement' in Rajeshwari Ghose (ed.), *Protest Movements in South and South-East Asia: Traditional and Modern Idioms of Expression*. Hong Kong: Centre of Asian Studies, University of Hong Kong.
Singh, Suresh. 1966. *The Dust Storm and Hanging Mist: A Study of Birsa Munda and His Movement in Chhotanagpur (1874–1901)*. Kolkata: Firma KLM.
Singha, Moni. 1983. *Jeeban-Sangram*. Dhaka: Jatiya Sahitya Prakashani.
Sinha Roy, Mallarika. 2012. *Gender and Radical Politics in India: Magic Moments of Naxalbari (1967–1975)* (Studies in South Asia Series). New York: Routledge.

Smith, Dorothy. 1987. *The Everyday World as Problematic: A Feminist Sociology*. Boston: Northeastern. University. Press.

Stree Shakti Sanghatana. 1989. *We Were Making History: Life Stories of Women in the Telengana People's Struggle*. New Delhi: Kali for Women.

Surjeet, H.S. 1984. *Major Jaspal Singh: A Tribute to a Revolutionary*. Delhi: CPM Publication.

Taneja, Anup. 2005. *Gandhi, Women, and the National Movement, 1920–47*. New Delhi, Har-Anand Publications.

*Telengana Tebhagar Subarna Jayantite Bishesh Sankhya Kalantar Krorpatra*. 1997. 5 April (special issue on the occasion of the golden jubilee of the Tebhaga and Telengana movements, with essays by Maleka Begum, Rani Dasgupta, Goutom Chattopadhyay, Asoke Basu, Abani Lahiri, Bhabani Sen, Nripen Bandyopadhyay, Ila Mitra and Ranajit Dasgupta; poems by Benoy Roy, Kangsari Haldar, Golam Kuddush and Kali Sarkar; sketches by artists Somenath Hore, Chittaprasad and Debabrata Mukhopadhyay; an editorial by Sunil Munshi; a letter from Kalishankar Das, editor, Kundia Union Krishak Samiti, Bangladesh; an interview of Tebhaga leader Bishwanath Roy; lists of men and women martyred during the movement; and details of the demands made during the movement, the present legal situation regarding land reform acts and the current demands of peasants).

Tronto, Joan C. 2009. *Moral Boundaries: A Political Argument for an Ethic of Care*. New York: Routledge (first published 1993).

Umar, Badruddin. 1984. *Bhasha Andolan Prasanga Katipoy Dalil*. Dhaka: Bangla Akademi.

———. 2004. *The Emergence of Bangladesh: Class Struggles in East Pakistan, 1947–58*. Karachi: Oxford University Press.

V. Geetha. 2008. 'Doing Gender in the Classroom: Issues at Stake'. Draft copy of the paper presented at the IAWS conference, Lucknow, February, pp. 1-10.

———. 2012. "Feminism: Where Life Worlds and Histories Meet', in Kavita Panjabi and Paromita Chakravarti (eds), *Women Contesting Culture: Changing Frames of Gender Politics in India*, pp. 243–58. Kolkata: Stree Publishers.

———. 2013. 'Invitation to Practice Social Fellowship', *Economic and Political Weekly*, 48(29): 35–37.

Wittgenstein, Ludwig. 1958. *The Blue and Brown Books*. Oxford: Blackwell.

Woodhead, John. 1984. *Famine Inquiry Commission Report on Bengal*. New Delhi: Usha Publications.

Young, James E. 1997. 'Between History and Memory: The Uncanny Voices of Historian and Survivor', *History and Memory*, 19(1): 47–58.

Zizek, Slavoj. 1997. 'Multiculturalism, or the Cultural Logic of Multinational Capitalism', *New Left Review*, 1(225): 28–51.

## Additional Readings

Abedin, Zainul. 1943. Famine Sketches (published and edited by Subir Choudhury, Department of Fine Arts, Bangladesh Shilpakala Akademi, Dhaka).

Ahmed, Shareef Uddin, Ahmed (ed.). 1996. *Dinajpur: Itihaas o Aitihijya*. Dhaka: Bangladesh Itihas Samiti.

Atik-uz-Jaman, Shareef. 1995. *Krishakneta Nurjalaler Atmakatha*. Dhaka: Ganaprakashani.

Bangladesh Krishak Samiti (ed.). 1988. *Tebhaga Sangram: 40 Barshik Smarakgatha*. Dhaka: Bangladesh Krishak Samiti, Papyrus Press (special edition on the occasion of the Fortieth Anniversary of the Tebhaga Movement, with press cuttings, photographs and essays by Shekhar Dutta, Abdus Salaam, Robi Niyogi, Moni Krishna Sen, Maleka Begum, Gurudas Talukdar, Nur-ul-Alam Lenin, Somenath Hore).

Bhattacharya, Annadashankar. 1947. *Tebhaga Sangrame Chhatra-Krishak Ek Hao*. Calcutta:Bangiya Pradeshik Chhatra Federation.

Bhattacharya, Jayanta. 1996. *Banglar 'Tebhaga': Tebhagar Sangram*. Calcutta: National Book Agency.

Bhattacharya, Shefali. 1997. "*Trinamule Sangathan*" in *Chalar Pathe*, August, pp. 64-67.

Bose, Sugata. 1993. 'Resistance and Consciousness', in *Peasant Labour and Colonial Capital: Rural Bengal since 1770, The New Cambridge History of India Series*, Cambridge: Cambridge University Press.

———. 1986. *Agrarian Bengal: Economy, Social Structure and Politics, 1919–1947*. Cambridge, Cambridge University Press.

Butler, Judith. 2004. *Precarious Life: The Powers of Mourning and Violence*. London: Verso.

———. 2011. 'Precarious Life and the Obligations of Cohabitation'. Nobel Museum, Stockholm. http://www.nobelmuseum.se/sites/nobelmuseet.se/files/page_file/Judith_Butler_NWW2011.pdf (accessed 9 April 2015).

Chandra, Bipan. 1984. *Communalism in Modern India*. New Delhi: Vikas Publishing House.

Chatterjee, Joya. 1995. *Bengal Divided: Hindu Communalism and Partition 1932–1947*. Cambridge: Cambridge University Press.

Chatterjee, Partha. 1997. *The Present History of W.Bengal: Essays in Political Criticism*. New Delhi: Oxford University Press.

———. 2001. 'The Nation in Heterogenous Time', *Indian Economic and Social History* Review, 36(4): 399–418.

———. 2004. *The Politics of the Governed: Reflections on Popular Politics in Most of the World*. New: Delhi: Permanent Black.

Chatterjee, Prabha. 1984. *Shahid Pratibha Ganguli*. Calcutta: The Orient Press.

———. 1994. 'Tebhaga Andolaner Dingulite', *Eksathe, Subarna Jayanti Sanhkya*, Baisakh 1801 (May).

Dasgupta, Kamala. 1963. *Swadhinata Sangrame Banglar Nari*. Calcutta: Basudhara Prakashani.

Dasgupta, Prashanta, Brajagopal Bhattacharya and Shashanka Mukhopadhyay (eds). 1987. *Manorama Basu Smarak-Grantha*. Calcutta: Samannway.

Dasgupta, Sachin. 1987. 'Jalpaigurir Adhiyar Andolan' (The Adhiyar Movement of Jalpaiguri), *Madhuparni, Bishesh Jalpaiguri Jela Sankhya*, December: 277–87.

Desai, A.R. 1979. *Peasant Struggles in India*. New Delhi: Oxford University Press.

Dhanagare, D.N. 1983. *Peasant Movements in India 1920–1950*. New Delhi: Oxford University Press

*Documents of the Communist Movement in India*. 2007. Eds Jyoti Basu, Sailen Dasgupta, Buddhadeva Bhattaxharya and Anil Biswas). Calcutta: National Book Agency.

*Eksathe*. 1997. March (special issue of the periodical commemorating the Golden Jubilee of the Tebhaga Movement with essays by Kanak Mukhopadhyay, Pranati Bhattacharya, Manjusri Dasgupta and Mamata Sen; poems by Kanak Mukhopadhyay, Ira Sarkar, Pranati Ghosh and Sufia Kamal; dance-dramas by Reba Roychoudhuri, Jayati Gupta, Manashi Chakraborty, Nilima Das and Rekha Goswami; and book reviews by Manjari Gupta and Bithi Sen).

Falguni, Aditi. 1995. 'Narir Rajnaitik Kshamatayan: Bangladesh Prekhsapat', *Unnayan Padakshep,* II (April–June).

———. 1996. 'Mahila Atmaraksha Samiti: Aitihijyer Anusandhaan', *Unnayan Padakshep,* V (April–June).

Ferguson, Kathy E. 1991. 'Interpretation and Genealogy in Feminism', *Signs: Journal of Women in Culture and Society,* 16 (2): 322–39.

*Ganashakti*. 1996. (Newspaper reports on the occasion of the fiftieth

anniversary celebrations of the Tebhaga movement in various parts of West Bengal).
29.10.96 "*Tebhagar Aagun*" reminiscences of the Tebhaga Movement by Purnendu Patri on the occasion of the 50th Anniversary
8.3.97 – announcement of the celebrations in Calcutta
9.3.97 -- report of the celebrations in Calcutta
10.3.97 -- Sunday's long report of the celebrations in Calcutta
12.3.97 -- report of the celebrations in Chandanpidi
14.3.97 -- report of the celebrations in Budhakhali
17.3.07 -- report of the celebrations in Bankura

Ginzburg, Carlo. 1997. 'Shared Memories, Private Recollections', *History and Memory*, 9(1/2): 53–63.

Government of East Bengal. 1955. Home (Political) C.R.B. Proceedings 532–37, March.

Guha, Ranajit. 1996. 'The Small Voice of History', in Shahid Amin and Dipesh Chakrabarty (eds), *Subaltern Studies IX: Writings on South Asian Hostory and Society*, pp. 1–12. New Delhi: Oxford University Press.

Gupta, Rabindra. 1949. *Tebhagar Laraiye: Sramik Sreni O Madhyabitter Pakkha Nirbachan*. Calcutta: Rangmashal Press.

Hore, Somnath. 1990. *Tebhaga Diary: An Artist's Diary and Sketchbook*.

Hossain, Mostafa Tofayel. 1996. *Kurigram Jelar Itihas o Samskriti*. Kurigram: Svatvaha Publishers.

Kandiyoti, Deniz. 1991. 'Identity and its Discontents: Women and the Nation', *Millenium: Journal of International Studies*, 20(3): 429–43.

Lucero-Montano, Alfredo. 'On Walter Benjamin's Concept of History'. http://www.philosophos.com/philosophy_article_69.html (accessed 23 February 2012).

Mokammel, Tanvir. 1987. *Khetmajur Andolan: Shrenigata O Rajnaitik Tatparja*. Dhaka: Jatiya Sahitya Prakashani.

Mukhopadhyay, Kanak. 1993. *Narimukti Andolan o Amra*. Calcutta: National Book Agency.

Mukhopadhyay, Saroj. 1987. *Bharater Communist Party O Amra: Dwitiya Khanda (19821987)*. Calcutta: National Book Agency.

Mukhopadhyay, Sudhir and Nripen Ghosh. 1985. *Rangpur Jelar Krishak Andolaner Itihas O Party*. Calcutta: National Book Agency.

*Nandan*. 1996. November (special issue on Tebhaga Movement with essays by D.L. Dhanagre, Binoybhushan Choudhuri, Jayanto Bhattacharya, Samir Rakshit and Baidyanath Kar).

Newman, Louise M. 1990. 'Dialogue: Critical Theory and the History of

Women: What's at Stake in Deconstructing Women's History', *Journal of Women's History*, 2(1): 58–66.

Paschimbanga Pradeshik Krishak Sabha (ed.). 1996. '*Tebhaga Sangram: Phire Dekha* (The Tebhaga Movement: Looking Back). Calcutta: Paschimbanga Pradeshik Krishak Sabha (collection of essays on the occasion of the golden jubilee of the Tebhaga movement, with essays by Mansur Habibullah, Muhammad Abdullah Rasul, Mani Singha, Bhupal Panda, Sunil Sen, Manikrishna Sen, Kalyani Dasgupta, Amal Sen, Manabesh Choudhiri, Sudhir Mukherjee, Rupnarayan Ray, Binoy Choudhuri, Krishnabinod Roy and Jyoti Basu).

*Paschimbanga: Tebhaga Sankhya.* 1997. 'Tathya o Sangskriti Bivagh, Paschimbanga Sarkar', 30(42–46) (special issue on Tebhaga movement, with essays, stories, memoirs, poems, songs, analyses by Jyoti Basu, Manik Bandyopadhyay, Muhammad Abdullah Rasul, Sachin Dasgupta, Sunil Sen, Kalyani Dasgupta, Bimal Dasgupta, Binoy Kongar, Hemanta Ghoshal, Golam Kuddush, Poritosh Dutta, Jiban Dey, Narahari Kobiraj, Sudhi Pradhan, Kalpataru Sengupta, Jayanto Bhattacharya, Bhaba Roy, Partha Roy, Anuradha Ray, Ranajit Samaddar, Sukanto Bhattacharya, Bishnu Dey, Nibaran Pondit, Binoy Roy, Salil Chowdhuri, Kali Sarkar, Sadhan Guha, and Probir Majumdar).

Patai, Daphne. 1988. 'Constructing a Self: A Brazilian Life Story', *Feminist Studies*, 14(1): 143–66.

Patel, Vibhuti. 1985. 'Indian Women on the Warpath', in *Reaching for Half the Sky: A Reader on the Women's Movement*. Baroda: Antar Rashtriya Prakashan.

Portelli, Alessandro. 1998. 'Oral History as a Genre,' in *Narrative and Genre*, (ed.) Mary Chamberlain and Paul Thomson. London and New York: Routledge, pp. 23–45.

Ranga, N.G. 1979. *The Modern Indian Peasant.* New Delhi: Anmol Publications.

Ray, Chhabi (Basu). 1995. 'Banglar Nari Andolan: Sangrami Bhoomikar Dedh-sho Bachhor', in *Chhabi Basur Rachana Samkalan*. Calcutta: Dey's and School of Women's Studies, Jadavpur University.

Roy, Krishnabinod. 1948. *Tebhagar Larai* (The Tebhaga Struggle). Calcutta.

Roy, Parama. 2005. 'Women, Hunger and Famine: Bengal, 1350/1943', in Bharati Ray (ed.), *Women of India: Colonial and Post-Colonial Periods*, pp. 392–423. New Delhi: Sage.

Samuel, Raphael. 1995. *Theatres of Memory, Vol. I: Past and Present in Contemporary Culture.* New York: Verso.

*Samvaad*. 1996. 4 November (special page in the newspaper published from Dhaka on the occasion of the golden jubilee of the Tebhaga movement, including essays by Sikandar Ali Haoladar, Robi Niyogi and Motahar Hossain Sufi).

Sangari Kumkum and Sudesh Vaid (eds). 1989. *Recasting Women: Essays in Colonial History*. New Delhi: Kali for Women.

Sarkar, Bikram. 1989. *Land Reforms in India: A Study of Legal Aspects of Land Reform Measures in West Bengal*. New Delhi: Ashish Publishing House.

Sen, Arindam and Partha Ghosh (eds). 1991. *Communist Movement in India: Historical Perspectives and Important Documents*, Vol. 1 (1917–39). Patna: Samkalin Prakashan.

Sen, Satyen. Undated. *Bangladesher Krishaker Sangram* (Bangladesh Peasants' Struggle). Dhaka: Alamgir Press.

Sujan Samaj (ed.). 1996. *Tebhaga Sangramer Ponchash Bachhar*. Jessore: Sujan Samaj (collection of essays on the occasion of the golden jubilee of the Tebhaga movement by Shamchir Rahman, Fakhre Alam and Mostafijur Rahman Kabul).

*Surjapur Barta*. Various. (With essays by Partha Sen, Maitreya Ghatak, Satya Chanda, Sevketu Singha, Sachindu Chakraborty and Swapan Guhaniyogi, among others).

*Surjapur Barta*: *Tebhaga Samkalan Sankhya*. 1990. (Special issue on Tebhaga with essays by Shachindu Chakraborty, Basanta Chatterjee, Himangshu Sarkar, Abani Bagchi, Partha Sen and Riyajul Islam and Sachin Dasgupta; memoirs of woman leader Ghiya Singha; and excerpts of Bachcha Munshi's diary).

*Tebhagar Larai*. (Collection of essays by Binoy Choudhuri, Bijoy Modak, Hemanta Ghoshal, Kangsari Haldar, Gunadhar Maiti, Gopal Das, Somenath Hore, Anil Roy, Khagendranath Maiti, Rani Dasgupta, Golam Kuddush, Subhash Choudhuri, Souri Ghatak, Sudhir Mukherjee, Manabesh Choudhuri, Anunay Chattopadhyay, Asokekumar Mukhopadhyay, Samiran Mukhopadhyay, Madhu Goswami and Jahar Nath). Calcutta.

*Tebhaga Sangram: Rajat-Jayanti Smarak Grantha*. 1973. (Collection of essays on the occasion of the silver jubilee of the Tebhaga Movement, with essays by Bhabani Sen, Krishnabinod Roy, Susheel Sen, Sunil Sen, Promotho Bhoumik, Mani Singha, Gurudas Talukdar, Maniklrishna Sen, Kangsari Haldar, Bhupal Panda, Ashu Dutta, Bibhuti Guha, Kali Sarkar, Ajit Roy, Bimal Dasgupta, Palash Roy, Subal Mitra, Rani Dasgupta, Souri Ghatak and Golam Kuddush). Calcutta: Kalantar.

Vansina, Jan. 1985. *Oral Tradition as History.* Madison: University of Wisconsin Press.

Weber, Rachel. 1995. 'Recreating the Home: Women's Role in the Development of Refugee Colonies in South Calcutta', *Indian Journal of Gender Studies*, 2(2): 195–210.

Williams, Walter. 1990. 'Documents: Women and Work in the Third World: Indonesian Women's Oral Histories', *Journal of Women's History*, 2(1): 183–85.

Yuval-Davis, Nira and Floya Anthias. 1989. 'Introduction', in *Woman–Nation–State.* London: Macmilan.

# Index

1857 72, 206
1917 xxii, xxix
1940s xxxix, xliii, vli, 8, 9, 13, 47, 49, 58, 63, 70, 72, 81, 109, 120, 123, 124, 142, 191, 201, 279, 280
1943 (also see Bengal famine) xlii, 4, 21, 23–25, 27, 31, 74, 86, 87, 96, 104, 108, 115, 186

Adhiar 4, 11, 172
Adivasi x, xiv, vliii, 62, 63, 175, 195, 224, 227
Adyashakti Mahamaya 226, 259
aesthetics 71, 77–79, 92, 261, 271, 275, 276, 278
affective xxvii, lii, liii, 17, 17, 18, 53, 60, 63, 73–75, 77, 79, 86, 91, 99, 103, 106, 107, 118, 119, 121–123, 128, 135, 137, 172, 184, 219, 241, 252, 254, 270, 271, 277, 280, 281, 283
Agarwala, Madanlal 114
agency xxxvii, 53, 60, 77, 93, 114, 126, 128–130, 133–137, 140, 147, 180–183, 192, 271
Ahalya xliv, 132, 226, 227, 258
Ahmed, Laila 24
Ahmed, Nazimunnesa 24
Akbar, Nurul 44, 164–167
alienation xix, xxiii, xxiv, 93, 185, 220, 240, 243, 264
All India Peasants' Conference 40, 153
All India Women's Conference (AIWC) 23, 29, 106
Ambedkarite politics xiii, vliii
*ananda* xxv, xliii, lii, liii, 8, 135, 181, 271, 279
Anandi, S. xiii
*anchal* lii, 110, 115, 116, 119

Anderson, Benedict 161
*andolan* 3, 11, 45, 128, 190, 271
*antarikata* lii, liv, lv, 8, 63, 64, 128, 131, 149, 180, 184, 263
anti-caste radicalism xiii
Anti-Fascist Writers' Union 9
anti-Sikh xii
Arendt, Hannah 282, 283
*atiter jed* lii, 67, 185, 204, 205, 209–211
Aveling, Edward xxx

Bagchi, Dipti 98, 99, 104, 106
Baidyerbazar 20, 96
*baithak* 21
Bamacharan 173
Bandyopadhyay, Manik 45, 46. 97, 98, 121, 149
Bandyopadhyay, Nripen xxxv, 47, 55
Bandyopadhyay, Ramen 46
Bandyopadhyay, Sekhar 5, 18, 39, 145, 146, 164, 223, 224, 261, 262
Banerjee, Prathama 215
Bangladesh War of Liberation 47
Bangladesh Workers' Party/ Workers' Party (WP) xxvi, 220, 221
Bankura 24, 25, 115, 206
*bargadar* 11, 33, 34
*bargadari* 11
Barisal 17, 21, 24, 28, 87, 115, 25, 251
Barman, Santosh Kumar 7
Barmani, Joymoni 139, 141, 147, 160–162
Baroligram 165
*basti* 25
Basu, Jyoti 34, 259
Basu, Manorama 41, 251, 252
Batasi xliv, 226
Begum, Anwara 168
Begum, Hajrah 29
Begum, Maleka xxxvi, 66, 75, 199, 253
Begum, Muksuda 24
Begum, Rabeya 24
Begum, Sakina 24
Begum, Shahzadi 24, 25
Bengal Bargadars' Temporary Regulation Bill (also known as Bargadars' Bill) 33, 34
Bengal Famine (also see 1943) xv, xlii, 4, 10, 23, 25, 74, 86, 89, 90, 94, 95
Bengal Muslim League (also see Muslim League) 29
Bengal Provincial Krishak Sabha 8, 11, 31, 32, 90
Bengal Provincial Mahila Atmaraksha Samiti (also see MARS) 23
Benhabib, Seyla 136, 155
Benjamin, Walter 53, 55, 6768, 71, 80, 81, 222, 270
Bhagini Bahinis 39
Bhandani 132
Bhasin, Kamla xiii, vl
Bhattacharya, Malini 149
Bhave, Vinobha 18, 27
Bhowmick, Suhrid Kumar 214
*bhukh michhil* (also see hunger march) 22, 109, 111, 112, 15, 116
Bhuteshwari 132
*bidi*-rollers/ *bidi* workers x, vliii
Bimala Majhi xxiv, 63, 100, 110, 131, 134, 157, 162, 163, 169–171, 173, 174

Biswas, Charu 30
Biswas, Anima xxv, xxvii-xxix, xxxi, liii, 44, 48, 51, 59, 75, 77, 94, 133, 135, 144,145, 150, 221–223, 228-233, 235–237, 239–243, 247, 249, 250, 254, 257, 262–265, 272, 280, 281
Biswas, Hemanga 269
Biswas, Sisir 30
Bohstedt, John xx, xxi
Bokul*er ma* 46
bonding xix, xxvi, liii, liv, lvi, 9, 56, 107, 124, 136, 148, 154, 157, 174, 179, 184, 203, 238, 276, 277, 280, 281
Bose, Ashok 261
Bose, Rahul 227
Bowie, Andrew 77, 78, 271, 276
Brecht, Bertolt 282, 283
bridging li, 71, 79, 151, 265
Budhakhali 86, 225, 256, 258
Burima 132
Butalia, Urvashi xiii, xxxix, vl, lx, 67, 212

Calcutta High Court 24
capitalism x, xxi, xxii
care work xvi, xix, 108, 109, 111, 119, 122, 159, 163
caste x, xiii, xv, xvii, xix, xlii, xliii, vli, vliii, li, liii, lv, 4–6, 8, 11, 20, 32, 61–64, 79, 86, 89, 90, 95, 130, 134–136, 138, 142, 145, 158, 163, 164, 172–175, 183, 185, 186, 188, 192, 196, 197, 200, 204, 217–219, 221, 222, 229, 230, 234, 248, 249, 255–257, 262, 264, 282
Chakravarti, Uma xiii, xxxix, 92, 255, 257
Chakravartty, Renu lii, 6, 12, 15, 18, 22, 26, 30, 40, 86, 87, 99, 101, 110, 124
Chakravarty, Arindam 128
Chakravarty, Asha 111, 269, 270
Chandals 5
Chandanpidhi xliv, 132, 225, 226, 258, 259
Chandpur 228
Chatterjee, Basanta 152
Chatterjee, Bishtu 228
Chatterjee, Partha 161
Chatterjee, Srilata 14
Chattopadhyay, Bankimchandra 193
Chattopadhyay, Birendra 95
Chattopadhyay, Kunal 6, 32, 131
Chaudhuri, Sita 30, 31
Chaudhuri, Supriya 86, 87, 90, 95, 97, 98, 121
Chauduri, Tripti 24
Chauhan, Subhadra Kumari 72
childcare x, xxii, xxvii
China xxviii, 43, 178
Choudhury, Salil 35
Chowdhury, Samsunnehar 111
Civil Disobedience Movement 12, 27, 39,
class x, xvi, xvii, xix, xxi, xxiii-xxv, xxvii, xxviii, xlii, li, liii, lv, 6–10, 14–16, 20, 22, 23, 25, 29, 32, 36, 40, 43, 46, 50, 55, 61, 63, 64, 80, 86–88, 92, 94, 95, 98, 103, 107, 111–113, 123, 135–139, 142, 143, 147, 150, 151, 154, 155, 157, 158, 161, 162–164, 176–180, 183, 85, 186, 188, 192, 193, 195–198, 207, 208, 217, 218, 230, 234, 249, 250, 255, 257, 260, 261, 262, 264, 277, 282

class consciousness xxiii, 94
Cominform 33
Comintern directive xvii
communalism 7, 165, 188
Communist Party (CP) xvi, xvii, xxiv, xxv, xxvii, xxxiii, xli, xliii, liv, 4, 6– 9, 11, 12, 16, 30–33, 35–37, 39–44, 46, 48, 49, 57, 58, 66, 69, 87, 99, 100, 103, 104, 106, 108, 110, 113, 123, 24, 131, 136, 137, 140–143, 147, 151–153, 159, 161, 167, 169, 176, 181, 186–188, 191, 193, 196–198, 202, 205, 208, 210, 211, 217, 218, 220–223, 228, 229, 231, 233–236, 239–241, 244–248, 250–252, 254, 255, 257–260, 262–264, 274, 275, 278, 281, 282,
Communist Party of Bangladesh (CPB) 221
Communist Party of India (CPI) xiv, xlii, 3, 48, 49, 223
Communist Party of India (Marxist) (CPM) 34, 48, 49
community lv, 5, 21, 28, 61, 90, 99, 133, 136, 146, 152, 157, 158, 163, 164, 171–173, 183, 195, 218, 234, 276
comradeship xv, xvii, xix, xxiii, xxvi, xxx, xxxi, xxxiii, lv, 41, 43, 63, 69, 123, 124, 128–130, 133, 135, 137, 138, 142, 143, 145, 147, 148, 151, 156, 157, 174, 175, 177, 180–184, 217, 218, 241, 263, 283
Cooper, Adrienne 4, 7, 11, 32, 34, 86, 90, 94, 131, 223
Cornell, Drucilla 136, 155
culture of silence 43, 281
Custers, Peter 6, 7, 131

Dalits ix, x, xiii, vli, 5, 62, 63, 101, 262
Dalmiya, Vrinda 91, 121, 128, 179, 181, 182
*daroga* 12, 46, 134, 257
Das, Basanti 225, 258
Das, Jamuna 226
Dasgupta, Ajoy 53–55, 57
Dasgupta, Atish 7
Dasgupta, Kalyani 25, 36, 44, 89, 148, 156, 158, 183, 275
Dasgupta, Ranajit 103
Dasgupta, Rani/Rani Mitra xxxiii, 16, 23, 25, 28, 36, 44, 50, 51, 53, 54, 56-58, 63, 99, 114, 131, 139, 143, 152, 153, 161, 162, 180, 183
Dasgupta, Sachin 148
Datar, Chaya x
Debi, Amiya 29
Deepeshwari 132
Deutscher, Issac xxx
Devi, Bhanu 251, 252
Dhaka xxxvi, vli, 38, 66, 199, 253
Dhaka/Dacca xxxvi, vli, 5, 24, 38, 66, 199, 253
*dhal* 257
Dhar, Adhir 173
*dhol* 186
dignity x, xviii, xx, xxiv, xxvi, xxxviii, lvi, 15, 51, 103, 107, 109, 116, 117, 120, 125–127, 145, 175, 180, 182, 251–253, 257
Dikshit, Sibarani/Sibarani Mitra 14, 220
Dinajpur xxxvi, vli, liv, 3–5, 8, 11, 16, 23–28, 31, 32, 36, 44,

46, 48–50, 54, 64, 95, 96, 98, 99, 105–107, 112–117, 128, 130–132, 138, 140, 142, 147, 149, 152–156, 164, 172, 180, 183, 218
Dissolution of Muslim Marriage Act, 1939 xii
domestic xv, xvii, xxii, xxiv
Dumurtala 164, 168, 169
Dutta, Shekhar 7, 190

Eagleton, Terry 89, 102
East Pakistan Committee 235, 236
Elias, Akhtaruzzaman il
epistemological (also see ontological) 60, 63–65, 71, 73, 76, 219
ethnicity li, lv, 61, 142, 155, 158, 163, 176, 188
external li, 129, 193, 272

familial x, 112, 117, 154–156
famine xv–xvii, xix, xx, xxii, xxiii, xlii, xliii, il, lii–lv, 4, 8–10, 12, 16, 21–27, 29-31, 36, 40, 48, 74, 85–96, 98, 100–111, 113, 115, 117–126, 129, 130, 137, 142, 152, 157, 159, 172, 180–182, 186, 276
famine relief work xix, 40, 107
Farnsworth, Beatrice xxii
female consciousness xxi, xxii
feminist ix–xiv, xvii, xviii, xxvii, xxviii, xxxii, xxxiii, xxxviii, xliv, vli–vliii, l, li, 19, 35, 56–58, 61, 63, 67, 70, 78, 98, 140, 147, 149, 179, 182, 184, 190, 257, 265
Fernandez-Armesto, Felipe 87, 92
feudalism x, 89
Floud Commission 11, 12, 34
food riots xx, xxi, xxiii, 95
Foucault, Michel 60, 62, 271, 275, 276
Friedlander, Saul 69, 70, 243

Gajol 187
Ganatantrik Mahila Samiti 48, 49
Gandhi ashram xxvi
Gandhi, Kasturba 25, 55
Gandhi, M.K. xlii, 12, 16–19, 24–26, 29, 39, 109, 110
Gandhi, Nandita xi
Gandhian xv, 9–11, 17, 18, 26, 27, 38, 39
Ganguly, Arati 6, 37
Ganguly, Jyotirmoyee 29
Ganguly, Snehalata 25, 116
*gaynbahinis* 6, 131
Geetha, V. 9, 63, 65, 94, 183, 216, 218, 254, 257, 281
gender x, xiii, xxi, xliv, vli, lv, lvi, 6–8, 13, 15, 42, 44, 46, 52, 57, 58, 61, 64, 66, 78, 94, 95, 135, 137–139, 143, 147, 150, 158, 188, 195, 230, 257, 262, 264
gendered xxviii, xliii, xliv, vl, lvi, 6–9, 11, 43, 47, 51, 52, 57, 61, 62, 64, 67, 77, 80, 81, 93, 94, 96, 122, 128, 129, 137, 146–148, 157, 169, 181, 188, 192, 221, 222, 255, 256, 272, 275
Ghandy, Anuradha xii
Ghatak, Maitreya 7, 32
Ghosh, Adhir 173
Ghosh, Purnendu 7
Ghosh, Sourin 86
Ghosh, Surendramohan 38

Goldar, Phuli Xxvi, 8, 48, 51, 94, 131, 133, 135, 140, 143–147, 150, 157, 181, 249
Greenough, Paul 86, 100
Guha, Bibhuti 106
Guha, Bina liv, lv, 3, 4, 8, 24, 25, 27, 36, 44, 46, 47, 51, 63, 106, 107, 112–117, 120, 128–131, 138–140, 142, 143, 149, 151, 160, 172, 181
Guha, Ramachandra 260
Gupta, Ashoka 9
Gupta, Dinesh 17
Guru, Gopal 256

Habibpur 187
Habibullah Mansur 235
Hajong peasants 4
Haldar 183
Haldar, Kangsari 261
Haoldar, Sekander Ali 7
Haq, Abdul 165
Haq, Fazlul 11, 33, 108, 110, 198
Harding, Sandra 78
Hartsock, Nancy 78
Hashem, Abdul 29
*hat tola* 4
Hatiara 47, 143, 145
Hattola 4, 11
Hazra, Matangini 39
Heleketu Singha xxvi, 44, 48–50, 112, 139, 149
Hindu xv, vli, 5, 9, 11, 47, 50, 63, 67, 88, 95, 146, 153, 164–167, 169, 170, 172–175, 177, 185–187, 193–197, 200, 206, 208, 212, 235, 251, 252
Hindu Mahasabha 88, 164
Holocaust xxxii, li, lii, liv, 69-71, 73, 78, 88, 192, 243, 245
Hossain, Selina Il, 190
Hossein, Azhar 187, 247, 262
Howrah 24
humiliation xxiii, xxiv, 42, 175, 237, 256, 257
hunger xiv, xvi, xxii-xxiv, xxxiii, xlii, li, lv, 22, 23, 74, 85–87, 90, 92–94, 96, 101, 108, 109, 111, 115–117, 120, 122, 125, 147, 152, 154, 181, 259
hunger march (also see *bhukh micchil*) xlii, 22, 108, 109, 111, 115, 120, 122
Hussein Badshah, Fazle xxxvi, 185, 211

*ichchhajanam* 273
imperialism 10, 48, 96, 103, 158, 159, 168,
Independence xiii, xvi, xli, xlii, vliii, 15, 24, 33, 44, 54, 89, 188, 207, 208, 229, 260
Indian People's Theatre Association (IPTA) 9, 106
Intelligence Branch (IB) 261
interiority xix, xxiv, xxv, xxvii, li, lv, 53, 60, 67, 74, 77, 79-81, 128, 129, 148, 151, 159, 183, 218, 248, 254, 272, 276, 277
internal 33, 53, 68, 122, 129, 193, 223, 229, 232, 242, 247–250, 254, 258, 259, 281, 282
intersubjectivity 65, 182, 183, 275, 276
intimate xv, xxv–xxvii, xxxi, lv, 53, 59, 67, 100, 101, 103, 112, 113, 116, 118, 120, 121, 129, 130, 147, 149, 151, 158, 159, 182, 183, 204

inwardness (also see *antarikata*) xxv, xxviii, lii, 128, 129, 148, 151, 271, 276
Islam, Nazrul xxxvi

Jalal, Nur 173, 227, 228
Jalpaiguri vli, 4, 5, 8, 11, 25–27, 36, 48, 89, 115, 148, 156, 157, 175, 183, 218
Jamuna 132
Jamuna Das 226, 259
Janaraksha Food Committee 24
Japanese invasion of India 21
Jean Dreze 86, 87, 94, 95
Jogisches, Leo xxx
Joshi, P.C. 16, 40–42, 153, 261, 263
jotedars xvi, xx, xxiii, xxv, xxviii, xliii, xliv, liv, lv, 4, 10, 12, 31, 32, 45, 48, 88–90, 93–95, 97, 98, 101, 123, 129, 131, 132, 138–143, 145, 147, 152, 153, 165, 166, 177, 181, 188, 195, 197, 206–208, 223–226, 245, 246, 256–258, 277, 282
Jugantar Party 38

Kakdwip vli, 4, 5, 31, 48, 183, 198, 218, 223, 225, 227, 255, 256, 258, 259, 261, 262, 264
Kamilya, Amulya 224
Kant, Immanuel 126, 271, 278
Kaplan, Temma xxi
Kardelj, Edward 33
*khaddar* 17
Khalistan problem xii
*khamar* 4, 153, 156, 168
Khatun, Riziya 157, 173, 257
Khatun, Sabeda 25
Khatun, Tasmina 24
Khudiram 17
Khulna 5, 101, 222, 228, 234, 251, 252
kisan sabha 4, 152
*kisani* 2
Kishore, Karuna 150, 173, 228–231, 233–242, 262,
Koch, Gertrud 69, 73, 243–245
Kochs 5
Kollontai, Alexandra xxii
*krishak sabha* 11
*krishak samitis* 6, 43, 138, 139, 141–143, 147
*kulobodhu* 20
Kurigram 26, 111, 269, 270

Lahiri, Abani 31, 36, 37, 42–45, 48–51, 103, 113, 131, 138, 143, 148, 151, 153, 155, 160, 180, 260
Lahiri, Animesh 176, 187
Land Reform Act 34
'Langal chalai' 269, 270
*langarkhanas* Xlii, 25, 26, 36, 74, 87, 99–104, 107–109, 111, 119, 276
Langer, Lawrence 248
*lathial* 152
Laub, Dori 75, 192
Layalganj/Layalgunge 224, 227, 258, 260
left, the xi, xii, xiv, xxiv, xxviii, xxx, xli, xlii, xliv, lv, 6, 10, 15, 16, 27, 28, 32, 47, 48, 50,69, 70, 92, 95, 105, 123, 139, 140, 143155, 85, 188, 189, 192, 193, 210, 216-218, 221, 222, 229, 244, 249, 251, 259, 263,

264, 269, 281, 282
liberation xli, 7, 9, 12, 16, 18, 19, 33, 61, 62, 97, 150, 162, 184, 229, 230, 258, 263, 264, 269, 271, 272, 274, 275, 277, 278
love xix, xxiv, xxvi, xxviii-xxxi, l, lii, 54, 77, 118, 125, 137, 144, 148–151, 156, 158, 159, 180, 197, 203, 220, 221, 229–231, 235, 238–240, 271, 272, 276–278, 280, 283
Lowenthal, David vlii
Luxemberg, Rosa xxx
Lyotard, Jean-Francoise liv

Madhumani 132
Mahila Atmaraksha Samiti (MARS) (also see Women's Self-Defence League) xvi, xvii, xxii, xxxix, xliii, lii, 3, 4, 8, 9, 12,13, 15–17, 20, 22–29, 31, 32, 36, 50, 38, 85, 87, 99, 100, 103–105, 108, 110, 115, 123–126, 131, 138, 142, 146, 160, 181, 186,
*mahila samiti* xliii, 3, 8, 19, 25, 27, 28, 30–32, 36, 46–49, 51, 106, 107, 117, 130, 131, 138, 140–142, 150, 160, 172, 270, 271
*mahilabahini* (also see *naribahini*) 45
Mahishyas 5, 38, 256, 259
Maity, Jatin 261
Maity, Sushila 259
Majhi, Bimala xxiv, 63, 100, 110, 131, 134, 157, 162, 163, 169–171, 173, 174
Majhi, Matla 176, 187, 216
Majhis 4, 5, 218
Majumdar, Alaka 114
Majumdar, Asok 7, 10, 11, 31, 33, 34, 90, 131, 142, 153, 156, 223–225, 261
Malda vli, 12, 186, 187, 206, 207, 221, 258
man-made famine xlii, 85, 87, 95, 98, 126
*Manushi* xii
Marcuse, Herbert 271, 277, 279
MARS xvii
Marx, Eleanor xxx
Marxism xii, 103, 136
*mazaa* xxvi, lii, 8, 135, 183, 271, 279
Mednipur vli, 4–6, 11, 14, 39, 87, 111, 115, 131, 134, 157, 169, 171–173, 183, 218, 220
memory xiv, xv, xvii–xix, xxiv, xxvi, xxvii, xxix, xxxi–xxxiii, xxxvii, xliv, vl, vli, il–liv, 8, 40, 52, 53, 59, 65–75, 78, 80, 81, 86, 136, 181, 182, 190, 192, 194, 195, 206, 208-212, 214–217, 235, 247, 248, 251, 252, 258, 265, 272, 280, 281
Menchu, Rigoberta vl
Menon, Ritu xiii, vl
middle-class activists xxiii, 139
middle-class women xix, xxiii, xxviii, 6, 9, 16, 23, 107, 177
Mitra, Ila xxv–xxvii, xxix, xxxi, xxxvi, xxxvii, il, liii, 13, 36, 44, 59, 63, 66, 67, 75, 78, 85, 86, 99, 103, 108, 125, 131, 132, 157, 175–177, 182, 183, 186–197, 199–201, 204, 205, 208–212, 214–219, 221–223, 227, 243–248, 251, 253–255,

258, 262–265, 280, 281, 287
Mitra, Mrigen 22
Mitra, Ramen 187, 196
Modachcher, Munshi 228
Mohanty, Chandra T. 179, 182
Mohanty, Satya P. 65
Moitra, Sitangshu 186
Momin, Hamida 29
Mondal, Bijoy 224, 227, 260, 262
Mondals 4, 5, 183, 218
Moon, Meenakshi vliii
Mukerjee, Madhushree 39, 88, 223
Mukherjee, Kamala/Kamala Chatterjee 22, 30, 31, 37, 109, 110, 186
Mukherjee, Kanak 41, 48
Mukherjee, Rani 36, 111, 162, 236
Mukhopadhyay, Bhudev 193
Mullah, Mohammed Mominuddin 44
*mushtibhiksha* 18, 26, 27, 105
Musim Women's Self-Defence League 108
Muslim xii, xiv, xv, xxvi, vli, 5, 9, 11, 12, 24, 25, 44, 63, 67, 88, 95, 106, 152, 153, 157, 164–174, 177, 183, 186, 187, 193–195, 199, 204–206, 208, 212, 235, 262
Muslim League 24, 29, 88, 187
Mymensingh xxxvi, 4, 5, 11, 21, 40, 115, 153, 222

Nachole xxxvi, vli, il, 5, 12, 13, 36, 59, 175, 176, 183, 185–190, 192, 193, 195, 197, 198, 200, 201, 205, 206, 208, 210, 211, 214, 216, 218, 221–223, 245, 251, 257, 262
Nag, Lila 38
Naidu, Sarojini 25, 105, 124
Namasudras xxix, 5, 8, 62, 95, 145, 146, 183, 218, 221, 225, 226, 230, 249, 255–27, 259, 263
Narail xxxvi, vli, liii, 4, 6, 8, 31, 32, 44, 47–49, 51, 59, 66, 94, 96, 130, 131, 133, 135, 140, 143–145, 150, 155, 157, 164–168, 173 183, 218, 220–222, 227, 229, 232, 242, 255, 257, 262, 263
Nari Seva Sangh 30, 110, 126
*naribahini* (also see *mahilabahini*, women's brigade) 6, 36, 45
*nasha* xliii, 271, 279
National Federation of Indian Women 49, 50
National Service Board 14
National Service Workers' Union 14
Nawabganj 186, 201, 204, 214
Naxalite vli, vliii, 35, 184, 282
Neelkantha 226, 256, 258
Netrakona 40, 42, 153, 263
Niyogi, Robi 7
Noakhali 21, 172, 194
nomadic Vaishnavism xv
Non-Cooperation Movement 13, 18
Nora, Pierre 65, 66, 68
Nrityamoyee Debi 29
Nurunnissa 24
Nussbaum, Martha 121

Odlabari 135
Omvedt, Gail x–xiii, vliii
ontological xix, xxvi, xxix, liv, 97, 102, 103, 135, 177, 183, 184, 195, 204, 215, 218, 280, 281

Operation Barga 34
Oraoni, Poko 8, 135, 181
Oraons 5, 175, 183, 218

Pabna 18, 21, 27, 115
Pakistan xxvi, xxxi, xxxix, vliii, 33, 47, 67, 187, 188, 194, 212, 232, 238, 251, 262
Pakistan Committee 235
Pakistani injection 200, 203
Pandey, Rekha 104
Pardesi, Pratima xiii
partition xii, xvii, xxix, xli, xlii, vl, il, 9, 10, 46–49, 67, 192, 211, 212, 221, 235, 236, 239, 280, 281
Partnoy, Alicia vl
Paschimbanga Mahila Samiti 3, 48, 49, 54, 56, 199
Passerini, Luisa 11, 60, 64, 71, 80, 217, 264, 265, 279
patriarchy x, vlii, 7, 19, 58, 59, 77, 167, 242
Pawar, Urmila xiii, vli, vliii
People's Relief Committee 24, 103, 227
Permanent Settlement Act of 1793 10
personal x, xii, xxv, xliii, 37, 41, 42, 51, 52, 56, 58, 60, 73, 74, 96, 109, 119, 124, 137, 142, 147, 149–151, 156, 157, 180–184, 221, 231, 235, 238, 241, 252–254, 258, 265, 278, 280
Phuleshwari 132
*phyan* 74, 85, 86, 99, 102, 120
political agency 128–130, 133–135, 137, 140, 147, 180–183, 271
Portelli, Alessandro 72
prabhat pheri 18, 21, 27
*premer jomir* (also see terrain of love) lii, 150
Progressive Writers' Association 9, 15

Quit India Movement 39

Rai, Nirmala 20, 96, 287
Rajbangshis 5, 95, 138, 139, 149, 153, 156, 164, 177, 183, 218
Rajshahi 24, 115, 201, 214, 251, 252
*ramda* 257
Ranadive 33, 187, 188, 221, 229, 232, 236, 243, 245, 246, 260, 263
Randall, Margaret vl
Rangpur xxxvi, vli, 4, 5, 20, 26, 36, 95, 96, 98, 104, 111, 162, 208, 218, 236, 269
Rani Dasgupta xxxiii, 16, 23, 25, 28, 36, 44, 50, 51, 53, 54, 56–58, 63, 99, 114, 131, 139, 143, 152, 153, 161, 162, 180, 183
Ranisainkel 46
Rasul, Muhammad Abdullah 7, 32, 223, 235
Ray, Khoka 235
Ray, Manas 211
Ray, Sabitri xv, vliii, 9
Red Cross 26, 100, 14
Rege, Sharmila xiii, 62, 257
Reid, Ela 22
Reid, John 22
*Report of the Bengal Land Revenue Commission* 11
Rohanpur 187, 200
Rowbotham, Sheila xxvii, xxxii

Roy, Bidhan 30
Roy, Sarat 111
Roy, Srila vliii
rural xiv, xvii, xxvii, xli–xliii, vli, li, liii, 3–5, 7–9, 20, 23–26, 28, 32, 47, 49, 63, 86, 96, 101, 102, 112, 113, 117, 124, 125, 130, 138, 151, 152, 154, 155, 158, 159, 162, 163, 172, 177, 179–183, 185, 192, 204, 210, 218, 221, 273, 279
rural–urban divide, bridging of xliii, 32, 112, 159
*ryot* 5

Saha, Brindaban 187
*sahadharmini* 9, 11
Sahu, Satish 260, 262
Samanta, Tulsi 86, 259
Santhal, Harek xxvi, 78, 157, 199, 202–204, 210, 218, 244, 248
Santals xv, xxv, xxvi, xxix, xxxi, l, 5, 12, 62, 67, 78, 79, 95, 132, 152, 153, 157, 175–177, 183, 185–197, 199, 202–218, 221, 223, 224, 244–246, 248, 252, 255, 257, 258, 272, 276
Sanyal, Nirmalabala 29
Saotia, Lakkhi 225, 226, 256, 258
Sardar, Jitu 207–210
Sarkar, Hemanta 17, 173
Sarkar, Shanti 22
Sarkar, Sumit 50, 51
Sarkar, Tanikapp xxxix
*sarki* 257
Sarvodaya vliii, 18, 27
Sayani, Kulsum 29
Sen, Amal 48, 49, 75, 77, 133, 143, 144, 150, 155, 173, 220, 222, 230–232, 235,237–242, 249, 262, 263, 265, 272–275, 281
Sen, Amartya 86, 87, 94, 95, 120
Sen, Ashalata 38
Sen, Bhawani 42
Sen, Ilina xi, xii, vlii, vliii
Sen, Manikuntala xvi, xxiv, xxviii, lii, 6, 8, 9, 12, 13, 17, 18, 21–23, 36, 40, 41, 42, 50, 63, 100, 102, 104, 115, 119, 120, 124–126, 135, 153, 162, 163, 177, 179, 182, 242, 263, 279, 281
Sen, Minakshi 7
Sen, Sunil 6, 261
Serge, Victor xxviii
sexual desire 144, 149, 184, 250
sexual exploitation xxv, xlii, xliii, liv, 20, 32, 96, 98, 117, 131, 137, 140, 142, 143, 147, 154, 181, 255, 256
sexual servitude xvi, xxiii, xxiv
sexual torture xxvi, liii, 66, 67, 177, 190, 191, 199, 200, 218, 244, 247, 252, 253
sexual violence xvi, xxxiii, xlii, 21, 192, 193, 202, 251, 255
sexuality x, 6, 60, 64, 98, 138, 145, 146, 150, 180, 195, 248–251, 254, 264, 280
Shah Bano controversy xii
Shah, Nandita xi
Shahzadi Begum 24, 25
Shakti/Kali 226, 258
*shanti* xxv, xliii, 8, 135, 181, 271
Siddiqui, Kamaluddin 7
sincerity 28, 104, 128, 145, 152, 196
Singh, Bhagat 17
Singha, Heleketu xxvi, 44, 48–50, 112, 139, 149

Singha, Moni 7
Singha, Sarala 48, 133, 144–147, 157, 249
Sinha Roy, Mallarika vliii
Smith, Dorothy 78, 278
socialist xi, xxii, xxx, 178
solidarity xxviii–xxx, xxxviii, xlii, l, 32, 66, 97, 98, 106, 111, 116, 124, 129, 131, 136, 137, 152, 153, 155, 157, 164, 178, 179, 180, 182–184, 195, 197, 199, 270, 272, 276, 277
Sonalkar, Wandana xiii
Soviet Union xxii, xxviii
Spashtaram 160
Stalin xxvii, xxix, xxx, xxxi
Stree Shakti Sanghatana (SSS) xi, xliv, vliii, 35, 184
stubbornness of the past (also see *atiter jed*) xxvi, 67, 204
subjectivity xxiv, xxvii, xxxi, 8, 11, 51, 56, 57, 59–61, 64, 65, 67, 68, 70, 74, 78–80, 87, 92, 97–99, 101, 108, 124, 129, 155, 156, 181–183, 192, 193, 198, 199, 218, 229, 244, 247, 251, 153, 254, 263, 264, 271, 274, 276, 279
Sudhir 256
Sufi xv
Suhrawarddi 34
Suhrud, Tridip 128
*swadeshi* 28, 39, 140
*swaraj* 26

Talukdar, Gurudas 180
Tamil self-respect movement xxvii
Tamluk 38, 39, 100, 162, 177,
Taneja, Anup 27
Tanka 4, 11, 34
*tanka* 4
*tebhag* 31, 141
Telengana xviii, xxiv, xxv, xxviii, 33, 35, 184, 223
terrain of love (also see *premer jomin*) xix, xxiv, xxvi, xxviii–xxxi, lii, 220, 221, 229, 235, 271, 272, 277, 280
*testimonio* vl, li
Thakurgaon 98, 106, 112, 141, 152
tribal 4–6, 32, 48, 95, 135, 142, 158, 185, 187, 190, 193, 196, 206, 212–214, 217, 219, 221, 229, 255, 257, 262, 264
tribe x, vli, 5, 8, 138, 142, 158, 187, 217, 219, 248, 262
Tronto, Joan C 91, 121, 122
Tularampur 164, 165
Tularampur Union Board 165

*ulu-dhvani* 186
Umar, Badruddin 7, 33, 187, 235, 239, 244, 251
urban x, xli, xlii, xliii, vli, li, liii, 3, 7–9, 16, 20, 25–29, 32, 35, 36, 42–44, 48, 49, 51, 52, 54, 56, 58, 59, 62–64, 66, 74, 79, 85, 86, 99–104, 108, 109, 112, 113, 116, 117, 120, 124, 125, 126, 128, 130, 131, 135–138, 148, 151, 153–155, 157–159, 162, 163, 175, 177–183, 185, 186, 192, 196, 204, 210, 216, 27, 221, 223, 229, 249, 250, 255, 260, 272, 275, 279

violence x, xii, xvi–xviii, xxv, xxx, xxxiii, xxviii, xlii, liv, lv, 21, 23, 49, 51, 67, 69, 89, 143, 187,

188, 190, 192, 193, 197, 198, 202, 207, 218, 220, 221–223, 225, 228, 229, 232, 233, 243–248, 251, 254, 255, 257, 259, 262, 263–265, 270, 276, 280–283
violence at home x, 143

Waddedar, Preetilata 17
West Bengal State Archives 261
Wittgenstein, Ludwig 126
women's brigade (also see *mahilabahini*, *naribahini*) xliv, 6, 36, 45
Women's Emergency Volunteers 24
women's experiences xi, xviii, xxii, xxviii, 8, 101, 272, 274, 280
women's groups lx, xi, xliii, 21, 25, 28, 48
women's movement x, xi, xii, xxxii, xxxiii, xxxix, xli–xliv, vlii–li, liii, lv, lvi, 3, 6–10, 13, 14, 18, 21, 27, 38–40, 46, 48,49, 51, 54–56, 58, 62, 69, 137, 140, 153, 283
women's question x, xii, xiii, xvii, xxviii
Women's Self-Defence League (also see MARS) xliii, 22, 23
Woodhead, John 88
World War II xlii, 87, 118,123, 129, 186

Young, James 69, 70, 72, 78, 247, 248
Yugoslav Communist Party 33

Zaheer, Sajjad 235
*zamindar* xliii, xliv, liv, lv, 10, 31, 34, 90, 94, 95, 98, 129, 131, 132, 139–141, 164, 165, 170, 177, 188, 195, 206–208, 223, 225, 245, 277
*zamindari* 6, 11, 34, 176, 224
Zizek, Slavoj 255